THE ORIGINS OF
BUSINESS, MONEY,
AND MARKETS

Keith Roberts

The Origins of
Business,
Money,
and Markets

❦ Columbia Business School
Publishing

Columbia University Press
Publishers Since 1893
New York   Chichester, West Sussex

Copyright © 2011 Keith Roberts
All rights reserved

Library of Congress Cataloging-in-Publication Data
Roberts, Keith, 1943–
The origins of business, money, and markets / Keith Roberts.
p. cm.
Includes bibliographical references and index
ISBN 978-0-231-15326-3 (cloth: alk. paper) —ISBN 978-0-231-52685-2 (e-book)
1. Commerce—History—To 500.   I. Title.
HF357.R63 2011
330.9'01—dc22
2011001127

Casebound editions of Columbia University Press books are printed on permanent
and durable acid-free paper.
Printed in the United States of America

c 10 9 8 7 6 5 4 3 2 1

References to Internet Web sites (URLs) were accurate at the time of writing. Neither
the author nor Columbia University Press is responsible for Web sites that may have
expired or changed since the book was prepared.

To my muse and my love, Verna MacCornack, who
"walks in beauty, like the night
of cloudless climes and starry skies"
—George Gordon

CONTENTS

FOREWORD

WILLIAM H. MCNEILL

I have had the pleasure of reading successive versions of this book across the past seven or eight years and watched with admiration as its proportions and literary elegance improved with each revision, eventually emerging as a masterpiece with no close parallel amid all the vast freight of classical learning and scholarship that burdens library shelves.

As a former professor of history myself, with nothing to do but teach and write, I was amazed to know that what I was reading came from the hand of a businessman and lawyer, who somehow found time in his busy schedule to seek the answer to a simple question he casually asked himself one day: "How did the life he was leading as a businessman get started?"

As is usual in historical inquiry, he began by reading what predecessors had to say about the general subject and looked into the sources they had used when that seemed needful. The more he read, the more subsidiary questions arose, and from time to time insights dawned on him that his predecessors had missed. Soon he recognized that he had a full-scale book to write, setting forth his findings and amending older understandings; and it was then that he approached me to read and comment on his writing.

Our relation resembled that between a history professor and a star student at work on a PhD dissertation, with the difference that Roberts was fully engaged in a successful professional career, while I had already retired. It was the last such relationship I will ever enjoy, and the best. To be sure, several of my students wrote excellent dissertations that were later published as books. But never before have I stayed with the process of revision from beginning to finish, nor felt greater satisfaction in witnessing the elegance and power of the end product after years of disciplined effort.

My contribution was rhetorical rather than substantive since I have only superficial acquaintance with ancient history. But pruning unnecessary passages and clarifying arguments was part of the revisory process, and my comments were mostly directed to those ends. Much in these pages was unfamiliar to me from the start. Some details struck home to me, like the way Bactrian camels at the time of the Assyrian Empire and Arabian camels under their Persian successors facilitated both warfare and trade by increasing the carrying capacity of caravans. These nuggets of information came from other scholars, as the endnotes show, and Roberts merely passed them on to me. But I am duly grateful, since I believe improvements in transport and communication like these are central to human history everywhere and always.

More important are insights that Roberts personally generated through his own inquiries into the history of business in antiquity. His two most important original ideas concern the roles played by Greek coins and by Roman clientage in forwarding business affairs. Like almost everyone else, I had assumed that a coin was a coin from the time they were first minted in the Lydian kingdom of Asia Minor in the sixth century B.C.E. and subsequently by Persian kings. To be sure they were of pure gold, but I had never recognized that they were therefore too valuable to be used in everyday transactions. Roberts taught me that the first gold coins were instead doled out one by one to mercenaries as pay for a year's military service and little else. Since the Persian kings did not depend on foreign mercenaries to fill the ranks of their armies, they had little need for coins. Accordingly, they hoarded nearly all their precious metal in the royal treasury, generation after generation. They stayed there until Alexander of Macedon (died 323 B.C.E.) defeated the Persian armies, seized the royal treasuries, and began recklessly disbursing the hoarded gold to his soldiers and others around him.

Greek cities, too, did not depend on mercenary soldiers in the sixth and fifth centuries B.C.E., but they found a different use for coinage by issuing silver and copper coins of far less value than the original Lydian ones.

Such coins made everyday exchanges of goods of common consumption far easier than ever before. Buyers and sellers no longer needed to possess some commodity the other partner wanted then and there. Instead, a sufficient number of standardized coins could buy anything, anywhere, and at any time.

Accordingly, market transactions took on a new character, affecting far more persons far more often than before and integrating human effort across time and space much more efficiently. Long-distance trade and, above all, massive exports of wine and oil from the Greek heartlands in exchange for grain, slaves, and raw materials from the periphery created an Aegean–Black Sea and then a Mediterranean-wide circulation. That exchange engaged rural producers as well as townsfolk in a commercial web that gave classical Greek and Roman society a novel, enduring, and distinctive character. Without small coins it could not have happened: that is what Roberts taught me, and, as far as I know, no one had previously made this fundamental transformation clear.

His argument that interpersonal ties created by patron-client relationships in Rome facilitated large-scale business under the late republic and early empire is just as new and convincing, if not quite as sweeping in its implication since Rome's patronage system was peculiarly its own. But political careers in Rome were built around clientage. Aspiring senators and other men of wealth and power sought to attract a following among the citizens by doing them favors and asking their loyal service and support in return. Every morning senators and lesser luminaries were greeted by their clients, exchanged news and gossip, and arranged any and all mutual services for the days ahead.

This relationship became lifelong, and breaking it off was almost unthinkable. Simply put, patrons and clients learned to trust each other and to do whatever they promised to do to help each other. So when collecting provincial taxes became big business (beginning with the annexation of Sicily in 241 B.C.E.), it is easy to see how patrons and clients could work together, organize large business enterprises, and collect large sums of money throughout the empire while still maintaining mutual trust and effective cooperation on a scale that family businesses could not match. Needless to say, the finances of the late republic and early Roman Empire depended on the efficiency of these private companies—hated though they were by taxpayers, as New Testament references to "publicans" make clear.

But the Roman peace and prosperity that remained almost unbroken until 80 C.E. was sustained by circulation of money and goods between taxpayers in the provinces and armies stationed on the frontiers. To be sure, tax collection by private companies gradually gave way to official tax collectors (often slaves or freedmen belonging to the imperial household itself). Whereupon the large multinational organizations dependent upon clientage ceased to play as much of a role in business affairs. Trustworthy bureaucratic officials were hard to find, however, and disease disasters in the second century c.e., followed by barbarian invasions, soon shattered the money economy in the western provinces of the empire, and Roberts's story comes to its close with business in full retreat and official command increasingly directing economic affairs.

It is worth asking how a practicing American businessman could use his spare time to write a history that casts so much new light on the past. Certainly, high intelligence and unusual diligence were at work. But there is something else. As he suggests when discussing the Homeric worldview, an aristocratic landowner's disdain for business and businessmen prevailed in ancient Greece and Rome, even though it was then that some of the distinctive forms of business activity that exist today first appeared. When Italian humanists revived classical studies in Western Europe during the Renaissance they reproduced the same dichotomy, living as they did in vibrant centers of business, but sharing the ancients' aristocratic heroic bias, while also claiming that their studies could show others how to lead a good, civilized life.

Many believed them, and humanistic learning in due course migrated north and became the core of higher education for the upper classes of Western Europe between about 1550 and 1950. Generations of English, French, German—and then American—gentlemen learned Latin and Greek in primary school and read Homer, Cicero, and other ancient authors as university students. They imbibed classical heroic ideals from these exercises and blended them variously with Christian charity and other moral doctrines to make them what they were.

But among the few who became lifelong classical scholars, the ancient aristocratic bias dominated completely. That accounts for the scant attention they paid to ancient businessmen and the disdain they accorded to the biblical "publicans and sinners," who, as Roberts points out, were the innovative big businessmen of Roman times.

Being a businessman himself, Roberts was predisposed to think otherwise. By asking simple questions about how things got done, what functions merchants and producers of goods for sale and export played in ancient times, how trade was organized, and how markets expanded and contracted across time, he was able to write this book. It is admirable on many grounds, not least because in departing from traditional disdain for businessmen, he does not go overboard in praising them. Instead he recognizes costs as well as gains arising from their activity, as well as the very conspicuous role of slavery and other sorts of violence involved in ancient business transactions.

In short, anyone curious to know how our business practices and attitudes got started can find persuasive answers in this book. That was exactly what Roberts set out to discover. Only an experienced businessman with relevant questions clearly in mind could have combed through so much scholarly (and often refractory) literature and found so many answers.

It makes a lively story, worth thinking and wondering about. I recommend it warmly.

PREFACE

I make no claim to offer information that will be new to specialists, nor can I do justice to the vast amount of primary research available. . . . At best, a volume like this can synthesize the better general studies of each area, try not to ignore too many detailed studies, and try not to add too many new inaccuracies.

—DAVID CHRISTIAN, *A HISTORY OF RUSSIA,*
CENTRAL ASIA, AND MONGOLIA

The great contemporary historian David Christian's modest disclaimer certainly applies to the present work. Once I realized that a history of early Western business would require delving into various ancient societies over long periods of time, it seemed presumptuous for me to attempt it. I prefer to view this work, therefore, as a report in story form, a report on what an inquiring businessman can learn from the historians who have studied such matters.

My hope was to trace the roots of modern business, meaning business as it developed in Europe and the United States after the Industrial Revolution and today exists in developed countries everywhere. Like the language, social culture, and political systems of Europe and the United States, the lineal ancestry of European and U.S. business traces clearly to Middle Eastern and Mediterranean antiquity. In India, China, and other places business also grew, but historians have not noted much cross-cultural influence.

Every book entails significant editorial choices. A fundamental choice here was to approach business history as a story and to tell it chronologically. The goal has been to report on a sequence of seminal places where influential changes of significance first emerged, rather than providing a comprehensive enumeration of businesses and their practices. The result is selective in its description of businesses and of the places where business was practiced.[1] Because knowledge about antiquity is often uncertain, those who aim to advance the state of scholarship often disagree about what things mean. As scholars they provide lengthy discussions and citations to justify their views. But since this is simply a report on what the scholars have found, rather than an effort to advance their learning, and since I doubt that most readers would find such discussions of value, I have limited references to the principal sources for each chapter and the particular sources I used for quotations and less obvious information.

I have been the happy beneficiary of enormous help from many people. Intellectually, I have formed my concepts of how history works from, among others, the great twentieth-century scholars Fernand Braudel, Alfred D. Chandler, Sir John Hicks, William H. McNeill, Douglass C. North, and Oliver Williamson.[2] I also owe a debt to the late Harvard Law School professor of legal history Samuel Thorne, whose careful standards of scholarship I have always tried to follow.

I began this study while operating a business. I could proceed only because of the hard and capable work of its managers, including Arthur Pirrone, Vincent Valicenti, the late Milton Linker, and Wilmer Pastoriza; and my ability to trust honorable business partners like Frank Gilfedder of Stiefel Laboratories, the late Richard Ottaviano of Genesis Management, Bill Weiss and Arturo Peralta-Ramos of Medtech Laboratories (now Prestige Brands Inc.), and Menelaos Kostarelos of the international cosmetics company Farmeco.

Quite a number of friends, colleagues, and teachers have most helpfully read and commented on drafts and chapters of this work. First and foremost has been my mentor, William H. McNeill, the great historian who read, reread, and read again these chapters. I cannot say enough for his guidance and friendship. And if I have misused the word *feudal*, it is not his fault. Another great historian and teacher who freely gave me his time and thought was the late Alfred Chandler, the inventor of modern business history. His early counsel and enthusiasm kept me going through times of grave doubt. My friend Clifford Brown, a distinguished political scientist with a particular love for Thucydides, provided many helpful comments, as did the learned Fred Terna and marketing professor Sashi Gadjil. I am also extremely grateful for the encouragement and friendship of professors Douglass North, the late Peter Drucker, and Karl Moore.

Several business executives, including the masterful entrepreneur Bob Kulperger, my friend Walter Sleeth, and Menos Kostarelos, read earlier version of the manuscript and gave me useful feedback. I received extensive editing help from Ken Atchity and Andrea McKeown of AEI Online, my wonderful agent/editor Paul McCarthy, and Bridget Flannery-McCoy of Columbia Business School Publishing. I would also like to thank Andras Bereznay of London for his maps.

My greatest debt of gratitude is to my wife Verna MacCornack, who first vetted many of my ideas as we jogged in Central Park. She encouraged me to read every chapter aloud to her, through revision after revision, and her sage advice, steady support, and constant enthusiasm for this project have, quite simply, made it possible.

Dear Reader, much as I might wish to blame the book's shortcomings on others, you and I know better.

LIST OF TERMS

agribusiness	farming for profit
asset	a saleable valuable; in accounting, a valuable possession that will not be used up within a year
business person	an investor (the one risking his wealth), manager, or employee in a business concern
business	the activity of selling to voluntary buyers for a profit, or an enterprise that survives by doing this activity
capital	resources available to fund a business; also, a business's assets
civil conditions	the conditions and rules governing conduct in society
credit	purchasing power that has been provided in exchange for a promise of repayment
demand	desire coupled with purchasing power
direct costs	the cost of producing what is to be sold, generally involving the payments for labor and materials
disposable wealth	wealth available for present exchange
East, West	Asia east or west of the Hellenistic or Roman border, as the case may be

east, west	the eastern or western part of the Roman Empire; the eastern part spoke Greek; the western, Latin; the dividing line ran down the Adriatic Sea and across the Mediterranean
Fertile Crescent	a swath of fertile land from Mesopotamia through the Levant to Egypt
finance	a discipline that gives economic value to possessions, protects and increases that value, and generates purchasing power from it
imperialism	the conquest and rule of new territories for the sake of profit
investment banker	an intermediary who brings together investors and business opportunities
investment	the use of present resources to create future benefits
latifundia	an extensive farm estate, usually including several farms, operated for profit
Levant	the lands along the Mediterranean coast from Egypt to Turkey
market	a trading place where prices depend on supply and demand
marketing	the presentation of what is to be sold, including design, advertising, selling, distribution, and customer support
monetized market	a market using coins
prehistoric societies	societies without writing
purchasing power	a form of wealth that serves as payment; most often, money or credit
role of business	the importance, prosperity, and function of business in a society
trade	the business of acquiring goods and reselling them at another place or time
trader	one who risks his capital in trade
transaction costs	costs of doing transactions, including the acquisition of information, use of agents, and the shirking or opportunism of people who affect the transaction
valuable	a desirable possession
wealth	a sum of desirable possessions

THE ORIGINS OF
BUSINESS, MONEY,
AND MARKETS

Introduction

As manager of a small manufacturing and distribution company, I was stomping around my office late one night, frustrated with our antiquated business practices. I heard myself mutter, "This place is run like a Roman blacksmith shop!" and I stopped pacing. How did they run blacksmith shops in Rome, I wondered? Did they even have any? What were they like? In fact, how did business, to which billions of us now devote our working lives, even begin? What are the important differences between ancient businesses like Roman blacksmith shops and the computerized, outsourced, Internet-linked, machine-based businesses of today? To find the answers, I started the research that led to this book. As I quickly discovered, virtually nobody has described the ancient origins and how it developed into a significant part of economic life. That is the story told here.

Business is the activity of selling to voluntary buyers at a profit. Businesses survive by attracting customers and earning the full cost of what they sell, generating enough profit to compensate for the effort, investment, and risk involved. Unlike governments, charities, and other entities that may sell things but do not require the proceeds for survival, businesses must direct continuous, urgent attention to achieving profitable sales. That characteristic distinguishes businesses from all other enterprises.

The concept and possibility of selling at a profit first arose in Mesopotamia about five thousand years ago. The mentality and skills essential to business operations developed in the Middle Eastern states, as did governmental accomplishments that expanded trade and other business activities (part 1).

But it took the Greek combination of coins and markets to make business more than a marginal activity. From the sixth century B.C.E. an entrepreneurial market system became central to the urban economy of Athens and other democratic city-states. By 200 B.C.E. Alexander the Great and his followers had spread this economic system to hundreds of cities throughout Western Asia and the Mediterranean region (part 2).

Roman sources provide most of what we know about early business operations, including Roman blacksmith shops. The Romans favored cities with entrepreneurial market systems and established them in the parts of Africa and Western Europe they conquered. They invented multinational business corporations, and between 200 B.C.E. and 200 C.E. their empire's favorable business environment allowed firms to attain considerable influence and importance. During that same period, from Roman Judea came Hillel and Jesus with their humanistic teachings, the Christian church, and the complete dispersal of Jewish communities throughout the Eurasian landmass. These developments would strongly influence later European business and provide moral justification for the consumerism that characterizes modern economies. After 200 C.E. Roman business declined, but the nexus between money, markets, and business remained firmly established (part 3).

For each part, I have asked a similar set of questions: What were the main businesses? How did they operate? What was business's role in the economy? What was the nature of business labor? How were business people regarded? In short, what was new about business, and why so?

To address such questions, we must range far beyond an account of business itself to account for impersonal forces that affected the business environment, such as climate, geography, and technology. To quote the editors of a grand recent survey of Greco-Roman economic history, this account like theirs "recognizes that classical antiquity saw one of the strongest economic efflorescences in premodern history but keeps this perspective, refusing to confuse the ancient economy with the modern. In short, it takes seriously Douglass North's injunction to explain the structure and performance of economies through time."[1]

Extraordinary individuals also changed the course of history. Given the times, they were almost all men: kings called "the great," such as Sargon, Cyrus, and Darius in the Middle East and, of course, Alexander of Macedonia; thinkers like Solon, Aristotle, and Archimedes; Roman emperors, including Augustus, Diocletian, and Constantine. Not many business people are known, but we encounter a few: the trader Imdi-ilum of 2000 B.C.E. Assur, the banker Balmonahse of Babylonia, Roman investors like Pliny the Younger and Cato the Elder, and the greatest ancient tycoon of all, Marcus Crassus. They all inhabited a world full of murder, cruelty, villainy, and perversion, as well as love, wisdom, courage, and heroism—and so, therefore, does this story.

The early history of money, markets, and business also offers the benefit that Niall Ferguson identifies: "Understand the origins of an institution or instrument and you will find its present-day role much easier to grasp."[2] By picturing business in earlier, simpler forms, we can better understand how money and markets work, and the relationship between business activities like manufacturing, trade, retailing, and finance. Businesses that primarily serve other businesses—shipping, banking, investment, and wholesaling—also emerge naturally as the story progresses.

Let us begin. The real beginning, though, is not with the simpler times when business originated, but before then. Why, indeed, was there ever a time before business?

Part 1

Business began in the earliest civilizations, those of the Middle East. Part 1 concerns three questions:

- Why did business begin when it did, and not before?
- Why and how did it begin there?
- What subsequent Middle Eastern developments were important to it?

The first part of chapter 1 argues that before societies organized on a scale larger than the tribe, living conditions and human mentality did not conceive of profits. There were plenty of activities that we now identify with business, such as manufacturing and trade, but like celebratory gift exchanges today, they was not conducted for profit as we conceive it, nor could they have been.

The possibility of profit first emerged in the organized irrigation societies of Egypt and southern Mesopotamia, an area known as Sumeria whose natural endowments made trade important. Their leaders—especially in Sumeria—began to accumulate material wealth. Traders could then earn profits, perhaps most often from buying and selling slaves, and use the profits for their own benefit. Other opportunities for profit, such as crop loans, shipping, and retailing followed. Nevertheless, the social and economic structure of these societies kept business in a marginal role. These were command economies, in which rulers and their supporters monopolized the wealth and, although normally respectful of tradition, distributed it as they saw fit. Business neither created much wealth nor played a significant part in distributing it.

Over the next thousand or so years, culminating in the reign of Babylonia's King Hammurabi, most key business developments followed improvements in government. One was Sargon of Akkad's recognition that in Sumeria a ruler who respected other religious views could govern a larger territory. Larger sovereign territories made for larger markets. Another crucial development was the invention, discovery, or creation of tools that would be essential to business becoming a common and competent activity: calculation, writing, forecasting, and legal systems. Yet another development came in the field of finance, where the needs of Assyrian and Babylonian merchants generated sophisticated innovations for transmitting credit over long distances, such as checks and letters of credit. Yet, even new kingdoms and cities adopted the old social and economic structures. In both old and new command economies, businesses remained economically marginal activities.

Chapter 2 concerns the expansion of business activity from Mesopotamia to the rest of the Middle East under the various empires that new military technology empowered shortly after Hammurabi's death. One truly innovative businesslike form emerged during this time—commercial states like those of the Minoans, Mycenaeans, and Phoenicians. As states that derived at least some of their support from sovereign powers, these were not true businesses. But they did derive much of their income from profitably selling goods and services to willing customers, and usually behaved accordingly.

The other critical business development during the twelve hundred years covered in chapter 2 was the further development of sovereign statecraft. This allowed rulers to govern increasingly large territories longer and more peacefully. In the process they built roads and improved communications, unified diverse communities, and forced many outlying people to join the exchange economy.

Although these measures greatly improved business conditions and led to much more business activity, the empires retained the old social structure, and the choices of the powerful continued to regulate economic life. It would take a more thorough social revolution than the advent of the Iron Age to subject economic life to the desires and purchasing power of the population at large.

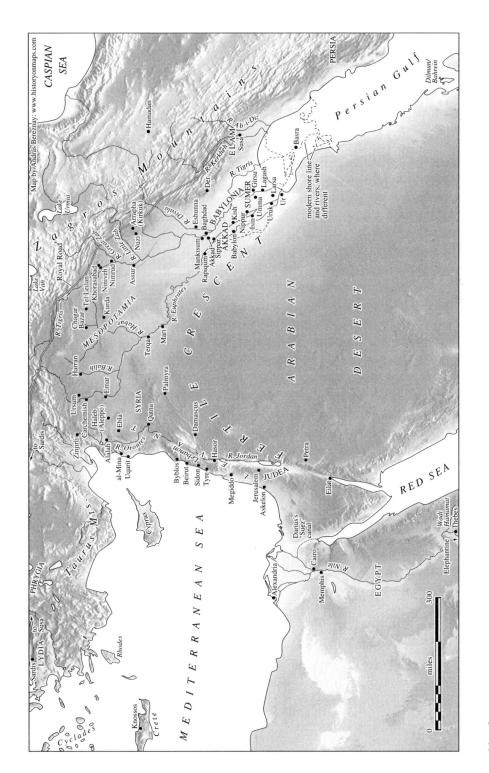

Map 1.

Ancient Middle East, 3000–1000 B.C.E.

1

The Beginning

Contrary to the implicit dogmas of current free-market triumphalists, free markets and businesses have not been with us since the dawn of time. Business—the activity of selling for a profit—dates from only the start of urban civilization in Mesopotamia, about five thousand years ago. There was certainly plenty of prehistoric manufacturing and trade, but profit and the desire for it were unknown. The conditions that made cities possible also made for wealthy elites, and the desire for profit took seed with the accumulation of wealth. What were these new conditions? Why in Mesopotamia, not Egypt? Which businesses arose first, and what were they like?

Why No Prehistoric Business?

As far as we can tell, primarily from the reports of nineteenth- and twentieth-century anthropologists who studied people living under presumably similar conditions, communities of prehistoric people treated economic, social, and religious life as an indistinguishable whole.[1] Struggling to survive under conditions they could not understand, predict, or control,[2] our ancestors formed communities of intense interdependency. They ascribed their fate to spirits, totems, witches, or the evil eye[3] and used shamans or priests to influence these powers.[4]

There was an "exquisite homogeneity and wholeness" to these communities.[5] People could not survive alone. They lived intensely communal lives and had little sense of themselves as individual actors.[6] Ideas, actions, responsibilities, and even interests belonged to the community or its gods, not the self. Some scholars even speculate that prehistoric individuals didn't perceive themselves as the source of their own thoughts and actions, but instead attributed them to dreams sent by gods.[7] This orientation made it difficult for people to formulate and pursue self-interested goals.[8] Besides, pervasive religious and communal norms rendered selfish calculation inconceivable.

In any case, wealth hardly existed. Land was held in common, food was perishable, slaves died quickly, clothing and shelter were barely more durable, and entertainment was communal.[9] The significance and value of ornaments and tokens was largely personal or communal. With little wealth, prehistoric societies were fairly egalitarian. No one had a great advantage of power, since muscular strength was the only major difference. The greatest differences were in the distribution of intangible social goods, like respect, status, sexual access, ceremonial priority, strength, and affection.[10]

Commerce was therefore an activity by and for the benefit of the entire community. Archeologists have found many ancient traces of it. New Guineans traded obsidian to nearby archipelagos at least twenty thousand years ago.[11] In Europe, Baltic amber found its way to Mediterranean sites,[12] and Ukrainian mammoth hunters wore Mediterranean shells. Flint was mined and flaked into tools in many places, like Grimes Graves in Great Britain, where miners dug shafts over fifty feet deep with picks made from red deer antlers.[13]

How such miners traded we don't know for sure, but an anthropologist describing nineteenth-century Australian aborigines gives a suggestion. Billi-billeri lived with his family at Mount William, where they quarried rock and shaped it into stone axes. They had to protect their inventory from thieves. When neighboring tribes wanted some, messages would be sent offering articles in exchange for the desired quantity, and a party would later come to the quarry and complete the barter.[14]

This type of barter wasn't a purely economic transaction. Without an active trading market, neither Billi-billeri nor his customers could determine a fair price for his axe heads. Even if the same things had been traded last year, their relative needs might have changed. Under these conditions, the pursuit of advantage could have been dangerous. People met and exchanged goods so rarely that perceptions about their value could differ radically.[15] In the absence of markets or other neutral mechanisms for determining value, the semblance of gain from an exchange might easily seem immoral, causing insult and perhaps even a fight. It was safer to obscure and cushion bargaining within diplomatic and religious ceremony. The ceremonial process itself often provided a dynamic leading to agreement, even when the parties couldn't truly calculate their own economic interests. Economic transactions, as Karl Polanyi famously put it, "were embedded and enmeshed in institutions economic and non-economic."[16] There was no "exchange," requiring equivalence of value, but what Polanyi called "reciprocation," requiring sufficiency of respect.[17]

Wedding gifts are a modern example of reciprocation at work. In Japan, for example, a manager's wedding gift to a subordinate must consist of new bank notes presented on the wedding day in a special envelope tied with a cord. The cord's color and the amount of money depend strictly on the manager's rank, and the couple must reciprocate on the spot with an item worth about half the money received.[18]

Both of these examples illustrate another feature of prehistoric trade: simultaneity. Nobody promised future performance, because the only relevant time was "now." This "perennial reality of the now," in anthropologist Jamake Highwater's phrase, characterized a prehistoric view of time based on the cyclical nature of the physical world. Oral traditions, like the legends of the Hopi and other American Indian tribes, contained little sense of past or future time. In fact, most native languages don't have terms to express the passage of time.[19]

Absent a linear sense of time, the sequential ordering necessary for reasoning from cause to effect becomes difficult. To quote Highwater again, "without a concept of past and future, of discrete events following each other temporally, it would be impossible to perform scientifically meaningful analyses."[20]

In sum, prehistoric economic transactions were indistinguishable from social, religious, and political relationships. People had little material wealth or desire for gain, and their sense of time made calculation difficult. The search for profits became conceivable only when these conditions began to change, with the birth of the first cities.

Sumeria: The Cradle of Business

After the last ice age, the curved slice of the Middle East known as the Fertile Crescent (see map 1) was more humid than now.[21] Lions, elephants, gazelles, hippopotami, crocodiles, and vast flocks of birds fed on its extensive pastures and wetlands.[22] There people domesticated many of the world's most valuable large animals: goats, sheep, pigs, cattle, and donkeys. Six major food crops (wheat, barley, oats, rye, millet, and sorghum) were native to the region, and the loose, mineral-rich soil was easy to cultivate with weak tools made of wood, bone, or horn.[23]

Before 3000 B.C.E. people living at the two ends of the Fertile Crescent, on the Nile in Egypt and near the rivers flowing through Mesopotamia to the Persian Gulf, began using irrigation to cultivate the rich soil left by annual floods. Their farming could support large, sedentary populations, including full-time leaders who organized the massive effort needed to build and maintain their irrigation works, maintained order among the gathered clans and tribes, and protected the community from plunderers.[24]

Priests were probably the first of these leaders, an extension of their prehistoric role. But as successful farmers acquired armaments and the training to use them, a military caste led by kings began to emerge. The priests claimed to represent the gods, who owned the land and created kings to protect the peasants who fed them all.[25]

Around 3100 B.C.E. the discovery that adding tin to copper made a harder metal, bronze, led to innovations like bronze armor, hardened shields, and metal-tipped spears and arrows, which along with powerful bows helped destroy the prehistoric equivalency of power.[26] Priests and warriors took the best land and resources for themselves and under the threat of force used tithes, rents, and taxes to extract surplus production from everyone else. Irrigation farming's abysmal conditions reinforced the new hierarchical order. Constant labor in the watery fields led to parasitic infections that sapped strength and energy. In time, the average peasant became smaller, weaker, slower, and less energetic than his healthier overlords.[27]

The ruler possessed 10–25 percent of the land, often hundreds of acres. Officials received some in tenancy, some was leased out, and peasants attached to the land as serfs farmed the rest or herded vast flocks of sheep and goats.[28] The ruler's enormous households supported relatives, courtiers, and slaves, who functioned as servants, artisans, soldiers, and bureaucrats. Monthly rations of barley, oil, and cloth were issued to retainers and serfs, based on the sex, age, and status of the recipient: for instance, sixty liters of barley for men, thirty for women.[29] The rulers also collected taxes and labor services from subsidiary chieftains and independent peasants.[30]

These conditions characterized both Egypt and Sumeria, but geography created important differences. Egypt's deserts, rich in gold, copper, and building stone, protected the fertile Nile River valley from outside attack. But its farmers, living in villages along the Nile's length, were readily accessible and easily conquered from the river. The first pharaoh, Menes, did so on the Upper Nile during the fourth millennium, and by 3000 B.C.E. his successors had extended their military and religious influence downstream, creating a large and homogeneous state[31] whose abundant resources made it largely self-sufficient. The trade that took place was primarily for wood, ships, and naval stores from Byblos in Syria.[32]

Sumeria, on the other hand, consisted of scattered settlements within the vast maze of marshes, lakes, and waterways that formed the delta of the Tigris and Euphrates rivers, an area larger than Great Britain. Nomads tended great flocks of sheep and goats on surrounding slopes, often raiding the delta farmers for food and slaves. The farmers, in turn, gathered together for safety and fortified the best situated villages. Some of these grew into cities like Sumer and Uruk. Uruk's walls enclosed 1,280 acres and harbored as many as 30,000 people.[33]

Sumeria had less wood than Egypt and no building stone or metals. Despite the sporadic seizures of distant goods by Sumerian adventurers like Gilgamesh, the only practical way to assure them was through trade, a solution that strikingly parallels the English solution to its eighteenth-century overpopulation, one that helped it create the Industrial Revolution. Where England lacked food, Sumeria lacked military and building materials. For each, the solution was to export manufactured goods.[34]

But what could Sumeria offer? Surplus food, except perhaps for dates, was not a reliable export, since communities generally fed themselves. Dates were, in fact, extensively cultivated.[35] A more important and reliable export policy was to take advantage of the large labor supply by specializing in processing and manufacturing. Temples and palaces marshaled hundreds of women and children to assemble everything from sieves to sandals.[36] At Girsu, 679 women and 89 men milled barley,[37] while other Sumerian factories made baskets, fragrances, jewelry, artwork, and paint.[38]

The most valuable Sumerian export was woolen cloth. It took a month to make a simple cloak, and years for more elaborate work.[39] The Sumerians had a clear competitive advantage in these goods, since they had plenty of wool and labor. This labor included the wives and children of peasant farmers,[40] as well as widows and orphans "dedicated" to the gods and worked to death in temple workshops. As in nineteenth-century New England nearly five thousand years later, Sumeria's factories ran on the female labor that its agricultural productivity made available.[41]

Early-third-millennium trade crossed amazing distances. In a valley leading from the Red Sea to gold mines in southern Egypt, there is a pre-3000 B.C.E. drawing of a Sumerian ship.[42] Sumeria apparently imported copper from the Harappan and Mohenjo-daro civilizations of the Indus River valley. Indian seals found on site suggest that much of it came through Dilmun, a port on Bahrein Island in the Persian Gulf.[43] Lapis lazuli, mined in Afghanistan and processed in eastern Persia, arrived overland.[44] The Sumerians also obtained conch shells from Ceylon, and timber, ivory, semi-precious stones, and gold from various other Asian and African sources.[45] Egypt was receiving ebony from Africa; burning frankincense and myrrh obtainable only in southern Arabia, the Sudan, or Ethiopia; and import-ing wood, ships, and naval stores from the Syrian port of Byblos.[46]

Such trade was not just for consumption. The Sumerians, for instance, profitably sold goods like lapis lazuli to Egypt. Entrepôts like Dilmun and the Euphrates river port Mari became wealthy middlemen. Mari imported timber, wine, and olive oil from the Levant, cloth from Crete, and copper from Cyprus, sending it down the Euphrates to Sumeria and, at least in the case of olive oil, on to Dilmun.[47] Mari's palace with terra-cotta baths and frescoed walls covered more than six acres.[48] There is even evidence of Su-merian trade in Denmark, and segmented ceramic beads manufactured in either Egypt or Mesopotamia dot trade routes that ran through central Europe to Cornwall.[49]

Long-distance trade generally took the form of gift exchanges be-tween rulers, as in the following letters between an Egyptian pharaoh and a Babylonian king:

> [from Egypt:] I have sent you as a present for the new house . . . one ebony bed, inlaid with ivory and gold; three ebony beds, inlaid with gold; one ebony headrest, inlaid with gold; one ebony armchair, in-laid with gold; five ebony chairs, inlaid with gold; . . . Altogether, these contain gold to the weight of seven minas and nine shekels. The weight of silver is one mina eight shekels.
>
> [from Babylon:] I have sent my brother four minas of fine lapis lazuli as an interim present. I have also sent my brother five teams of

horses. . . . Let my brother send me much fine gold, so that I may use it for my project.[50]

Rulers negotiated access and protection for the agents, known as *tamkaru*, who negotiated these deals and carried the goods. King Ilushuma of Assur claimed to have "established the freedom" of several Babylonian cities, meaning that he had gained trading rights there.[51] Many treaties guaranteed tamkaru safety and stipulated the taxes they would pay.

Tamkaru routinely spent long periods abroad on their trading missions, since movement was agonizingly slow. A Sumerian trip to southeastern Turkey for copper, for instance, could take months. The copper would then float for weeks down the Euphrates River in skin-covered rafts. Round, to accommodate the greatest weight with the least building material, these vessels were then packed onto donkeys and returned home.[52]

Twice a year, tamkaru took wool, silver, dates, barley, and other commodities for the temple at Umma to Syria or Persia, returning with perfume resins, wood, bitumen, gypsum, honey, raisins, and precious metals.[53] While they had to account for the quantities and value of their inventory, and how much they used for expenses,[54] tamkaru necessarily operated with great independence. They had to be skillful and trustworthy, since many lives and fortunes might rest on their success.[55] High status was also obligatory, since trade was still enmeshed with diplomacy, and bargains were normally sealed with solemn ceremonies and religious oaths. Their travels, fraught with danger and uncertainty, required courage and enterprise, becoming the stuff of legendary tales like the *Epic of Gilgamesh*. Not surprisingly, tamkaru were often friends or relatives of the ruler, well rewarded for their work with grants of land and other assets.[56]

These were probably the first real businessmen. At a time when most wealth consisted of land, slaves, or goods in use, their commissions and trading gains provided them an unusual amount of disposable wealth. This, along with their political connections and independence, gave them the opportunity to seek profit for themselves along the way.[57] In fact, the earliest recorded business was a trading venture to Dilmun for copper, privately financed by investors from Ur around 3000 B.C.E.[58] Private trade then became common, especially under weaker sovereigns.[59]

In time, intensive farming spread to the rain-watered lands of northern Mesopotamia and the Levant. By 2600 B.C.E. Tel Leilan, in a dry-farming area of northern Mesopotamia, had ten to twenty thousand people. New cities like Akkad, Babylon, and Assur appeared.[60] By 2400 B.C.E. the Syrian

Table 1
Early Middle Eastern Population

Region/Dynasty	Year (B.C.E.)	City Population	Region Population
Sumeria	3000	Uruk: 30,000	500,000[a]
Third Dynasty of Ur	2100	Ur: 65,000[b]	1,000,000[c]
Old Babylonia	1750	Babylon: 60,000[d]	1,500,000[e]
Egypt	1750		2,000,000–3,000,000[f]
Levant and Syria	1750/2250	Ebla: 30,000[g]	1,000,000[h]
total			4,000,000–5,500,000

a. McNeill 1977: 54–55.
b. Saggs 1989: 144.
c. Diakonoff 1991: 92.
d. T. Chandler 1987: table 60.
e. Assumes that Old Babylonia ruled twice Sumeria's population and grew at an average rate of
   0.036%/year, as per North 1981.
f. An extrapolation backward from Egypt's 7,000,000 as of 1 B.C.E.
g. T. Chandler 1987: table 60. Ebla population ca. 2250 B.C.E.
h. Assumes that the population of the Levant and Syria was proportionately the same as in
   Alexander's day, or 86% of Egypt's; Peters 1970: 517 and Grant 1990c: 39.

oasis of Ebla had become the leading commercial center between Egypt and Sumeria. The palace owned some seventy to eighty thousand sheep grazing on the lush pastures and operated a textile factory.[61] The rulers of Ebla, its temples, and tamkaru exported fabrics, arms, and metal products; coordinated the flow of goods from Egypt, Cyprus, Sumer, and Elam; and earned vast quantities of gold and silver.[62] Temples and palaces continued to sponsor major expeditions, but as rural chieftains developed "a taste for the goods of civilization" and traded wood, meat, building stones, and slaves for them,[63] ever-denser commercial networks allowed private traders to make shorter excursions with just one or two loaded donkeys.[64]

Many undoubtedly traded slaves.[65] There was no moral taint to slavery: it was considered a natural disaster that might befall anyone.[66] Tribal chieftains commonly sold subjects or captives into slavery in return for weaponry and other manufactured goods; creditors sold defaulting debtors, often tenant farmers, who had borrowed against themselves and their families to pay expenses while awaiting harvest.[67] There were also war captives, kidnap victims, unwanted children, and even some who sold them-selves into slavery as a way to emigrate.[68]

Slaves were in steady demand, their price varying by age, gender, train-ing, or physical condition. Their ability to move themselves and the trader's goods was extremely useful at a time when the transport of goods was very expensive. This convenience, plus assured demand and ready supply, made slave trading an easy business to enter.

The profits of trade soon found varied business investments. One was tax farming. Rulers found it easier to let merchants collect their taxes for a share of the proceeds, as in sharecropping, than to support the necessary bureaucracy themselves. At Sumer, merchants collected taxes in the form of crops, gave the palace what it demanded, and sold the rest for themselves, about two thirds of the total. The silver or barley proceeds went into loans and other investments.[69] The eighteenth-century B.C.E. ruler of Babylonia, Hammurabi, delegated tax collection to those who governed his cities, and they in turn farmed out the job to local merchants and bankers.[70] These merchants engaged in a large variety of activities, partly because there was little need for specialized knowledge or equipment, and partly because the difficulty of trusting strangers in this early day made it easier to do many things oneself.[71] So, for instance, one Balmonahme owned ships, hired out slaves trained as artisans, and lived in a fortified house in the middle of a village he owned near Lagash.[72]

Retailing became a business slightly later. The concentration of pur-chasing power in temples and palaces and the rise of urban life created a new demand for goods and services. Shops soon appeared. Bakers were probably first, due to the cost and danger of ovens.[73] But unlike well-born tamkaru, such early vendors were almost certainly slaves or serfs. The temple or palace provided the wheat, the ovens, and perhaps even the shops that the first bak-ers used. The goldsmith was undoubtedly moonlighting from his job at the palace, and the merchant vessel at the quay probably belonged to an estate, carried the estate's produce, and was staffed by the estate's people. Gradu-ally, though, fully private markets appeared at city gates, along particular streets, and at riverfront quays. Goldsmiths lined a specific street in Sippur, fowlers had their own street in nearby Nuzi, and roaming peddlers hawked salt, wine, beer, and roasted grain.[74]

Even so, "markets, if present at all, would have played a peripheral role only."[75] The distribution of goods in early civilizations was almost entirely by the ruler's command, not the consumer's demand.

Old Babylonia: The Expanded State, Fundamental Business Tools, and Finance

The economic development of Mesopotamia brought new opportunities for trade, but as city-states and jurisdictional borders multiplied, so did wars over land and water. Unlike Egyptian villages strung along the Nile, the small theocracies of Sumeria found consolidation difficult. Well fortified and scattered amid vast, impenetrable marshes and waterways, they were hard to conquer and harder to control. Their theocratic leaders fervently protected their own gods, constantly revolted, and kept the region divided into small city-states.[76]

This began to change around 2300 B.C.E., when Akkad's ruler, Sargon the Great, first secularized sovereign authority.[77] Instead of trampling defeated gods, he honored them and claimed their support. In doing so he sidestepped religious objections to his legitimacy. The conquered could accept his rule, at least so long as he governed adequately, keeping rents and taxes tolerable while providing security, justice, and welfare.[78] Indeed, Sargon was so successful that his state maintained the most extensive irrigation works in southern Babylonia prior to Sasanian rule twenty-five hundred years later.[79] Performance replaced family as the basis for sovereign legitimacy, finally making consolidation possible in Sumeria.[80]

Enlarged political jurisdictions triggered a cascade of improving economic and business conditions, just as some economists credit larger political units with technological success in modern times.[81] Businesses gained larger markets. Trading costs diminished as borders disappeared and subjects came to share customs, laws, languages, and measurement systems. They also identified their gods with each other, as when Nippur's Enlil came to be thought the same as Babylon's Marduk. Known as syncretization, this process fostered trust. Since parties commonly safeguarded their contracts by exchanging oaths and denouncing violators at the local temple, syncretization allowed parties from different religions to believe in this procedure.[82]

Hammurabi: Tools of Accountability and Calculation

The need to maintain legitimacy by performing sovereign functions inspired technical and managerial innovations. By the time Hammurabi (1792–1750 B.C.E.) established his dynasty in Babylon, these were largely in place. Approximately five million people were living in the Fertile Crescent by then (table 1). Growing ports on the Euphrates (Mari, Carchemish) and the Mediterranean (Tyre, Byblos), oasis cities (Damascus, Ebla), and dynastic capitals (Babylon, Uruk, Larsa) numbered between thirty thousand and sixty thousand people each.

Like Sargon, Hammurabi carefully cultivated religious support. His god Marduk was said to have anointed the king's family, while a forged genealogy called the *Sumerian King List* justified his rule through hered-ity.[83] But underlying Hammurabi's legitimacy was administrative compe-tence. His kingdom was a bureaucratic entity, independent of tribe or church, whose network of alliances with neighboring tribes and cities covered far more territory than Sargon's.[84] Cuneiform writing, invented for priests by 3000 B.C.E., had been simplified for use in rulings and orders and to keep track of soldiers, record receipts and disbursements, and me-morialize landholding rights, contracts, judicial decisions, and adminis-trative orders.[85]

Bureaucratic needs also stimulated the development of mathematics. Taxes were based on agricultural production, so rulers needed to calculate the size and yield of every parcel of land.[86] The state's effectiveness in col-lecting taxes gave it a central role in providing welfare, primarily famine protection.[87] For instance, Joseph's suggestion that Pharaoh "take up the fifth part of the land of Egypt in the seven plenteous years"[88] required as-sessors to calculate average yields over seven years and then set taxes at 20 percent of the result. And to help the government manage irrigation and harvests, Babylonian priests invented the measurement of time in seconds, minutes, hours, and days that we still use.

These computational and managerial innovations became essential business tools. Written contracts, bills, receipts, and letters allowed entrepre-neurs to control distant agents and made it more likely that laws would re-ceive predictable and relatively uniform application. Mathematics brought accuracy to calculations, and astronomy gave Babylonians a more linear understanding of time. Babylonian schoolboys were taught to calculate sim-ple and compound interest, evidencing an ability to plan for future revenues and profits.[89]

Hammurabi and other rulers created written legal codes, probably based upon prior oral responses to the complexities of irrigation and urbanism[90] and derived from earlier religious strictures. In other ancient civilizations like Egypt and China, local officials also recorded the residents, owner-ship, and productivity of every plot of land.[91] But to the Egyptians, and many others, it was the gods who kept order. As Charles Seife put it, "In

Egypt, filching your neighbor's land was considered as grave an offense as breaking an oath, murdering somebody, or masturbating in a temple," and according to the *Book of the Dead* the gods would feed your heart to a horrible beast called the Devourer.[92]

In the famous dictum of the Victorian legal scholar Sir Henry Sumner Maine, however, "the movement of the progressive societies has hitherto been a movement from Status to Contract."[93] Under Hammurabi scribes shaped commercial agreements to comply with code requirements, like lawyers today.[94] Hammurabi also created legal procedures and maintained a network of courts, magistrates, and officials.[95] These legal systems improved the scope and trustworthiness of business activity. One of Hammurabi's laws, for example, reimbursed those who ransomed captured citizens, no doubt a comfort to traders venturing abroad.[96] Another law strengthened trust by forbidding any challenge to a properly notarized promissory note.[97] By protecting the ownership and orderly transfer of property, legal systems created wealth. By enforcing agreements, they allowed people to hire agents, work with others, and obtain financing. And by dispensing justice they helped reduce the risks of loss from theft, bad faith, or chicanery.[98]

Legal systems also allocated risks, a service of great benefit to business. Since the cost of risk differs from one person to another, its proper allocation can significantly reduce the total cost of a business venture or increase the willingness of customers to transact business. One approach was to provide bankruptcy protection when crops failed, pledged property was stolen, or natural disasters caused loss. The Code of Hammurabi contains perhaps the earliest bankruptcy provision:

> If a man owe a debt and [should] Adad inundate his field and carry away the produce, or, through lack of water, grain have not grown in the field, in that year he shall not make any return of grain to the creditor, he shall alter his contract-tablet and he shall not pay the interest for that year."[99]

Finance: The Infrastructure of Business

For a sale to happen, the buyer must both desire what is offered and possess wealth to pay for it in the form of purchasing power: money or credit. Economists normally take desire for granted, but purchasing power has been harder to come by. It is finance, the discipline of manipulating wealth, that makes most of this purchasing power available.

Money

Before money there was barter, a slow and uncertain method of exchange. One party may not want what the other offers, or the offers may not have equivalent values. Money, however, is a reliably valuable, divisible, and portable form of wealth. These qualities make it easy to exchange because its value is trustworthy. Indeed, one expert calls it "trust inscribed."[100] As a result, values measured in money are widely understood, and money is a reliable way to hold wealth.[101]

Many items have served as money. The Egyptians and Sumerians initially used dates, olive oil, and barley.[102] But food was too bulky and its value too uncertain for long-distance trade, so by 2000 B.C.E. traders were using silver or gold instead.[103] These metals were widely considered so precious that small amounts provided great purchasing power while being easy to carry and conceal. Their value also remained fairly constant, because new sources were rare and the technology of mining and refining changed very slowly.[104] Even just as units of account, precious metals facilitated transactions; any item to be traded could be valued in terms of the value of silver or gold. By Hammurabi's day, barley was for everyday transactions, while large payments and long-distance trade involved precious metals.[105] Perhaps because his code forgave barley loans if the crop was destroyed by natural disasters, and thus made the loans riskier, Hammurabi allowed interest on barley to reach 33 percent while restricting interest on silver to 20 percent per annum.[106]

Gold and silver were probably first valued as adornments. Most of the Fertile Crescent's gold came from Egypt, where the hieroglyph for gold was a bead necklace.[107] Gold was beautiful and easy to work. Artisans could melt gold dust at mere campfire temperatures or shape nuggets with nothing more than stone tools. At first it was panned from the Nile, but by 4000 B.C.E. it was being mined upstream in Nubia.[108] Silver, also beautiful and workable, was more abundant and therefore less valuable than gold. Coming primarily from India, Persia, and Armenia, it joined barley as Mesopotamia's money.

Early civilizations made precious metals divisible in several ways. By 3200 B.C.E., the Egyptians formed gold into rings of standard weight[109] and chopped the coils into desired lesser weights. Later on the Mesopotamians made both gold and silver coils in integer multiples of shekels, their unit of weight.[110] Merchants also put specified weights of silver into sealed bags. If the merchant was trustworthy, the sacks could serve as local currency. Well into the Middle Ages, artists routinely identified merchants by their holding such moneybags.[111] But fraud also abounded. As early as 1800 B.C.E. one merchant complained to another, "You said, 'I will give good ingots to Gimil-Sin.' That is what you said, but you have not done so; you offered bad ingots to my messenger saying 'Take it or leave it.' Who am I that you should treat me so? Are we not both gentlemen?"[112] Rampant tampering with purity, and chicanery with weights, required the prudent trader to weigh and assay every ingot, bag, ring, or necklace, a tedious and time-consuming process. The scale became another artist's symbol for a merchant.

Credit

One of the great innovations of modern life has been the emergence of credit as the dominant form of purchasing power. In 2004 it constituted about 85 percent of the best measure of purchasing power in the United States, the M3 money supply.[113] Credit was much scarcer in ancient societies, but the Babylonians and their neighbors were financial innovators.[114]

Credit is purchasing power provided in return for a promise of repayment. It comes in many forms, not just loans. These include pledges, investments, guarantees, and the advance of goods or services. The supply of credit depends on the amount of wealth available for temporary use and on the borrower's access to it. But primarily it depends on the trustworthiness of repayment. Generally speaking, the more trust, the more credit.[115] This trust rests partly on realities like the debtor's ability to repay, the effectiveness of collection mechanisms, and the quality of information about the debtor. It also depends, however, on the creditor's mood, an imponderable that has often caused rapid and otherwise inexplicable shifts in asset values.

The major Mesopotamian financiers of long-distance trade were temples and royal agencies. But by 3000 B.C.E. private individuals and professional moneylenders also supplied credit to trading ventures,[116] sometimes in tiny amounts, a bracelet or two.[117] Most commercial loans were secured to guarantee the promise of repayment. Pledged assets might include houses, orchards, fields, slaves, or even the borrower and his family.[118] Farmers often borrowed against their standing crops, with repayment due at harvest time.[119] All pledged assets became the creditor's property upon default in any amount.[120]

The first known financial instruments, representations of a promise to pay, date from about 2800 B.C.E., excavated at Gilgamesh's home city of Uruk. These were tokens shaped like lambs, loaves of bread, honey jars, and other promised goods, encased in clay balls. Some tokens even represent units of work. Marks on the balls probably represent adjustments made after the initial loan.

Most of the loans represented in these clay softballs were for personal emergencies, but many were for business: an investment for partnership, an advance to a baker, an investment to hire a boat and crew for a trading venture.[121] As the word for "interest" in many ancient languages shows, these largely pastoral societies readily accepted the payment of interest on such loans, considering it similar to the offspring of livestock.[122] Oil, wool, animals, real estate, and slaves could be bought on credit. Credit normally had a fixed duration, although demand loans were not unknown. Partnerships usually liquidated annually, with the proceeds distributed under legal supervision.[123]

Mesopotamian financial sophistication was unrivaled until the heyday of Rome, two thousand years later. Not only was credit readily available, the loan instrument was readily salable as well. For instance, in 1796 B.C.E. one Dimuzi-gamal, probably a banker living in Ur under Larsa's powerful King Rim Sin, invested in bakeries serving Rim Sin's palace at Larsa, a day's journey north, as well as the local temple. At one point he and a partner borrowed 250 grams of silver, each promising to repay 297.3g five years later. Dimuzi then made loans to farmers and fishermen at rates up to 20 percent per month. His lender, meanwhile, sold Dimuzi's loan to other merchants, who duly collected in 1791 B.C.E.[124]

The Babylonians also used "structured finance," a method of reducing investment costs that the chairman of J. P. Morgan Chase recently described as a modern innovation for the "pooling, segregation or reallocation of expected cash flows in ways that reduce uncertainty or diversify or reallocate risk."[125] Here is the Babylonian version:

Lu-meshlamtae and Nigsisanabsa have borrowed from Ur-ninmar 2 minas of silver (in the form of) 5 gur of oil and 30 garments as capital for a partnership for an expedition to Tilmun to buy copper. After safe return of the expedition, [Ur-ninmur] will not recognize any loss incurred by the merchants; they have agreed to satisfy Ur-nin-mar with 4 minas of copper for each shekel of silver as a just price. They have sworn by the king. Before [five named witnesses].[126]

While sophisticated mathematical, accounting, and legal tools made such contracts possible, the unusual trading environment of Mesopotamia probably explains the demand for them. Elsewhere, self-financing elites conducted most of the long-distance trade at infrequent intervals, and largely by sea. But Mesopotamia's greater need for trade had spawned many private traders, who often needed credit.[127] They traded by land, where low-capacity donkey caravans made frequent trips necessary, crossing bandit-infested terrain and passing rapacious customs barriers. These circumstances made it important to minimize bullion shipments, leading to the creation of financial instruments to make this possible. These instruments anticipated modern methods of payment like checks, letters of credit, and negotiable bills of exchange.

Kanesh

Mesopotamia's financial sophistication is clearly reflected in a vast trove of cuneiform tablets found at Kanesh, the seat of a copper- and silver-mining region in eastern Turkey, where merchants from Assur had a trading post between 2000 B.C.E. and 1800 B.C.E.[128] The tablets provide our fullest picture of Babylonian trade and finance.

It was a difficult trek for the Damascus-bred black donkeys of the Assyrians to cross eight hundred miles of barren, bandit-infested hills from Assur to Kanesh. The dangerous trip took months, even with stations along the way to replenish scarce water and fodder.[129] Still, the copper and silver of Kanesh was worth the trouble, because investors could double their money.

Kanesh's Hittite ruler confined the traders to their own quarter in the town, which they governed through a council called a *karum*. By segregating them, he could control their interactions with his subjects until familiarity made informal contact safer.[130] Karum officials escorted arriving merchants to the palace, where they negotiated exchange rates and other terms of trade and paid about 10 percent of their goods for access to the territory and use of the ruler's warehouses.[131]

The merchants' main concern was receiving the right trade goods from home in a timely fashion. They often requested cloth from Babylonia, which was superior to their own,[132] and they repeatedly urged the Assyrian king to remain on good terms with Babylon's ruler.[133] They fretted about when inventory would ship, the speed and safety of its transport, and how to finance it all. Typically, a partnership with outside investors financed the inventory, which was shipped in sealed containers to protect against pilferage en route. The trader himself was often only a minority partner, in one instance owning 57 of the 410 talents of tin he carried in his caravan.

One prolific correspondent was Imdi-ilum,[134] whose grandfather, a royal favorite, had founded the family business. After Imdi-ilum's young father died, one uncle directed affairs in Assur while Imdi-ilum accompanied the other to Kanesh and throughout the mining district. One of Imdi-ilum's brothers, stationed at a caravansary along the way, probably hired out idle donkeys and smuggled goods.

As usual throughout history, the family constituted the basic business unit.[135] Family members were more available, easier to manage, and usually more trustworthy than outsiders.[136] The women could play active, even dominant roles. Queen Barnamatara of Umma sold imported copper and bought cattle from Elam around 2300 B.C.E. Elam's queen ran a textile factory, and another queen named Iltani operated a textile factory with twenty-five workers, owned more than one thousand sheep, along with shepherds, donkeys, and drivers, and exported textiles as far away as Babylon, Assyria, and Anatolia.[137] Families and allied houses could number hundreds of people, including dependents like servants and slaves. For instance, in Genesis 14.14 Abraham "armed his trained servants, born in his own house, three hundred and eighteen" and pursued the capturers of Lot.

Sisters managed affairs in Assur. Imdi-ilum's sister was his purchasing agent, invested his money, and collected rents and loans. His wife did the same for her brothers. As in modern agricultural communities, real estate was a major focus, and investments centered on houses, gardens, orchards, and fields. The forms of landholding were the same as today: outright ownership and leases of various terms and conditions.[138]

Labor's Love Lost: Slavery and Other Jobs

In all ancient societies, most people did most of their work as self-employed peasants or their families. In Mesopotamia, the most common form of employment was forced labor. Peasants were recruited during idle periods to staff palace workshops, repair canals, or perform other public functions.[139] In an era of meager surpluses, it required the effort of several peasant families to maintain one full-time employee.[140]

Most full-time employees were therefore slaves, who could be forced to work the long hours necessary to compensate for their expense. Many were servants; by 2000 B.C.E. Babylonian households often had three or four.[141] Employees in the palaces and temples included scribes, who served as the clerks, lawyers, and accountants of the day. The first professionals, they created and recorded agreements on moist clay tablets, which the principals then stamped with personal seals to signify assent. They also notarized important events like land sales, which an agent could make only after notifying the owner of the price by sealed writing.[142] Skilled artisans like masons, carpenters, and artists were sometimes retained as well and might form craft associations that performed religious or civic functions.[143]

Difficult, dangerous, and unpleasant work like mining, quarrying, and construction fell to slaves and convicts throughout all of ancient history. But slaves were too expensive for agricultural labor in Mesopotamia. During the Third Dynasty of Ur, around 2000 B.C.E., one slave cost about six times as much as an acre of land.[144] There was also the expense of supervision. Except for shepherds, who tended sheep or goats in return for a share in the flock,[145] these costs could not be recovered.[146]

The kind of social and economic forces that shape the behavior of modern businesses were already operating when private profit first appeared. So the exports of ancient Sumeria, which paid for the building materials and baubles that the elite imported, reflected the region's special advantages: a fine growing environment for date palms, on the one hand, and plentiful sheep combined with surplus labor, on the other.

The profits from long-distance trading ventures, the first private businesses, quickly poured into loans and ownership interests in other investments. The first private retail enterprises appeared slightly later. Other forms of business emerged more gradually. The ruling elites controlled the economic activities within their reach and distributed virtually all the benefits. Business long remained a marginal activity in these command societies.

Contrary to the apparent assumption of *Wall Street Journal* editorial writers, business did not precede government on this earth. Rather, the growing competence of governments created the fundamental circumstances and skills that make business possible. Sargon's secularization of sovereignty allowed conquerors to stabilize and control larger populations, a step that increased the size of markets and made transactions more secure. By the time of Babylon's Hammurabi and his dynasty, governmental bureaucracies had created the basic legal framework and computational skills that businesses rely upon to this day. Under special circumstances, as in the Assyrian outposts at Kanesh, businesses themselves generated notable financial innovations.

2

Middle Eastern Empires,
1600–323 B.C.E.

Great technological and political disruptions introduced successively larger, better-governed Middle Eastern empires, including the first truly colonial power. Trade, rising in volume but frustrated by imperial rivalries, increasingly fell to favorably located commercial states like those of the Phoenicians. Though not strictly businesses, they avidly pursued commercial profit, even inventing our alphabet to simplify mercantile recordkeeping. As the Assyrian and Persian Empires created larger markets, trading costs fell. Within the enormous Persian Empire "the umbrella of the Persian peace"[1] quickened commercial activity despite the lingering command economy, setting the stage for the transformations that Alexander the Great would bring.

Chariot Empires

The invention of war chariots allowed raiders from the horse country of Anatolia, Persia, and central Asia to evict many of the Middle East's rulers.[2] The Hyksos conquered Egypt, the Mitanni overran northern Mesopotamia and Syria, and the Hittites sacked Babylon, killing Hammurabi's grandson in 1595 B.C.E.[3]

Table 2
Middle Eastern Dynasties and Rulers

Dynasty	Period (B.C.E.)	Selected Rulers (Dates)
Hittites (Anatolia)	1800–1200	
Mittanis (Syria)	1550–1330	
New Kingdom (Egypt)	1600–1000	Ahmose (1550–1525) Queen Hatsephut (1504–1482) Thutmoses III (1479–1429) Amenophis III (1417–1367) Akhenaton (1353–1333) Ramses II (1304–1237)
Assyrian Empire	1114–609	Tiglath-pilesar I (1114–1076) Assurnasirpal I (1049–1031) Tiglath-pilesar II (966–935) Tiglath-pilesar III (745–727) Sargon II (709–705) Sennacherib (705–681) Esarhadon (681–668) Ashurbanipal (668–626)
Neo-Babylonian Dynasty	625–539	Nebuchadnezzar II (630–562)
Persian Empire	538–331	Cyrus (538–529) Cambyses (529–522) Darius I (521–486) Xerxes I (486–465) Darius III (338–330)

Note: for Egyptian New Kingdom chronology, I relied on Reeves and Wilkinson 1998. For other chronologies, see the texts cited in the relevant discussions.

It took the Egyptians about a century to expel the Hyksos. The victorious New Kingdom pharaohs, realizing that chariot horses did not breed well in Egypt's climate, ended Egypt's traditional isolationism. Over the following centuries, they would compete with Hittites to extract slaves, loot, and tribute from the Levant. In fact, at Megiddo in northern Israel, also known as Armageddon, Egyptian charioteers won history's first recorded battle in 1469 B.C.E. Egyptian traders ventured to Syria and Mesopotamia, south to the Sudan, and west into Libya.[4] Egypt also welcomed foreign merchants. By 1400 B.C.E. the pharaoh's coast guard in the Nile Delta protected trading vessels from pirates,[5] and the capital of Memphis hosted foreign merchants near the temple of Byblos's goddess, Astarte the Stranger.[6]

This commercial awakening poured luxuries and exotica into Egypt. A wall painting in the tomb of Queen Hatsephut depicts a trading expedition to Punt, probably in Ethiopia, which obtained ebony, ivory, gold, incense (including live myrrh trees), cosmetics, animal skins, thirty-three hundred head of cattle, Ethiopians with spears and children, apes, monkeys, dogs, and even a live panther.[7]

The pharaoh's emissaries had long procured wood, timber, and naval supplies by following prevailing sea currents north to Levantine ports like Byblos, located on the wooded shores of the Lebanon mountains, whence summer breezes blew them home again. In fact, Egyptians called their sea-going vessels "Byblos ships,"[8] and the Greeks knew Egypt's principal export, papyrus, as "byblos." But when Hittites blocked access, Egyptians turned their oared galleys to the next accessible source of naval supplies, the forested island of Crete.[9]

Minoans and Mycenaeans

The early discovery of copper on Cyprus, Crete, and the nearby Cyclades islands had allowed the island farmers and fishermen to make bronze weapons and tools for building large, seaworthy ships.[10] As pirates and traders, Crete's Minoans roamed the eastern Mediterranean and perhaps even reached Sicily and Sardinia.[11] By 1550 B.C.E., with colonies on Rhodes and Cyprus, they were trading with the Hittites, Mittanis, and Levantine city-states. The main customer, though, was Egypt, which supplied gold, linen, papyrus, and rope in exchange for their timber, wine, olive oil, hides, and purple dye.[12]

The Minoans built citadels, including a huge complex at Knossos apparently modeled after one at Mari,[13] with running water, toilets, drainage, heat, and light.[14] The ruler and his officials lived there, as well as hundreds of scribes, accountants, and craftsmen. They anointed themselves with imported oils and perfumes, wore intricate gold and silver adornments, and drank from elaborate silver vessels. Surviving traces of their language, Linear B, consist primarily of accounting records. The complex provided outfitted workshops for shipwrights, weapons specialists, cloth-makers, potters, and goldsmiths. Residents received ration cards, and the accountants kept detailed records of inputs and outputs.[15]

Around 1440 B.C.E. an earthquake destroyed Knossos. Mycenaeans invaded and completed the Minoan destruction. The Mycenaeans were Homer's Achaeans, who had built cleverly fortified stone palaces in the

Peloponnesus, like Nestor's at Pylos and Agamemnon's at Mycenae about 1600 B.C.E. They evidently prospered as pirates, warriors, and perhaps mercenaries, since their graves have yielded gold ornaments in amounts that compare to the Scythian hoards or the Macedonian royal treasury.[16] They quickly replaced the Minoans on Crete, Cyprus, and Rhodes and in trade with the Middle East for the next two centuries. A Mycenaean vessel, recovered off the coast of Turkey in 1982, carried six tons of copper ingots from Cyprus, hundreds of tin ingots from Persia, and a ton of perfume resin from southern Arabia or Africa, plus glass, scrap metal, gold and silver objects from the Levant, Cypriot ceramics, and ebony logs, ivory, and hippopotamus teeth from Africa.[17]

Ugarit

Probably the greatest commercial state of the day was Ugarit, a Syrian port at the hub of many trade routes. Caravans from Mesopotamia, ships from the Mediterranean, donkey trains laden with silver and copper from Urartu (a kingdom encompassing Kanesh and Lake Van), and merchants from Damascus and other cities all converged there.[18] By around 1500 B.C.E. trade had become Ugarit's main activity.[19]

As a small but independent city-state, Ugarit offered a safe and orderly place for traders from the surrounding empires to mingle. Its kings, whose palace occupied a quarter of the city's area,[20] posed no military threat to others. Ugarit offered growing returns to scale: the more people used it, the more useful it became. As traders and goods flowed into its markets, the city could increasingly provide one-stop shopping and valuable information about prices, supplies, demand, political conditions, and other relevant matters. Economists and historians call such places ports of trade; Ugarit was the first.

Ugarit maintained first-class commercial services. The king provided trustworthy weights and measures, policed the markets, and made treaties to protect travelers.[21] Visitors could buy, repair, and outfit their ships; expert money changers and assayers of precious metals were available; and food, lodging, wine, women, and song were plentiful. Ugarit also invented the original version of our alphabet to simplify merchants' recordkeeping.[22]

The harbor was full of ships loading and unloading, and workmen repairing or building others. Some ships reached two-hundred-tons displacement, equivalent to the average size of those in the Atlantic trade during the American Revolutionary War.[23] Bordering the harbor were jumbled streets

and alleys lined with two-story stone or masonry buildings, which served
as stores, workshops, dye works, and boarding houses. Goldsmiths, silversmiths, engravers, and sculptors worked nearby.[24] Vendors of metal and
metalwares, timber cut to measure, and other goods filled the streets by day.
Food markets offered wheat, fruit, olives, oils, wine, spices, and cheeses. A
livestock market sold horses, donkeys, mules, cattle, sheep, and birds.[25]

In addition to selling local resources like timber and salt, Ugarit's elite
financed long-distance trading ventures, including the manufacture and
sale of armaments like war chariots to Egyptians, Hittites, and others.[26]
Trade was not always honest. An exasperated Hittite king wrote, "What is
this business about which you have kept sending messages to [me], saying,
'Herewith I have sent you lapis lazuli'? . . . Is [your king] having a joke with
me, that he has picked up stones from the ground and sent them, saying
'Herewith I have sent you lapis lazuli'?" Similarly, a Mitanni ruler protested
to Egypt's pharaoh that the solid gold statues his agent had purchased arrived gold-plated instead.[27]

The great private merchants of Ugarit operated as royal partners.
Abdihaqab, a long-distance trader who made enormous profits for himself
and the king, acquired large estates, held high offices, and gained lucrative
concessions. Sinarunu handled royal real estate transactions and traded
on behalf of the king and himself in Crete. He also collected taxes, subcontracting the work to lesser merchants.[28] The palace dominated capital-in-
tensive production such as armaments, shipbuilding, chariotmaking, and
lumber. Private merchants marketed the produce of royal estates and on
their behalf or for themselves operated saltworks, wove textiles, made copper and bronze wares, and traded livestock.[29] Many goods were normally
handled privately: purple wool, carpets, bolts of woolen or linen cloth, and
finished garments.[30] Merchants were respectable; the most successful might
join the elite chariot corps and were sometimes ennobled.[31]

With the thirteenth century, however, drought on the Romanian
steppes would unleash a complete disruption of the Middle East's elite trading system and leave Ugarit in ruins.

Thirteenth-Century Convulsion

Phrygians, possibly fleeing other tribes, overran the Hittites. Egypt's trade,
disrupted by internal unrest, virtually collapsed, plunging the Mycenaean

world into depression, piracy, and mass emigration.[32] Agamemnon's father Atreus ravaged Cyprus, as Hittite chronicles mention,[33] and the *Iliad's* famous attack on Troy soon followed. Then the Dorians, possibly fleeing Romanian drought, invaded Greece and overwhelmed the Mycenaeans.[34] Refugees, known to the Egyptians as Sea People, descended on the Nile Delta. Called Philistines in the Levant, they gave Palestine its name, settled Ashkelon, and sacked Ugarit.[35]

The destruction of Hittite and Egyptian power allowed Levantine communities to enjoy a golden age. The Israelites prospered under David and Solomon, Aramaic Damascus flourished, and Phoenician city-states grew in size and wealth. Around 975 B.C.E. the invention of rainwater cisterns, attributed to King Hiram of Tyre, greatly improved irrigation agriculture and helped the region support a considerably larger urban population.[36] A disruptive new technology was coming, however.

Iron Age and the Assyrian Empire

To Achilles, a bronze cooking tripod was worth three women or twelve oxen,[37] the tin and copper needed to make bronze being that scarce and expensive. Iron, widely available and inexpensive, could make far cheaper cooking pots and equip much larger armies than the Bronze Age could afford.[38] The technology of working iron had long been a Hittite secret.[39] But with their collapse the secret dispersed, reaching the Assyrians by 1000 B.C.E., the Greeks after 900 B.C.E., the Etruscans by 800 B.C.E., and the Celts of northern Europe by 640 B.C.E.[40]

Military advantage shifted to those who could organize their armies and military logistics to make the best use of iron's potential. With plentiful iron deposits, the Assyrians of northwestern Mesopotamia reacted first. They armed thousands of foot soldiers who overwhelmed Syria and Babylonia, conquered the Levant, and took Egypt, whose lack of iron ore badly hampered the pharaoh's power.[41] As Byron put it in "The Destruction of Sennacherib":

> The Assyrian came down like the wolf on the fold,
> And his cohorts were gleaming in purple and gold;
> And the sheen of their spears was like stars on the sea,
> When the blue wave rolls nightly on deep Galilee.

The size of the Assyrian forces also changed the nature of their domination. Where the Bronze Age's hundreds of charioteers had been light on the land and quick to leave with their plunder, the thousands of Assyrians devoured resources like locusts and had to live off the lands they conquered. The result was colonization.[42]

As colonizers, the Assyrians greatly improved the business environment in the lands they seized. Occupiers seeking sustenance, rather than raiders seeking plunder, they promoted productivity. They built new irrigation systems, restored old ones, and imported peasants to farm abandoned fields. By taxing potential rather than actual crop yields, they forced landowners to maintain production.[43] They greatly reduced transport costs by importing two-humped Bactrian camels, which could carry more goods over longer distances,[44] and for military reasons built new roads and improved old ones, paving and widening the most heavily used so that chariots could pass each other.[45]

But their greatest contribution to business was the consolidation of their lands into a large trading network governed under a common law derived from the Code of Hammurabi.[46] Many subsistence farmers and somnolent backwaters, forced to pay Assyrian taxes and furnish food, clothing, and other necessities to military garrisons, began generating surpluses and receiving Assyrian silver in compliance with Assyrian laws.[47] This happened, for instance, at Elephantine on the upper Nile, where Esarhadon (681–669 B.C.E.) had stationed Israelite soldiers and their families. Even the notorious Assyrian mass deportations increased regional coherence. Those deported communicated with their homelands, while the forced mixing of people from different cultures and religions reduced old barriers of alienation and xenophobia.[48]

The construction of an empirewide common market clearly raised the amount of wealth generated, converted much of it into goods and services, and resulted in heightened levels of trade. As colonial wealth flowed into Assyria's royal treasuries, the rulers lavishly adorned Assur and built themselves monumental new capitals at Nineveh, Nimrud, and Khorasabad. Nineveh had twenty-five-meter-high double walls and fifteen monumental gates. Its water came from a fifty-kilometer canal that crossed one valley on an aqueduct 22 meters wide and 280 meters long.[49] Artisans were gathered from all over the empire: carpenters, potters, scribes, musicians, physicians, augurs and diviners, smiths, jewelry workers, and leatherworkers.[50]

But in spite of all these improvements to the business environment, the structure of the Assyrian economy remained virtually unchanged. Goods and services continued to be allocated by the ruling elites, money was still used only rarely, and business remained marginal. The royal residences were far from population centers and well off the major trade routes. Although loot and wealth may have pooled in the Assyrian capitals, most manufacturing and trade took place in Levantine ports like Sidon, Tyre, Byblos, and Beirut.[51]

Phoenicians

Beirut may date from approximately 3000 B.C.E., Tyre was known by 2750 B.C.E., and the Egyptians wrote about Byblos as early as 2700 B.C.E.[52] Each city-state controlled hinterland villages nestled between the cedar- and pine-timbered Lebanon Mountains and the Mediterranean Sea, where most of the inhabitants fished, farmed, tended sheep, or cut timber. The Israelites called these people *canaani*, the Aramaic word for merchants. Our term *Phoenician* comes from the Greek word for red, the color of their famous purple dye.[53]

Due to their favorable environment, the Phoenicians succeeded the Minoans and Mycenaeans as the preeminent sailors, shipwrights, and carpenters of the eastern Mediterranean. Around 1075 B.C.E. the king of Sidon boasted to the Egyptian priest Wen-Amon that he had no fewer than twenty ships in Byblos and fifty in Sidon.[54] King Hiram I of Tyre (969–936 B.C.E.) supplied both wood and carpenters for Solomon's Temple in Jerusalem,[55] and they jointly sponsored trade with Ophir (Yemen, perhaps) from Eilat on the Red Sea, receiving gold, silver, ivory, monkeys, and precious stones from Somalia and India.[56]

The Phoenician cities were also the preeminent manufacturers of the day. Ancient cloth usually came in one shade: dark for wool, off-white for linen. But the eastern Mediterranean's now-extinct Murex clam, when left to putrefy in the sun, secreted a dark liquid that made "royal purple," the most vivid and valuable textile dye then known.[57] By 1000 B.C.E. the Phoenicians had learned about it, and no one else could produce such color. Everybody wanted it,[58] so Phoenicians like Hanunu of Sidon obliged. He became the Assyrian court's principal supplier of dyed cloth.[59] Sidon and Tyre, with access to royal purple, as well as vegetable dyes, Egyptian linen, and abundant local wool, became the Paris and Milan of the day.

Once the Phoenicians were shipping cloth, they added lesser luxury goods like carved ivory to their offerings.[60] In shipping these goods they came to handle most of the Assyrian Empire's slave trade and gained a virtual monopoly over the metal trade.[61] This created expertise in mining and the fabrication of armor, tools, and metalwares. Tyre's experts advised Solomon and turned Damascus's iron into exports of weapons and tools.[62]

Phoenician cities hummed with workshops, and their traders built a network of shipping and trading firms.[63] They dominated the Mediterranean sea routes, and their traders gained privileges in Babylonia[64] and Egypt, including the establishment of temples to their gods.[65] These gods protected their ventures, especially Tyre's Melkart, who cursed contract violators. His temples may have coordinated and financed Tyre's trade throughout the Fertile Crescent, operating like the *keiratsu* and *chaebols* of Japan and Korea today.[66]

In any event, Phoenicians were clearly buying, selling, manufacturing, distributing, negotiating, and trading more intensively than their contemporaries. Honed for centuries, their commercial skills became a source of gain in themselves, perhaps the most lucrative of all. Tyre, for one, negotiated independence from the Assyrians in return for annual tribute payments and also gained exclusive trading rights in Urartu (biblical Ararat), which controlled the rich iron, copper, and silver mines of the Armenian mountains and was noted for its weapons and armor.[67]

To the prophet Ezekiel, Tyre was "of perfect beauty":

> Thy borders are in the midst of the seas, thy builders have perfected thy beauty. They have made all thy ship boards of fir trees of Senir [Mount Hermon]: they have taken cedars from Lebanon to make masts for thee. Of the oaks of Bashan [near Lake Tiberias] have they made thine oars; the company of the Ashurites have thy benches of ivory, brought of the isles of Chittim [Cyprus]. Fine linen with broidered work from Egypt was that which thou spreadest forth to be thy sail; blue and purple from the isles of Elishash [Cyprus also] was that which covered thee. The inhabitants of Sidon and Aradus were thy mariners; thy wise men, O Tyre, that were in thee, were thy pilots.[68]

In Tyre, as in Ugarit, the royalty and nobility owned and sponsored the most valuable businesses, but private merchants could also own ships and sponsor voyages.[69] Commercial ships often sailed as a fleet for protection from piracy.[70] Although insurance would remain unknown to antiquity, Phoenician financiers reduced risk by diversifying their investments across many ships, each usually laden with trade goods from numerous merchants.[71]

Trading techniques varied. Herodotus described a silent trade for African gold or ivory. A Phoenician ship would anchor offshore while sailors placed wares on the beach and lit a signal fire. As they waited on their ship, the Africans would arrive, inspect the wares, deposit some gold, and withdraw. The Phoenicians then inspected the offer, leaving it if too little. The process repeated itself until everyone was satisfied.[72]

Trade with the more familiar Greek, Etruscan, and Spanish tribes took the form of exchanging gifts with their chieftains, much as Europeans would later do with North American Indians.[73] The gifts were typically manufactured tools and trinkets in return for copper, gold, or access to silver mines.[74] The Phoenicians, seeking profit, tried to give the least necessary to satisfy the chieftain's pride.[75] An outraged Homer, foreshadowing agrarian society's perennial complaints about business practices, called the Phoenicians "greedy knaves, bringing countless trinkets in their black ship."[76] Paradoxically, since the tribesmen got what they valued and could not make for themselves, the trades were unfair only from a perspective that values precious metals more highly than the tribesmen did; in other words, from the commercial perspective that Homer and his agrarian progeny professed to disdain![77]

With organized states, terms of trade were usually negotiated. As at Kanesh, the trader/diplomat initially met the ruler in a ceremonial encounter similar to meetings between heads of state today, replete with gifts and flowery speeches. Later would come prolonged haggling over what could be bought and sold, when, and for how long. Other terms covered the traders' lodging, provisions, and safety.[78] The agreement might specify approximate equivalences between items, since barter did not allow for exactitude, but the Phoenicians controlled their costs by standardizing the goods they provided.[79]

Wen-Amon's journey shows the practice in operation. In 1025 B.C.E. Egypt's pharaoh sent this priest to Byblos for timber. He requested an audience with the king, and five months later it took place. The king agreed to send samples of timber for inspection. The ship returned to Byblos with "gold, five silver jugs, ten garments of royal linen; ten kherd of good linen from upper Egypt; five hundred rolls of finished papyrus, five hundred cow hides; five hundred ropes; twenty bags of lentils and thirty baskets of fish." Byblos's king "rejoiced and . . . detailed 300 men and 300 beasts and appointed supervisors over them that they should fell the trees."[80]

Due to their resources and skills, for centuries Tyre's merchant families, with agents in towns like Carchemish, Aleppo, Nineveh, and Babylon, dominated Fertile Crescent trade.[81] Many cities would later follow the pattern of Tyre's success. Initially, prosperity came from natural resources—a great harbor, nearby conifer forests, and an accessible location within a growing region. The murex clams provided a manufacturing advantage, which in turn became the foundation of further manufacturing and trade. In pursuing these activities, Tyre's citizens acquired commercial skills that increased the value of their work and attracted other profitable opportunities, like the metal trade. These in turn led to new skills like diplomacy, metal fabrication, and distribution.

The next step, typical of later commercial centers like Rhodes, Florence, Venice, Amsterdam, London, and New York, would have been putting its wealth to use as a financial center. But since coins and readily exchangeable money did not yet exist, this was not feasible for Tyre.

In time, then, political changes chipped away at Tyre's privileges, as when Egypt seized Judea in 930 B.C.E. and blocked Tyre's access to the Red Sea fleet at Eilat. Others acquired Phoenician commercial acumen, most notably the Arameans, who lived throughout Syria and Mesopotamia. Since supplying black donkeys to the Assyrian traders at Kanesh, they had become the Fertile Crescent's principal transporters of overland trade.[82] Their language became the commercial tongue,[83] and around 800 B.C.E. Damascus even replaced Tyre as the exclusive Assyrian agent for trade with Urartu.[84]

Tyre's response was a speculative search for new silver resources in the western Mediterranean. It proved spectacularly successful, leading to the greatest pre-Columbian discovery of treasure in history.

Carthage

In 814 B.C.E., it seems, Tyre's Princess Elissa fled her murderous brother, King Pygmalion, for the superb, well-protected harbor site of Carthage (modern Tunis).[85] According to a Greek pun, she offered to buy a hill upon which to build a citadel, or *byrsa* in Phoenician. The local chief would sell her only what she could cover with an oxhide, *byrsa* in Greek, so Elissa cut one into strips thin enough to reach around the hill she wanted.[86] Carthage shared nearby Sicily's productive climate and soil, and Phoenician irrigation techniques soon turned the hinterland into a thriving garden of wheat fields, fruit orchards, vineyards, olive groves, and pastures.[87]

Not long afterward, the Phoenicians heard of immensely rich ore deposits in the Rio Tinto and Guadalquivir River basins of Spain. Diodorus, a Roman Era Greek historian, attributed the discovery to a huge forest fire that sent pure silver flowing down the hills: "The natives did not know how to exploit it, but once the Phoenicians heard of the affair they bought the silver in exchange for objects of negligible value. . . . It is said that such was the cupidity of the traders that they replaced the lead anchors of their ships with silver ones after there was no more room for silver in the vessels."[88] In fact the local Tarrascans had long used these mines, which also produced gold, copper, lead, iron, and, to this day, mercury. But the Phoenicians used iron tools, better smelting techniques, and systematic mining practices to greatly increase production.[89] In 770 B.C.E. they founded Cadiz on an offshore island to refine and ship the ore.[90]

To protect and supply their mines, the Phoenicians settled colonies around the western Mediterranean and maintained control there for hundreds of years.[91] They developed a commercial network, transshipping Cornish tin, mining Sardinia's lead and silver, manufacturing trade goods like the ceramics of Toscanos,[92] importing all kinds of manufactured goods to Spain.

Carthage became a port of trade like Tyre. Indeed, after murex clams were transplanted there from Phoenicia, it became known for its colorful cushions, carpets, and embroidery. Metal factories produced weapons and armor, scissors, mirrors, forks, and knives, and Carthaginian craftsmen also made pottery, glass, and jewelry. As traders, the Carthaginians inherited both the high skills and shady reputation of their Phoenician forebears. But they remained intensely loyal to Tyre, sending tribute and military support.

Eventually, however, the flood of silver into Assyria reduced its price so much that after 734 B.C.E. the Assyrians demanded ever more tribute from Tyre, and ultimately the Spanish mines closed.[93] The Assyrians installed customs officials at Tyre, besieged the city in 701, and annexed its hinterland in 640. Heroic searches for new metal sources, including a probable circumnavigation of Africa in 600 and a probe to Britain and the Baltic Sea in 450,[94] discovered nothing comparable to the Spanish mines.

Assyrian Downfall

As the first colonial power, the Assyrians made many mistakes. They demanded excessive rents and taxes, tolerated corruption, and incited hatred with their cruelty. King Assurnasirpal had the skins of rebels hung from his walls,[95] and the stone monument celebrating victory over the Mitanni boasts that 14,400 of them were blinded.[96] About 10 percent of the empire's population fell victim to their main punitive tactic, mass deportations.[97]

Most fatally, Assyria's colonial governors controlled their own military forces and led revolts at every opportunity. Many succeeded; Assyria managed to rule Egypt for only twenty years; and Babylonia, Judea, and the Phoenician city-states often regained independence as well.[98] By 614 B.C.E. Babylonia and Egypt were again independent, and in 612 the Chaldean rulers of Babylonia and the Medes of Persia jointly sacked Nineveh.[99]

While the Babylonians seized the Levant, sacking Jerusalem in 586 B.C.E. (deporting many Jews to Babylonia) and taking Tyre in 583, the Medes pushed into Anatolia, attacking the western kingdom of Lydia. According to Herodotus,[100] their King Cyaxeres had upbraided his Scythian hunters for failing to find game. In revenge, they barbecued a Mede child and fed him to Cyaxeres, then fled to Lydia. When Lydia's king refused to extradite the culprits, war ensued. It ended on May 28, 585 B.C.E., one of the few certain dates in ancient history, when an eclipse predicted by Thales of Miletus stopped a pitched battle.

Mede leadership fell to the Persian leader Cyrus the Great (559–530 B.C.E.), who with unprecedented statesmanship adopted the Mede title "king of kings" and kept many Medes in office, effectively unifying his tribal forces. According to Herodotus, Lydia's King Croesus then asked the Delphic Oracle if he should attack Cyrus. Told that he "would destroy a great empire," he foolishly did so. Cyrus annexed both Lydia and the Ionian Greek city-states on Anatolia's Aegean coast.[101] He next secured Persia's eastern frontier on the Indus River and turned to Babylonia in 546 B.C.E.

The Babylonians, even more brutal than the Assyrians, had forgotten the lesson of Sargon and demanded obeisance to their religion, inspiring widespread hatred. They fled as Babylon welcomed Cyrus, whose reputation for toleration and statesmanship made him enormously popular. Acclaimed Babylonia's king, he quickly gained the submission of its colonies as well. By his death Cyrus ruled from the Hellespont to India, and from the Aral Sea to the borders of Egypt, which his son Cambyses (530–522 B.C.E.) soon conquered.

Persian Empire

The great contribution of the Persian Empire to business history was to legitimize Persian rule over the empire's many tribes and nationalities, implementing often-innovative policies that later rulers would copy. Improved sovereign legitimacy allowed for larger markets, fewer barriers to trade, and lower transaction costs.[102]

Even though the Persian economy retained a traditional command-economy organization, it occupied a larger territory for longer periods than any before it. It stretched from Anatolia to the Indus River, south to the Levant, and for much of its time included Egypt, first captured after Cyrus's death by his son Cambyses. About nineteen million people lived within the empire at its largest. At its center was Babylon, the city of Sargon and Hammurabi. With three hundred thousand people,[103] it presented "a vista of high white terraces, luxuriant greenery, great crenellated walls and towers."[104] The walls, stretching across the Euphrates River, formed a rough square fifteen miles to a side and were wide enough that two four-horse chariots could pass abreast along the top. Tyre, with about fifty thousand people, was probably the empire's next largest city.[105]

Darius the Great (521–486 B.C.E.) won a civil war to gain the throne after Cambyses died. In Herodotus's charming version of events, the contenders agreed to meet at dawn, and whoever's horse whinnied first would

Table 3
Population, ca. 400 B.C.E.

Region	Population
Egypt	5,000,000+[a]
Syria and the Levant	3,000,000[b]
Persia and Anatolia	7,000,000–8,000,000[c]
Mesopotamia	3,000,000[d]

a. Bowman 1989: 17.
b. Peters 1970: 517 puts the population of Syria plus the Levant at 6,000,000 by Alexander's day.
c. For Persia and Anatolia in Alexander's day, Aperghis 2001: 76 estimates some 11,000,000, so 8,000,000 seems reasonable for the earlier time.
d. Aperghis's estimate (2001: 76) for Mesopotamia is 3,500,000.

become king. The night before, Darius had his stallion mate his favorite mare at the meeting place. When the princes came riding up at dawn, Darius's stallion "started forward and neighed."

The West remembers Darius primarily for his failure to invade Greece. But Darius joined Cyrus as "the Great" because together they instituted many new measures to legitimize their rule, allowing their dynasty to control vastly larger territories more peacefully than ever before. These innovations in statecraft were undoubtedly the most important Persian contributions to ancient business in that they expanded the population of customers available to business, their integration of territories reduced barriers to trade, and the voluntary support they earned for their rule facilitated tax collections and the integration of remote populations into territorial market activities. Subsequent rulers, including the Roman emperors, would emulate these measures.[106]

From the beginning, they treated subject peoples and their gods respectfully. Cyrus freed Jews and other deported peoples, letting them return home if they wished, and gave conquered leaders high office. In Babylon he offered sacrifices to local gods like Marduk and added Akkadian titles to those of the Medes. Inscriptions were written in Akkadian, and he proclaimed, "I am Cyrus, the king of the world, great king, legitimate king, king of Babylon, king of Sumer and Akkad, king of the four rims."[107] Darius similarly adopted Egyptian names that associated him with the god Re.[108]

Cyrus created an elite guard known as the "Ten Thousand Immortals," consisting of aristocratic youths from throughout the empire. His harem was the female equivalent, with one great family's daughter for each night of the year.[109] These posts became avidly sought honors and tied the leading families directly to the king. This personal connection bypassed tribes and gave the king a personal power base that enjoyed widespread acceptance.[110]

The lavish "oriental" court was probably Darius's most original contribution. It transformed the king from military leader into a majesty within ostentatiously luxurious trappings and elaborate ceremonies. To further elevate the king and curtail rebelliousness, the nobility had to attend his court for prolonged periods and show humbling obeisance to him. The Greeks disdained such luxuries and carryings-on as "gesture[s] reserved exclusively for the adoration of a god."[111] That was the point. Pomp and ceremony had been associated with worship from time immemorial, so by surrounding the king with the splendor of a Croesus, the solemn ritual of a pharaoh, and the mysterious ceremonies of his own Zoroastrian tradition, Darius made the king a godlike being with universal appeal.[112] Whereas Sargon of Akkad had secularized the sovereign to transcend divisive religious loyalties, Darius deified him to transcend divisive tribal loyalties.

While bolstering the public's emotional ties to the Persian monarchy, Darius markedly improved sovereign performance. He divided provinces into smaller and more manageable units called satrapies and sent inspectors known as "the king's eyes" to ensure the loyalty and performance of the satraps, or governors.[113] Tax reforms reduced corruption and gave landowners more incentive to make improvements.[114] And he extended throughout his realm what the Bible calls "the law of the Medes and the Persians," an improved version of the Code of Hammurabi under a system of courts that he personally supervised as the judge of last appeal.[115]

Persian Commerce

Transportation systems notably improved. Cyrus sent a Greek sailor named Scylax to find a route down the Indus River to the Indian Ocean and on to Egypt,[116] and Darius opened trade along this route. It would remain the principal channel for east-west trade until Vasco da Gama circumnavigated Africa in 1498. Darius also built the first Suez Canal, linking the Mediterranean to the Red Sea via the Nile.[117] There were many new roads, most notably the 1,600-mile Royal Road between Anatolian Sardis and Persian Susa.[118] Inns, called caravansaries, were placed a day apart along the way, as were military garrisons for security.[119]

Arabian dromedaries began to supplement Bactrian camels. Far more tolerant of thirst,[120] they could cross the Syrian Desert directly via Palmyra instead of zigzagging between oases. Dromedaries could also travel from Mecca and Medina to the Mediterranean, stimulating commerce between those towns and new ones like Petra.[121]

Such improvements helped long-distance trade, but populations and prosperity had grown so much that local trade now far outweighed its importance.[122] One study of three Babylonian merchants' accounts concludes, for example, that "about 90 percent of the goods acquired were of local Mesopotamian origin (fish, grain, leather, wool) and only about 10 percent were of foreign origin (fruits, spices, metals)."[123] Hence no merchant city dominated trade, although Phoenician cities, led by Sidon, remained vital.[124] Damascus and Babylon were also notable centers of manufacturing and trade. Carchemish replaced Mari as the principal port on the Euphrates, and a market culture prevailed along Anatolia's Aegean coast in cities that included Sardis, Lydia's former capital, and the Greek ports of Rhodes, Ephesus, and Miletus.[125]

As in Hammurabi's time, the most successful businesses were family firms in trade, banking, and real estate. In Babylon, Iddun-Marduk's family conducted an import-export business in garlic, barley, dates, wool, livestock, and bricks that spanned four generations between 603 B.C.E. and 507 B.C.E. Sometimes they advanced silver against the harvest to help farmers pay taxes.[126] At nearby Nuzi, Shilwa-teshup's family employed eighty shepherds, sold hides, wool, and hair, and bought and sold real estate. They also made loans of silver and barley.[127]

Persia's one important new type of business was farm management. A Persian grandee like Arsames, satrap of Egypt, owned huge estates in Egypt and Mesopotamia, but spent his time on campaign or followed the roving royal court.[128] Land agents like the Murasu family, which operated near Nippur in Babylonia between 454 B.C.E. and 404 B.C.E.,[129] arose to manage property for such men, often under master leases. They in turn hired sharecroppers and advanced them loans, livestock, equipment, and seed. Like the Sumerian tax farmers, they traded the rent that they received in kind for silver or barley, which they used to loan out and to pay their own rent and taxes.[130] Interestingly, land agents were still operating the same way in twentieth-century Australia.[131]

Herodotus famously remarked that the Persians "never buy in open market, and indeed have not a single marketplace in the whole country."[132] He exaggerated.[133] Jerusalem, for instance, had a fish market at one city gate, markets for sheep and pottery at others, and a baker's street.[134] But although one Barrekub had minted the first coins at Zinjirli in northern Syria around 730 B.C.E.,[135] barter generally prevailed, assuring desultory markets with few transactions.[136] A few Greek and Phoenician commercial centers minted small coins for everyday use, but in the larger Persian world, status and affiliation outdid purchasing power in providing access to goods and services.[137] Persian coins—*darics* (Persian for "gold") and silver *shekels* (the old Babylonian unit of weight)—were too large and valuable for everyday use[138] and existed mainly to pay taxes or Greek mercenaries.

Downfall

The Persian rulers insisted that rents, taxes, and fees be paid in gold or silver. This precious metal was mostly hoarded, not spent.[139] Over time, then, it took increasing amounts of production to acquire gold or silver. As when the central bankers of France, Germany, the United Kingdom, and the United States hoarded gold early in the Depression, the economy began to stagnate, perhaps even decline.[140] Public support for Persian rule dwindled, and rebellions following the king's death became more frequent and successful.[141] Egypt regained independence in 404 B.C.E., and in 345 B.C.E. the Persians had to suppress a rebellion in Sidon, sending its inhabitants to slavery in Babylon and Susa.[142]

The Greeks, hating the Persians and avid for loot, were always looking to foment trouble.[143] Their mercenaries got to know the Persians well and quickly spotted weakness. In 401 B.C.E. the satrap of Lydia hired a band of Greek mercenaries to overthrow his brother, the king. They marched twelve hundred miles to Babylon, marveling at the prosperity on view en route, and won the battle. But their sponsor was killed. The king then lured the mercenary leaders to a feast and had them slaughtered. The Athenian general Xenophon led the survivors on a harrowing flight for home. His famous *Anabasis* graphically described both the wealth and weakness of Persia, showing Greeks that it was ripe for plucking, while the perfidy he depicted reinforced anti-Persian sentiment.[144] The die was cast in 338 B.C.E., when a sinister eunuch named Bagoas assassinated the Persian royals and enthroned his own proxy, Darius III.[145] In the same year, King Philip II of Macedonia defeated Athens and Thebes in the Battle of Chaeronaea, setting the stage for his son Alexander's subsequent conquest of the Middle East.

Despite the enormous technological and political changes that made large empires possible and greatly increased wealth, old economic and social structures remained, including command economies. Business therefore remained a marginal activity.

The extraordinary persistence of social and economic structures continues. As I write, efforts to change the structure of healthcare in the United States have fallen short and floundered once again. Virtually everyone despises this structure, which imposes huge and apparently unnecessary costs that threaten to destroy the economy, but it remains impervious to reform. As with the economic and social structures of the ancient Middle East, healthcare took shape under particular historical circumstances that no longer exist. But it so rewards its beneficiaries that they can defeat any unpleasant changes, thus preserving the structure itself.

At the same time, this conservatism is sometimes outflanked. The Minoans, Mycenaeans, and Phoenician city-states fulfilled needs that traditional economic structures could not, crossing borders closed to more dangerous entities or offering themselves as neutral trading grounds when direct contacts were forbidden. Modern ports of trade like Hong Kong, Singapore, and Dubai serve the same functions and through their sovereign funds operate as quasi businesses as well.

Part 2

Business first took modern form in ancient Greece, where money, markets, and entrepreneurial businesses began coming together in the early sixth century. Entrepreneurial businesses vied to sell their wares in public markets to the populace at large. Goods were allocated by purchase, rather than by status or political consideration. With Alexander the Great's conquest of the Persian Empire, the civilized Western world experienced an unprecedented political, social, and economic revolution. The Macedonian kingdoms that divided up Alexander's empire after his death largely replaced the command economies of the Middle East with a modified version of the free-market economic model developed in Greece. Called "Hellenistic" by modern historians, these kingdoms remained significant powers for only about 150 years. But their culture endured for centuries more in the Greek-speaking parts of the Roman Empire, and their urban economies spread throughout all parts of the empire.

Chapter 3 explains how a free-market business economy arose in Athens and other Greek city-states. Chapter 4 describes business there. Chapter 5 serves as an historical prologue to the Hellenistic Era. Chapter 6 discusses its distinctive business environment, and chapter 7 describes Hellenistic business, emphasizing the major new developments

Table 4
Greek Chronology

Date (B.C.E.)	Event
1200	Mycenaean "decapitation"
1000	Dorian invasion of Peloponnese
825	oldest Greek writing
800–700	Homer transcribed
776	first Olympic Games
775	Ischia and Cumae colonized
733	Syracuse colonized by Corinth
668	Battle of Hysiae: Argos's phalanx defeats Sparta
632	Cylon's revolt and murder
631	Thera colonizes Cyrene in Libya
625	Megara colonizes Byzantium
620?	first coins struck in Lydia
616?	Gyges sends 30,000 Greek mercenaries to Egypt
594	Solon elected archon of Athens
511	Sybaris destroyed
510	Cleisthenes made tyrant of Athens
490	Battle of Marathon: Darius's invasion stopped
480	Battle of Thermopylae; Battle of Salamis
479	Battle of Plataea: Xerxes retreats
460–429	age of Pericles
431–404	Peloponnesian War
371	Battle of Leuctra: Thebes defeats Sparta
338	Battle of Chaeronaea

Map 2.
Greek Communities

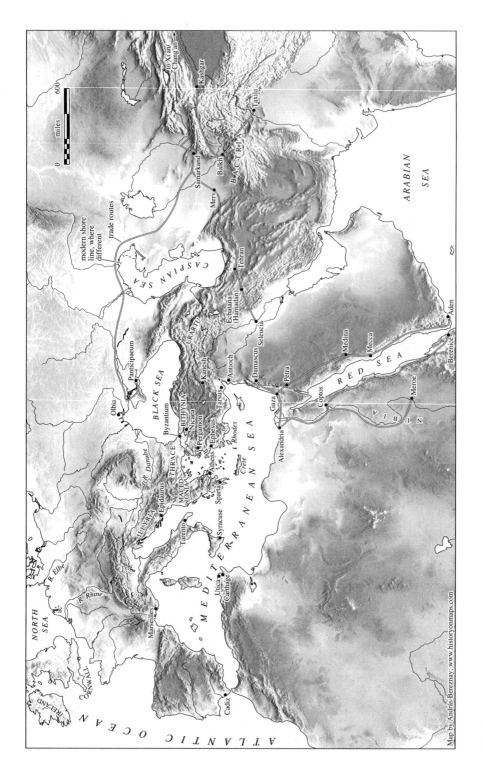

Map 3.
Hellenistic World

3

Markets and Greece

Business in its modern guise first appeared in the small, weak, and poor city-states of ancient Greece.[1] There, for the first time, money-based markets gave entrepreneurial businesses a central economic position. It's a complex story that includes

- the geography, culture and social structure of early Greece
- the education and opportunities provided by Greece's Middle Eastern neighbors
- new military technology and mercenary earnings
- changing political structures
- the invention of coinage

Like much of business history, this story begins with the underlying social, political, and technological framework.

Geography and Social Structure

Centered on the Aegean Sea, ancient Greece included not just the southern end of the Balkan peninsula, but the shores of Anatolia, the islands of the

Aegean and eastern Mediterranean, and colonies from the Crimea to Spain. In Plato's happy phrase, the Greeks settled around the seas "like frogs around a pond."[2] Herodotus noted that Greeks were "of the same stock and the same speech, with common shrines of the gods and rituals, with similar customs."[3] Similar climates, terrains, and resources produced a common lifestyle.[4]

The Aegean homeland consisted of small plains and valleys divided by rocky hills and impenetrable mountain ranges. The light soil in the valleys and the Aegean's hot, dry climate permitted a meager but varied agriculture of winter wheat, barley, grapes, figs, honey, and olives. Livestock included goats and sheep, but rarely cattle. In this terrain cultivation could not expand to accommodate larger populations, and the meager output generated little surplus. The entire mainland population reckoned "in thousands instead of millions" throughout ancient times.[5]

Sparta and Athens occupied the two largest territories, but even these could be traversed by foot in a day or two. Sparta's home, Laconia, sprawled across 3,200 square miles in the central Peloponnesus; Attica, the Athenian land, was only a third the size but far more arable.[6] Sparta was never crowded,[7] but Athens may have supported as many as 350,000 people at its height of wealth and power, when it ruled an empire of 179 city-states with a combined population of about 2,000,000.[8] Syracuse, in Sicily, had perhaps 260,000 people by the fourth century. Other large *poleis*, or city-states, included Rhodes, Ephesus, Smyrna, and Corinth, but most were much smaller, with an average population of about 5,000 people.[9] At their most populous, the Greeks altogether probably numbered fewer than 5,500,000.[10]

This Greek diaspora inhabited a myriad of pine-forested islands and valleys, which provided timber and pitch for building ships, all linked by sea routes that kept them in close communication with one another. As the motto of modern Greece says, "the sea unites us." A couple of days' journey from any Aegean island would reach as many cities as could be found on a journey taking months throughout the entire Middle East. Communication was also quick for the times. In normal weather a ship could sail forty miles in less than a day, compared to the weeks of upriver hauling required in Mesopotamia or the ten to twenty miles a laden donkey could cover.[11] Ships could also carry the equivalent of thousands of donkey loads.[12] The Greek Aegean was an extraordinary natural resource, a facilitator of transport and communication that far surpassed anything available elsewhere. And unlike the Nile, which provided easy access to villages in all seasons, the Greek seas became impassible during the stormy winter and protected the independence of virtually all Greek city-states, however small, for many centuries.[13]

The limited food production of the Greek homeland led to recurring waves of emigration, beginning once the population recovered from the destruction of Mycenaean society around 1200 B.C.E. and the Dorian invasion after 1000. While some survivors became the conquerors' serfs, called "helots" in Sparta,[14] others remained free. Their city-states gradually recovered and then sent colonists to the Aegean Islands and the coast of Anatolia, where they occupied naturally defensible promontories amid fertile river valleys and plains. By the ninth century nearly 700 Greek city-states dotted Greece and the Aegean.[15]

These were tiny farming settlements of extended households and clans,[16] much like the New Guineans of Diamond's *Guns, Germs, and Steel*. Smyrna, one of the largest, consisted of five hundred mean hovels huddled together behind the city wall.[17] Hereditary clan leaders normally controlled and allocated the choicest land and jointly governed the community. Each community had its patron god or goddess, but all maintained an animistic concept of competitive gods controlling natural forces.[18]

These settlements were too small and poor to generate much of an agricultural surplus, and the difficulty of reaching and subjugating neighbors usually made conquest unprofitable (with Sparta the major exception). "Poverty and Greece," said Herodotus, "are stepsisters."[19] Unable to support military specialists, citizens did their own fighting between planting and harvesting. Their temporary war leaders, called kings, rarely accumulated much personal power,[20] and the title retained little meaning (again, excepting Sparta).

The most important forms of wealth were social goods like leisure and honor. The high value placed on leisure promoted interest in artistic production, natural investigation, and speculative thought. Honor was even more valuable.[21] Men earned it by excelling in athleticism, valor, leadership, and other manly activities, usually through competition—a Greek mania unique among the ancients. In fact, the earliest recorded Greek event was the founding of the Olympic Games in 776 B.C.E.[22] With prosperity, prominent citizens also competed for public office by providing benefactions, called liturgies, like games, religious festivals, and plays. The competition to sponsor ever more magnificent liturgies ultimately financed many public buildings, temples, monuments, and even warships.[23] The ultimate competitive prize was victory in battle. Where other primitive warriors put their own safety first, the Greeks strove for the honor of victory, accepting personal risk. According to military historian John Keegan, they fought with unprecedented frequency and savagery, creating "the Western way of war."[24]

Each household provided virtually all its own food, shelter, and clothing. In fact *oikos*, the word for household, is the root of our term *economy*.[25] Homer and Hesiod, the first Greek writers, list only nine occupations other than farming: priest, seer, bard, herald, doctor, carpenter, potter, leatherworker, and smith.[26] For metalwares, luxury goods, and slaves, Homer's Greeks depended on war, piracy, or Phoenician traders.

Early encounters with trade were not entirely happy. The Phoenicians were pirates if possible, traders if necessary.[27] In dealings with isolated Greek clan leaders whom they were unlikely to see again, they were often deceitful and predatory. Unfortunately for their future reputation, a great poet was watching. Homer set the *Iliad* and the *Odyssey* in contemporary eleventh- and tenth-century B.C.E. Greek society. Indeed, scientists have recently dated Odysseus's homecoming to April 16, 1178 B.C.E., based on astronomical and eclipse references in the *Odyssey*.[28] Homer depicted the Phoenicians, and all traders, as wily and dishonorable, and his writings sealed a general distaste for trade into the foundations of Western thought.[29] Justice Oliver Wendell Holmes Jr. once spoke of "the secret isolated joy of the thinker, who knows that, a hundred years after he is dead and forgotten, men who never heard of him will be moving to the measure of his thought."[30] Just so, Homer's disdain for trade and traders has moved many generations "to the measure of his thought."

Colonies and Trade

Homer's tales, recorded in the eighth century B.C.E., were the first Greek writings after Mycenaean account books.[31] They marked a new phase in Greek development. Greek traders had begun venturing to the Syrian port of Al-Mina, near the ruins of Ugarit, returning with the new alphabet used in recording Homer's tales. The linear sense of time, so integral to business thought, was perhaps incorporated into Hellenic thought at this point.[32] Perhaps the Greeks also learned about interest on loans there as well.[33] Middle Eastern trade brought new techniques for improving agricultural yields, including better breeds of livestock, new feeding methods, improved plants and grafting techniques, and the use of irrigation and cisterns.[34]

Meanwhile, itinerant ironsmiths introduced new and better tools. Cultivation spread to the hillsides, and by the late fifth century B.C.E. a greater percentage of Attica's acreage was devoted to agriculture than modern California's.[35] The population grew rapidly, and Greece became overpopulated once again.[36]

This time colonization headed west, where local resistance was weak and Greek sailors already knew the coasts.[37] The straits of Messina between Sicily and Italy, for instance, were thought to be the site of Homer's Scylla and Charybdis. The first new colonies were on Ischia and, by the Graei, at Cumae on the Bay of Naples around 775 B.C.E., which is probably where the Romans got the name *Greek*. Many other colonies followed, including Syracuse in 733 B.C.E. and Sybaris in southern Italy, which became so rich that its name is now a byword for decadent opulence. Seventh-century colonies included Marseilles, Byzantium, the chokepoint for traffic between the Aegean and the Black Sea due to currents in the Hellespont, and Black Sea ports settled from Ionian cities like Ephesus and Miletus.

The new colonies enjoyed agricultural and mineral resources beyond all previous imagining. Their lands have served as granaries to Europe and the Mediterranean ever since. There was also gold and silver from Egypt, Anatolia, and Spain; copper from Cyprus, Spain, and Sardinia; iron from Cyprus, Anatolia, the Black Sea, and Italy; and luxury goods from Carthage. Ischia was settled as much for its proximity to Etruscan iron mines as for its agricultural and defensive properties, and other colonies, like the Lipari Islands off Sicily, seem to have lived off piracy.

Colonists were independent sorts who often married local women and established their new homes in a frontier spirit of rough-and-ready individualism and equality. They owned the land and the mines, the inventories, slaves, warehouses, and ships. For instance, the king of Thera (modern Santorini, an island near Crete) sent colonists to Cyrene in Libya in 631 B.C.E., proclaiming that they

> sail as [the King's] companions: that they sail on fair and equal terms, according to family; that one son be conscripted from each family; that those who sail be in the prime of life; and that, of the rest of the [mother city citizens], any free man who wishes may sail. If the colonists establish the settlement, any of their fellow-citizens who later sails to Libya shall have a share in citizenship and honors and shall be allotted a portion of the unoccupied land.

The colonies retained close ties to their mother cities, linked by easy travel upon the seas, and trade was part of their life. As Hesiod wrote, "On occasions a man may have to load his surplus produce on a ship and dispose of it abroad." One such was Kolaios, a merchant from Samos who, blown off course to Spain, returned around 600 B.C.E. with a windfall of sixty talents.[38] But where Carthage sent tribute to its mother city Tyre for hundreds of years, Greek colonial trade was private, voluntary, and competitive. Traders like Kolaios were individuals seeking their own profit, and buyers, including those in the mother cities, had to pay for what they wanted. And so they did; indeed, trade soon reached such volumes that specialized merchant ships came into use, broader of beam and carrying more freight than contemporary warships.[39]

To pay their colonies, the mother cities began to produce or resell trade goods. An outstanding example was Corinth, which founded Syracuse and colonies on the Adriatic islands of Ithaca and Corfu in the eighth century B.C.E. Located on the narrow isthmus that separates the Aegean and the Adriatic Sea, Corinth prospered from the traffic across the isthmus. Around 600 B.C.E. a Greek merchant from Aegina named Sostratus, who lived at Gravisca in Italy, apparently built a log haulway across the peninsula for his ships,[40] and by the sixth century Corinth was the leading commercial city of Greece, selling pottery and other manufactured goods and reselling artifacts like terra-cottas, scarabs, and amulets from Egypt to pay for Sicilian wheat and Etruscan iron. The Corinthians, famed for their prostitutes, assured their eastern visitors that the city's patron goddess Aphrodite was really the Phoenician goddess Astarte by another name.[41]

This trade liberated many Greek communities from a Malthusian cycle of poverty. It began with people needing male children to support them in old age and infirmity. To have boys survive the high infant mortality rates, they produced as many babies as they could feed. More production quickly led to more children, leaving no surplus. Production equaled consumption. But with colonial trade, some families began to save something from current consumption to produce goods like olives, wine, and manufactured articles. By devoting resources to producing those goods, they fed fewer children, but accumulated wealth. Production equaled consumption *plus* surplus.

The invested surplus generated new wealth. To sell olive oil abroad, for instance, Greek farmers devoted land to olive trees, dug irrigation ditches, saved and planted seeds, fashioned plows and other tools, built jars and ships to get the produce to market, bought inventories, set up shops, and otherwise invested time and resources. The resulting oil and its proceeds constituted new wealth.

Colonial trade stimulated manufacturing in the mother cities. Since Greek custom was to divide land among all the children, population growth led to such a minute subdivision of the arable land that idle labor was plentiful.[42] By contrast, the colonies had plenty of land and raw materials, but a shortage of labor. If the cities devoted their idle labor to manufacturing, much as the Sumerians had, and the colonies traded the bounty of their land for those goods, both would benefit. As usual, once trade began, merchants could diversify and sell other less valuable goods as well.

To some degree, aristocrats could best take advantage of the new opportunities in trade and manufacturing. They could more easily devote a portion of their lands to cash crops than could a small farmer whose own family would bear any food shortages. They could also afford the investment required. Some cash crops like grapevines and olive orchards required years of cultivation to become productive.

Yet the landed gentry were not the chief beneficiaries of these new developments. For the small farmer, the landless poor, and resident foreigners called "metics," who could not own land, manufacturing and trade provided new sources of wealth. Many people participated and shared in the benefits: carriers, warehousemen, sailors, artisans, carpenters, loggers, and so forth. But since work was often dull or difficult, the landed gentry preferred pastimes like war, sports, poetry, and love, leaving commerce to the lower classes.[43]

So, too, for trade. Trading voyages could last for months or even years. Sailing in a cramped and stinking boat with verminous, perhaps disease-ridden companions, often drafted from the dregs of humanity, travelers were at the mercy of vast and overwhelming seas, reportedly full of whirlpools, clashing rocks, murderous sirens, vengeful gods, and man-eating monsters, not to mention pirates. As Shylock comments in *The Merchant of Venice*, "Ships are but boards, sailors but men; there be land-rats and water-rats, water-thieves and land-thieves, I mean pirates, and then there is the peril of waters, winds and rocks."[44] Rowing from port to port along the coasts, their reception was always uncertain. Would there be welcome and trade; or famine, war, and plague? Food and water for the journey; or violence, slavery, and death? Traders encountered strange people, strange food, and strange customs, which could lead to dire results. (Recall the movie *Indiana Jones and the Temple of Doom*, where Indiana Jones, visiting a savage chief and his warriors, must eat a disgusting plate of eyeballs *au jus* to avoid dishonoring his touchy host.) And as all Greeks knew from the story of Odysseus, the homecomer could find his family imperiled (or worse), wealth consumed, and himself a stranger to all. For those with property, it was far better to leave such unsavory adventures to others and live in leisure off one's property.

Commerce began to change the nature of Greek wealth. Land, flocks, and slaves remained valuable, but now came disposable goods like gold, silver, and inventories, as well as financial assets: in a word, purchasing power. Some artisans even accumulated more of these goods than the nobility.[45] By the fourth century B.C.E., Demosthenes' inheritance could include not only his parents' house, furniture and jewelry, but also $929,000 worth of raw materials for his factories, $372,000 on loan at 12 percent, a maritime loan of $434,000, and $285,000 on deposit with a relative and two banks. He also received a sword factory whose thirty-three slaves brought in $187,000 per year and a furniture factory of twenty slaves that earned $76,000 a year.[46]

Hoplites

As ordinary people gained wealth through manufacturing and trade, improved metallurgy was making swords, shields, and armor more affordable.[47] By the end of the fifth century B.C.E. the arms and armor of a foot soldier cost little more than an unskilled slave or a pair of oxen.[48] Honor through warfare, previously reserved for the nobility, became a privilege of citizenship.[49]

The new warriors were called hoplites after their *hoplons*, round shields that soldiers held on one arm. Since it protected only half the body, the hoplites developed a close-order formation, the phalanx, which allowed the shield of each man's neighbor to protect the other half of his body. To maneuver effectively in this close formation of highly coordinated foot soldiers required hours of drill. With leisure for practice and a love of sport, the Greeks learned to use phalanxes in battle, initially when Argos defeated a much larger army of Spartans at the Battle of Hysiae in 668 B.C.E.[50]

With the phalanx, hoplites became the most formidable fighters of the day.[51] Soon every Greek city was raising and training such forces. This investment of time and skill turned idle time into a valuable asset. Moreover, it gave the Greeks a lasting source of revenue. Since the phalanx rested on the culture, motivation, and training of the Greeks, Middle Eastern societies could not imitate it, but had to hire Greek mercenaries. Mercenary earnings added significantly to Greek wealth.

(An aside: as a product of Greek culture, the phalanx was difficult for competing armies or would-be mercenaries to replicate. It therefore conveyed a lasting advantage to Greek mercenaries over the would-be mercenaries of other places. The phalanx strategy is one that many modern businesses would like to imitate. They know that, apart from patentable goods, their innovative goods or services may be quickly and inexpensively copied, even improved upon. According to many a business book and article, the solution is to create a lasting competitive advantage from one's corporate culture. Cisco is envied for its system of acquiring and integrating smaller technology companies; Apple for its systems of innovation and marketing; MMM for its system of invention; and so forth. The Greeks, as in so many areas, seem to have gotten there first.)

Modern mercenaries are often portrayed as marginal sociopaths who scrounge for loot in Third World hellholes, "red-eyed deviants that modern societies wheel out in times of crises, only to closet when dust settles,"[52] and this perception makes it easy to underestimate their early importance. Mercenaries were in fact the first large class of employees,[53] and mercenary service "accounts for a large part of the increase of wealth for Greek states."[54] Greek mercenaries served in Egypt, the Persian Empire, Rome, and Carthage. In one case of late-seventh-century B.C.E. geopolitical maneuvering, Lydia's King Gyges sent thirty thousand mercenaries to help Egypt rebel against the Assyrians. (Gyges, a palace guard to the king, apparently seduced the queen while her husband was away at war. With her help he seized the throne and founded a new Lydian dynasty.)[55] While Gyges' enlistment bonuses and other payments flowed into their cities of origin, the mercenaries themselves, whose descendents' graffiti can still be seen on the feet of Ramses II at Abu Simbel in Nubia, colonized the city of Naucratis in the Nile Delta.[56]

Mercenaries became the most valuable of all Greek exports. Their remittances elevated Greek wealth,[57] much as the earnings of "guest workers" flow back to impoverished lands today. In 2006, for instance, the Philippine Republic received 10 percent of its gross national product this way.[58] Greek mercenary captains sometimes amassed such huge fortunes that to avoid taxes they retired instead to Cyprus, Lesbos, Thrace, or Egypt.[59]

In time, though, the growing wealth of Greek society enabled more people to acquire the necessary armor and weapons for mercenary service. Pay fell, at least for the common troops, until by the end of the fourth century it was little more than that for slave labor, four obols compared to three for slave labor.[60] In Greek comedy, as in Flaubert's *Salammbô*, the mercenary became "a boaster, a deep-drinker, and at all times a clumsy fool."[61]

The phalanx's emergence had dramatic political implications. It accentuated the equal status of citizens; whatever their differences of birth and wealth, each depended on the others in his phalanx.[62] The aristocrats became dependent on hoplites for military protection. They, in turn, demanded an end to the political dominance of clan leaders, forcing a transition from oligarchy toward "democracy" in many Greek cities during the seventh and sixth centuries B.C.E.

The transition toward democracy, by reducing the power of the landed aristocracy, assured a broader distribution of wealth, permitted entrepreneurs to enjoy a central economic role, and protected commercial activity and employment. Institutions created to replace aristocratic dominance, such as written legal codes and government-operated welfare systems, also proved more supportive of markets and businesses than in city-states like Sparta, where aristocrats retained their absolute power.

Most of what we know about the process of democratization comes from Athens,[63] where an oligarchy of clan leaders originally controlled the land. They provided welfare by lending seeds and food to their clansmen when crops were poor, and dispensed justice. From these aristocrats the male heads of household annually elected magistrates and an executive, called the *archon*; this was their government.

Due to its rich silver mines at Laureion, Athens grew and prospered more during the eighth and seventh centuries B.C.E. than most Greek city-states. Silver paid for the food and other requirements to sustain a rapidly growing urban population, which by some estimates multiplied eightfold during this time.[64] But the practice of dividing patrimonies equally among children created ever-smaller farms, making it increasingly difficult for farmers to survive bad years without borrowing from their clan leaders. Farmers might have to secure these loans with their bodies. Default cast the farmer, his wife, and his children into slavery, much to the profit of the clan leader.[65]

Hoplites had other grievances. Within the city they protected, the clan leader had always been litigator, sheriff, prosecutor, and judge as he saw fit, with ordinary men helpless to punish any crime or obtain redress without the leader's sanction. Hoplite protests therefore grew more strident as they gained military and social importance. Some clan leaders thought reforms would preserve their privileges, but others refused any concessions. In many of the cities that failed to act, aristocrats who promised reforms and other benefits seized power with hoplite support. In Corinth, at the time larger and richer than Athens, hoplites helped Kypselos banish or kill many of his rivals. He then seized the rivals' property and ruled as tyrant, passing the office to his brutal son Periander thirty years later. Periander, who gave tyranny a bad name among the Greeks, took revenge on restive aristocrats "by sending 300 sons of noble families to Alyattes of Lydia to serve as eunuchs at his court."[66]

In Athens, Cylon and his followers seized the Acropolis in 632 B.C.E., but a rival named Megacles then slaughtered them at the temple of Athena. Lest Megacles become tyrant, the ruling council accused Megacles of defiling the temple with those murders and banished him and his family forever. They exhumed his ancestors and scattered their remains for good measure. (Nonetheless, his descendents included such Athenian leaders as Cleisthenes and Pericles.)[67] To still continued Hoplite unrest, the clan leaders elected Draco as archon. He sought to reduce discontent by making prosecution for murder a state responsibility. He also promulgated written laws. But they were so harsh and limited that such measures are still called "draconian." For instance, Draco said that since murder defiled the gods and made the killer impure, it was a state matter, but punishment for accidental killing remained an aristocratic prerogative.[68] Draco, therefore, only whetted the public's appetite for change.

Democracy

In 594 B.C.E. continuing public discontent and frightening examples of tyranny elsewhere finally persuaded the aristocrats to support Solon's much more thorough program of reform. Solon, described as "the morningstar of the Greek intellect,"[69] is usually credited with transforming Athenian society to the meritocratic and individualistic model that has been the conceptual core of Western beliefs, and certainly of Western business, ever since.[70]

Solon began with the immediate cancellation of debts, the restoration of debtors to their farms, and the redemption of slaves sold for debt. He limited interest rates and prohibited debt slavery, perhaps the first human-rights measure in history. He had all Athenian laws written and posted, so that their protections became a *right* of citizenship, not just an aristocrat's favor. As Euripides optimistically wrote: "When the laws are written, both the weak and the wealthy have equal justice."[71]

To effectively reduce aristocratic dominance, Solon transferred explicit powers from the clan leader to the individual. He made ordinary citizens full landowners by allowing them to bequeath it to their heirs. He also terminated the privilege of clan leaders to seek vengeance for manslaughter. This privilege had allowed them to run amok as private sheriffs, commandeering the time, property, and lives of clan relatives in their posses. Most critically of all, individuals gained the power to protect their own rights and property by initiating litigation without the clan leader's approval.

These shifts of power from clan leaders to individuals made the government more important. But as the only public officials, the clan leaders could always thwart or rescind these reforms. To complete his program, therefore, Solon also had to implement political changes. He gave the vote to all propertied citizens and required political candidates to meet only property qualifications rather than the hereditary clan positions formerly specified.[72] As the major landowners, the aristocrats did not strenuously oppose this measure, but in the dawning era of trade and mercenary service it made political power and social status theoretically accessible to any commoner who could accumulate wealth, as many later did.

When Solon abolished debt slavery, emergency loans became harder to obtain (an outcome that credit card lobbyists use to oppose restrictions today). Faced with terrifying prospects of famine and starvation, the city-state took over responsibility for assuring the food supply—in effect, welfare. To that end, Solon initiated various mercantilist and commerce-friendly policies. He prohibited the export of fish and grain, but encouraged Athenians to grow olives and grapes for export, in places grain could not. He also offered citizenship to foreign-born artisans, an invitation that soon made Athens the leading Greek pottery producer.[73]

Later Athenian leaders took further steps, most notably securing favorable trade terms with the city's principal grain source, the Bosporan kingdom in the Crimea. Much like the relationship between the United States and the Saudi royal family today, Athens gave privileges to Bosporan royalty, including a highly coveted honorary Athenian citizenship. In return, Athens received discounted harbor fees and preferential access to grain.[74] After the Peloponnesian War, Athens further encouraged shipping by allowing foreign traders to testify and bring suit in a special court meant to resolve commercial disputes before the sailing season came to an end.[75]

In Athens, as in other Greek cities, commercial measures consisted primarily of regulations, rather than direct ownership of production or distribution facilities.[76] Those who handled grain and fish were licensed. Thasos, the island that produced the finest Greek wine, even instituted trademark regulation, forbidding the import of foreign wine. Its merchants didn't want cheap wine reexported under the Thasos name, diluting the value of their brand.[77]

At the end of his term, Solon refused requests to become dictator and instead traveled to Egypt, the Ionian Greek cities, and Lydia, trading to pay his expenses. As the story goes, when Lydia's King Croesus showed Solon his treasures and proudly asked him who was the happiest of men, Solon named certain men who had died honorably. Croesus criticized Solon for preferring commoners to a great king. Solon replied that the gods were jealous of human prosperity and warned, "In every matter one must look to see how the end will turn out, for the deity, after giving a glimpse of happiness to many, destroys them root and branch."[78] Croesus soon met his doom at the hands of Cyrus the Great.

Despite Solon's efforts the real circumstances of peoples' lives had not changed much. Political strife in Athens continued, and finally the wealthy Peisistratus, who owned silver mines at Mount Pangaeus in Thrace, made himself tyrant by entering the city with a statuesque young woman dressed as Athena after spreading the rumor that she favored him and was bringing him to her home on the Acropolis.[79]

Peisistratus turned out to be a largely benevolent ruler during thirty-three years of rising prosperity. He installed a municipal water system and the first public library in Athens, among other improvements.[80] He encouraged production, making it a capital crime to leave one's land idle,[81] while providing credit on favorable terms to farmers who planted grapes or olives.[82] Pottery exports increased, reflecting wine and oil sales, and Athens began routinely importing grain and fish from the Black Sea along routes that he secured. His sons continued these policies until forced from power.

In 510 B.C.E. Cleisthenes, a grandson of the banished Megacles, became tyrant with hoplite support and extended the vote to perhaps 20 percent of the population.[83] Pericles, also descended from Megacles, increased popular participation in government even more, especially by paying men for their services as jurors, members of the assembly, soldiers, sailors, and magistrates.[84]

Such measures helped protect the property and freedom of common citizens,[85] and Pericles' welfare measures enabled many citizens to live in the city and buy necessities on the market. Also dependent on the markets were the many metics who had come to work in trade or manufacturing. A recent estimate suggests that out of a population of 150,000 in Athens and its territory, perhaps 20,000 were slaves and 10,000–30,000 were metics.[86]

Athens versus Sparta

By the time Pericles banished the oligarchs' favorite Cimon in the election for archon in 460 B.C.E., Athens and Sparta had become the two most powerful Greek city-states. Together with allies, they had repelled Persian attacks in the famous battles of Marathon (490), Thermopylae (480), Salamis (480), Plataea (479), and Mycale (479). Then they launched numerous raids into Persian territory. The clever Persian response was to finance conflicts within and between the Greek city-states. For 150 years, until the arrival of Alexander the Great, this strategy contained Greek hostilities to the nuisance level.

Spartan political and economic institutions differed greatly from those of Athens. Sparta prospered by military conquest and seizing the surpluses of those it subjugated, known as helots. With helots to do the farming, Spartans could maximize family wealth by keeping their own citizenry small. Sickly babies were exposed to die, and even though Spartans might lend their wives to others for stud purposes, the city-state never fielded more than eight thousand citizen soldiers.[87]

Sparta's only respected trade was war. A rigid military regimen had made it the strongest city-state in Greece. Virtually alone among Greek city-states, it retained a permanent war leader, or king—in fact, two of them. Boys left home at age seven to live with others in barracks under the tutelage, including sexual, of an older boy. They wore one tunic, both winter and summer, slept on a bed of reeds, and received little but wheat porridge to eat, a diet they supplemented by stealing from the farms of helots. If caught, they were severely punished—not for stealing but for doing it badly. Between the ages of eighteen and twenty they trained as soldiers and policed the helots. They could marry at twenty, but remained in the barracks until age thirty, when they were elected to "messes," where they took their meals until age sixty. Girls also engaged in sports and competition, but lived at home until marriage.[88] The Greek envoys who met Cyrus after his conquest of Lydia were Spartans, and when Xerxes' army threatened to conquer Athens and all of Greece in 480 B.C.E., Sparta's King Leonidas and his three hundred men heroically delayed them at Thermopylae, allowing Athens to muster its forces and ultimately repel the Persian attack.

Under the guise of creating a coalition against Persia, Athens then assembled an Aegean empire known as the Delian League, whose tribute financed the splendors of the Periclean Age and Athenian attacks on Persia. In response, Persia financed Sparta's coalition of oligarchic city-states against Athens and its allies during the long Peloponnesian War (431–404 B.C.E.), which ended with the razing of the walls of Athens. Then Sparta attacked Persia, which financed an Athenian revival. And so it went. Ultimately, the northern city-state of Thebes, under its brilliant military commander Epaminandos, defeated Sparta in 362 B.C.E. at the Battle of Mantinea.[89] Thebes and Athens then competed for Greek leadership, but only twenty-three years later they both succumbed to Epaminandos's student, King Philip II of Macedonia. With the help of his son Alexander, Philip defeated their combined armies in 338 B.C.E. at the Battle of Chaeronaea, inaugurating the Hellenistic age.

Wealth, Money, and Markets

Amid their frequent wars, the farmers and fishermen of Greece went from penury to splendor in the span of about two centuries. This wasn't because their wealth rivaled the Persian Empire's. Athens, even at the height of its empire, rarely received more than 400 talents per year in tribute,[90] compared to Persia's 14,560,[91] and in 378 B.C.E., according to Polybius, the total value of Athenian property was a mere 5,725 talents.[92]

But Greek purchasing power seems to have grown very rapidly between the sixth and fourth centuries B.C.E. Mercenary service in neighboring empires was one reason; in Athens, silver mining and coining was another. The city's silver four-drachma pieces known as "owls" became the Greek monetary standard of the day, and profits from their sale helped finance a vast public building program that spread the wealth to many artisans and laborers.[93]

This building took place in the cities. Greeks valued the sociability of city life and designed their cities around central plazas, temples, gymnasiums, theaters, and forums where people could meet and mingle. With purchasing power, markets naturally followed. The Athenian Acropolis was perhaps the first of them.[94]

Money in the form of coins was the catalyst for these markets. When most trade consisted of gift exchanges designed for reciprocity rather than exactitude, money in imprecise and hard-to-value bulk forms, whether precious metal bullion or the iron pellets that Greeks called obols, had served well enough.[95] Likewise, Solon had measured wealth crudely by the number of wet or dry "measures" one's land produced.[96]

But such forms of money were impractical for those seeking to hire hoplite mercenaries, who wanted exact compensation that worked back home, not local tokens or vague reciprocity. If precious metals were to be offered, their true assay had to be known; approximations would not do. In the kingdoms of western Anatolia where many Greek mercenaries served, the difficulty was compounded by the nature of their precious metal, a variable mixture of gold and silver called electrum. Carried down the rushing Pactolus River to the city of Sardis, this electrum so enriched the Phrygian King Midas and the Lydian King Croesus that their names became bywords for fabulous wealth. But when these rulers sought to pay Greek mercenaries, electrum proved to be a nuisance. The precise value of each nugget was difficult to determine because the proportion of gold and silver varied from one nugget to another.

Late in the seventh century, the Lydians learned to refine electrum into pure gold and pure silver. They then poured the metals into molds embossed with the royal symbol—facing heads of a bull and a lion—to guarantee the weight and purity of the resulting coins.[97] The oldest known Lydian coin was worth twelve sheep, not coincidentally a year's pay for a mercenary.[98]

Coins quickly became emblems of civic pride,[99] used for large public expenditures like mercenary wages, construction costs, or gifts and prizes.[100] Commercial Greek cities soon began to issue their own: Lydia's neighbor Ephesus in 600, Corinth in 575, Athens by 560, and eventually more than eleven hundred other cities.[101]

Athens, with its silver mines at Laureion and Mount Pangaeus, fabricated much of its silver into coins like the famous four-drachma piece called the "owl" because of the emblem of Athena stamped on one side. Owls were so valued for their purity that they became the most widely used coins in the Greek world. The Athenian unit of value was the drachma, meaning "fistful," which referred to a fistful of obols.[102] (Other drachmas

Table 5
Greek Weights and Coins

Unit	Obols	Drachmas	Other	Silver
1 drachma[a]	6			5g
1 stater	150	25		125g
1 shekel	10	1.66		8.33g
1 mina	600	100	60 shekels	0.5 kg
1 talent	36,000	6,000	60 minas	30 kg/43 lb.
1 gram gold				12g[b]

Note: this table is valid for the period ca. 600 B.C.E.–200 C.E., during which inflation was mild.
Main sources: Aubet 1993; Grant 1987; Vilar 1976; and Grant 1990b.
a. The Greeks had two drachma weights, the Athenian and Aegina's, which was 70% of the
   Athenian. I refer to the Athenian drachma throughout. Based on equating the cost of
   maintaining a slave with the U.S. minimum wage as of 2006, 1 Athenian drachma = U.S. $61.77.
   The upkeep of a slave was ⅔ of a drachma per day (Ste. Croix 1981: 187). The 2006 minimum
   wage was $5.15/hour, or $10,506/year, or about $61.77/drachma for 2,040 hours per year of work.
b. The ratio of gold to silver varied, of course. It was 1:9 around 2700 B.C.E., 1:6 in Hammurabi's
   Babylon, and about 1:12 from the sixth century on.

had slightly different weights, such as the Aegina drachma and, later, the
Ptolemaic drachma, but I refer throughout to the Athenian drachma.) The
most common Lydian coin was worth twelve drachmas, but Greek cities
soon issued smaller ones useful for market transactions. Many sixth-
century denominations were worth only two or four drachmas,[103] and
other issues came in smaller denominations yet.[104]

    As coin denominations became smaller and more useful for daily
commercial transactions, they became mediums of exchange, greatly sim-
plifying and speeding the process. By the end of the sixth century B.C.E.,
coins had made markets so informative and efficient that they became indispensable features of Greek urban life.[105]

    Unlike bartered goods, coins were widely accepted. Since everyone val-
ued them, they could readily pay any cost. Their uniformity and the issuer's
guaranty of purity made them faster and easier to assay than bullion. As
coins made sales faster and easier, money-based markets became livelier,
more useful for their participants, and more popular. Economists call this
effect "positive returns to scale," meaning the more that money and markets
are used, the more beneficial they become; their growth is self-reinforcing.[106]

Coins also improved the quality of information about prices. Barter provides little pricing information—if a helmet was traded for a goat once, another would fetch a goat only if the buyer was offering one and the seller needed another one or could dispose of it. But trade for coins offered a common calibration, since the helmet maker who accepted five drachmas last month would probably accept about the same amount again. One result was to stimulate investment. With coins, producers could better estimate future sales and make appropriate investments of time and resources. The investment stimulated economic growth. Indeed, the 1994 Nobel prize for economics rewarded the mathematical demonstration of how buyers at a market would pay more money if they had better information about values (one of the three winners, John Nash, is the subject of the popular movie *A Beautiful Mind*).

As markets began to flourish, they stimulated consumer demand, which, in turn, supported more specialization. Compared to Homer's nine occupations, no fewer than 170 different occupations have been identified for classical Athens, not counting government, religious, or military offices.[107] Specialization, as Xenophon noted at the time, led to higher quality and more productivity:

In small towns the same man makes couches, doors, ploughs and tables, and often he even builds houses, and still he is thankful if only he can find enough work to support himself. And it is impossible for a man of many trades to do all of them well. In large cities, however, because many make demands on each trade, one alone is enough to support a man, and often less than one: for instance one man makes shoes for men, another for women, there are places even where one man earns a living just by mending shoes, another by cutting them out, another just by sewing the uppers together, while there is another who performs none of these operations but assembles the parts. Of necessity he who pursues a very specialized task will do it best.[108]

By the middle of the fifth century, Pericles was selling produce at the Athenian market and buying his daily necessities there.[109] A century later, Aristotle described the passing away of the earlier barter economy.[110]

Market demand also stimulated more investment—often, at this early date, of resources that were otherwise unused. This investment came about both because suppliers noticed and responded to demand and because consumers tempted by market wares became creative in using their fallow land, spare time, idle servants, or hidden artistic skills to earn the needed purchasing power. Just as a pile of gold, useless to a marooned Robinson Crusoe, was valuable in London, so previously overlooked resources became productive assets in the presence of markets.

Much of the new Greek wealth took the form of coins or moveable assets like silver objects, imported lumber, cash on deposit, ships, maritime cargo, and household furnishings.[111] As Aristotle noted, there was "wealth in slaves and livestock and money and there is much holding in what is called furnishings."[112] The wealth of bankers and merchants consisted largely of trade inventories and cash[113] and of considerable amounts of credit as well.[114] Many of these forms of wealth were so easily exchangeable that by modern definitions they would be considered part of the money supply. For instance, what the Federal Reserve until recently called M3 money was cash, bank deposits, certificates of deposit, credit card debt, and short-term promissory notes.[115]

This relatively large money supply was extremely important for business. Simply put, the economic demand that fuels business activity comes from a desire for what business offers, plus the ability to buy it—purchasing power. Desire usually exists: normally, therefore, business activity is a function of purchasing power. The more purchasing power, the more business. The money supply is one form of purchasing power. By contrast, the land that constituted most of the ancient world's wealth was harder to use as purchasing power. Formalities made it slow and difficult to sell or pledge, and most ancient societies sharply restricted the right to own land. In other words, the form of Greek wealth brought its money supply and purchasing power far closer to Persia's than the disparity in their total wealth might suggest, and the volume of business per capita was accordingly much greater.

Democracies like Athens had other financial advantages. Their wealth, even in land, was far more equally distributed than Persia's. Seventy-five percent of Athenian citizens owned an average of 25 acres of arable acreage, with 45- to 70-acre holdings common.[116] None was more than 750 acres.[117] Landless Athenians could earn purchasing power as craftsmen or through petty trade, and Pericles provided stipends for even the poorest if they served on juries, rowed in the galleys, or attended assemblies.[118] The richest Athenians, like Kallias and Hipponicus in the Periclean Age,[119] each owned about 200 talents worth of land and other assets. With the upkeep of a slave at about 175 drachmas,[120] this fortune was worth about six thousand times the annual Athenian wage. By contrast, a billionaire today has nearly one hundred thousand times the U.S. minimum wage. Nor did prosperous Athenians retire from the market or hoard their purchasing power. Many were metics, who could not own land and held their wealth in investments.[121] The richest man in Periclean Athens was a Cypriot named Zenon, a metic who invested his one thousand talents primarily in shipping.[122]

With purchasing power in the hands of such businessmen or of consumers shopping in the markets, demand was strong. It attracted production, and investment created new wealth. With the market's temptations always before them, Athenians readily translated their money into business activity. In Persia, by contrast, virtually all wealth belonged to a tiny elite, who hoarded their valuables and bought fewer goods and services than they could afford.

The nature and distribution of wealth was the principal reason why the combination of money, markets, and businesses assumed a recognizable modern appearance and economic role in Athens and other Greek democracies. Colonial trade had indeed given business a greater role in Greece than in the Middle East, but it was no coincidence that business thrived in democratic Athens, not in oligarchic Sparta. Democracy protected voters' purchasing power, safeguarding it from clan leaders. With coinage, then, their demand enlivened urban markets in democracies, expanding wealth and business opportunities far beyond anything previously known. Sparta had trade, coins, and markets too, but nothing like the level of demand. The next chapter describes how money, markets, and business actually looked in ancient Athens.

4

Business in Athens

Since the key to Athenian business activity was the widespread purchasing power of its residents, I will start with its money and credit institutions. That fueled the trade, manufacturing, and retail businesses. Next I will look at the workforce: citizens, women, slaves, and resident metics, those foreigners allowed to live and work there. Finally, I'll contemplate the rather ambivalent social status of business.

Banking

The money supply described in the previous chapter was one of two main forms of purchasing power.[1] The other was credit. Coins made credit easier to provide, so there were "thousands upon thousands of . . . loans made and received in the 4th and 3rd centuries."[2] In fact, credit became a major enabling condition for business. As consumer credit, usually provided by friends for personal reasons or as emergency aid, it fueled sales. As commercial credit, usually provided by investors for a profit, but sometimes also by temples like that of Nemesis in Africa, it financed investment.[3] Bankers served as investors, as intermediaries who put together private investors and entrepreneurs, and even occasionally as consumer lenders.

Greek banking began with money changing. By 480 B.C.E. major ports were awash in different coins minted in some ninety-three places.[4] Ultimately, more than eleven hundred Greek cities and several hundred petty monarchs would issue their own coins.[5] Traders needed them, but there were difficulties. Coins naturally wore thin with use, and since coinage was a largely manual art, even new ones varied in weight and assay. Impurities and counterfeits abounded, and information was hard to get, making exchange values fluctuate dramatically.

The first money changers appeared around 527 B.C.E. in Byzantium.[6] Within decades, several money changers operated in the marketplaces of Athens and its port, Piraeus, and in at least nine other Greek cities. They worked behind tables—*trapeza* in Greek, *banc* in medieval Italian—and charged a regulated commission of 5–6 percent, less than foreign exchange usually costs travelers today.[7]

Experts at keeping their own cash secure, money changers began safeguarding valuables for others, like traders away on long voyages. By Athenian law these were demand deposits, and the evidence for them—usually a ledger book entry—became a type of money itself. A bank's customers could pay each other with a simple transfer on its ledgers. These ledger entries became part of the money supply. Even today, economists describe the M1 core money supply as currency *plus* bank deposits.[8]

Because they handled cash, money changers were the obvious source for petty loans in the marketplace, holding objects in pawn for security. The final step to becoming full-fledged bankers was to make larger loans, risking both their own funds and their customers' deposits. In Demosthenes' words, "The Athenian bank is a business operation that produces risk-laden revenues from other people's money."[9]

The most intrepid Athenian bankers also acted as investment bankers, intermediaries who connected businessmen needing funds to investors. Such banking flourished in Athens because of the relatively equal distribution of wealth. Few Athenians could fully finance a trading voyage or the construction of a ship, but many could invest if properly advised. Investment bankers knew who had the money and who needed it, and they were expert judges of risk because of their intimacy with the market.

Bankers also provided fiduciary services. In one instance, when one Epikrates needed forty-two thousand drachmas to buy a perfumery, the investors deposited the money with a banker who made sure that Epikrates used it as promised, by personally witnessing the purchase transaction.[10] Epikrates then tried to get out of the deal, claiming that he had been hornswoggled into it "when all he wanted was sex with [the seller's] son." Bankers also seized opportunities for chicanery. One famous scandal involved investment bankers gone bad. The treasurers of Athens had loaned them funds in return for a cut of the profits. When the bankers defaulted, the treasurers tried burning the treasury to hide the loss.

Because reputation was so important a banking asset, the value of a banker's business far exceeded its tangible assets. This made selling the business after his death very difficult, because Athenian law didn't recognize this "good will" as saleable property. Only the bench and strongbox could be sold, not the real assets—his reputation and relationships. The widow's best financial recourse, as a woman who lacked the legal right to operate the bank, was to stay well informed about the business and marry the best slave, in this way realizing some of the business's intangible value.

So Pasion's bank, the largest in Athens, passed through four generations that we know about. Two citizen bankers originally bought Pasion as a slave and left him the bank in 394 B.C.E. He did so well that he gained citizenship, bought land, and retired while his slave Phormion ran the bank. Phormion later married Pasion's widow, retired around 370, and leased the bank to four of his own slaves.

Slaves who worked for banks could enjoy great authority and importance. Unlike other slaves or women, Athenian law allowed them to appear as parties or witnesses at court and to make contracts that bound their masters. They controlled and dispensed large sums at their own discretion, interrogated important customers, and sometimes traveled abroad to negotiate with high dignitaries. Due to their opportunities for manumission and inheritance, bank slaves were probably the most socially mobile businessmen in ancient Greece. Pasion and Phormion became two of the richest Athenians of their day. Pasion had revenues of about 54,000 drachmas per year and supported five Athenian warships.[11] His estate included 120,000 drachmas in mortgage loans and 300,000 drachmas in maritime commercial loans. Phormion was also a civic benefactor, but he never gained citizenship in Athens, so most of his funds were invested in maritime loans and other commercial activities.

Credit

Creditors need two things: purchasing power to offer, and trust in the borrower's promise of repayment. This trust in repayment is a psychological factor that can range from the infinitely small to the infinitely large. When trust is high, easy credit greatly multiplies available purchasing power; when trust is low, tight credit contracts, as the 2008–2009 recession so dramatically showed. Since credit is such an important component of the purchasing power that business depends upon, mechanisms that enhance trust have benefited business, while deteriorations in trust have hurt it.

Greek commercial law enforced mortgages and debt repayments and revoked the sale of any slave whose physical defects were not disclosed. But it was otherwise devoid of trust-building measures. And unlike their Middle Eastern counterparts, Greek gods cared nothing about the violation of oaths, perhaps the reason Romans made *Graeca fides* ("Greek faith") a synonym for dishonest dealing. Yet even in a city the size of Athens, the commercial community was small and close-knit; everyone knew if credit was not repaid. Informal community norms and social accountability enforced whatever laws and gods did not, regardless of the Roman view.[12]

The Greek concept of a sale derived from gift exchanges; *domai*, the word for "gift," became *apodidomai*, the word for "sale."[13] Most sales were strictly for cash undoubtedly, but the unusually large money supply made credit readily available. Stone boundary monuments memorialize thousands of mortgage loans in Athens alone during the fourth and third centuries B.C.E.[14] Many other loans and investments went undocumented or were recorded on perishable papyrus.

Credit took two forms: consumer credit for current consumption, and business credit for investment purposes. Consumer credit is more visible on the historical record because it was often secured by mortgages whose evidence survives. Mortgages secured major transfers of wealth, like dowries for daughters or bequests to children who would not inherit land.[15] They also secured emergency funds, as did unsecured loans from friends. For example, one Nikostratos fell into the hands of pirates while pursuing his escaped slaves and was himself sold into slavery. After promising to pay twenty-six hundred drachmas for his release to the ancient equivalent of Somali pirates, he raised sixteen hundred drachmas by taking a mortgage at 16 percent interest and borrowed the rest for a year, interest free, from his friend and neighbor Apollodorus. We know of this because Nikostratos repaid the mortgage, but not Apollodorus, who brought suit.[16]

The mortgage loan, evidently an arm's length business transaction, was expected to generate a profit. But the unsecured personal loan, which should have cost even more due to the greater risk, was free. Such personal loans, normally a form of private welfare to cope with emergencies and disasters, were considered moral obligations. Charging for them, or even demanding repayment, was thought indecent.[17] As one Greek wrote, "Where a loan is involved, there is no friend; for if a man is a friend he does not lend but gives."[18] The Hebrews made a similar distinction: "To a foreigner you may charge interest, but to your brother you shall not charge interest."[19] The Code of Hammurabi even required a trader who returned no profit "to give the banker double what had been advanced."[20] Less commercial cultures did not recognize commercial loans, however, holding that any charge was usury, a wrongful act. This was the church's long-held position and that of Islam today. But as commerce increased during the Renaissance, the church began to exempt business loans from the prohibition. Since the time of Adam Smith, the question has been how high interest rates should go without legal prohibition.[21]

But in commercial Greek cities like Athens, profits from commercial credit came free of moral taint. Studies of wills and inheritances show that "the profits of moneylending at interest were a regular part of the income of the upper classes."[22] Many banks appeared during the fourth century B.C.E., and some thirty Athenian bankers have been identified by name, compared to eighty in medieval Florence when that city was the banking center of Europe or the ten banking houses and their 150 affiliated bankers in seventeenth-century Osaka, the banking capital of Japan's 25,000,000 people.[23] Pasion's bank had eleven talents on deposit and fifty on loan ($18,500,000), mostly for commercial credit secured by moveable assets.[24]

By the fourth century B.C.E. Athenian businessmen commonly relied on banks for their financial needs and kept their accounts there.[25] These accounts, inventories, freight in transit, and even entire business enterprises like workshops, mining concessions, and proto-employment agencies that hired out slaves could be pledged for commercial credit.[26] Historians calculate that perhaps one in twenty Athenians used a banker, compared to one in thirty-five or forty in medieval Bruges, one in thirty at Venice, and one in fifteen at Barcelona.[27] With an estimated four million to six million drachmas on loan at any one time, commercial credit obviously financed much of the fourteen million drachmas per year in foreign trade by Athens.[28]

Most of this activity was invisible. Some involved tiny sums like half-obols (one-twelfth of a drachma) that pawnbrokers in the marketplace advanced for hours or days, recorded if at all on perishable papyrus ledgers.[29] Other loans, which Greeks called "obligations in the sky," were completely unsecured.[30] Even large advances were rarely secured by mortgages or recorded in a permanent way, since the metics who dominated banking could not take ownership of land. Moreover, secrecy was highly valued to avoid taxes and evade creditors.[31] A banker's accounting records might well be kept in his head or at a secure, undisclosed location. Only the banker knew, and he wasn't talking.[32]

Most large advances were maritime loans, secured by liens on ships or cargo. Cargo was typically owned by several merchants, thirty of them in one case. But unlike the stone monuments that marked mortgaged property, the agreements securing these advances usually disappeared after payment. The few known advances averaged some 3,000 drachmas, roughly $185,000 in 2006 dollars. They bore interest at anywhere from 12.5 percent to over 30 percent for terms of three to six months. At these rates, actually, they were venture capital investments for returns of 40 percent or 60 percent in a year.[33] Such high rates reflected the risk of trading voyages,[34] both the inherent danger of the briny deep and a legal risk: to encourage shipping, commercial cities customarily forgave maritime loans if the ship or its cargo was lost due to shipwreck or piracy.[35]

Naturally, creditors tried to limit legal risk. One who financed a voyage from Athens to the Crimea required a majority vote of the merchants on board before cargo could be jettisoned.[36] Nevertheless, the law was ripe for gaming. In one such case, Demosthenes' client had advanced Protus the money to buy grain in Syracuse, taking a lien on the grain. But once Protus loaded the grain in Syracuse, the ship's two owners pledged it repeatedly to secure loans from bankers there. Since a loss at sea would void these debts, they planned to scuttle the ship and keep the money. Indeed, once at sea one tried to distract the passengers on deck with loud talk while the other began sawing through the hold. Discovered, he leapt overboard. His partner tried to panic everyone into abandoning ship but Protus bribed the crew to continue to Athens. There, Protus, the bankers from Syracuse, and even the surviving shipowner each claimed the grain. Sadly, the outcome was never reported.[37]

Trade, Manufacturing, and Retail

Markets were usually located on city property, with stalls rented to the merchants. Shops in the *stoa*, the portico set up in the central marketplace of Athens, sold food and imports every day and stayed open well into the cooler hours of the night. As in other large cities, shops also lined the nearby streets.[38] Specialized markets arose in outlying districts, sometimes due to the unpleasant or dangerous processes required for manufacturing. Athens had a potters' quarter and a tanners' quarter as well as separate markets for wine, olive oil, cheese, soft cheese, and bedding.[39] Peddlers also called out their wares with distinctive cries as they walked, much like the opening scene of Gershwin's *Porgy and Bess*.[40]

Markets had restaurants and comfortable gathering spots and sold all the necessities of daily life, including baked bread, hardware, housewares, and furniture.[41] Retailers were often poor widows who had neither the space in their tiny booths nor the cash for much more than a day's worth of inventory.[42] If a customer ordered a good bottle of wine, the retailer might well have to run to a nearby wholesaler for it.[43] Produce reached Athens from other parts of Greece and abroad: jars of wine from the Aegean Islands and Anatolia, mackerel and salted fish from the Hellespont and the Black Sea, cypress wood from Crete, pine logs and pitch from Macedonia, spices and coconuts from India, Arabia, and Ethiopia, wheat from Phoenicia, sail cloth and papyrus from Egypt, ivory from Libya, pigs and cheese from Syracuse, and carpets and cushions from Carthage.[44]

Most goods reached Athens through Piraeus's large and protected harbor. Port officials boarded arriving ships to inspect their cargoes and collect customs dues, which usually amounted to about 2 percent of the cargo's value. Customs dues constituted the bulk of tax revenues in Athens and many other cities.[45] With the Athenian navy on one side of the harbor, the merchant ships then docked on the other at a long stone-paved quay, and heaps of diverse merchandise alongside or stored in colonnades behind the quay—bales of wool, bolts of cloth, amphoras of wine and oil, etc.—awaited transport by donkey or mule-drawn cart.[46] An open-air bazaar, the *deigma*, from which a babble of Mediterranean languages arose, formed adjacent to the quay. After unloading his goods, a merchant could sell from the quay, the colonnades, or the *deigma*, or sell everything to a wholesaler, whose donkeys or mule-drawn carts stood waiting to transport the merchandise to the central market in Athens.[47]

Public officials, guarded by a famous contingent of Scythian bowmen, maintained the access roads to the markets, policed the premises, and flogged offenders on the spot. Citizens were exempt from flogging, an important privilege given the brutal injuries that resulted. The city also provided a measure of quality control by supplying weights and measures for the market, and sometimes, especially when fine wines arrived from

Chios, the inspectors insisted on approving samples before sales could begin.[48]

Before the Peloponnesian War, Athens imported an estimated 800 silver talents' worth of goods per year, including grain worth 700 talents and some 5,000 slaves costing 70 talents ($26,000,000). It paid with tribute from its Aegean empire, the provision of services like shipping and prostitution, and the sale of exports, including jars of wine or olive oil, crocks of honey, and carefully wrapped batches of ceramic ware that were decorated in the city's inimitable style.[49]

Grain was by far the most important trade item. As city-state populations grew, their demand for grain strained the capacity of their farmlands. People normally got 65–70 percent of their calories from grain,[50] but crop failures occurred every third year or so.[51] These constituted emergencies that city officials had to alleviate with imports. Although the right to buy grain usually came through a diplomatic process, as when Athens bribed the Bosporan princes, those who actually imported, retailed, warehoused, and processed it were private merchants.

In Athens and presumably other cities, merchants were regulated through licensing. When famine threatened, the government might prohibit investment in shipping other than grain and allocate imports between the port of Piraeus and Athens itself. Grain wardens supervised these markets—fifteen in Athens and twelve in Piraeus by the fourth century B.C.E.—ensuring, upon penalty of death, that everyone in the distribution chain was selling on a fixed cost-plus basis. To prevent hoarding, grain dealers were prohibited from acquiring more than fifty measures of wheat, and their profit had to be less than one obol per measure.

Except for construction and shipbuilding, manufacturing took place in craft workshops that often doubled as retail outlets. The din of manufacturing filled the markets. Workshops used very little equipment—a bag of tools and maybe an easily constructed movable kiln, furnace, or forge. In fact, the simplicity of the manufacturing process allowed many owners the spare time for politics, an Athenian man's first love.[52] Craftsmen generally worked with family members, an apprentice, and perhaps slaves. A number of workshops had twenty to thirty of them, all working side by side, naked in hot weather. To maintain a good pace, large shops provided rhythmical music and whip-wielding supervisors, often slaves themselves.[53] Shops manufactured both inventory for the local market and made-to-order goods for exporters,[54] who generally supplied the materials.[55]

The most numerous Athenian craftsmen were probably potters; roughly 450–500 at the height of pottery exports during the fifth century B.C.E.[56] The largest manufacturing facility in Athens, however, was a shield factory. It belonged to Plato's friend, the Syracusan metic Cephalos, whose sons Lysias and Polemarchus employed 120 slaves there in 404 B.C.E., near the end of the Peloponnesian War.[57] That was about the upper limit of factory size, because without mechanization the only way to increase production was to hire more workers. Beyond a certain number of workers, another layer of supervision became necessary, raising costs above those of smaller rivals.[58]

Even though Greek scientists made important contributions to military technology and other practical applications,[59] they never concerned themselves with production.[60] Scientists belonged to the leisured classes, while people concerned with production were usually slaves and metics. Moreover, the labor of family and slaves was so inexpensive that labor-saving improvements would hardly reduce unit costs. Evidently nobody imagined that they might increase output without adding supervision costs. So the processes and techniques of production remained traditional, modified over the long run only by chance learning.

Labor and Status

Most citizens cultivated land as owners or sharecroppers. They set their own schedules, organized their work, and determined the nature and quantity of their output. If displaced to become artisans in the city, they continued to organize and control their own work. Even Sparta's helots organized their own work.[61]

Sharecropping made sense in a world primarily concerned with survival and self-sufficiency. Its administrative costs were negligible, and everyone shared the fate that war and weather decreed. But sharecropping also kept productivity low. Sharecroppers tried only to support themselves and pay their share to the landlord. Any display of wealth to powerful landlords and envious neighbors risked catastrophe.

But the rise of markets and the enrichment of many Greeks began to change this philosophy. When market temptations beckoned and the possibilities for making money expanded, subsistence no longer sufficed. Hiring more labor to increase production and profits became logical.

Free Greeks normally disliked working as employees, which they regarded as slavish.[62] When they worked for others, they typically did so as independent contractors—arrangements that protected their pride and independence. The main exceptions were for public construction and seasonal farm labor. The Colonos Misthios district of Athens had a labor market for these jobs, and records show that fully a quarter of those who built the Erectheum on the Acropolis were citizens.[63]

After Solon's day, the growing demand for employees was primarily satisfied by slaves. Slavery was nothing new, of course. The average 5-foot 6-inch, 150-pound hoplite marching to war needed slaves to carry the seventy pounds of armor and weapons he would don for battle,[64] and slaves worked as servants in many Greek households.[65]

Slaves came into heavy use in almost every aspect of Greek life, especially in the cities. By the fifth century B.C.E. Athens may have had some sixty thousand, roughly a third of the population.[66] They were easy to discipline, and the organization and supervision they required also made them very productive.[67] In commerce, manufacturing, and domestic service, the dependent labor force consisted almost entirely of slaves.[68] Even the Scythian archers who kept order in the Athenian markets were slaves. Slaves staffed such major manufacturing plants as Pasion's shield factory (about sixty-five slaves), the shield factory of Demosthenes' father (thirty-two or thirty-three), his bedding factory (twenty), the pottery factory of Duris (nine or ten), and the shoemaker Herondas's factory (thirteen). Mining used larger numbers—one thousand slaves worked Nicias's mining concessions at Laureion.[69] Slaves also constituted a lucrative form of investment, whether leased to others or allowed to work independently and remit a percentage of their earnings. Known as "those who live apart," such slaves lived at large as craftsmen alongside metics and citizens.[70]

The largest slave market was on the Aegean island of Chios, once Homer's home. Chios had long sold its fine wines throughout the Greek world, and early in the sixth century B.C.E. it also became a supplier of armor after a citizen named Glaucus invented welding and soldering, which eliminated the need for nails and rivets in armor. A rising demand for slaves assured their easy and profitable resale, so the wine and armor merchants of Chios started accepting slaves in trade and reselling them through their home market. As slave buyers flocked to Chios, they in turn attracted vendors who sought to dispose of their captives and enemies. In time, the slave market became Chios's most important economic activity.[71]

Slave trading joined the grain and timber trades as among the most important. Most of the Athenian slave traders probably lived in Piraeus, a town that "was 'a world apart,' a 'sacrilege'" to the Athenian elite, "full of foreign cults, brothels, and unconventional views about money-making and working for a living." Many traders there were neither Athenians nor even Athenian metics, but simply foreigners like the slave traders of Chios—that is, foreigners privileged enough *not* to be enrolled as metics or liable to the obligations and taxes imposed on the metics.[72]

Women constituted a dependent labor force in a position similar to that of slaves, especially since strong emotional bonds between men and women were probably not as common as in modern Western societies. In this context women had little power, and in fact their formal status approximated slavery. Both a new slave and a new bride were welcomed into an Athenian household by a ceremony called *katachysmata*.[73] Women, like slaves, couldn't own property or make legal commitments on their own behalf.[74] For men, the strongest emotional bonds seem to have arisen through military service, when new recruits normally paired off with veterans as military and sexual apprentices. The famous Sacred Band of Thebes, which helped Epaminandas defeat Sparta, "lived and fought as 150 pairs of lovers."[75]

But like bankers' wives, women *did* participate in business, especially in work that could be performed within the context of home and family.[76] Indeed, both women and slaves probably ran many a business, if only because Greek men considered gainful employment feminizing. For real men, only military, cultural, and political pursuits were masculine.[77] We know of female cobblers, painters, and gilders of helmets in Athens, as well as retailers of salt, groceries, hemp, wreaths, and perfumes.[78] Women actually predominated in retail,[79] where they could simultaneously tend the shop, watch their children, and perform chores like spinning, sewing, cleaning, cooking, or supervising the help.[80]

Apart from women in retail, most business entrepreneurs were metics, who numbered 6–20 percent of the Athenian population, depending on the time.[81] These resident foreigners performed military service and paid a head tax, but could not own land, use the courts for noncommercial purposes, or enjoy such informal benefits as holding good seats at the theater and stadium. Since metics also paid customs dues, they probably accounted for much of the city's tax revenues.[82] Some achieved great wealth, moved in the highest circles of society, and received many of the privileges of citizenship— even, occasionally, honorary citizenship itself.

The metics' status reflects Greeks' general ambivalence about business.[83] Having imbibed Homer practically with their mothers' milk, they shared his distaste for trade. Thebes banned from public office anyone who had pursued a trade within the preceding ten years.[84] As Aristotle put the aristocratic view, leisure was "more desirable and more fully an end than business."[85]

On the other hand, commercial cities were full of business activities, revenues derived from business were normal, and business could lead to wealth, leisure, and prestige. In a democracy like Athens, where virtually everyone worked, idlers faced condemnation for not using their talents.[86] Artisans and tradesmen who earned enough could serve as hoplites alongside free farmers, and the social barrier between the highest levels of society and the world of business was permeable. Socrates was a stonemason by trade, while the families of men like Pasion and Phormion could erase the stigma of their banking origins with time and good works.[87]

Abetting Greek ambivalence about business was uncertainty about business ethics. Homer condemned the Phoenicians for greed and dishonesty, but Greek traders treated strangers the same way.[88] Yet bankers were usually scrupulous and honest, sometimes famed for their probity, and business people were mostly scrupulous in dealing with fellow Greeks, at least. We are dealing here with

> the contrast between the institutions and beliefs geared to confronting the uncertainties of the physical environment and those constructed to confront the human environment. . . . The collectivist cultural beliefs that characterized the former environment produced an institutional structure geared to personal exchange whose cohesion and structure were built around strong personal ties. In contrast, the individualistic framework that evolved in response to the new human environment relied less on personal ties and more on a formal structure of rules and enforcement mechanisms.[89]

Might the perplexities of business ethics have spurred the development of Greek moral philosophy? It may not have been merely fortuitous that one of the core moral treatises of civilization, the dialogues of Plato's *Republic*, took place in the house of Cephalus, a wealthy metic trader.[90]

From a modern perspective we can see that accountability had much to do with the uncertainty of business ethics. Greeks were accountable to each other through the web of relationships that bound them together, but no such web tied them to strangers. Accountability made ethical behavior important; as later business history reveals, the ethical behavior of business people within their own cohesive groups has often contributed to the commercial success of Jews, Armenians, Quakers, Jains, and overseas Chinese, among others.[91]

The Athenian economy's unusually high level and broad distribution of purchasing power led to markets supplied by business entrepreneurs with ready access to credit. Its marketplaces were remarkably similar to modern malls, selling a vast diversity of products from many places. A sophisticated banking industry served it through money changing, depository safekeeping, trust services, investment banking, and finance. Slaves and women provided the bulk of the commercial workforce. Business, while considered somewhat distasteful, also served as a common and often rigorously ethical activity that fostered social mobility.

Unfortunately for the Greek democracies, however, their democratic idyll would soon end. While the concepts of money, markets, and business that they pioneered would flourish, their proponents would not be democracies, and the benefits for ordinary people would greatly diminish.

5

Hellenistic History
Prologue to Revolution

The markets and businesses that supplied democratic Greek city-states might well have remained a regional curiosity had Alexander the Great and his successors not wrought a social and economic revolution in the Middle East. The fascinating story begins with politics and power. The Middle East's social and economic structures had always outlasted its many conquerors and major technological changes. This chapter, while providing a brisk summary of Hellenistic political history, addresses the question of why the Macedonians had so much more profound an impact than others and how it happened that a modified version of the Greek business environment spread throughout virtually all of Western civilization.[1]

Alexander's Conquests

Philip II, Alexander the Great's father, received military training and a Greek education from Epaminandos of Thebes, vanquisher of Sparta and perhaps Greece's finest military mind. After the rest of his family had died or murdered each other, Phillip inherited the throne of Macedonia. This was a large, feudalistic land north of Greece known for cattle herds and pine forests. Xenophon had called it "the timberyard of Athens," foreshadowing its future naval importance.[2] Philip capitalized on his Greek culture, military skills, and diplomatic alliances (such as marrying Olympias, a princess of neighboring Epirus and future mother of Alexander the Great) to build Macedonia into a formidable military power. With Alexander's help he defeated Athens and Thebes in 338 B.C.E. at the Battle of Chaeronaea, becoming master of Greece.

Philip then made the mistake of announcing that he would marry a new wife and substitute her son for Alexander as his heir. With that, Alexander and his fiery mother Olympias plotted Philip's assassination. They knew a spurned lover of Philip's, a youth named Pausanius who had come to hate him. It seems that Pausanius had called his replacement in Philip's arms "a hermaphrodite and a promiscuous little tart." In revenge, Philip's new father-in-law, a friend of the "promiscuous little tart," invited Pausanius to dinner and, with his guests, gang-raped him. Then the servants got a turn. When Philip disregarded Pausanius's pleas for justice, Pausanius became his enemy. Alexander promised to help Pausanius escape if he assassinated the king. Pausanius did, but instead of helping him escape Alexander's men pursued and killed him, nailing his body to the public gibbet. The barons accepted Alexander as king; afterward, Olympias secretly placed a gold crown on Pausanius's head and had the body burned over Philip's ashes and buried. She poured libations over the grave ever after.[3]

The barons held vast tracts of Macedonia subject to obligations like providing soldiers, arms, and provisions in times of war. To placate them, Alexander reduced their taxes.[4] But since he also found the crown 500 talents in debt, a deficit he could not overcome even by selling virtually the entire population of rebellious Thebes into slavery (sparing only the poet Pindar's widow), he soon faced a desperate choice. As his biographer Peter Green put it, "To solve his economic crisis, Alexander must either sink back into obscurity, or wage a successful war of aggression."[5]

Greek propaganda had long painted the Persians as wickedness incarnate, while mercenaries like Xenophon had detailed their wealth and their weakness. In March 334 B.C.E., therefore, Alexander led about thirty thousand Macedonian and Greek troops across the Hellespont and swiftly won his way through Anatolia. For two years he besieged Tyre, home to Persia's fleet, and then slaughtered or enslaved its inhabitants. The Levant and Egypt rapidly surrendered, and in Egypt's ancient capital of Memphis, Alexander accepted the title of Pharaoh, descendant of the gods. Then he invaded Babylonia, defeating Darius III's army in the decisive 331 B.C.E. Battle of Gaugamela.

Table 6
Hellenistic Dynasties

Area	323 B.C.E.	301–282 B.C.E.	281 B.C.E.	263 B.C.E.	145 B.C.E.	Romans
Macedonia	Antipater	conflict	Antigonids →			165 B.C.E.
Thrace	Lysimachus →					4 B.C.E.
Anatolia	Antigonus	Lysimachus	Seleucus	Attalids→		133 B.C.E.
Babylonia/ Persia	Seleucus →				Parthians →	
Syria		Seleucids				69 B.C.E.
Levant	Ptolemy →		conflict →			69 B.C.E.
Egypt	Ptolemy →					30 B.C.E.

Note: based on Green 1990.

The greatest gamble in history had paid off. He had turned the eastern Mediterranean "into an Hellenic lake,"[6] and the Persian Empire was his, along with the emperor's harem and treasuries brimming with centuries of accumulated valuables. Arriving with 70 silver talents, Alexander found 59,000 in the treasury at Susa (150 times the gross national product of Athens at its height)[7], double that amount at Persepolis, and untold thousands more in Babylon, the wealthiest city of all.

Alexander soon departed to hunt down Darius III near the site of modern Tehran. In central Asia he married a beauty named Roxanne, then crossed Afghanistan and fought his way down the Indus River to the Indian Ocean. At age thirty-three, Alexander returned to Babylon and died. Typhus from salmonella poisoning is the current theory.[8]

Alexander left an enormous empire of twenty-five to thirty million people, but no competent heir.[9] His viceroys and generals, using the Persian hoards to pay mercenary armies, spent the next fifty years fighting over it, and after the murder of his mother, wife, half-brother, and infant child, proclaimed themselves kings. Four dynasties emerged: the Ptolemies in Egypt and the Levant; the Seleucids, who ruled the more populated valleys

Table 7
Hellenistic Population

Territory	City	323 B.C.E.	1 C.E.
Greece and Macedonia[a]		2,000,000–3,000,000	2,000,000–3,000,000
	Athens	100,000–200,000	100,000–200,000
Anatolia[b]		5,000,000–6,000,000	10,000,000–13,000,000
	Ephesus	100,000	100,000–400,000
	Smyrna	—	100,000–400,000
	Pergamum	—	100,000–120,000
	Rhodes	100,000–200,000	—
Levant[c]		4,000,000–6,000,000	7,000,000–10,000,000
	Antioch	200,000	200,000–400,000
	Tyre	20,000–55,000	—
	Jerusalem	—	100,000
Mesopotamia and Persia[d]		3,000,000–4,000,000	—
	Seleucia	—	600,000
Egypt[e]		5,000,000–7,000,000	7,000,000–8,000,000
	total	22,000,000–30,000,000	26,000,000–34,000,000

Note: population estimates for these eras are extraordinarily variable. Those provided here represent my estimates based on the sources cited in the notes.

a. Pounds 1990: 53 estimates 3,000,000–6,000,000 for Greece in the second century C.E. Extrapolating backward using North's normal growth rate of 0.036%/year for the ancient world (North 1981: 14) yields a Greek population of about 1,500,000, and hence my estimate of 2,000,000–3,000,000, including Macedonia. For Athens, see Sallares 1991: 6 and W. Ferguson 1969: 316–17.

b. Anatolia had 5,000,000–6,000,000 in 188 B.C.E. according to Grant 1990c: 6. For the 1 C.E. and Ephesus and Smyrna estimates, see Peters 1970: 520; for Pergamum, see Alfoldy 1988: 98.

c. Levant estimates based on Peters 1970: 517. Aperghis 2001: 76 provides estimates for Babylonia (1,000,000), northern Mesopotamia (ca. 1,000,000), northern Syria (500,000 increasing to 2,000,000), Phoenicia and southern Syria (ca. 2,000,000), Cilicia (2,000,000+), and western Persia (ca. 2,000,000). For later population, see Kaegi 1992: 27. Peters 1970: 520 says Syria alone had 6,000,000 at the time of Augustus. For the Antioch population in 323 B.C.E., see Brown 1992: 12; for 1 C.E. see Peters 1970: 520. For Jerusalem and Tyre, see Peters 1970: 517; Dudley 1993: 197; and Aperghis 2001: 76 (a sharply lower estimate of 20,000).

d. The estimated population of Mesopotamia and Persia is probably equally split, derived from Grant 1990c: 48; see also Aperghis 2001: 76. For Seleucia on the Tigris, see Grant 1990c: 60.

e. Egypt had 3,500,000 at 400 B.C.E. according to Bowman 1989: 17; for 7,000,000–8,000,000 at 1 C.E., see Bowman 1989: 17; Peters 1970: 173; and Aperghis 2001: 76.

of Anatolia, Syria, Mesopotamia, and Persia; the Antigonids in Macedonia; and the Attalids, who carved the kingdom of Pergamum from the rich southwestern parts of Seleucid Anatolia.[10]

The Hellenistic Political Revolution

Macedonian kings and Middle Eastern rulers had always exercised power and control through subordinates who provided manpower and loyalty in return for land, authority, and privilege. Such dispersed power led, however, to frequent revolts. Alexander's father Philip began to alter that arrangement. His army, although conscripted in the time-honored way, received a thoroughly Greek regimen of arduous training and prolonged service, making it more like a mercenary army loyal to the king alone.[11] And once Alexander captured the Persian treasury, the balance of power between king and baron changed forever.

His successors put this treasury to use by hiring mercenary armies, whose loyalty ran more to their paymasters than to their homelands. This gave the Hellenistic kings far more power than anything their subordinate governors, or any conceivable alliance among them, could hope to match. They were now powerful kings who governed through comparatively weak subordinates.

This revolution in royal power inaugurated an era that most ordinary people experienced as remarkably calm and stable. Despite the rulers' frequent wars, city-state economies, commercial relationships, and business continuity were rarely disrupted.

One reason was that the monetized treasure that each king initially accumulated continued to circulate through their hands even after the Persian hoards had disappeared. For hundreds of years the kings' disbursements returned to them through the sale of produce from royal estates, rents, and taxes. In fact, Hellenistic kings were the first to replace opportunistic levies with periodic taxation to ensure a continuous cash flow.[12] By maintaining their overwhelming military superiority, the kings discouraged revolts, and the few that occurred all failed.

Apart from Gallic war bands early in the third century B.C.E., barbarian attacks were also rare. Not until the Parthians seized Persia and then Mesopotamia from the Seleucids nearly two centuries later did outsiders seriously challenge the Hellenistic kingdoms again.

The many wars between kingdoms were often fought at sea or confined to certain contested borderlands—Palestine alone suffered more than 200 invasions, for example.[13] Confining warfare to these locales obviously reduced its economic disruptiveness. Moreover, these wars rarely resulted in complete conquest, if only because other powers usually intervened to prevent it. The most likely threats to the kings came from lovers and relatives, a threat often deflected by incestuous marriages. Not surprisingly, then, all the major dynasties lasted for generations: the Antigonids in Macedonia for 110 years, the Attalids in Pergamum for 135 years, and the Seleucids and the Ptolemies each for over 250 years.

In general, then, the Hellenistic age provided a political environment that allowed businesses to accumulate wealth and purchasing power. The lack of military disruption encouraged specialization and trade, which increased productivity and reduced transaction costs by allowing people to establish long-term commercial relationships. Let us now look more closely at each of the four main kingdoms, along with the commercial hub of the Hellenistic world, the independent city-state of Rhodes.

Greece and Macedonia

Although Macedonia and Greece constituted the smallest, poorest, and least populous of the Hellenistic kingdoms, the Balkan peninsula's strife-torn history after Alexander's death had profound consequences. It made possible the extension of money, markets, and business to vast numbers of new cities in the Middle East; it brought the commercialization of agriculture, agribusiness, to Greece; and it ultimately pushed the Hellenistic kingdoms into the Roman Empire.

For nearly fifty years after Alexander's death, Macedonia and Greece served as a battleground for rival claimants to the Macedonian throne. Gallic war bands, which Rome had driven from northern Italy, rampaged there with impunity. Only in 277 B.C.E. did Antigonus Gonatus, by expelling them, secure the Antigonid claim to Macedonia's throne.

Even more destructive were repeated civil wars, sparked by Macedonian support for oligarchic rule in the democracies. No doubt Greek and Macedonian aristocrats shared a disdain for the masses,[14] a view Cicero later expressed in attributing the fall of Greece to the "immoderate liberty and license" of "uneducated men," cobblers, belt-makers, artisans, shopkeepers, and all such "dregs of the state."[15] More fundamentally, however, the rulers knew that the rich, with more to lose, were more pliable than popular democrats.[16] They therefore favored oligarchic rule in all their cities, especially after Demosthenes led democratic Athens in a failed uprising upon Alexander's death.

This uprising was financed by Harpalus, who as Alexander's treasurer had embezzled vast amounts of treasure. Under the influence of his Athenian mistress, Harpalus had become a benefactor and honorary citizen of Athens and fled there with six thousand mercenaries and five thousand talents of silver once Alexander discovered his thievery. The Athenians were preparing to surrender him to Alexander's emissary when Demosthenes saved him with the caustic remark, "What will they do on seeing the sun who are dazzled by a lamp?"[17]

After this revolt failed and Demosthenes committed suicide, the Macedonian viceroy Antipater imposed oligarchy on Athens, inspiring similar efforts elsewhere. But since people never meekly surrender what they have, democrats fiercely resisted their loss, often with the support of Macedonia's Hellenistic rivals. Persistent and exceptionally destructive warfare resulted, depopulating large areas and undermining the prosperity of Greece. In the century after Alexander, Greece lost an estimated 25 percent of its population as hundreds of thousands of its countrymen emigrated to the courts, cities, and armies of the East, leaving large areas deserted or impoverished.[18] As chapter 7 will describe, these conditions made it possible for entrepreneurs to acquire property at bargain prices, import slaves, and install agribusiness.

Athens was nearly the only Greek city that maintained some degree of prosperity, its population remaining between one and two hundred thousand.[19] Silver from its mines at Laureion was in great demand; and as the revered fount of Greek culture, Athens also attracted munificent gifts from wealthy patrons abroad. It became a tourist stop for overseas Greeks returning to the old country, and a lively trade in Athenian artwork crisscrossed the Mediterranean. In one instance, the Ptolemies borrowed the original works of Aeschylus to copy for their library at Alexandria. They returned the copy and kept the originals, forfeiting their security deposit of four hundred talents—possibly the largest library fine in history.[20]

The Ptolemaic Empire

Some of the era's most original and important business developments arose in Egypt. In the division of spoils after Alexander's death, this richest of all Mediterranean lands fell to Alexander's schoolmate Ptolemy. His dynasty would rule for more than three centuries.

Ptolemy hoped to succeed Alexander. He claimed to be Alexander's half-brother and, since Macedonian custom held that a king must bury his predecessor, hijacked Alexander's funeral bier (a colonnaded, golden-roofed Greek temple on wheels) as sixty-four mules pulled it across the Syrian desert on the way to Macedonia.[21] He took the body to Memphis for a pharaoh's funeral and then enshrined it in a solid gold coffin at Alexandria.[22]

Despite Egypt's vast wealth, though, it lacked many resources that Ptolemy needed to support those ambitions or even to keep his kingdom. Hellenic mercenaries preferred wine and olive oil to the local barley beer and sesame oil. Gold production was now meager, and other essentials like silver, wood, ships, iron, and horses were available only through trade, a requirement that would shape many Ptolemaic policies.[23] To secure access to markets, as well as resources like iron, copper, and naval stores, therefore, Ptolemy quickly seized the Phoenician cities of the Levant and Cyprus, with their seafaring fleets. He then built a mercantile empire that helped stimulate entrepreneurial suppliers, shippers, manufacturers, and artisans in virtually every part of the Hellenistic world.

To maximize purchasing power for trade, Ptolemy and his descendents ran Egypt as a giant family business. They emphasized cash crops like wheat, papyrus, and oils and imported spices and luxury goods for resale abroad. Important as food preservatives, spices were so valuable that Ptolemaic officials kept them in guarded warehouses and strip-searched departing workers.[24] This was an extreme example of their close supervision of the workforce; other cost-control measures included regulating imports and excluding foreign coinage.

Such policies proved immensely successful. Although Ptolemy never ruled Alexander's empire, he ably defended his realm and added the Levant, Cyprus, important Aegean islands, and strategic holdings in eastern Anatolia.[25] By 245 B.C.E. the Ptolemaic empire was the wealthiest and strongest of all the Hellenistic kingdoms. It controlled the eastern Mediterranean and conducted robust trade throughout the Mediterranean and Black Sea region.[26] Ptolemy II's annual revenue of 14,800 talents, some $5,600,000,000 per year in today's currency, was 21 times the revenue paid to the last Persian king. He also collected 12 times the grain.[27] Under Ptolemaic rule, Egypt's population steadily grew from 6,000,000 to 8,000,000; the Levant's from 2,000,000 to 4,000,000.[28]

The magnificent capital of Alexandria reflected this success. Founded by Alexander in 331 B.C.E., it became the ancient world's most important manufacturing center. Much the largest Hellenistic city, with 500,000 people by 200 B.C.E., it had more Greeks than Athens and more Jews than Jerusalem.[29] The Pharos, Alexandria's 120-meter-tall lighthouse, was one of the Seven Wonders of the Ancient World, with a resinous flame that copper mirrors amplified into visibility 35 miles away. The library contained many of the existing written works, some half million scrolls, and the city's famous Serapaeum led the worship of Serapis, a Ptolemaic synthesis of Greek and Egyptian mythology that became a popular religion throughout the Mediterranean.

Guilds

The Ptolemies perceived the advantages of using local entities to collect taxes, draft labor, and maintain local order. But lacking city-states in Egypt, they created there instead one of the most enduring, distinctive, and powerful business institutions in history: the guild.

Guilds evolved from the social and service associations that became popular with the Greeks after Macedonia's victory at Chaeronaea. For the Greeks, as for many other peoples at the time, the gods were considered their city's protectors, and defeat undermined faith. A poem to Demetrius, a Macedonian ruler of Athens, made this plain:

> The other gods either are not, or are far away;
> Either they hear not, or they give no heed;
> But thou art here, and we can see thee,
> Not in wood or stone, but in very truth.[30]

The "fall of the Olympians," as Tarn calls it, led to a scramble for other social affiliations. New philosophical schools emerged as scholars in the Athenian academies of Aristotle, Plato, and Socrates formulated new philosophies in which gods played little role. The main ones were Epicureanism, Stoicism, and Scepticism. There were also the less popular views of the Cynics and the Peripatetics and, late in the Hellenistic day, Neoplatonism, a "syncretic mishmash" in Green's phrase.[31] People also flocked to the temples of Middle Eastern gods like Zoroaster, Mithras, Serapis, and Cybele. Dinner clubs and funeral societies became very popular as well, especially among metics, who were strangers in societies and constantly feared starvation and had few coreligionists to ensure a proper funeral.

Indeed, if these societies functioned anything like the similar social societies that proliferated in Britain during the Industrial Revolution and the Lions, Elks, and other service clubs of early-twentieth-century America, they would have facilitated business by enhancing trust and accountability between people who would otherwise remain strangers.[32] As Joel Mokyr says of such informal associations in eighteenth-century Britain, the transfer of trust from social to economic relationships helped develop "a level of trust that made it possible to transact with nonkin, and increasingly with people who were, if not strangers, certainly not close acquaintances."[33]

In Ptolemaic Egypt, such societies readily evolved into trade associations when, for instance, one prestigious grain merchant joined and others, even from diverse origins, would follow.[34] These associations often gained the right to own and dispose of land, a right that allowed metics far more integration with the community of citizens than would otherwise be possible.[35]

In their organization and operation, associations often adopted city-state forms: magistrates, laws, a council, and quasireligious ceremonies.[36] Perhaps these features reminded the Ptolemies of city-states. In any event, they made trade associations into guilds by granting them coercive powers and carefully defined monopolies or other economic privileges; in return, the guilds enforced public regulations and collected taxes.[37]

For example, the salt merchants of Tebtunis, from the part of Egypt known as the Fayum, obtained a monopoly over the sale of salt and elected Apunchis to collect the salt tax. They also ruled

> that all alike shall sell salt in . . . Tebtunis . . . upon condition that they shall sell the good salt at the rate of 2½ obols, the light salt at 2 obols, and the lighter salt at 1½ obols, by our measure or that of the warehouse. And if anyone shall sell at a lower price than these, let him be fined 8 drachmae in silver for the common fund and the same for the public treasury. . . . But if anyone is in default . . . it shall be permissible for the same Apunchis to arrest him in the main street or in his house or in the field, and to hand him over as aforesaid.[38]

Arrangements like this made the guild, like the city-state, a cheap and effective administrative agent for the government, while profiting and protecting guild members. Consumers paid higher prices, of course, but there was little they could do about it.

Rhodes

Much of the wealth that beautified Alexandria funneled through the independent city-state of Rhodes, an island between the Aegean Sea and the eastern Mediterranean with a population similar to that of Athens.[39] Winds and tides made it accessible from Alexandria in all seasons. Ships could then head west via Crete and Malta to Rome, Sicily, and Carthage or north into the Aegean and the Black Sea. Rhodes served as Egypt's main trading outlet and the commercial center of the entire Hellenistic world.

Rhodes had a proud military tradition. Both Mentor and Memnon, the best Persian commanders against Alexander, were Rhodians. Its small but effective navy prevented both Byzantium and Pergamum from levying tolls on the Bosporus, patrolled commercial waterways to control piracy, and played a significant role in Great Power confrontations.[40] The Louvre's famed Winged Victory of Samothrace, by a Rhodian sculptor, probably commemorates a naval victory over the Seleucids around 190 B.C.E.[41] Service on the rowing benches was a proud and unifying rite of citizenship.[42]

Rhodes served the Hellenistic powers the way Ugarit had served the Egyptian, Mitanni, and Hittite powers a thousand years earlier. It was a port of trade that provided a neutral market and communications center for rivals reluctant to visit each other's ports. Foreigners visiting Alexandria, for instance, had to surrender their books to the library for copying, exchange all their money for Ptolemaic coins, and follow regulations specifying what they could buy and sell and the prices they could charge. Trade was easier in Rhodes, whose stable leadership consistently sought to promote and protect business activity.

Many foreigners settled at Rhodes to facilitate trade, while the citizens of Rhodes were themselves the most formidable merchants of all. As merchants and sea captains, they dispersed Ptolemaic exports throughout the Mediterranean. They dominated the grain trade of Egypt, Cyprus, and the Black Sea and turned the distant cities of Carthage and Rome into Egypt's most important market.[43]

In its heyday, over eight thousand talents' worth of cargo passed through Rhodes annually.[44] Its role in trade allowed Rhodian seafarers to develop a lucrative shipping business. The busy port also attracted slave traders. After one Seleucid king's mistress was abducted from Ankara, he soon found her in the slave market of Rhodes.[45] As it accumulated wealth from these activities, Rhodes also became the Hellenistic world's financial clearinghouse.

Like Alexandria, its appearance reflected its prosperity. Rhodes was built on hills that formed an amphitheater around one of its three natural harbors. It was filled with squares, temples, statues, and paintings. The acropolis, the harbors enclosed by walls, and the quays loaded with international merchandise were famous everywhere. Even more so was the Colossus, one of the Seven Wonders of the Ancient World. This gigantic statue of Helios, the city's sun god, bestrode the harbor entrance. Two-thirds the height of the Statue of Liberty, it celebrated the escape of Rhodes from a terrifying, yearlong siege in 306 B.C.E., its three-hundred-talent cost paid by realized from selling the abandoned siege engines.

The besieger arrived with 40,000 soldiers, 30,000 workmen, a flotilla of 200 warships, and 170 transport ships that were carrying the greatest assortment of siege engines ever seen. One was an armored tower, loaded with catapults and slingers, called Helepolis, the "Taker of Cities."[46] The huge balls of stone that it flung are still there. Diodorus describes his forces as "joined by a host of pirates and almost a thousand craft belonging to merchants and others drawn by the hope of rich plunder."[47] Its resistance undoubtedly fortified by this horrifying specter and the certain knowledge of what would follow a breach of its walls, Rhodes held out until Ptolemy could lift the siege.

The earthquake of 228 B.C.E. flattened Rhodes and toppled the Colossus. Although all the Hellenistic states sent generous amounts of help to rebuild Rhodes and its naval power in a testament to its central role, the Colossus lay there for centuries until the Arabs hired a Jewish merchant to haul the pieces to Syria on 900 camels.[48] The Venice of the ancient world, grown rich on commerce, Rhodes would remain a tourist destination long after its commercial decline.[49]

The Seleucid Empire and Pergamum

In the two decades after Alexander's death, Ptolemy's main rival for Hellenistic power was Antigonus the One Eyed, whose grandson Antigonus

Gonatus would found the Antigonid dynasty in Macedonia. After Alexander's death, Antigonus had quickly gained control of the richest Middle Eastern regions outside Egypt, a northern tier of the Middle East stretching from the former kingdom of Lydia in Anatolia through Syria, Mesopotamia, and Persia to India. One enemy that he made in the process, however, was Seleucus, whom he had accused of embezzlement. Seleucus fled and joined Ptolemy in Alexandria. Although Antigonus repeatedly sent his son Demetrius to attack Ptolemy, most famously in the 306 B.C.E. siege of Rhodes, Ptolemy survived these attacks and returned Seleucus to Mesopotamia.

Seleucus prevailed in the East and claimed Alexander's territories there for himself. He built himself a capital, Seleucia-on-the-Tigris, to replace the malarial Babylon. Seleucus became even more powerful after making peace with the Indian ruler Chandragupta, ceding him Pakistan in exchange for a wife and five hundred war elephants. This alliance gave the Seleucids exclusive access to Indian elephants, much larger than their African cousins. The tanks of ancient warfare, they conferred military superiority to the Seleucids for many decades.[50]

In 301 B.C.E. Ptolemy and Seleucus, along with another of Alexander's old companions, King Lysimachus of Thrace, invaded Anatolia. Antigonus was killed in the decisive Battle of Ipsus, near Ankara, where some 150,000 soldiers fought in perhaps the largest of all ancient Western battles.[51] Demetrius fled, ultimately to drink himself to death at Seleucus's court, and the victors divided up Antigonus's territories.

Ptolemy gained his Aegean islands and eastern Anatolian forests and ports (including Tarsus, where Cleopatra would meet Antony). Seleucus took Syria, which he turned into an agricultural powerhouse by introducing the waterwheel from Persia and irrigating vast new acreage, where he grew imported Persian crops like peaches, lemons, and alfalfa.[52] He built a new capital at Antioch, named for his son Antiochus, which became a beautiful city of 250,000–400,000 people, and Syria's population eventually reached some 6,000,000 people.[53]

Lysimachus received the former Lydia and Antigonus's treasure, which he sent under a trusted aide to the cliff-top fortress city of Pergamum. He built a new capital on the Hellespont named Nicea after his first wife and soon made himself king of Macedonia as well. But his rule lasted only another twenty years, to 281 B.C.E.

A sordid intrigue led to Lysimachus's death and the last major rearrangement of Hellenistic territories. After Nicea died, Lysimachus married Ptolemy's daughter Arsinoë, and they had two children. She then plotted with her half-brother Ptolemy Ceraunus, who was also at court, to split the kingdom after old Lysimachus died. To inherit, they had to remove his grown son and heir, so they framed him for treason and persuaded Lysimachus to execute the popular young prince. At that point, however, the kingdom's dismayed barons offered the throne to Seleucus, who invaded and killed Lysimachus in 281 B.C.E. At that moment, Seleucus ruled from the Adriatic Sea to the Indus River.

The moment ended, however, when Seleucus stepped ashore after crossing the Hellespont to Thrace. Ptolemy Ceraunus had grown up at Seleucus's court in Antioch, and Seleucus invited him to join his little trip. As Seleucus stepped ashore, Ceraunus stabbed him to death, and the waiting Thracians acclaimed Ceraunus king. To legitimize his rule he offered to marry Arsinoë and make her children his heirs. At the first opportunity, however, he murdered them. Arsinoë fled to Egypt, married her full brother Ptolemy II, and ruled competently for many years on his behalf. Ptolemy II gained the sobriquet "Philadelphus" or sister lover. When she died, he had her declared the first Hellenistic goddess. Ceraunus was later killed by marauding Gauls who toured Macedonia with his bloody head on a pike.

The Seleucid conquest of southwestern Anatolia led to a long succession of Syrian Wars between the Ptolemies and the Seleucids. They competed to control the eastern Mediterranean: the Ptolemies for access to resources and markets, the Seleucids for travel between their territories. The first Syrian War, which erupted upon Seleucus's death, confined the Seleucid Empire to Anatolia and regions east, with the Levant remaining disputed territory. The second Syrian War distracted the Seleucids while Gauls raided the richest part of Anatolia. Instead, Attalus of Pergamum defended the region and in 241 B.C.E. proclaimed it the kingdom of Pergamum.

But in 228 B.C.E. Rhodes suffered its earthquake, and ten years after that the Second Carthaginian War cut off the Ptolemies' main source of silver in Spain. Lacking silver to pay mercenaries, they had to fight the Seleucids with native Egyptian recruits. Their victory in the 217 Battle of Rafia led them, like Greek hoplites, to demand more rights in reward for their service. Ptolemy IV's response to the silver shortage made matters worse. He debased his drachmas, forcing soldiers, peasants, and workers to accept ever less valuable payments. Temples led the protests despite efforts to placate them with tax exemptions like those decreed around 200 B.C.E. in Greek and hieroglyphics on the Rosetta Stone.[54]

By then the teenaged Antiochus III had taken the Seleucid throne. The greatest Hellenistic conqueror since Alexander, he retraced Alexander's march to India, thrilling Hellenes everywhere. He returned to find that his uncle had revolted; with Pergamum's help he captured the traitor, who was castrated and beheaded, wrapped in an ass's skin, and crucified. Antiochus then joined with Philip V of Macedonia to attack Pergamum, recovering Seleucid lands in southwestern Anatolia.[55] Next he marched through Cyprus and the Levant to Egypt, where Ptolemy IV only forestalled invasion by marrying Antiochus's daughter Cleopatra (the first of seven Ptolemaic Cleopatras) and promising his throne to their future son.

At this triumphant moment, however, Antiochus III made the mistake of defying Rome. He hired Rome's enemy Hannibal and despite Roman warnings invaded Greece. Rome swept him out of Greece and invaded Anatolia. At Magnesia in 189 B.C.E., thirty thousand Romans annihilated his seventy-five thousand troops, stampeding their war elephants. Hannibal fled to nearby Bithynia, where Roman agents found and assassinated him.[56] Rome forced Antiochus to cede all his Anatolian territories to Pergamum. He promised to destroy his fleet and the remaining elephant corps, and to pay Rome fifteen thousand talents of silver. A few years later he was lynched while looting temples for the money.

With Rome's support, Pergamum was now expanding its empire in Anatolia and becoming enormously wealthy. The city rivaled Alexandria in splendor, prestige, and commercial power. Its library, at two hundred thousand volumes, was second only to Alexandria's. The Ptolemies tried to stunt the library's growth by embargoing papyrus, the paper of the day; Pergamum thereupon invented parchment, made from the skin of its plentiful sheep. But the last Attalid ruler of Pergamum died childless in 133 B.C.E. and bequeathed it to Rome. A long popular revolt ended only when the Romans poisoned all the wells in rebel territory.[57] The Attalid kingdom became the Roman province of Asia. A century later, Mark Antony gave Pergamum's library to Cleopatra.[58]

Hellenistic Decline

Rome's imperial ambitions toward the Hellenistic kingdoms were first kindled by the endless wars of the Greek city-states and Macedonia. They received irresistible impetus after Rome responded to Antiochus III's invasion of Greece by invading Anatolia. What the legions saw in Macedonia and Anatolia led Roman leaders to the same conclusion about the Hellenistic world that Alexander had reached about Persia: it was rich, weak, and ripe for the taking.

Within a few years of the Anatolian invasion, therefore, Pergamum's king easily stirred the Senate to attack Macedonia. Finally defeated in 167 B.C.E., its King Perseus and his son were led to Rome in chains, along with stupendous spoils. The Senate also punished several smaller Hellenistic powers that had questioned this war. One thousand skeptical Greeks, among them the historian Polybius, were exiled to Italy. The cities of Epirus, which had supported Macedonia, were all sacked, their 150,000 inhabitants sold into slavery. Even Pergamum lost territories after objecting to the abolition of Macedonia's monarchy.[59]

Rhodes had repeatedly tried to broker a peace between Rome and Macedonia. With exquisitely unfortunate timing, its ambassadors brought new peace proposals to Rome just as news of Macedonia's surrender arrived. In punishment, Rhodes was stripped of its Anatolian possessions; worse, Rome declared nearby Delos a free port and installed shrewd Athenian management there. Delos's competition soon reduced the harbor receipts of Rhodes by 85 percent.[60] Its navy declined, unable to police piracy any more,[61] and after grain ships began sailing directly from Alexandria to Rome, it became little more than a museum of Hellenistic achievement. Rome incorporated Rhodes into its province of Asia in 44 C.E.[62]

The Seleucids made one last attempt to regain their power. Still rich and powerful, they finished paying their indemnity to Rome in 176 B.C.E., and an opportunity to finally unite with the Ptolemaic lands immediately materialized. With Ptolemy IV's death, Antiochus III's infant grandson had become heir to the Ptolemaic throne. But sinister advisers—one a eunuch, the other an ex-slave, nearly always bad signs in ancient history—killed Cleopatra and forged a will naming themselves them his guardians.[63] These developments encouraged Antiochus IV to invade Egypt, launching the sixth (and final) Syrian War.

Looting 1,800 talents from the temple in Jerusalem on his way to Egypt, the Seleucid king arrived at Eleusis before the gates of Alexandria. There he met a Roman envoy, who ordered him to relinquish his gains and go home. While the king pondered, the Roman drew a circle around him in the sand and told him to decide before stepping out. Antiochus IV capitulated.[64]

The consequences were dire. Retreating in humiliated rage, Antiochus IV fell upon Jerusalem and sacked the city, sparing no one. A three-day orgy of destruction commenced, according to the Book of the Maccabees, with up to eighty thousand dead and another forty thousand sold into slavery.[65] The Maccabean Revolt followed. In 145 B.C.E., after a long guerilla war, Judea became independent under the hereditary high priests of Judas Maccabee's family, the Hasmoneans.

In Persia, a nationalistic revival had already begun. By 200 B.C.E. the Pahlevi dialect had largely replaced Aramaic as the second language of trade, and after Antiochus III's defeat at Magnesia, a group known as the Parthians gradually gained control. They invaded Babylonia in 141 B.C.E. and razed Babylon itself in 125 B.C.E.[66] Reduced to Syria, the Seleucids turned to dynastic struggles, as had the Ptolemies in Egypt. Hellenistic city-states now looked to Rome for privileges and aid; welcomed Roman financiers, traders, and merchants; and joined a Roman-dominated commercial network long before Rome's sufferance for the remaining kingdoms ran out—in 64 B.C.E. for Syria and in 32 B.C.E. for Cleopatra VII, the last Ptolemy—as the political lines were officially redrawn.

It was not necessary and inevitable that free markets and private businesses should have gained a central role in the creation and allocation of material wealth in the Western world. Although there are many reasons why that did happen, and many threats to that form of economy that were closely avoided, the Hellenistic political revolution described in this chapter was critical. That revolution made money, markets, and business common to urban economies throughout virtually all of the civilized Western world. It also had a profound impact on long-lasting features of business life like the guild system and the disrepute of business practitioners. The forces and circumstances shaping the Hellenistic environment largely derived from the political upheavals of the age as outlined here. This chapter is therefore the prologue to the story of how Alexander the Great and his followers gave business to Western civilization.

6

The Hellenistic Business Environment

The innovations in royal power discussed in the last chapter made possible a series of social and practical changes that transformed the nature of business. The main changes took place in the role played by city-states, the use of technology, the amount and distribution of wealth, and the development of international trade law.

City-States

Hellenic culture was imposed throughout much of the territory that Alexander had conquered through a local administrative structure of city-states. The Macedonian conquerors, who despised the native elites and rejected their society, sought to supplant them root and branch, except in religious institutions. To this end, instead of hoarding the land's surplus and accumulating treasure as the Persians had done, they used it to lure vast numbers of Hellenes to hundreds of new cities modeled after those in Greece. Alexander founded several Alexandrias; Seleucus founded nine Seleucias, sixteen Antiochs named for his son, three Apamaeas named for his mother, and one Stratonica named for his wife. The immigrants served as mercenary soldiers, bureaucrats, landowners, merchants, and tradesmen.[1] As in America's history, they were not simply pulled by the exciting opportunities of the frontier, in this case an eastern one; they were also pushed by the deplorable conditions in the old country, Greece and Macedonia.

Hellenistic cities differed sharply from those already there. Middle Eastern cities, with a few exceptions, were just agglomerations of people around the palaces of the mighty.[2] Hardly any owned or allocated land; operated, supported, or policed markets; or provided entertainment, welfare, police, sanitation, or justice.[3]

But the cities beloved of Hellenes performed all such sovereign functions and also maintained diplomatic relations.[4] They were not just cities; they were city-states. For Hellenes, citizenship in a city-state was the defining relationship of a man's life. Aristotle's very definition of a man was *zoon politikon*: "a being whose highest goal, whose *telos* [end], is by nature to live in a *polis* [city-state]."[5] Alexander, to emphasize how far Macedonians had progressed, remarked that while once they had been "vagabonds and poor shepherds," now they were "city-dwellers."[6] Most importantly for business, they all operated market-based free enterprise economies through which passed the greater part of the enormous wealth that the Hellenistic kingdoms produced.[7]

Given their distrust of democrats like Demosthenes and their belief that oligarchs were more trustworthy and loyal, the Hellenistic kings gave their new city-states oligarchic constitutions, under which a limited number of propertied citizens elected magistrates to govern. These magistrates enjoyed valuable benefits. As sovereigns in all but war, they could control properties, shape laws, and allocate opportunities to themselves and their friends. A lucrative perquisite was to collect taxes for the king, keeping any excess they procured.[8] Magistrates could also protect their families from such calamities as forced labor or billeting the army's rough mercenaries.[9]

Not surprisingly, election was avidly sought. Campaigns took the form of performing religious or charitable chores called liturgies. One common liturgy was to subsidize the grain supply. Others paid for public entertainment, ships of war, even buildings. The cost and splendor of liturgies inevitably escalated and put magistracies beyond the means of most people, much like campaign costs in modern democracies.[10] The victors, heavily dependent on the kings for protection, were naturally subservient to them while diligent in discharging their administrative duties.

City-states were initially "islands of Hellenism in an Oriental sea"[11] and were treated like other great landowners. When Cyrene donated grain to

famine victims around 330 B.C.E., for instance, the recipients were indis-
criminately listed as Athens, Alexander's mother Olympias, Corinth, Rhodes,
Alexander's wife Roxanne, and Argos.[12] But the rulers soon realized how
the structure and leadership of city-states made them both more effective
and more docile than priests, barons, or princes.[13] The kings therefore attached many temples and properties to them and granted them extraordinary privileges, rights, and powers that attracted other property owners.[14]
In divorcing Antiochus II, for example, his wife gained certain property
with the agreement that she would "have the right to join the land to any
city she wishes."[15] The peasants on such lands often gained personal freedom and the right to legal ownership of their farms.[16] City-states ultimately
governed most of the Seleucid and Attalid lands, as well as Ptolemaic holdings in Anatolia and the Levant.

Businesses blossomed there.[17] Apart from mercenary soldiers, possibly
30–40 percent of their residents worked as traders, artisans, retailers, merchants, performers, and orators who served the population at large rather
than any one person. The rest were servants, usually slaves.[18] As more and
more land fell within city-state jurisdiction, most of the Seleucid population
may have participated from time to time in market exchanges, either as free
peasants, artisans, or shopkeepers.[19] In the markets, vendors sold to all com-
ers for cash, subject only to taxes and limited regulation. Behind the vendors, and similarly free to set prices and amass wealth if possible, stood a
commercial network: the merchants who imported slaves, provided the raw
materials for manufacturing, and brought luxury goods from afar; transporters like caravan leaders, muleteers, and ship captains; money changers
and bankers who facilitated the cash economy; and landowners whose
agents sold food, bricks, wool, metals, wood, and other raw materials.[20]

Even as business activity flourished, though, entrepreneurs lost social
status. Most of the purchasing power accrued to the dozens or hundreds of
richest citizens, depending on the city's size, and through slaves or freedmen
(former slaves) they owned the largest, most profitable businesses. Only the
riskiest, dullest, and least profitable ones were left to other entrepreneurs. Nor
could petty entrepreneurs easily obtain financing. The concentration of wealth
left few potential investors, and they had feasible investment alternatives like
slave-operated enterprises or real estate purchases. Such investors could
therefore demand a larger share of the profits.[21]

Under these circumstances business ceased to offer entrepreneurs a
good living or social advancement. Markets in the stately civic centers
increasingly resembled modern flea markets—thriving and active, per-

haps, but with a high-volume, low-value trade that consumed vast quantities of time and attention in return for a modest living. Offering scarce opportunity for gain, leisure, or personal development, business conferred little prestige; even its profits came to seem somewhat disreputable.[22]

Technology

Never before, and not for many centuries afterward, did technology contribute so importantly to productivity and wealth.[23] In fact, Hellenistic technology was so much more important to business than that of the Romans that, for simplicity, this discussion will anticipate Rome's technological contributions as well.

There was nothing new about Greek rationality or scientific curiosity. Many Greek contributions to science predated the Hellenistic Age, and since many of the Hellenistic kings, however brutal, were also sophisticated and learned men who enjoyed the company of great thinkers, they avidly sponsored scientists and even competed to attract them. The Attalids of Pergamum competed with the Ptolemies to attract the greatest scholars and build the largest library, while other Hellenistic kings were patrons of the best and the brightest and were considerable intellectuals themselves. These included the sensual Demetrius, who drank himself to death, and his rival Cassander, who killed off Alexander's mother, wife, and child. The most famous of all was Demetrius's son Antigonus Gonatus, a student of the Stoic philosopher Zeno. Hailed as a godly offspring of the sun, he replied: "The man who empties my chamber-pot has not noticed it."[24] He viewed kingship as noble servitude, a philosophy that the Roman Emperor Marcus Aurelius would adopt. Working in the royal museums, academies, and universities, Hellenistic scholars, as well as private inventors, studied the natural world with unprecedented success. They reached new understandings about the way things worked and generated many ideas and inventions:[25]

- Astronomers produced what is essentially our modern-day calendar, down to the hours, minutes, and seconds.[26]
- Cstesibus of Alexandria invented the water clock, a vast improvement in accurate timekeeping. He also created a pump, improved Ptolemaic siege weaponry, and discovered steam power, which he (or Hero) used to create mechanical toys.[27]

- Aristarchus of Samos, in the early third century B.C.E., hypothesized that the earth revolved around the sun.
- Eratosthenes of Cyrene accurately calculated the earth's circumference using Euclidian geometry.[28]
- Hippodamus of Miletus proposed laying out cities on grids, a concept immediately and widely put to use.[29]
- Mathematicians expanded the boundaries of mathematical knowledge: Euclid systematized geometry and established a school in Alexandria around 300 B.C.E., and Diophantus of Alexandria's *Arithmetica* was the book in which Pierre de Fermat scribbled his famous last theorem.[30]
- Greek astronomer Ptolemy, writing in the 140s C.E., catalogued approximately eight thousand places, complete with latitude and longitude, creating a view of the world that lasted until the age of Galileo.[31]
- A profound new understanding of mechanics, exemplified by Archimedes, led to such innovations as windlasses, pulleys, levers, wedges, balances, and pneumatic devices.[32]

Many of these discoveries were the byproduct of intellectual play. The scientists and engineers of the Hellenistic Era were aristocrats seeking to satisfy their private curiosity and saw discoveries like steam power more as toys or parlor tricks than as practical applications. But some of their work was also meant to help their royal patrons, mainly in the practical fields of health, armaments, and productivity.

Hellenistic medical advances include such fundamental biological discoveries as the function of the brain and the relation between the pulse and the heartbeat—often achieved, it must be said, by experimenting on living slaves. Around 30 B.C.E. the physician Celsus compiled a medical textbook, *de Artibus*, that became a foundation of modern medicine after its rediscovery in the fifteenth century.[33] Galen, the most famous ancient physician, came from Pergamum in the second century C.E.[34] The preeminent military technologist was Archimedes, who worked as a defense engineer in Alexandria and died in 212 B.C.E. fighting the Romans on ramparts he had designed and built for his home city of Syracuse in Sicily.[35]

Productivity

The most novel use of scientific thought, however, was for productivity, using rational methods to achieve economic goals. The main reason seems to have been financial. While the Persian windfall had allowed Alexander's successors to secure their kingdoms with mercenary forces, the continuing need to pay them gave the kings an unprecedented desire to increase the productivity of their lands, which flourished as a result.

Business benefited greatly from the resulting contributions to productivity. While people had previously thought carefully about such matters as the farming calendar, the timing of Nile floods, and the mining of precious metals, most productivity advances had always resulted from chance discovery or accumulated experience. With abundant slave labor and rulers dependent on their own estates or those of henchmen to supply military power, there was no demand for improved productivity. Unlike previous rulers, however, the Hellenistic kings depended on paid mercenaries and wanted productive estates to generate cash. They were therefore the first to use systematic observations of nature, the recording and publication of useful measurements, mathematical calculations, and other rational techniques to raise productivity.

They introduced slave labor when feasible and improved peasant efficiency by providing better tools made of iron[36] and using water- or animal-powered wheels to replace hand querns to grind grain,[37] as an 85 B.C.E. poem by Antipater of Thessalonica charmingly noted:

> Cease from grinding, ye women who toil at the mill.
> Sleep late even if the crowing cocks announce the dawn,
> For Demeter has ordered the [water] nymphs to perform
> the work of your hands
> And they, leaping down on the top of the wheel,
> Turn its axle which with its revolving spokes,
> Turns the heavy concave Nysarian millstone.[38]

Virtually all the kings initiated massive reclamation projects to increase their arable acreage, draining swamps and lakes, repairing old irrigation works, and building new ones.[39] A Ptolemaic invention, an animal-powered contraption called a *saqia* that lifted buckets of water, became common throughout the Middle East.[40] The Archimedes screw, a device for pumping water, became so popular that Egyptians simply called it "the machine." In Spain, it helped quadruple the output of mines that Rome captured from Carthage after defeating Hannibal.[41] New tools like pumps and pulley-equipped cranes facilitated a vast expansion of arable lands, the construction of large buildings like the six- and seven-story tenements that Strabo saw in Tyre, and monuments like the Pharos of Alexandria and the Colossus of Rhodes.

Hellenistic agronomists developed improved olive and grape seeds, and wheat yields from their seeds apparently doubled.[42] In Egypt, the Ptolemies introduced sheep-raising for the wool they preferred,[43] as well as viticulture and new fruit crops.[44] The Attalids of Pergamum constantly improved their agriculture and pasturage[45] and used technical handbooks to create profitable businesses in woolen textiles and parchment.[46] The Seleucids introduced new crops like rice, alfalfa, peaches, and lemons into Syria and Mesopotamia.[47] Another new crop was cotton, which had apparently come to Alexander's attention during his march down the Indus Valley, where the oldest known cotton fabric has been found at Mohenjo-daro, dated to 2500 B.C.E.[48]

The kings also tended their forests, fisheries, and mines with care. The Antigonids of Macedonia paid particular attention to their natural resources, harvesting their forests on a sustained yield basis,[49] opening new mines, building mints in their cities to exploit them, and harvesting grain, salt, and timber for export.[50] With the wide distribution of Aristotle's manual on the cultivation and harvesting of commercial fish, fisheries were studied and sustained everywhere. Aristotle also produced a manual on beekeeping, honey being the ancient world's sugar;[51] and Theophrastus of Alexandria wrote a treatise entitled *On Odors*, concerning perfumes, medicinal oils, and olive oil.[52]

Transport

Transportation, a matter of prime concern in trade because of its great cost, received various benefits from Hellenistic and Roman technology. Land travel was vastly slower than travel by sea, of course, and much more expensive. On a good Roman road, a 1,200-pound ox-drawn cartload of grain took nearly two weeks to cover 300 miles, doubling the grain's cost. In just five days, a ship could deliver vastly more over the same distance.[53] It could carry grain from one end of the Mediterranean to the other for less than a quarter of the ox cart's charge for 300 miles on land.[54] John the

Almoner, the seventh-century C.E. archbishop of Alexandria, could relieve a famine in England more easily than a famine in villages 100 miles inland, although his charitable impulse might have been influenced by grain being sold in England for thirty times its price in Alexandria.[55]

The Hellenistic Era invention of lateen sails, which swung from side to side, probably helped ship speeds a bit,[56] but since transport remained determined by muscles, winds, and tides, it was always slow and unpredictable. A trip from the Indus to the Mediterranean took some two months: forty days by sail from the Indus to Babylonia, and another fifteen by boat and caravan up the Euphrates and across the Syrian desert to Antioch.[57] From Athens to Rhodes, a prime trade route, normally took six–seven days, but Cicero's trip during optimal sailing weather from Athens to the closer port of Ephesus took sixteen days.[58] On the most important trade route of all, from Alexandria to Rome, weather effectively prevented sailings from October to April, allowing time for only one sailing per season, and this could be a chancy one, as Lucian's fictionalized account of such a voyage in the second century C.E. illustrates. His grain freighter followed the coast north from Alexandria, sighting Cyprus seven days out. Just then a strong gale forced it back to Sidon, and it took ten more days to reach Anatolia. The captain then headed to Athens, arriving in Piraeus seventy days after leaving Alexandria.[59]

The main technological improvements to speed were on land. Under the Hellenistic rulers, camel caravans continued a long-standing trend of replacing mules on overland trade routes through Persia and central Asia to China and India.[60] The camels could carry more than the mules they replaced, and their tolerance for thirst allowed them to proceed more directly.[61] Road improvements were also important. Except for a few Persian roads, overland routes before Alexander had been incredibly bad. The main road between Corinth and Athens was just a narrow track along cliffs that plunged into the sea. According to legend, a bandit named Sciron stopped all travelers on this road, robbed them, and made them wash his feet. As they did so, he kicked them over the edge.[62] The Hellenes improved many such roads, but the Romans, of course, did far more. Hadrian broadened the track between Corinth and Athens into a dual carriageway,[63] and the vast Roman military road network was a marvel. They were the first to pave their main roads, which were built ten feet wide and sometimes widened to a majestic thirty feet as they approached the gates of a city.[64] Italy alone had 12,500 miles of paved roads, and the empire had 51,000. These good roads made fast travel possible, at least for soldiers and messengers. We are told that Caesar once took a carriage 800 miles in eight days, and Tiberius allegedly galloped 600 miles in three.[65] Indeed, Caesar's 54 B.C.E. letter from Britain reached Rome in twenty-nine days, while in 1834 Sir Robert Peel took one day longer to rush from Rome to London.[66]

There were other important Hellenistic improvements to transport. Greeks had improved harbors as early as the eighth century B.C.E.,[67] but the Hellenes regularly built lighthouses like Alexandria's Pharos and compiled maps, charts, geographies, and atlases to aid navigation. These devices helped them pioneer important new trade routes.[68] Alexander and the Seleucids secured the caravan route through Persia to India by founding many cities along the way.[69] The Ptolemies reopened Darius's old canal between the Nile and the Red Sea, and their navigators learned the monsoon patterns of the Indian Ocean, permitting scheduled trading voyages to India.[70]

Merchant ships increased from a standard size of 100 tons to 120–50 tons by the end of the second century C.E.,[71] but many were larger. The Romans used 1,300-ton ships for the grain trade between Alexandria and Ostia.[72] One carried 1,300 passengers and a crew of 200 sailors along with 93,000 bushels of wheat, a granite obelisk the size of Cleopatra's Needle in New York's Central Park—a 193-ton monolith that stands 77 feet tall[73]—plus cargoes of linen, pepper, paper, and glass.[74]

The remarkable 3,000-ton ship that Archimedes built for the dictator of Syracuse was too large for most ports, so it was sent to Ptolemy IV, fully laden with supplies. Named the *Syracusia*, its timber came from Mount Etna, hemp and pitch from the Rhone Valley. Lead sheathing was attached by 10- or 15-pound copper spikes. It had four wooden anchors and eight of iron. It carried more than 4,000 oarsmen, 2,850 marines on deck, and 400 guests,[75] with stables for their horses, a gymnasium, a garden, baths, a reading room and library, a chapel to Aphrodite, kitchens equipped with a saltwater fish tank, and artworks, including mosaic floors that depicted the entire *Iliad*. Its eight towers were loaded with stones and missiles for defense, and its three masts had platforms for dropping stones, grapples, or chunks of lead on the enemy. One catapult that Archimedes designed could throw a 180-pound stone or an 18-foot dart 200 yards; others could hurl grappling hooks to pull an enemy ship alongside.[76]

Increasing volumes of trade probably sped travel more than technology. Travel took much longer than the trip itself, because people had to wait for sailings or caravans. While a fast ship could reach Alexandria directly from Naples in nine days,[77] it took fifty-seven days on average for Alexandria to receive the important news of a Roman emperor's death. Even so, the days or weeks required for Hellenistic and Roman communications were vast improvements over the months required during times of infrequent sailings.[78]

Technology Withers

Despite all its advances, technology had nothing to do with the most remarkable developments of the age, like Alexander's conquest of Asia, the rise of Rome, or the endurance of the Roman Empire that followed. In fact, the Greeks and Romans were often at a technological disadvantage. Nothing of Alexander's compared to the terrifying war elephants he encountered in India,[79] and Roman armorers had to import the superior steel of Pontus and Scythia. Even the Damascene steel of medieval Crusader dreams and legends was invented in India before 125 B.C.E.[80] Instead of creating an ancient industrial revolution, the flowering of Greek technology withered within a century.

Unlike the eighteenth-century industrialization of Europe, with its thousands of manufacturers clamoring for innovations, the demand for new technology in ancient times came almost entirely from rulers, whose interests were limited and personal.[81] In one famous instance, an inventor of shatterproof glass asked the Roman emperor Tiberius for a reward. Tiberius ascertained that nobody else knew the secret and had the man executed, lest "gold be reduced to the value of mud."[82] The public benefit of such an invention weighed little against its threat to the value of his glass collection.

Kings would buy technology to improve their property, but with plenty of cheap manpower available, they had little interest in technology to improve labor productivity. That is probably why animal-powered wheels for grinding grain, a second-century B.C.E. Persian innovation that increased labor productivity sevenfold,[83] which historian Perry Anderson called the "major single advance in the agrarian technology of classical Antiquity,"[84] took centuries to spread.[85] Laborsaving innovations could also create political difficulties. The Roman Emperor Vespasian opposed new technology on the ground that it would reduce work for artisans.[86]

Laborsaving innovations did appear, as in all periods, due to chance discovery or trial and error. Grinding stones were improved, as were screw presses for crushing grapes and olives. And sometimes, as when cranes and compound pulleys for lifting heavy weights were invented to erect fortifications otherwise impossible to build, innovation made labor more efficient as a byproduct. But the demand for new technology came from a small number of rather similar rulers, so improvements to labor productivity were not high on the agenda. Virtually all Hellenistic kings were educated in Athens, competed in athletic games, and knew, imagined, valued, and wanted improvements in pretty much the same fields: medicine, military devices, and the productivity of land.

Innovation also lagged because there was little accumulated knowledge and technology to support it.[87] The steam engine remained a toy at least in part because no one could build the large, strong boilers needed for steam usable in the real world.[88] Technological innovation usually builds on an available stock of ideas, knowledge, materials, and interactions within a community of technologists.[89] This stock was simply too small to achieve the critical mass necessary for sustained innovation. Scientists, engineers, and manufacturers were also scarce. Few people in any agrarian society have the leisure and education to pursue scientific speculation; fewer still wish to do so. Only in the largest cities could enough of them gather to create a technological community that might stimulate and support innovation.[90]

Quite apart from these problems, the optimism underlying rational scientific thought did not last. This optimism came from the self-confident belief that applying intelligence to the natural environment could improve man's fate, a view that took wing with the extraordinary triumphs of the Hellenes, from victories over Darius and Xerxes to the conquests of Alexander and the refinement of Hellenistic life during the subsequent century. It found expression in the philosophy of Stoicism, which proclaims the rationality of the universe.[91] But once the leading Hellenistic powers began dancing to Rome's tune and their wealth increasingly flowed west, optimism turned to gloom. Late Hellenism distrusted Greek rationalism.[92] Even the most brilliant men turned to magic, rather than nature, for understanding and peace of mind. Saint Augustine noted that when twins fell ill and recovered from the same malady at the same time, the sixth-century B.C.E. doctor Hippocrates attributed the phenomenon to their physical similarity, whereas a first-century B.C.E. astrologer, Poseidonius, believed it was related to the power of the stars.[93]

The spirit of scientific inquiry did not revive under Roman rule. As Vergil famously wrote in the *Aeneid*:

Let others make bronze statues that can breathe,
Carve marble to become a human face,
Be better orators, and chart the heavens,
Astronomers predicting when stars rise.
Remember, Roman, *your* task, ruling nations,
Your artistry to set the terms for peace,
Spare those who yield, and beat resisters down.[94]

The Roman Republic had no such need for productivity as did the Hellenistic kings. Its armies lived on the spoils of conquest, not the profits of property. In fact, conquest allowed the Senate to rescind property taxes in Italy and lease land to political insiders at crony rates. The Romans never bothered to translate the technical works of Euclid, Aristotle, Archimedes, or many other Greek scientists.[95] Apart from military roads, the major technological contributions during the Roman period came primarily from other cultures: "Arabic" mathematical notation developed in India by 269 C.E., improved horse harnesses developed in China before Augustus was born, and the Chinese magnetic compass developed before 271 C.E.[96]

Wealth

This chapter has so far described conditions that fostered economic growth and generated unprecedented levels of wealth, as population growth suggests. Except in Greece and Macedonia, populations virtually doubled during the three centuries between Alexander's death and the Roman census at the time of Jesus's birth.

The rapid growth of Hellenistic wealth also appears from various suggestive facts. We know, for instance, that Antioch's port could pay Ptolemy III three times what Athens had collected from all its colonies. Whereas Persia's richest civilian, probably the tax collector Zeno of Dardanus, reputedly had a buying power of 300–400 talents,[97] several Hellenistic civilians had fortunes in the thousands.[98] Indemnities paid to Rome, over a period without notable inflation, also suggest rapidly growing wealth. In 201 B.C.E. Rome fined Macedonia's king the then-vast sum of 1,000 talents. The Seleucid King Antiochus III, however, had to pay 15,000 talents, and a century later the former kingdom of Pergamum coughed up 120,000 talents.[99]

Improved agricultural productivity was undoubtedly the main reason for this growth. The monetization of the Persian treasury also helped. The coins allowed markets to flourish down to the village level wherever money circulated through mercenary salaries and government purchases.[100] They also became the desired medium for rents and taxes. Rulers preferred coin to in-kind payment since it didn't spoil or get eaten by vermin and was less expensive to carry and store. In these ways, coins induced many farmers to generate new wealth through surplus production. In fact, output grew so quickly that the flood of new coins only briefly changed price levels.[101]

The resulting purchasing power circulated through the city-states where the mercenaries and other recipients of the king's payments lived and served to fuel business activity there. In turn, the demand stimulated by these new urban markets encouraged investments, trade, and specialization. Efficiencies improved in all business activities, including manufacture, transport, and trade.[102]

Law and Trade

At any city from Sicily to the Indus River, merchants could do business in Greek or Aramaic; use familiar currencies, weights, and measures; and cater to predictable preferences in goods and services. Most Hellenistic city-states were accessible through ports, where permanent colonies of foreign traders resided. An integral part of Hellenistic city life, these colonies spun a web of international relationships, ameliorating differences, reducing fear, and giving important citizens a stake in stable, peaceful relations with other nations. All the Hellenistic city-states used similar denominations of coins, weights, and measures, and their residents, including the many metics, shared Greek customs, tastes, laws, and even language—a host of common understandings and assumptions that simplified doing business together.

Along with fewer borders, more frequent sailings, and better roads, this common culture drastically reduced transaction costs. Not surprisingly, the Hellenistic world enjoyed unprecedented levels of trade. Both a cause and consequence of that development was the creation of an enduring system of international commercial law.

Oddly enough, this system owed more to the meager legal tradition of Greece than to the highly developed legal systems of the Middle East. In the Greek city-states, social norms had regulated private conduct more than public laws.[103] The legal system, such as it was, operated more as a political institution than as a mechanism to provide consistent and impartial rules of private conduct.

In classical Athens, juries of hundreds or even thousands of people could determine both law and facts. Trials became popularity contests and morality lessons. They didn't produce consistent rules and predictable results that could guide business behavior.[104] In the words of eighteenth-century English jurist William Blackstone, "if the power of the judicature was placed in the hands of the multitude, their decisions would be wild and capricious, and a new rule of action would be every day established in our courts."[105]

As political institutions, juries checked the power of magistrates, voiding official actions and even laws procured through corruption, and limited the ruthlessness of creditors.[106] Juries could punish powerful landowners who seized their neighbors' property by "sending in cattle to trample down the unfortunate man's crops and thus ruin him and compel him to part with his land cheaply," in the Roman poet Juvenal's words,[107] regardless of their legalistic justifications. That is why Demosthenes' famous legal speeches centered on the character and public benevolence of his clients, not on the facts or law of the case.

As today, elites naturally detested juries and tried to curb them.[108] But after savage riots greeted a Macedonian effort to limit Athenian juries to men of property,[109] their attacks took subtler forms that are also familiar today.[110] Magistrates eliminated compensation for jury duty,[111] and when juries refused to enforce new laws that favored the rich and the powerful, they removed cases altogether, sending them instead to neutral judicial commissions—one or more judges who came from another city and heard all the cases awaiting trial.[112]

While the commissions did enforce unfair laws if duly enacted, they also provided fairer and more consistent judgments than juries. These virtues made them popular arbitrators of intercity boundary disputes, which were life-and-death conflicts that had caused many earlier wars.[113] Merchants, who also needed effective mechanisms for resolving international disputes, adopted the same commissions for their own uses.

Rhodes, with its commercial expertise and international involvement, provided many of these jurists, who became famous for their skill. Their commercial decisions provided reliable guidance for future conduct.[114] City laws often incorporated their reasoning into local commercial rules,[115] effectively establishing the maritime code of Rhodes as the accepted principles of international commercial law. Rome adopted these rules as well and bequeathed them to the modern world.[116] As one Roman said, "Rhodes gave its laws to the sea."[117]

This chapter has described several new conditions that increased Hellenistic wealth and made the performance of money, markets, and business more efficient and effective. These virtues no doubt strengthened acceptance of the free-market system and thereby helped weave business into the economic fabric of the Western world.

As a lawyer and a lover of the law, I was struck by the Hellenistic transition from juries to professional jurists, arbitrators. The efforts of Antipater and the Greek aristocrats to abolish juries resemble the removal of business litigation from the regular trial courts today. Juries are not abolished; they are simply pushed aside as business litigation is increasingly pursued before specialized judges and private arbitrators or mediators. As in Hellenistic Greece, these professionals no doubt apply the law more impartially than juries, but also more mechanically, regardless of the consequences.

Another development during the Hellenistic period struck me. While business improved, its practitioners did worse. The greater concentration of wealth in Hellenistic cities, as compared to the democracies of classical Greece, allowed the few who could invest to capture most of the business profits available, leaving only the dregs for entrepreneurs. No longer did business lead to wealth or social advancement; instead it became an occupation for slaves and lowlifes.

7

Hellenistic Business

The Hellenistic kingdoms formed a large new market for goods and services. Trade networks multiplied, as did new trade routes. The major new business categories of the era were agribusiness and professions like architecture, art, theater, poetry, medicine, and athletics. There were also significant innovations in banking, financial operations, and labor management. The concentration of wealth had made financing more expensive for entrepreneurs, as previously noted, and business activities had generally become less profitable as they had become more common.[1]

Trade

Since cities lived on food from their hinterlands, most trade was for locally produced food and cloth. Still, with the eastern Mediterranean a "Hellenic lake,"[2] the Ptolemies and other elites greatly stimulated long-distance trade with their demands. Apollonius, Ptolemy II's prime minister, imported wines from Thrace and Chios, honey from Rhodes and Athens, slaves purchased in Rhodes, copper from Spain, soap from Marseilles, and foreign foods like cheese, tuna, mullet, wild boar, venison, and goat.[3] The upper classes in all the Hellenistic city-states shared Apollonius's tastes. Preserved fish from the Black Sea and Spain found markets everywhere. Other frequent trade items included linen from Tarsus, wool exported by Pergamum through Miletus, and Egypt's papyrus, which was used not only for writing paper but also for sails, mats, ropes, baskets, and clothes. With famines every third year on average and food emergencies even more frequent, and the Ptolemies eager to sell their grain, even bulk-food imports became common.[4] Other items were commonly traded: preservatives like salt, pepper and other spices, metals, and naval stores. There was also a brisk trade in luxury goods, including purple cloth, pearls and other jewels, cosmetics, marble, and works of art.

The great demand for luxury goods led to pioneering explorations and new trade routes. Around 300 B.C.E., Pytheas of Marseilles eluded the Carthaginians to sail through the Straits of Gibraltar and north to Britain, where he discovered that Carthage's tin was coming from Cornwall. He reached Ireland, skirted Scotland, and then "pushed on to an 'island of Thule,' six days north of Britain and one day south of the 'frozen sea,' where the sun went down for only two or three hours at night." Then he turned south across the North Sea and found amber at the mouth of the Elbe River.[5]

The voyages of Eudoxus on behalf of the Ptolemies proved even more fruitful. Alexandria's spice traders had always bought from Aden, the port of Yemen, from which caravans plodded up the Red Sea coast past Mecca and Medina to Petra. From there caravans could proceed to Alexandria by way of Gaza or to Damascus and Antioch. Around 120 B.C.E. a half-drowned Indian was nursed back to health at the court in Alexandria and taught Greek. He offered to show the way to Aden by sea.

The king sent Eudoxus, a skipper from Cyzicus on the Black Sea. Following the sailor's instructions, he proceeded up the Nile, crossed the desert to the Red Sea (the canal built by Darius that once connected the Nile with the Red Sea long since silted over), and sailed to Aden. This showed how to bypass the caravan routes at much lower costs. Like many pioneers, however, Eudoxus did not profit. Upon his return from this and a later voyage, Ptolemaic customs officials confiscated his cargo. Next he loaded his ship with trade goods, including dancing girls, and apparently tried to sail around Africa. But he had to turn back when his sailors refused to go beyond Morocco's Atlantic coast.

Ptolemaic traders eventually learned that many of Aden's spices came from India or even farther east.[6] But direct trips to India didn't begin until an Arab slave explained the monsoon winds to a mariner named Hippalus in Roman times. Large fleets then sailed up the Nile to Coptos, where a caravan route led to Red Sea ports like Berenice. From there, the monsoon winds took ships across the Arabian Sea to India and returned them in another season. Another trading post was Meroë in Nubia, where caravans laden with gold, ivory, ebony, and elephants from central Africa reached the Nile. A town by 500 B.C.E., Meroë was a major commercial center from 270 B.C.E. to 350 C.E.[7]

The Seleucids also pioneered important trade routes.[8] From India the overland route west ran from Taxila on the Indus River through Bactria, Merv, and the Persian resort of Ecbatana (modern Hamadan) to Seleucia on the Tigris. But after the Parthians took Persia and Mesopotamia around 140 B.C.E., the Seleucids developed the famous Silk Road that Marco Polo would later traverse. The Silk Road, neither a road nor a path, consisted of ever-changing caravan routes heading west from the Chinese city of Xi'an (known then as Chang'an). At the Stone Tower near Balkh, halfway along the Silk Road, the route divided. One part led south to India and its ports; the other continued west through major oases like Kashkar, Samarqand, and Merv to destinations in Persia or ports on the Black Sea like Olbia and Panticipaeum.[9]

The silk trade began when the kingdom of Bactria, formerly a Seleucid satrapy, came under attack from steppe nomads pushed west by the Hsiung-nu people, later known as the Huns, who were themselves being dislodged by the expanding Han Empire (206 B.C.E.–220 C.E.) of China.[10] In 128 B.C.E. Chang K'ien traveled through the valleys of the Oxus and Jaxartes Rivers to Bactria, where he proposed an alliance. He returned to China with information about Parthia, Babylonia, and Syria. Within a decade, ten caravans a year were traversing the Silk Road.[11] A little later, the Chinese opened a sea route to India as well.[12]

Traders could not usually afford enough security to protect themselves from organized attack. Although the nomads controlling much of the route generally gained more by protecting traders than robbing them, each stage was a gamble of all that the trader had, including perhaps his life or liberty. Few dared to risk a long sequence of such gambles instead of taking their profits at the first opportunity and going home. Normally, therefore, people and animals traveled only one stage of the journey, and a new caravan then formed for the next.[13]

By any route, trading operations were similar. With funds from a buyer, financier, or investment group, the trader would purchase trade goods and charter a ship or caravan or rent space on one. Upon return, customs officials would assess his cargo and levy duties. Finally, after selling his wares, the trader would pay his investors, who could expect a 60–90 percent annualized profit.[14] On the Nile, members of the royal family and high officials frequently owned the ships, captains were often Egyptian and comparatively low in status, and the merchant shipper was usually a Hellene.[15] It was common to buy the cargo at its source, pay the duties, and sell it at the destination, normally a royal warehouse in Alexandria.

Since trade passed through a limited number of portals, and even though smuggling was common—a small cove just outside Piraeus was known as "Thieves' Harbor"—duties were the most easily collected taxes and often became the largest source of tax revenues. As one historian remarks, "Every Seleucid king was a tycoon on an enormous scale, making millions from the great trade routes from the Mediterranean to central Asia, India and Arabia."[16] The Parthians, after driving the Seleucids out of Persia, even located their capital at Hecamtopylos near Tehran, along the main caravan route from Bactria to Seleucia, to capture these duties.[17]

Agribusiness

The most distinctive business development during the Hellenistic Era was the shift, in certain places, from peasant-controlled subsistence farming designed to minimize the risk of famine to landowner-controlled farming designed for cash crops and profit: agribusiness. This shift wasn't a matter of monoculture, the dedication to one particular crop that chemicals make possible today. Rather, it was a change in the mix of crops from one optimized to prevent famine toward one optimized for the market, thereby forcing cultivators to more dependence on trade than they felt was safe.[18] In third-century B.C.E. Spain, for instance, the Carthaginians required peasants to grow grain instead of grapes, oil, and fruit, making these necessities available only through the market.[19]

For this change to take place, landowners had to be seeking more profits than sharecropping yielded. They also had to be capable of imposing their desires on the cultivators and have access to markets.

Today, we usually assume that the more we have, the better our lives will be.[20] But before the Hellenistic Era, few if any landowners thought this way.[21] At that time, wealth beyond a certain level was largely superfluous, which is why the Persians hoarded so much.[22] Only so many months of food could be stored before vermin and rot nullified the effort. Even the appeal of purchasing power was limited. As the great historian of Hellenism

Michael Rostovtzeff says, "Articles of clothing continued to be few and plain. . . . House furniture was very scanty. . . . Table and domestic utensils, including lamps, were mostly of clay and of comparatively few shapes and plainly made."[23] Absent the need to increase profits, large landowners normally preferred the simplicity of sharecropping, which yielded reliable payments at virtually no managerial cost.[24]

Changing traditional practices was also very difficult. The ever-present danger of famine presented a terrifying obstacle to innovation at a time when grain crops supplied 65–70 percent of food calories[25] and failed every third year or so. When famine struck, the peasantry bore most of the burden. Their fixed rent and tax assessments did not abate, and they were exceedingly vulnerable, as graphically described by Galen, a second-century c.e. physician from Pergamum:

> Immediately summer was over, those who live in the cities, in accordance with their universal practice of collecting a sufficient supply of corn to last a whole year, took from the fields all the wheat, with the barley, beans and lentils, and left to the rustics only those annual products which are called pulses and leguminous fruits; they even took away a good part of these to the city. So the people in the countryside, after consuming during the winter what had been left, were compelled to use unhealthy forms of nourishment. Through the spring they ate twigs and shoots of trees, bulbs and roots of unwholesome plants, and they made unsparing use of what are called wild vegetables, whatever they could get hold of, until they were surfeited; they ate them after boiling them whole like green grasses, of which they had not tasted before even as an experiment.[26]

Facing such dangers, and with emergency aid uncertain at best, peasants emphasized self-sufficiency, resisted change, and kept close control over cultivation.[27] Even Sparta's helots decided what to grow, when and where to plant, what tools to use, and when to harvest.[28] To be sure, peasants happily sold surpluses when they could, but to orient farming toward commonly saleable produce meant increasing the risk of famine. Farming could become agribusiness only by coercing farmers to shift the mix of crops from one optimized to prevent famine toward one optimized for profits in the market.[29]

Evidence of agribusiness appears only after Alexander, when the proliferation of Hellenistic cities and markets, the spread of Greek tastes and culture, and the ease of international trade created conditions more favorable to it. Access to markets became easier in many more places, and the markets generated new demand for cash crops. To pay for the new goods appearing on the market and for their mercenaries, kings and other major landowners sought increased earnings from their estates.[30]

Carthage, now within the Hellenistic orbit, imposed a cash-crop regime on its Spanish colonies, restricting most cultivation to grain and requiring the peasants to purchase such staples as grapes, oil, and fruit.[31] Among Hellenistic states, the power to impose more profitable farming practices on a reluctant peasantry proved feasible only under the unique conditions that prevailed in Egypt. There, the export-oriented Ptolemies created "the most elaborate and far-reaching bureaucracy the world had ever known" to oversee the peasants and other workers.[32]

While kings in other territories presided over diverse landowners who jealously guarded their traditional rights, the Ptolemies had inherited from the pharaohs a country that "belonged to the kings, who had the full right to use it for the general good."[33] Royal estates alone fed five hundred thousand people, and the Ptolemies leased large tracts to dependents like Apollonius, who master-leased about two thousand acres of newly reclaimed land in the Fayum, formerly a huge marshy lake.[34] Peasants received seeds, cattle, and tools. Leases specified what and when they would plant. Officials monitored compliance, supervised the harvests, and collected the king's share.[35] They also dispensed the spices used for preserving meat and other perishable foods.

Oil was one of the most important products in ancient agriculture, used for cooking, indoor lighting, and soap. To maximize output and minimize waste of the safflower and sesame oil that Egypt produced, Ptolemaic officials determined the price of oil, the amount of land allocated to the plants, the times of planting and harvesting, the share of profits that the workers would receive, where they lived, and who could sell the oil.[36] In similar ways, the government regulated textiles, perfumes, fish curing, beer, bricks, glazing, metalworking, many other kinds of manufacturing, and even bath management.

That virtually all production funneled through the Nile River, where checking it was easy, undoubtedly facilitated regulation. All boats could be inspected and were required to retain samples of their cargoes.[37]

But all this regulation came at a very high cost. With the peasant families as cultivators, many more people lived off the land than were needed to do the work.[38] Only because the Nile Valley was the richest farmland in the ancient world could its output repay the expense. The Ptolemies didn't impose their huge bureaucracy on their other territories, and no other states even attempted such regulation. By contrast, modern technology, and perhaps a more widespread acceptance of public interests, greatly simplifies health and safety oversight today.

The alternative to regulation was to replace the peasants with slaves. This proved feasible only in Greece and Pergamum, after warfare depopulated the land. Elsewhere, traditional farming still prevailed.

In Greece the catastrophic conditions after Alexander's death killed or drove off many peasants, leaving their farms to be acquired at fire-sale prices by businessmen who had prospered through trade.[39] These men, who habitually sought to maximize profits and productivity,[40] then acquired workers in the teeming slave markets of Delos, Rhodes, and Chios. Their slave-operated farm complexes, which Romans called *latifundia*, proved so profitable that the Hellenistic writer Varro disparaged the farming of Greek peasants as "primitive" and extolled the efficiency of the agribusinesses that replaced them.[41]

Pergamum turned to agribusiness for remarkably similar reasons.[42] The Gauls, as in Greece, had depopulated rural areas with their raids. In 263 B.C.E. Attalus I, like Antigonus Gonatus, made himself king by driving them away. With pressing military requirements, Attalus and his successors became preoccupied with improving their properties and staffed the depopulated royal estates with slave labor.[43] Many became shepherds, since Pergamum's main cash crop was wool—the finest grown anywhere around the Mediterranean.[44] Others worked to manufacture cloth and parchment,[45] which were exported through Tarsus, Ephesus, and Smyrna, making the Attalids extremely wealthy.

Professions

Professionals make a business of using specialized skills to help or entertain others. Homer was one, singing his tales in the courts of Dark Age princelings. In the sixth century B.C.E., when the greatest Athenian fortunes totaled 100–200 talents, the physician Democides of Croton received medical fees of 1 talent from Aegina, 1⅔ talents from Athens, and 2 talents from the tyrant Polycrates of Samos.[46] The seventy to eighty sculptors who worked on the Parthenon's frieze, at a time when Athens had perhaps thirty boatwrights, were also professionals.[47] Another was Aristotle, a teacher at the Lyceum at Athens, then a tutor to Alexander. He owned fifteen slaves[48] and the first private library of any size.[49]

The Hellenistic world's great purchasing power created much more demand for professional services. The medical school founded at Alexandria remained famous for hundreds of years. As late as the fourth century C.E., the Roman Senator Ammianus Marcellinus wrote, as though speaking of Harvard Medical School, "it is enough to commend a physician's skill if he can say that he was trained at Alexandria."[50] Other professionals included engineers, scholars, judges, teachers, architects, painters, and actors. Royal courts vied to attract the most famous, commissioned them for grand projects, and built them academies, museums, and libraries. The museum at Alexandria supported a hundred scholars.[51]

Some professionals were landowners, supported by their own estates, but often scholars and teachers were metics or slaves, probably paid about the same as mercenary soldiers. A few fared better, of course: in Athens, at a time when the usual working wage was about half a drachma per day, architects normally earned two to four drachmas,[52] and the son of the renowned sculptor Praxiteles was one of the city's wealthiest men during early Hellenistic times.[53]

An international art market arose as collecting became fashionable in cities like Alexandria. Rome later became so enamored of Greek and Hellenistic art that at least one Roman firm, the Cossutti, set up agencies throughout Greece to turn out marble statues for sale in Rome.[54] Archeologists have discovered many sunken ships on the sealanes between Athens and Rome carrying statues of bronze and marble, furniture, decorative bowls, candelabra, bas-reliefs, columns, and marble bases, capitals, and slabs.

Perhaps the most numerous professionals were entertainers. Initially associated with religious celebrations, entertainment became a major enterprise after Alexander. The multitude of cities implanted in the Middle East, many too small or too new to have their own traditions and pageants, looked to Greek sites like Athens, Delphi, and the temples of Apollo at Delos and Dydyma for inspiration. The new religions of the age did the same.[55] Traveling entertainers offered both a classical repertory drawn from traditional Greek religious ceremonies and popular entertainments like athletic games, comedies, and mime.[56] The Broadway musical "A Funny Thing Happened on the Way to the Forum" derives from

Menander, the most popular comic author, by way of Plautus, a Roman. Menander was "witty, elegant, more at home with men's mistresses than with their wives, [and] set a mark on literary history which lasted till Shakespeare and Molière."[57]

Liturgies, the religious and public benefactions provided by wealthy men, supported 97 annual festivals in Demosthenes' day, 118 every fourth year.[58] This number increased, especially as the religious nature of festivals gave way to pure entertainment.[59] On the enlarged stage of the Hellenistic world, with soldiering no longer the main route to civic honor, wealthy men competed all the harder to provide lavish entertainments at these festivals.[60] Their efforts employed an ever-growing number of impresarios and entertainers.

Artists, actors, singers, theatrical troupes from the homeland, philosophers, and poets and poetesses—the Hellenistic equivalent of modern pop singers—toured the Greek-speaking world's circuit to charm Hellenistic courts and fill municipal theaters, much as Jenny Lind, Sarah Bernhardt, and other representatives of Old World culture barnstormed the American West in the nineteenth century.

Some performers formed guilds called Dionysiac associations. The first arose in 279 B.C.E. Athens. The Isthmian association of Corinth embraced much of Greece until the Corinth's destruction in 146 B.C.E. Pergamum had the Dionysiacs of Teos, who eventually amalgamated with Pergamum's court players. These guilds would exchange "ambassadors" with the kings and cities that hired them and receive honors, privileges, immunities, and safe-conducts. The Athenian association even earned the right to wear purple. Kings and cities subsidized them.[61]

Like modern buskers, freelancers congregated wherever crowds were likely and sought to eke out a living from the public's handouts. Diogenes described those entertaining the crowd around Poseidon's temple at the Isthmian Games as "many writers reading aloud their stupid works, many poets reciting their poems while others applauded them, many jugglers showing their tricks, many fortunetellers interpreting fortunes."[62] Command appearances for kings or other rich patrons were probably much desired, like today. One 56 B.C.E. performance, of Euripides' *The Bacchae*, was dramatically interrupted when a messenger arrived after the Battle of Carrhae and presented the bloody head of the defeated Roman general Crassus to the Parthian king. Jason, one of the actors, earned a generous reward by seizing the head and dancing it around like a bacchante.[63]

Money

By allowing markets to flourish, the Hellenistic world's abundant coinage assured a market for agribusiness and traveling professionals.[64] Except for the Ptolemies, the kings left coinage to their city-states. Since most of them adopted the Athenian standard of 4.3 grams of silver per drachma, Hellenistic coins were far more uniform than earlier ones.[65] In fact, the competitive market for coins assured weights and purity, since any debasement would quickly lead to disuse. Consequently, prices outside of Egypt remained stable throughout the Hellenistic period, except during about ten years after the Persian treasuries were converted into a flood of new coins.[66]

The Ptolemies, by contrast, allowed the use of only their own coins. They minted gold coins for foreign exchange and turned copper from the Sinai and Cyprus into small-denomination coins for domestic use. Their Phoenician mints, using worn coins and Carthaginian silver, created new silver drachmas. After 285 B.C.E. anyone bringing drachmas from elsewhere into Egypt had to exchange them for these Ptolemaic drachmas. Since these weighed slightly less than the Athenian standard, the Ptolemies reaped a profit on each exchange.

This system worked fine until the Ptolemies lost access to Carthage's silver around 210 B.C.E., when Rome began battering Hannibal's armies. That loss, along with other setbacks, tempted Ptolemy V to reduce the silver content of his drachmas while requiring soldiers and other suppliers to accept them at face value. The value of salaries and other payments fell, generating endless strife.[67]

Banking

Despite the universal reign of the drachma, money changers remained necessary.[68] In the typical market of the early Hellenistic age,

> amidst the clamor of hawking and bargaining could be heard the clink of coins as sharp-eyed clerks exchanged darics from Persia or staters from Cyzicus or the coinages of Sicilian cities for Attic four-drachma pieces with the old-fashioned picture of Athena and her owl that Athens kept using since it was accepted everywhere as the mark of a trustworthy currency.[69]

Even in the later Roman Empire, when just one gold currency pre-vailed, the priest John Cassian (360–435 C.E.) could poetically describe the money changer's task:

> to distinguish which the purest gold . . . and which has been less re-fined by the fire; to remain undeceived, through the exercise of a most practiced discernment, by the copper and base denarius if it should happen to imitate the precious nomisma under the color of gleaming gold; to not only recognize, judiciously, the nomismata of tyrants from the portraits they carry, but—with an even greater degree of perception—to discover those which, although stamped with the por-trait of a legitimate emperor, were struck unlawfully; and finally, through the decision of the balance, to carefully examine whether any among them are of less than the legitimate weight.[70]

Currencies of strictly local circulation, like Egypt's copper coins, re-quired money-changing services as well.[71] Rates were often regulated, and kept to about 6 percent—less than banks usually charge for the infinitely easier performance of this same function today. Not surprisingly, then, money changers sought to extend their activities to more lucrative finan-cial functions like safekeeping, pawnbroking, lending larger sums, and notarizing payments and other important transactions.

Deposits

As money became a common medium for payment, merchants found it especially convenient to keep their valuables with marketplace bankers, usually metics like themselves. Since many deposits included cash that the banker could lend out, private bankers paid interest to attract them. The epitaph of Caecus, a banker in Rhodes, boasted that he kept his bank open even at night, and "for three decades he kept on deposit gold for foreigners and citizens alike, with purest honesty."[72]

Since at least the Third Dynasty of Ur in 2000 B.C.E., people had sought the protection of the gods for their valuables.[73] It seemed safer to put depos-its in temples than anywhere else, and wealthy people and cities often did so. One noted temple, that of Artemis in Ephesus, held deposits from Aris-totle, Xenophon, Caesar, Plautus, Plutarch, Strabo, and Dio Chrysostomus. Those who violated temple precincts suffered swift and violent responses,

Table 8
Ancient Currency

Unit (Symbol)	Material	Weight	Ancient Value	Value in U.S. Dollars[a]
Athenian obol	silver	1g	—	$12.35
Athenian drachma (d)	silver	4.3g	5 obols	$61.77
Egyptian drachma	silver	3.5g	—	$50.28
Roman as	copper	varied	1/60th HS	$0.26
Roman sestercius (HS)	silver	1.075g	60 as	$15.44
Roman denarius (d)	silver	4.3g	4 HS or 1 drachma	$61.77
Phoenician shekel	silver	8.33g	2 drachmas/ denarii	$123.54
Mina	silver	500g	60 shekels	$6,175
Talent	silver	30 kg	7,000 drachmas/ denarii	$432,390
Roman aureus	gold	8.2g	25 denarii	$1,544.25
Solidus	gold	6.3g	72/lb.	$1,186.44
Argentus	silver	43g	10 drachmas/ denarii	$617.70
Nomismata	gold	6.3g	—	$1,186.44
Kenteriaria	gold	45.4 kg	7,200 nomismata	$8,542,338

a. Based on equating the cost of maintaining a slave with the U.S. minimum wage as of 2006, 1 Athenian drachma = U.S. $61.77. The upkeep of a slave was ⅔ of a drachma per day (Ste. Croix 1981: 187). The 2006 minimum wage was $5.15/hour, or $10,506/year, or about $61.77/drachma for 2,040 hours per year of work.

as Antiochus III fatally discovered. Indeed, his son Antiochus IV's plundering of the temple in Jerusalem provoked the ferocious revolt of the Maccabees in Judea.

Many deposits consisted of valuables stored in jars, leather bags, or bronze drawers, much like safe-deposit boxes today. They were available only for designated financial uses, such as to finance festivals or other religious activities. Temples could, however, use donations to extend credit, primarily to governments. Their loans were usually for specified purposes like defense against pirates or repairs to local temples.[74] The most important temple bank was that of Apollo on Delos, a major shrine that received donations as well as deposits from throughout the Hellenistic world[75] and made numerous loans to neighboring municipalities.[76] The temple of Apollo helped Delos buy golden crowns to honor such Hellenistic rulers as Eumenes of Pergamum, Prusias of Bithynia, and Philip V and Perseus of Macedonia. Mostly, though, temple banks and city banks helped public entities with current expenditures, not investment. Elected magistrates often supervised the local temple bank's performance, while some entities, including Athens and the Ptolemaic kingdom, established public banks that operated similarly.

Payments

An important banking service, in a day before checks and receipts, was to make and witness payments. The banker usually paid only in the presence of both depositor and payee and then recorded the action in his ledger. Even bankers who were metics or slaves could testify in court to the fact of payment.[77]

Since city magistrates were usually elected for only one year, the magistrate who had deposited funds might not be available to validate payment. In those situations, therefore, some bankers relaxed the requirement that the depositor himself authorize payment and would accept the authorization of a new magistrate after verifying his authority. Others would pay directly upon official request, in effect emulating Assyrian practices at Kanesh in 2000 B.C.E. and foreshadowing modern checks. For instance, in 257 B.C.E., having deposited their Halicarnassus tax receipts with the banker Sapolis, Ptolemy's bureaucrats wrote him to disburse three thousand drachmas to their naval captain Xanthippus for delivery to Alexandria.[78] Similar orders were sometimes possible in the private sector. Lycan of Epidaurus agreed with a depositor that upon receiving his sealed order he would purchase a young slave girl and hand her over to the order's bearer.[79]

The most innovative financial institution was the Bank of the Ptolemies, headquartered in Alexandria. It had branches in the provincial capitals and major villages of Egypt that accepted tax deposits and disbursed government funds. They also accepted deposits and disbursed payments for private clients.[80] The branch system allowed deposits at one place to be paid out elsewhere without an actual transfer of coins. But this convenience for traders and travelers was evidently insufficient to motivate any other ancient banks to establish branches or to develop an interbank transfer system. Travelers had to obtain local funds privately.[81]

Lending

Monetization and the spread of cash markets led to a tremendous expansion of credit. In Egypt, farmers borrowed against standing crops, workers pledged their future labor, and consumers pawned personal or household goods, including jewelry, clothing, and kitchenware.[82] Most consumer loans were from private sources, but bankers recorded some, in amounts between 1,300 and 2,700 drachmas. Private bankers also made public loans, usually for little or no interest, out of civic loyalty.

On the other hand, Hellenistic banks rarely participated in large commercial undertakings. These were now privately financed by the rich, who possessed most of the purchasing power and often kept the best ventures for their own slaves and freedmen to run.[83] Only two large commercial loans are known to have involved bankers, and one was the Athenian banker Sosinomos's previously described involvement in the purchase of a perfumery. The other was an advance of two thousand drachmas for the purchase of a mining concession.[84]

Bankers were probably more active as brokers. With their intimate knowledge of the market, they remained well positioned to bring rich people together with trustworthy merchants and reliable guarantors. For instance, a first-century Italian banker in Alexandria arranged for Archippus of Marseilles to finance a trip by five metics to buy goods in Somaliland. The banker found another merchant from Marseilles, one from Carthage, and three army officers to guarantee the loan.[85]

Most often, Hellenistic bankers served as pawnbrokers and personal lenders in the marketplace, frequently advancing tiny sums at interest rates that may have averaged as high as 18 percent.[86] This rate was due less to the risk of default—most loans were secured—than to the risk that deposits, which carried no fixed terms, might be withdrawn before loans were repaid. Bankers were often mired in disputes, lawsuits, and bankruptcies because of such mistiming.

The Business of Banking

A banker's equipment consisted of a table in the market or port, scales, abacus, ledger book, coins, and strongboxes that he undoubtedly kept in secure, undisclosed locations elsewhere. The ledger was essentially a diary, a chronological record of deposits, loans, and payments. There were few other documents, since payment orders were verbal. The Bank of the Ptolemies was an exception, its size and branch system making extensive documentation necessary.[87]

As Hellenistic cities proliferated, many new banks appeared, especially in trading centers. Delos, a city of only five thousand citizens in the early second century B.C.E., had at least three banks in addition to the temple of Apollo. Three more were established by the next century. Rhodes had even more. In fact, thirty-three Hellenistic cities are known to have had private banks.[88]

Banking was the trade that most closely approached respectability. The practice required literacy and mathematical skill, and since success was closely related to trustworthiness, banking also favored those whose manner and education made them appealing. As about the only really profitable business not monopolized by the elite, it attracted dynamic men who were eager to make money. Not many were citizens, however, due to the low prestige of banking's sedentary nature as a trade. Most were metics, sometimes from illustrious families in other city-states whose service abroad was less embarrassing than it would be at home.[89]

Many banks had two or more owners; six on Delos were partnerships. Slaves and apprentices guarded the valuables, ran back and forth to deliver money, helped with mechanical tasks like weighing and assaying coins, and might even spell the banker at his table.

Labor

There was one important innovation in labor practices during the Hellenistic period, apart from the Ptolemaic use of guilds described earlier. This was the elaboration of policies using both incentives and punishments to harness the intelligence and energy of slaves in trusted positions, while preventing losses to opportunism. The Carthaginian writer Mago, who derived his teachings from Hellenistic models,[90] advocated letting managerial slaves accumulate money and buy their own freedom as a way to inspire more productive labor. Such ideas would find their fullest expression at Rome.

In trade, an enthusiastic expansion of international procurement inspired trade routes to Yemen, the Sudan, India, and China. Farms became agribusinesses where conditions in Egypt, Greece, and Pergamum created reliable access to the cash purchasing power of urban markets, to landowners eager to increase their wealth, and to opportunities to regulate or coerce farmers into a more cash crop orientation. The Hellenistic Era provided expanded opportunities for the professions, and in banking the Bank of the Ptolemies became the ancient world's first and only branch banking system.

Part 3

Roman business originated in war, flourished in peace, and foundered in disorder. For approximately four centuries, from the time Rome first acquired an overseas empire in 200 B.C.E. to the near-disintegration of the empire in the third century C.E., business played an increasingly significant role in Roman economic life. But Roman business was not just Hellenism writ large. During the first two centuries C.E., a crucial reason for its success was the extraordinary imperial achievement called the Roman Peace. Some fifty million people throughout the empire enjoyed a largely peaceful and orderly state, with common languages, currencies, laws, and customs, where a money-based market economy prevailed. Not until the European Union in 1992 did Europe possess a common market of comparable geographic size.

Another Roman innovation was its patronage system, a binding norm of relationships that regulated social and organizational life. This loyalty-based type of relationship so effectively inspired trust that it allowed Roman businesses to transcend the family-based model of earlier times, while ensuring a far more meritocratic and free flowing distribution of credit.

Yet another Roman difference was the public sector's heavy use of private business. In the ancient Middle East, the rulers had largely operated the production and distribution of goods and services, leaving private business only a marginal role. In Greek and Hellenistic cities, by contrast, the state left virtually all production and distribution to private entities. During the heyday of Roman business, however, the public sector became, like modern governments, business's most important customer.

The six chapters of part 3 proceed chronologically. Chapter 8 concerns the rise of Rome to dominance throughout Italy and its first victory over Carthage. It explains patronage, describes the origin of corporations, known in Rome as publican societies, and traces the development of the most novel and important Roman businesses, agribusiness and public contracting.

Chapter 9 covers the period from the Carthaginian wars to the victory of Octavian at the Battle of Actium in 31 B.C.E., which marks a major turning point in Roman governance. It describes how colonial rule and structural reforms led to the republic's demise and tells the cautionary tale of business's political influence during this period, a story with obvious modern implications.

Chapter 10's focus is on the early empire under Augustus and his successors, a two-century period known as the Principate. Three developments of fundamental importance to business occurred during this period: the creation of the Roman Peace, the extension of a market economy to North Africa and Europe, and the birth of Christianity along with the dispersal of the Jews from their homeland in Judea.

Chapter 11 discusses key business conditions that impacted business life during the Principate. These included the distribution and uses of Roman wealth, the status of business, aspects of Roman law that impacted business, and the nature of labor, especially slavery.

Chapter 12 describes important Roman businesses other than agribusiness and public contracting. None of these originated in Rome, but the available information often allows the first full description of how such businesses were conducted. The businesses fall into the categories of manufacturing, trade, and services, and it is striking to see how closely these business activities foreshadow those of the present.

Chapter 13 concludes the book. It has two main objectives. The first is to explain the downfall of business that occurred during the third century C.E., a sad and complicated tale of disease, disorder, and the disappearance of money. The second describes how the Principate became the Dominate, the restructured Roman state that emerged from the travails of the third century. While its institutions, including the church, once again relegated business to a marginal role, the foundations of Hellenistic and Roman business remained alive in the parts of the empire that fell to the Arab conquest in the seventh century.

Map 4.
Roman Empire

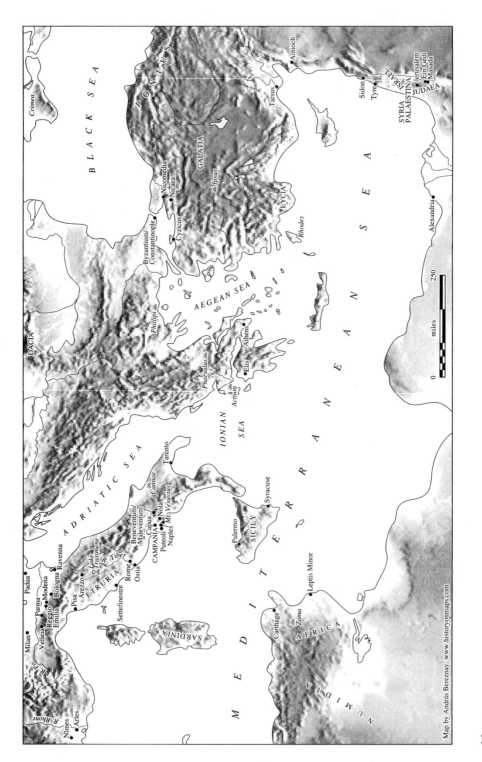

Map 5.
Roman Italy

Map by András Bereznay: www.historyonmaps.com

NORTH
SEA

BALTIC SEA

Helgö

York

London

modern shore
line, where
different

*Teutoburg
Forest*

BELGICA

Treves

Orleans Sens

Vienna

GAUL

RAETIA

Lezoux Geneva

Aquileia

Lyon

Padua

Milan

Parma

Bordeaux

Velleia Modena

La Graufresenque

Reggio Ravenna

Aveyron

Emilia Bologna

Narbo

Nimes Arles

Pisa

Arezzo

*Lake
Trasimene*

Settefinestre

Beneventum/
Maleventum

Porta

Rome

Ostia

Tarraco

Capua

Cannae

Puteoli Nola

SPAIN

Naples

Tarento

Mt. Vesuvius

Lisbon

Palermo

Cordoba

Seville

Syracuse

MEDITERRANEAN SEA

0   miles   300

Map 6.
Western Europe in the Roman Empire

8

The Early Roman Republic

Roman business was truly distinctive. For most of the city-state's first five centuries, business hardly existed; then, as Rome fought Carthage for dominance in the western Mediterranean, Roman business got its start supplying the war effort. From these wars, agribusiness emerged, its management the model for all Roman businesses. That said, the unusual nature of Roman business sprang from three features of Roman culture. One was patronage, a set of behaviors and understandings that underlay the remarkable entrepreneurship, scope, and scale that Roman businesses achieved. The second was the extensive use of public contractors to do the state's work, thereby channeling much of Rome's growing imperial bounty into the hands of business financiers and managers. The need for them to be large and enduring enterprises led to the third distinctive feature: Roman law's creation of the corporate form for such contractors.

Rome's Origins

Central and northern Italy had some of the richest lands in the Mediterranean region, but with few natural barriers tribal warfare prevented economic development until the Etruscans began exploiting iron deposits

Table 9
Roman Chronology: Republic, 750–31 B.C.E.

750	Etruscans emerge in Tuscany
575	Tarquinius founds Rome
509	Romans expel Tarquin the Proud
387	Celts damage Etruscan civilization in Tuscany, sack most of Rome
340	Rome dominates Italy
323	Alexander dies in Babylon; Greeks unsuccessfully revolt against Antipater
294	statue of Asclepius brought to Rome and set in a temple
280–275	Pyrrhic War gives Rome control of central and southern Italy
275	Battle of Beneventum: Rome beats Pyrrhus
264	First Carthaginian War: Rome gets Sicily, Sardinia, Corsica, and navy
247	Parthians penetrate Persia and Babylonia from steppes near Caspian Sea
241	Rome wins First Carthaginian War with naval victory
227	Rome makes Sicily its first colony
219–202	Second Carthaginian War: Hannibal invades Italy
215–205	First Macedonian War: Rome disciplines Philip V for helping Hannibal
202	Battle of Zama ends Second Punic War
200–197	Second Macedonian War at behest of Pergamum and Rhodes
172–168	Third Macedonian War
168	Battle of Pydna ends Third Macedonian War and Macedonian independence
168	Roman consul Popilus Laenas rebuffs Antiochus IV, gives Egypt to Ptolemy V
155	King Mithridates I of Parthia takes Media
149	beginning of Third Carthaginian War
146	Achaean revolt; Rome destroys Carthage and Corinth
146	Rome seizes Carthage, sells survivors to slavery, makes its territory province of Africa
136–132	Sicilian slave revolt; First Slave War
133	Attalus wills Pergamum to Rome

Table 9
(*continued*)

133	Tiberius Gracchus elected tribune, advocates land redistribution, is assassinated
123	Gaius Gracchus elected tribune, initiates food dole and tax farming
118	Rome founds Narbo, creates province of Gallia Narbonensis
113	Cimbri and Teutoni attack Narbo; Battle of Orange
111	Jugurtha War begins in Numidia
107	Marius elected consul, begins reform of army
105	Jugurtha War ends, Jugurtha captured and paraded in Rome
103	Marius annexes Cilicia as province
102	Cimbri and Teutoni expelled from Italy; pirates and slave revolts suppressed
101	Chinese armies reach west of Jaxartes, contact West, open Silk Route
96	Sulla repels Mithridates from Cappadocia, makes it a Roman province
95	Tigranes becomes Armenian king
88	Mithridates launches war by slaughtering 80,000 Romans in Asia
86	Sulla sacks Athens
84	end of First Mithridatic War; Second Mithridatic War in 83–81 to enforce terms
83	Tigranes takes Seleucid possessions in Syria
79	King of Bithynia dies, leaves it to Rome
74	Third Mithridatic War begins
73–71	Spartacus slave revolt
69–68	Lucullus of Rome defeats Tigranes, annexes Armenia
67	Pompey sweeps pirates from Mediterranean
66	Pompey defeats Mithridates on Euphrates; East becomes Roman provinces and clients
63	Rome annexes Syria
60	First Triumvirate: Caesar, Pompey, Crassus
59	Caesar creates first newspaper, posting "Daily Doings" on forum walls
58	Caesar begins Gallic campaign

(*continued*)

Table 9
(*continued*)

53	Battle of Carrhae: Parthians kill Crassus
52	Caesar defeats Vercingetorix in Battle of Alesia
49	civil war between Caesar and Pompey begins
48	Battle of Pharsalus: Caesar beats Pompey in Thessaly
48	Caesar pursues Pompey to Alexandria, where library is burnt in the battle
47	Battle of Zela: Caesar beats Pharnaces of Pontus—veni, vidi, vinci
44	Caesar murdered
43	Second Triumvirate: Octavian, Antony, Lepidus
42	Battle of Phillipi: Brutus and Cassius lose
40	Parthians invade Levant and Anatolia; Antony counterattacks
37	Antony installs Herod as king at Jerusalem, marries Cleo VII in 36
31	Battle of Actium: Octavian beats Antony

in Tuscany in the eighth century B.C.E.[1] They invented iron anchors and put iron ramming beaks on galleys. The Italians mined Etruscan slag heaps for iron during World War I.

Etruscans became intrepid pirates and traders who sold iron implements across the Alps and as far away as Poland and Scandinavia. They occupied Elba, Corsica, and Sardinia; planted colonies on the Spanish coast; were said to have sacked Athens; and may have fought the Carthaginians over Madeira, which lies far out in the Atlantic.[2] Their extensive travels apparently led them to discover advanced irrigation and farming techniques in the Middle East, which allowed them to relieve the poor drainage that drowned much of Italy's best farmland. In this manner, Etruscan and other Italian tribes achieved a degree of prosperity and economic development.[3]

The Etruscan lands straddled the fertile watershed of the Tiber River, which supported several small, Latin-speaking communities. One was Rome, traditionally formed by twelve tribes in 753 B.C.E. and ruled by an Etruscan prince. Located astride the first inland ford across the Tiber, commercial traffic allowed Rome to grow to a population of about fifty thousand by 500 B.C.E.[4]

About then, according to the story, the prince's son raped the virtuous housewife Lucretia, who killed herself. The outraged Romans expelled the Etruscans and elected a Senate, which in turn elected two annual consuls and a few lesser officials to lead the new republic's government and its army.

Like Sparta, Rome was a martial society in which all citizens served in the militia, including about two thousand so-called equestrians who owned the horses and equipment necessary to become chariot and cavalry troops.[5] No one could be elected to public office without ten years in the militia, and military historian John Keegan writes that "a higher proportion of Roman citizens was under arms for longer than I have found in any other pre-industrial state." The Romans, he adds, were exceptionally ferocious, comparable only to the Mongol hordes and Tamerlane's followers.[6]

The republic proceeded to beat or threaten the nearby Latins and other Italians into submission, receiving the inadvertent help of another militant group. The Gauls (also known as Celts) were emigrating from Gaul into the Po River valley, where they founded Milan and constantly attacked Rome's Etruscan neighbors and other powerful tribes north of Rome. Indeed, they attacked and in 410 B.C.E. sacked Rome itself. Eventually Rome prevailed, expelling most of the Gauls to Macedonia, Greece, and Thrace. But those who remained, and other Italian tribes, continued to resent Roman domination. They had to pay tribute to Rome, supply auxiliary troops in its wars, and grant special rights and privileges to Roman citizens.[7] Many would support Hannibal's invasion, and as late as 82 B.C.E. the Samnites of southern Italy were besieging Rome itself. Such cities as Parma, Bologna, and Aquilaea (the predecessor to Venice) began as Roman garrisons to pacify the countryside.

Political and Social Structure

Within Rome the ordinary citizens, like the Greek hoplites, tried to leverage their military role into political power.[8] Rome's patricians liked sharing power with these plebeians no more than their Greek counterparts, but Italy's geography made it easier. The Greek city-states, islands of fertility in a semiarid land, had no arable land to distribute. Concessions to the hoplites necessarily reduced the holdings of their ruling aristocrats, who objected. Insurrections often followed, leading to the confiscation of estates and the formalization of hoplite power. But the Tiber River basin's large and fertile terrain allowed Rome's patricians to pay off plebeian leaders with arable land seized from other Latins, like the Sabines of rape fame. Along with moderate reforms, this effectively contained plebeian discontent.

These moderate reforms led to a governmental structure that loosely resembled democracy, with annually elected magistrates, a patrician Senate of former officials, and popular Assemblies wielding formal power. Still, patrician control was never in doubt. Thanks to rigged rules and, if necessary, the bribery or intimidation of voters, the Assemblies usually elected only patricians to office and routinely followed patrician orders. They rarely exercised their veto powers.

Patronage

Patrician dominance owed less to voter manipulation than to patronage,[9] a customary system based on the private right to use physical force. In the Middle Eastern empires and the Hellenistic kingdoms, where the use of force was reserved to central authorities, patronage had little function, while in Greek city-states the triumph of either tyranny or democracy reduced its importance. In Athens, for instance, patronage was very much the issue in Pericles' opposition to Cimon. Pericles engineered Cimon's banishment when his promise of public patronage, in the form of stipends for jury service, trumped Cimon's generosity as a private patron.[10] Public law replaced private force.

But the Romans had no such notion. In a system that the National Rifle Association would adore, every Roman had the right to use as much physical power as he could, however he chose. The richer and more powerful he was, the more slaves, freedmen, relatives, clients, and friends he could call upon; the more secure a villa he could build; and the more ruthlessly he could treat his neighbors. Due to geography, the patricians could accommodate plebeian political desires without surrendering this right. Neither assault, theft, nor the destruction of property became crimes, and it's not even clear what—if anything—the authorities did about murder.[11] Private life in Rome was every man for himself.[12]

For protection, the weak had to affiliate with the powerful. As Epictetus of Antioch later put it, "there are many robber-bands, tyrants, storms, difficulties, losses of what is most dear. Where shall a man flee for refuge? How shall he travel secure against robbery? What company shall he wait for that he may pass through in safety? To whom shall he attach himself? To so and so, the rich man, or the proconsul?"[13] So people sought patrons and became their clients. Patrons likewise sought clients to enhance their power and influence. All Romans were either patrons or clients.

Clients could even include towns or cities. By law, freed slaves were clients of their former masters.[14] The clients closest to their patron's status were politely termed *amici*, or "friends," but they were clients nonetheless.[15] Clients were expected to consult their patrons on a broad range of issues. Cicero's consulted him about law, marriage, property, and farming, among other social and business matters.[16] A failure to heed the patron's advice on important matters, presumably including Assembly votes, was considered a serious breach.

During the late republic, these consultations became an extraordinary spectacle, the *salutatio*. Every dawn saw flocks of clients gathering at their patrons' homes.[17] They were admitted in order of status, which mainly depended on the number and status of *their* clients. An infinite variety of transactions occurred during these meetings. A poor client might hope for food; those of higher status sought more, perhaps a bequest or the grant of an office within the patron's giving—for which, according to Plutarch, most politicians "grew old haunting the doors of other men's houses."[18]

Because patronage was such a crucial source of power, Roman patricians imbued the relationship with high moral authority and legal backing. According to the jurist Servius, a patron to his client was like a father to his son.[19] Vergil foretold harsh underworld punishments for patrons who cheated their clients.[20] To Seneca, "Homicides, tyrants and traitors there always will be; but worse than all these is the crime of ingratitude."[21] The closest modern equivalent to Roman patronage is *giri*, the sense of obligation to another that governs political and business relationships in Japan.[22]

Patronage so shaped the Roman understanding of relationships that even treaties were viewed as patronage relationships. Accordingly, Romans were less concerned with strict compliance than with the loyalty they thought it commanded. The Greeks, by contrast, believed that treaty terms defined the relationship. Accordingly, they often mistook mild treaty terms and Rome's indifference to infractions as weakness or inattention, a serious mistake that led Philip V of Macedonia, Antiochus III, and Perseus of Macedonia, each of whom ignored Roman warnings, to their disastrous clashes with the Roman army. Perceived disloyalty like theirs also motivated Rome's furious punishment of both Epirus and Rhodes after the last Macedonian War.

In business, though, patronage had more benign consequences. It allowed unrelated people to trust one other. Patrons could confidently entrust money to employees, agents, and contractors who were clients, and as patrons employers could enlarge their organizations and undertake distant operations through client agents and managers. As a result, some Roman businesses grew into large, far-flung enterprises.

One such firm, that of Cnaeus Aetius of Arezzo, had ceramics workshops in Arezzo, Pisa, Lyons, and perhaps Aveyron around 10 B.C.E. Freemen and freedmen ran their Italian workshops, producing high quality, finely decorated wares for the Mediterranean markets. Slaves managed the workshops in Gaul, which made coarser products for the northern European markets.[23] Another far-flung operation was that of Cnaeus Domitius Afer. His family, whose most illustrious member would be Marcus Aurelius, dominated Italian brick production between 40 and 190 C.E. Their far-flung sales network could have been organized and maintained only by patronage.[24]

As a mechanism for instilling trust, patronage also facilitated credit. Roman patrons readily advanced funds to their slaves, freedmen, and other clients for personal and business purposes. Business advances, though called gifts, were actually investments: extensions of credit that required repayment as surely as any today. A *peculium*, advanced a slave or freedman, was a stake that became the founding capital for many a Roman business, and probably most of the small ones.[25]

The Carthaginian Wars (264–201 B.C.E.)

Even while gaining control over central and northern Italy, nearly all Romans were subsistence farmers.[26] The militia returned home every year for planting and harvesting. Rome had little trade, no consistent coinage, and few artisans, public employees, or professional soldiers.[27] The Samnites, with a manufacturing center at Capua, and Greek city-states around the southern coast from Naples to Tarento, were far more commercialized. But Rome finally defeated the Samnites and attacked the Greek city-states. At first, the Greeks hired the extravagant King Pyrrhus of Epirus to defend them. But after he lost a major battle at Maleventum in 275 B.C.E. (which the victorious Romans immediately renamed Beneventum),[28] the city-states fired Pyrrhus and came to terms with Rome. Pyrrhus, who renewed his war for the Macedonian throne, was beaned with a chamber pot in Argos, and his pursuers decapitated him.[29]

As usual, the Greek city-states became clients. Their tribute, more silver than Rome had ever seen, went to mint a new coin, the denarius. Weighing the same as the popular Athenian drachma, it entered the Mediterranean economy. Two years later, the Ptolemies became the first Hellenistic kings to establish diplomatic relations with Rome.[30] Their new clients also brought Rome a more troublesome relationship. As patron of the Italian Greeks, the Romans felt obliged to protect Greek city-states on nearby Sicily. The enemy there was Carthage.[31]

Contemporaries thought Carthage the richest of all cities.[32] Its colonies in North Africa, Spain, Sicily, and Sardinia yielded annual revenues of 12,000 talents, comparable to those of the Ptolemaic Empire at its height.[33] Its vast fleet of up to 100 merchant ships sheltered in a port of 220 docks, each fronted with two marble Ionic pillars.[34] From there a broad avenue led to the Forum, a colonnaded square adorned with Greek sculptures. Six-story houses crowded the narrow alleys around it, which rang with the din of shops and traders. The center of the city was the Byrsa, or citadel, containing the treasury, mint, various shrines, more colonnades, and the city's greatest temple, that of the Phoenician god Eshmun. Girding Carthage was a forty-five-foot-tall triple wall topped with towers and battlements. It sheltered 300 elephants, 4,000 horses, and 20,000 troops.[35]

Like Rome, Carthage maintained military alliances with other cities. In 264 B.C.E., after Carthage defended one from an attack by Syracuse, Syracuse appealed to Rome and the First Carthaginian War began. Fighting overseas for the first time, Rome was forced to build an enormous number of ships, 220 in just one three-month period during 255 B.C.E. This required importing and training many specialized craftsmen.[36] Italian merchants, mostly of Greek origin, supplied much of the naval expertise, and over the long course of the hostilities these merchants also profited by supplying arms and provisions, purchasing booty, and trading with the warring armies. They formed Rome's first business community.[37]

The war ended in 241 B.C.E., with Carthage ceding to Rome its holdings in Sicily and Sardinia and paying an indemnity of 4,750 silver talents over the next twenty years. To rule and profit from its new colonies, the Senate devised a combination of military governance and civilian exploitation that would become the model for all the republic's later territorial acquisitions.

Local allies like Syracuse joined Italian tribes and city-states as clients. They owed Rome loyalty and military help, but were otherwise free to conduct their own business. But no government remained in Sardinia and the Carthaginian portions of Sicily. There Rome ruled and taxed the peasant farmers through the *provincia*, or "authority," of the senators who served as military governors, while their social friends gained control of the best properties.[38]

Carthage, despite its defeat, still held its colonies in Africa and Spain. Its leader Hamilcar and his son Hannibal plotted revenge. In 219 B.C.E., with the indemnity paid, Hannibal launched the Second Carthaginian War by leading troops and elephants from Spain into Italy. This merciless war killed about 20 percent of Rome's population, and the city-state often faced extinction.[39] In such early battles as Lake Trasimene (217) and Cannae (216), Hannibal demolished entire Roman armies, slaughtering tens of thousands. For fifteen years, with the aid of Syracuse and many Italians, Hannibal remained on the attack, allowing no respite for harvest or winter. But Rome gradually turned the tide. Scipio Africanus cut off Hannibal's supplies in Spain and drove him from Italy. His victory in the 202 B.C.E. Battle of Zama in Tunisia forced Carthage's surrender.

The spoils were enormous. Carthage agreed to pay ten thousand silver talents over fifty years and ceded its major colonies in Africa and Spain, which became Roman provinces. Disloyal Roman clients like Syracuse were sacked. Spanish silver mines, which covered about one hundred square miles in the Guadalquivir River basin, poured a fortune into Rome, especially after Roman managers used forty thousand slaves to quintuple production from three hundred to fifteen hundred talents per year.[40] Cadiz, the main shipping port, became one of the Roman world's largest and most important cities.

The province of Africa, an arable strip about 200 miles deep that ran along the coast from western Libya to Morocco, was just as valuable. It shared the fertile soils of Sicily and southern Spain while enjoying more rainfall than today, and grew an abundance of crops. From Libya's Leptis Minor alone Carthage had reaped 365 talents a year.[41] In Roman hands, Africa became a major supplier of olives, wine, fruit, and later of wheat, and when Carthage became the provincial capital its 250,000 residents made it the fourth largest city in the empire after Rome, Alexandria, and Antioch.[42]

Rome had begun to enjoy a market economy during and after the First Carthaginian War. The sustained effort to defeat Hannibal in the Second Carthaginian War brought forth two important new businesses: agribusiness, which became the chief supplier to the growing city and its armies; and public contractors, firms that the still-tiny government hired to provision the military forces. These became the greatest businesses yet to appear in the Western world.

Public Contractors, Publican Societies

During the war, the Roman army, which had previously provided its own food and clothing, needed others to provision, arm, and supply it. Since there were few public employees, the Senate turned to private businesses. The need for public contractors became even greater after the war, when Rome required managers, accountants, and tax collectors to operate its captured mines, quarries, forests, grazing meadows, and fisheries. The army, keeping order,[43] had little capacity to manage these new resources. Its forces consisted only of militias raised for particular expeditions.[44] The governors, who served only a year or so, rarely cared enough to build managerial staffs. Their eyes remained firmly fixed on a future in Rome.

The contracts for managing state resources, ultimately extended to providing public supplies and services, including the collection of customs dues and other levies, were auctioned off around the Ides of March, when an official would solicit bids in the Roman Forum. The bidder, known as the *manceps*, had to provide guarantees of performance, secured with pledged property. A guarantor's liability passed to his heirs, and title to the pledged property was held under seal in the temple of Mercury.

Many of these contracts were too large, risky, long lasting, and complex for individuals. Nor could individuals or partnerships risk the open-ended financial liabilities that the contracts could entail. Partnerships, which dissolved when any partner died, were also too unreliable. Roman lawyers instead found and adapted an ancient entity, the *societas publicani*. Publican societies became the first business corporations in Western history.

According to legend, the original publican society was created around 390 B.C.E. A Celtic war party was creeping up to the citadel on the Capitoline Hill when geese raised the alarm, allowing the Romans to save themselves. Grateful senators formed a society to feed the geese. It became a club that took on a perpetual life as new members joined and old ones died. Unlike partnerships, members were liable only for their dues.[45]

As public contractors, publican societies could hire employees; own necessary assets like cash, land, buildings, and slaves; and make contracts. Limited liability and perpetual life allowed them to attract the large investments they needed.[46] They profited not only from contracts, but also seized every business opportunity that their large staff and financial power could turn to profit. They supplied and traded with the Roman legions and their soldiers and often dominated local commerce as well.[47]

Publican societies came to manage many of the forests, quarries, fisheries, grazing meadows, and mines that Rome acquired. They constructed public works and provided various public services.[48]

Their most valuable public contracts were for tax farming: private tax collection.[49] As early as 2300 B.C.E. the Sumerian merchant Balmonahme had farmed the king's levies, and the business remained common in the Middle East down to the late years of the Hellenistic kingdoms. Tax farming was also known in early Greece.[50] Although the sale of tax farms would become a financial device for rulers during the late Middle Ages, in Rome it remained just a simple way to collect taxes.

Roman taxes took many forms. Property taxes were the most important, although the Senate, whose members owned a great deal of Italian land, used the spoils of victory over Macedonia to eliminate property taxes in Italy, an exemption they enjoyed for several centuries. There were also border tolls, customs duties, and sales taxes on slaves. Augustus created the inheritance tax for Roman citizens in 6 C.E.[51] Caligula taxed food, lawsuits, porters' wages, and prostitutes, and his successor Vespasian added vegetables and public toilets.[52]

At first, each tax in a territory was auctioned, but eventually all the area's taxes were offered as a package.[53] Since property taxes were the earliest ones farmed, the term of the contract was set to coincide with the census that set property values every five years. The contract specified how the *manceps* was to secure and pay the government, penalties for nonpayment, the basis and rate of the tax, the farmer's profit (between 6 percent and 10 percent), and enforcement powers.[54] Collection methods were harsh.

Publican societies became so profitable that virtually the entire Roman elite, including senators who were theoretically prohibited from commerce,[55] avidly invested in them.[56] Shares of ownership, called *particulae* ("little parts"), were traded in the Forum, making it perhaps the world's first stock exchange. Equestrians, who faced no bar to active involvement even if they belonged to senatorial families,[57] often sponsored the societies and managed operations.[58]

Publican societies were headquartered in Rome.[59] Every year, just as the Senate elected consuls who appointed provincial governors, the society's owners elected managers who appointed provincial magistrates. Like governors, magistrates enjoyed considerable authority and headed bureaucratic staffs.[60] Regional offices consisted mainly of slaves and freedmen who supervised collection posts in cities and harbors and along borders.[61] For instance, the slave bailiff of a publican-owned border post in second-century-C.E. Bulgaria supervised scribes, inspectors, search officers, and clerks, plus their personal servants. They assessed and collected customs fees, caught smugglers, and fined them.[62]

The government's relationship to publicans evolved over time in a way that strikingly resembles the evolution of international business by modern corporations. Initially, the government sold territories to the publicans, who like independent distributors ran their own operations and took a large share of the revenues. These deals were often corrupt and costly to the treasury.[63] Later, when a large imperial staff allowed closer supervision, the publicans merely earned a commission on the revenues collected. By the third century C.E. the imperial staff had taken over collections completely[64] and publican societies disappeared.[65]

Agribusiness

Roman agribusiness also began with the Second Carthaginian War. As in Greece and Pergamum, war's slaughter of peasants made it possible. Italian deaths numbered in the hundreds of thousands,[66] and even survivors were often absent for seven years or more while Hannibal's armies ravaged their families and farms.[67] Many peasants lost their land or sold it at distressed prices, and others fared worse, as noted by Sallust: "While the generals and the cliques seized the spoils of war, their soldiers' parents and children were driven from house and home if they had stronger neighbors."[68]

Just as this calamity for peasants was allowing those who profited from the war—patricians whose estates supplied the city and the army, officers enriched with Carthage's booty, and sundry war profiteers—to acquire land at fire-sale prices, the market system that had replaced subsistence farming around Rome was making it feasible to generate profits by raising crops for sale. The value of supplying that market would only increase during the republic's remaining centuries as more and more Romans got their provisions from it: 60–90 percent of Rome's residents by the end of the republic in 31 B.C.E.[69]

Patrician eagerness for profit helped drive this commercialization.[70] Rome enjoyed an explosion of wealth as publican societies won huge new contracts to operate the mines, forests, fisheries, and other facilities captured from the Carthaginians in Spain. Newly prosperous landowners, publican shareholders, and military officers flush with Carthaginian booty financed increasingly extravagant displays of luxury. An intense new interest in money took hold while conservatives like the historian Sallust complained that avarice was "the root of all evil. Greed undermined loyalty, honesty and the other virtues. In their place it taught arrogance, cruelty, disregard for the gods and the view that everything was for sale."[71]

Nonetheless, social standing became increasingly dependent on wealth and its public display through a lavish lifestyle. As explained by the late Renaissance aristocrat Alessandro Piccolomini in 1552: "The munificent should make every effort so that his works cannot be easily imitated, and should always seek to outdo what has already been done by others on similar occasions. His country houses must be magnificent and splendid, the gardens sumptuous, the town house grand and splendid and furnished in accordance with his degree and something over."[72] Heroes like Cato the Elder or Emperor Augustus might live in simplicity and deplore extravagance, but for everyone else extravagance helped attract clients, friends, and support. In short, social standing equated to the power required for everything of value in the Roman world.

A related route to social standing was to hold increasingly important public offices. Each rung obliged its holder to make commensurately large expenditures, and ridicule destroyed shirkers like the Praetor Fabricius Veiento, who tried to substitute dog races for the chariot races a praetor was expected to sponsor.[73] In the power struggles that constituted Roman civil life, such a man's ability to protect family and property would dwindle as clients and patrons melted away and lucrative offices went to others. Consequently, honor was so valuable that some sacrificed everything for it. As Dio Cassius reported of one Julius Solon: "It was said . . . that he had been stripped of all his property and banished to the Senate."[74] Apart from the cash to finance ornate public celebrations, such a senator needed to maintain a mansion in Rome, a nearby country estate, and preferably a seaside villa. Naturally, the price of these properties was very high, since the size, appearance, and location had to demonstrate the man's position. He also needed an impressive retinue of slaves and attendants and an open hand to attract a respectable following of clients.

After the war with Hannibal, patricians with access to markets were therefore keen to make farming pay.[75] They read agricultural manuals, used cultivation methods recommended by Greek science,[76] and invested for productivity. Iron tools and the donkey-powered water mill came into widespread use, and mills and presses were introduced as Italian production shifted to an emphasis on wine and oil.[77] The greatest innovation, however, was to use enslaved farm labor.

This became feasible where land acquired in the wake of the war came largely free of peasants, clearing the way to use slaves.[78] Slaves were more productive than peasants. Peasants came with hungry families, set their own work schedules, and produced no more than they had to. They participated only marginally in the cash economy,[79] consuming roughly 60 percent of what they produced, using 20 percent for seed, and paying rent and taxes before they could make the occasional purchase.[80] They stoutly resisted change, and as citizens they could not be easily coerced. Slaves, on the other hand, did what they were told. They were normally single men fed five pounds of mostly cheap gruel per day.[81] It has been estimated that twenty slaves could be fed on what eight peasants and their families consumed.[82] Moreover, in the decades after the war little or nothing was spent to clothe or house field slaves, who were branded in the face, slept in chicken coops, and normally went chained and naked under the overseer's whip.[83] Although they quickly died, replacements were cheap.[84] In Italy, the use of slaves even cut the one tax landowners had to pay, a head tax on peasants.[85] According to most historians, the Italian slave population, most of them on farms,[86] rapidly grew to what contemporaries estimated at two million by the late republic and remained at that level for centuries afterward.[87]

The most profitable cash crop, according to Pliny the Elder, was animal husbandry.[88] Some of the richest Romans owned vast properties devoted to sheep.[89] In addition, publican societies and other entrepreneurs, in a practice called transhumance, which would prevail in remote areas of Italy and Spain until modern times, would lease upland acreage for the summer, assemble herds numbering hundreds of thousands from many farms, and drive them up along rights-of-way known as *calles*. In the fall they would return and sell their wool, hides, and meat.[90] The shepherds were mostly slaves, who often became the leaders of slave revolts because they had relatively independent and healthy lives and kept arms against wolves and rustlers. Some were free peasants, who often lived even worse than slaves.[91]

Apart from transhumance, agribusiness represented a shift in emphasis among mixed field and orchard crops, nothing like modern monoculture. Farms were very small, including those devoted to agribusiness. This was mainly because cultivation was so slow. A pair of yoked oxen could only plow about five-eighths of an acre per day, and most plowing was even slower.[92] Consequently, Egyptian farms averaged only forty-three acres; Sicilian, thirty-five.[93] Less than half a farm was cultivated at any time. Some of the land was devoted to buildings, pastures, and woodland,

and half the arable land remained fallow every year to suppress weeds and restore its fertility. The poet Horace kept oxen, sheep, goats, and pigs in the meadows and woods of his beloved Sabine farm and planted grain, a vineyard, and a fruit and vegetable garden.[94] This diversity was necessary for subsistence, since high transport costs made it prohibitive to obtain food from outside.[95]

The main difference between the subsistence farms of independent peasants and the agribusiness-oriented villas was the larger proportion of land that villas devoted to cash crops like grapes and olives instead of commodities like grain.[96] Grain accounted for 75 percent of the Roman diet, but even the urban poor spent as much on oil and wine.[97] Accordingly, these were highly profitable. The agricultural writer Columella explained that anyone who carefully and intelligently cultivated vineyards would easily earn more than from hay or vegetables.[98]

The Greeks had brought olives to Italy around 580 B.C.E., according to Pliny the Elder, and wine was long a Greek export to Italy.[99] Each had important uses beyond culinary pleasure. Olive oil fueled lamps and made soap. Wine made the widely contaminated waters potable, which is why the Greeks and Romans so often diluted their water with it.[100] Wine had become Italy's main cash crop by the first century B.C.E.,[101] with vineyards covering more than 123,000 acres around Rome.[102]

Even agribusinesses dared not operate entirely with slaves, since the enormous variety and seasonal nature of Roman farming made it impossible to keep them fully occupied,[103] and masters feared idle slaves. Instead, as agricultural writers suggested, wealthy landowners created estates, known as villas, that included a cluster of tenant farms to absorb excess slave time.[104] The five largest villas at Veleia, near Rome, averaged sixteen farms each.[105] Horace's relatively small villa had six farms. His bailiff operated the home farm with eight slaves and supervised sharecroppers who leased the other five farms.[106] The large villa at Settefinestre, north of Rome, had twenty-eight slaves: eleven on the home farm and seventeen in the vineyard.[107] Hence most Italian farms, even near Rome, remained in peasant hands.[108]

Villas were complex enterprises. In addition to their farm revenues they could also provide lodging, food, fodder, fresh horses, and draft animals to travelers and exploit resources like woodlots and clay, stone, metal, and salt deposits.[109] Their slaves produced bricks; manufactured flour, bread, wool, shoes, and clothing; and repaired carts and tools.[110] Many villas kept fish hatcheries and, near Rome and other large cities, sold flowers, fruits, vegetables, poultry, milk, and more exotic products. Birds for the Roman table should not be fed dried figs, advised Columella, "because it costs not a little to hire people to chew the figs, and they themselves tend to swallow a fair quantity because of the nice taste."[111]

With their cash revenues, villas participated fully in the market economy. Cato the Elder, describing a model villa, listed purchases as "clothing, shoes, iron implements, bronze utensils, ropes of fiber and leather, ploughshares, ploughs and yokes, wagon-frames, threshing sledges, oil mills and millstones for the grain mill. Other miscellaneous items in the list include iron nails and bolts, and . . . roof-tiles, large basins and large storage jars."[112]

A patrician might own several villas, visiting them for recreation or to check accounts and consult on strategic issues like the acquisition of neighboring properties. As Columella recommended, a procurator might oversee them all and keep track of their iron tools, performing management, accounting, and audit functions much like a modern billionaire's estate manager, whose role "usually involves overseeing multiple residences."[113]

The villa bailiff was the model for all other Roman business managers. Called *vilicus* or *institore*, he was comparable to a divisional manager. He managed the villa and kept detailed records for the owner. His accounting was a rational effort to collect information for guiding the villa's business tactics and strategy. He noted yields, recorded tasks, and registered transactions. He trained the slaves, organized them into gangs under slave foremen, and designed incentives like money for their own use and the right to take a mate. He bought and sold slaves, equipment, tools, seeds, fodder, and draft animals and hired seasonal labor. He also borrowed money, found tenants, collected rents, and made contracts.

Marketing was an important responsibility. The bailiff sold many items locally, like poles, reeds, and props for trees and manufactured goods like hampers, baskets, threshing sledges, rakes, fans, pottery, and bricks. The sale of cash crops was more complicated. It was most profitable to sell after the harvest, but selling beforehand minimized risk. Wholesalers commonly bought grapes this way, sending their crews to pick the fruit using the villa's equipment and leaving the grapes there to ferment before taking the wine away in their own amphoras within the year.[114] As Rome grew, villas increasingly sold to such wholesalers, bypassing local markets.[115]

Bailiffs also had to decide where to sell other crops and arrange to transport them. Spoilage required most food to be sold within a day's trip by oxcart, about nine miles, but durable items like grain, hard cheese, salted meat, animals on the hoof, wool, wine, and oil could travel much farther.[116] The villas in the Valle d'Oro, like Settefinestre, shipped their wine on six or seven boats, quite possibly to the provinces.[117] By the middle of the second century B.C.E., Italy was exporting hundreds of thousands of hectoliters of wine, much of it to buy slaves in Gaul.[118]

Some bailiffs were freeborn, some were freedmen, but most were slaves. The job required a mate, but since a slave couldn't marry, his mate was only a concubine with no legal standing. The hope of giving her legal rights and social standing through manumission doubtlessly helped motivate many a slave bailiff, but all were proud of their position. They insisted on the title *vilicus* rather than *institore*, since Roman literature commonly depicted *institores* as greedy and debauched characters. Although accounts were rarely examined, owners could punish their slaves for any reason and as sadistically as they wanted. In Apuleus's novel *Metamorphoses*, for example, a master punished his bailiff's sexual infidelities by having him covered in honey and eaten by ants.[119]

The most extraordinary aspect of Roman business is the institution of patronage, a relationship based primarily on social norms that has its closest modern equivalent in *giri*, the sense of obligation that binds Japanese businesses together. While we celebrate Rome for its law—and indeed Rome's limited liability corporations known as publican societies are one of the law's great achievements—the institution of patronage was at the heart of its business operations.

The expansion, wealth, and institutional structure of Rome that formed during the early Roman Republic set the stage for the four hundred years of flourishing Roman business that followed the defeat of Hannibal. The next chapter takes up what happened as Rome's imperial reach expanded and civil war erupted during the late Roman Republic.

9

The Late Roman Republic, 201–31 B.C.E.

Business wielded more power and political influence during the last two centuries of the Roman Republic than at any other time before the Renaissance. Italian agribusiness, with leaders like Cato the Elder, suppressed overseas competition; and publican societies helped persuade the Senate to adopt imperialist policies. Then, using its power to free itself from regulation, Roman big business destroyed much of what it had achieved. Its excesses inspired colonial hatred and bloody uprisings, which led to radical changes in Rome's political structure and world outlook.[1]

Cato and Agribusiness

Cato the Elder (234–149 B.C.E.) was Rome's leading politician in the decades after the war with Hannibal. Cato inherited a proud old name and won patronage that advanced his wealth, military career, and political standing. Upon reaching the Senate, his forceful oratory, biting wit, and honorable reputation made him a leader.[2] As the first Roman investor about whose affairs much information survives, and one who shaped the late republic's business environment, his life deserves examination.

Table 10
Roman Chronology: Early Empire, 31 B.C.E.–192 C.E.

20	peace with Parthians; Crassus's standards returned
9 B.C.E.	Battle of Teutoberger Forest: Germans drive Romans back across Rhine
18 C.E.	Augustus dies
50	Hippalus charts monsoons in Indian Ocean, making regular navigation feasible (Durant 1944: 325)
68–69	civil wars after Nero: Vespasian establishes Flavian dynasty
70	Titus sacks Jerusalem
79	Vesuvius erupts, buries Pompeii and Herculaneum
106	Trajan destroys Petra, annexes Nabateans
114–115	Trajan annexes Armenia and Mesopotamia, captures Babylon and Assyria from Parthians
135	Hadrian suppresses revolt of Bar Kochba, disperses Jews
165–180	measles and smallpox plagues decimate Rome for first time
180	death of Marcus Aurelius
192–193	civil wars after Marcus Aurelius, Severans triumph

During the Second Carthaginian War, Cato cannily bought distressed farms and inexpensive slaves to work their orchards and vineyards. He became an expert in agriculture and wrote the first Roman manual on the subject. To reduce the risk of natural catastrophes, he diversified his portfolio with holdings all over Italy. These included farms and "ponds, hot baths, grounds full of fuller's earth [used in finishing cloth]."[3] Cato also leased out or sold slaves he had trained as skilled artisans. Through his freedman Quintio, he bought 2 percent interests in many overseas trading ventures. Quintio often went along to watch them.

Like many conservatives today, Cato honored the old virtues born of toil and poverty. He idolized a childhood neighbor, a war hero who lived in a simple cottage, ate his own boiled turnips for supper, and had famously refused a lucrative Samnite offer with the comment that he preferred winning their gold through conquest to earning it through employment. Similarly frugal, Cato boasted that his clothes never cost more than 100 denarii, he never paid more than two denarii for meat or fish, and he drank the same wine as his slaves. To the disgust of Plutarch, however, this rich miser routinely dismissed or sold his slaves when they could no longer work.[4] Still, Cato was not selfish. In Spain he distributed the spoils of victory to all the troops instead of keeping them for himself and his officers in the customary way. He explained: "I had rather compete in valor with the best, than in wealth with the richest, or with the most covetous in love of money."

Many Greeks, Persians, Jews, and Romans welcomed luxury, sensuality, and the pleasures of the flesh; to this day, Jewish prayers thank God for providing wine. But Cato despised such departures from the flinty old virtues. He was the first to advocate sumptuary laws to repress luxury, ostentation, and vulgar display, and in office he ruthlessly opposed waste and licentiousness. He scolded Hannibal's conqueror Scipio Africanus for idle luxuriousness, and had Diogenes and another Athenian banished from Rome lest they corrupt the youth. He even got a fellow senator impeached and ruined for kissing his own wife in front of their daughter in broad daylight.

As censor, the official who assessed property, supervised public contracts, and enforced public morals, Cato's harsh frugality served the public well. He destroyed houses that obstructed the streets, severed pipes that diverted public water to private use, and heavily taxed luxury goods. He put tough terms on public contracts and extracted large payments from tax farmers, earning the epigraph on his statue, "This was Cato the Censor, who, by his good discipline and wise and temperate ordinances, reclaimed the Roman commonwealth when it was declining and sinking down into vice."

In the Senate, Cato advocated his own interests. Carthage had shown how to increase farm values at home by forbidding its provinces from growing grapes and olives, leaving these and other lucrative crops like fruit trees to its homeland. Cato persuaded the Senate to do likewise, allowing patrician farms in Italy to monopolize these more valuable crops.[5] He long advocated the final destruction of Carthage to protect Italian agribusiness as well. Once, he brought some lovely Carthaginian figs to the Senate, where his colleagues admired them. He then warned that they grew only three days from Rome, and from then on would end every address by thundering, "Carthage must be destroyed." Three years after his death Rome did so, planting the province of Africa entirely to grain.

Publicans and Colonization

While generating huge profits, the publican societies were causing the military considerable grief in the provinces. Publicans aimed to maximize revenues, and the short term of their five-year contracts made exploitation rather than cultivation the method of choice. With revenue a simple measure of success, their agents had to be ruthless or lose their jobs, whatever their personal sympathies. The managers and financiers back in Rome lived far away, like the upper management of multinationals today, and could easily ignore the hardships they imposed. The result was that the publicans "were often dishonest and probably always cruel."[6] In Spain, where powerful tribes remained hostile to Rome, the publicans provoked such frequent rebellions that the Romans called it the *horrida et bellicosa provincia* ("horrible and warlike province").[7]

Uprisings were of little concern to publican management so long as the army suppressed them. Normally, then, publicans reaped the benefits of their ruthlessness while largely escaping its costs. The soldiers, on the other hand, were endangered.[8] They also suffered personally from dishonest publican suppliers. In one horrible instance, when Rome was on the brink of destruction by Hannibal, it hired publicans to gather and deliver urgently needed provisions for Scipio's army in Spain where it was desperately trying to cut Hannibal's supply route. Instead, the patriots bought and sank rotting old ships to simulate a natural loss, sold the provisions on the black market, and claimed compensation for the alleged loss.[9]

Governors had difficulty controlling publicans. Short terms and minuscule staffs made supervision difficult. Moreover, they or their families were often investors. Governors also depended on publican societies. Publican couriers carried their mail, and the societies often provided branch banking, funding governors abroad and collecting reimbursement in Rome.[10] As Cicero wrote to his brother Quintus, the governor of Asia, "If we oppose [the publicans], we alienate from ourselves and the state an order which has deserved exceedingly well of us and which has been linked to the state by our efforts; if on the other hand we comply with them in every case, we shall allow the complete ruin of those for whose welfare and interests we are bound to have regard."[11] Indeed, many governors less scrupulous than Cicero joined the publicans in exploiting the provinces for themselves.[12] So despite enormous military antagonism, the publicans usually had a free hand.

In Rome, during the decades after defeating Hannibal, the Senate had opposed new military interventions abroad. Fighting in Spain and on the frontiers of Africa kept the militia busy, burdening the Roman citizens who comprised it. The Senate authorized foreign expeditions only reluctantly, and quickly withdrew the army afterward.

Moreover, the conspicuous consumption of the newly rich displeased many upper-class conservatives. As one of them, the writer Sallust, put it: "The love of money grew first: the love of power followed. This was, so to speak, the root of all evil. Greed undermined loyalty, honesty and the other virtues. In their place it taught arrogance, cruelty, disregard for the gods and the view that everything was for sale."[13]

But many were making serious money from their investments in publican societies.[14] Polybius wrote that "there is hardly anyone who is not involved either in the sale of these [public] contracts or in the kind of business to which they give rise. Some buy the contracts in person from the censors; some become partners of the purchasers; others stand surety or pledge their own property on their behalf."[15]

In addition, a military foray against Philip V of Macedonia and Scipio Africanus's spectacular victory over Hannibal and Antiochus III at Magnesia in 189 B.C.E. revealed the easy pickings available in the Hellenistic kingdoms, just as Xenophon's *Anabasis* had earlier whetted Hellenic appetites for Persian conquest.[16] Scipio Africanus, prosecuted for skimming off a portion of the Seleucid booty, took enough to leave senatorial fortunes to each of his daughters.[17] By 171 B.C.E., when Pergamum's persuasive King Eumenes II advocated a preemptive war against Philip V's successor Perseus of Macedonia, the Senate's resistance to imperialism had vanished.

After a surprisingly difficult struggle, Rome prevailed. The legions looted Macedonia's royal palace, seizing more than six thousand talents of silver from the treasury,[18] and triumphantly sailed the Macedonian royal barge up the Tiber. King Perseus was paraded in chains before a thrilled Roman populace, along with booty officially totaling almost twelve thousand talents.[19] The Senate annexed Macedonia's royal estates, and publican tax farmers turned the tactics honed in Sicily, Spain, and Carthage to collecting Macedonia's taxes. The new revenues allowed the Senate to abolish Italian property taxes.[20]

After this, Rome's colonial empire expanded steadily. Macedonia and later Greece were made provinces, the Seleucid and Ptolemaic rulers became

Roman dependents, and in 133, 96, and 74 B.C.E. respectively, Pergamum, Bithynia, and Cyrenaica in North Africa were bequeathed to Rome. Hellenistic city-states sought Roman patrons[21] and lobbied the Senate with bribes and offers of market access in ways now common in Washington and Brussels.[22]

Roman and Italian businessmen came to command the raw materials and labor forces in virtually every Hellenistic land.[23] The filaments of commerce, linking the personal interests of influential Romans with the Eastern upper classes, rapidly multiplied and strengthened.[24] Romans served as bankers to businessmen, cities, and kings; invested in mortgages, land, ships, and trade; and worked as merchants and farmers.[25] Athens flourished as a cultural tutor to Rome, much as London and Paris were to early-twentieth-century America. Romans bought Greek art[26] and became so Hellenized that many contemporaries thought Rome a Greek city.[27]

Despite their love for Greek culture, Romans treated the Hellenistic states with no more consideration than they did the provinces in Spain and Africa. The effect was actually worse, since there was much more to steal or destroy. Deprived under Roman rule of police, welfare, or justice, Hellenistic lands were thrown into chaos, while the Senate blandly ignored pleas for help and intervened only to protect Romans and their aristocratic friends.[28] Some historians even suspect a deliberate indifference, since these conditions generated so many slaves for agribusiness.[29] The Hellenes, used to governing themselves under the limited sovereignty of the Eastern kings, bitterly detested these policies.

They rose up in outrage, and Rome responded in force. In the 146 B.C.E. the legions brutally suppressed uprisings in Macedonia and Greece[30]— leaving Corinth so crushed that Cicero found it a heap of ruins seventy years later—and finally destroyed Carthage. They plowed the city under, sowed it with salt, and pronounced a curse on anyone who tried to restore it. Its fifty thousand survivors were sold into slavery.[31]

Provincials were not the only ones to suffer appalling losses. Few Romans apart from governors, certain traders, and publican society investors actually benefited, and Rome's police actions were so expensive and unrewarding that only Sicily and Asia were profitable provinces.[32] One hundred thousand Roman and Italian men died between 200 and 150 B.C.E., proportional to nearly 3,000,000 deaths in modern America.[33] The survivors gained little, even from their triumphs. The troops who sold 150,000 Epirotes into slavery netted about two weeks' wage each (16 denarii).

Even the pound of silver that Cato gave his troops in Spain paid only three months' living expenses, hardly fabulous spoils of war.[34] Upon returning home, Roman veterans continued to find destroyed farms, stolen property, and scattered families. Italians endured even harsher military service and returned to similar losses.[35] But lacking Roman citizenship, they were also denied access to the food, shelter, and employment available in Rome itself.[36]

The most miserable of all were the slaves. The supply of unskilled laborers was so large that their lives were cheap. They were chained, fed starvation wages, whipped to work, and left virtually naked and unsheltered. A slave could be tortured to death on the mere suspicion of misbehavior, while all of an owner's slaves would be tortured to death if he was murdered. Such treatment drove slaves to desperate revolts. In 135 B.C.E. a Syrian slave styling himself King Eunus of Antioch led two hundred thousand followers in capturing several Sicilian cities and holding off Roman armies for three years. This revolt inspired uprisings at Rome, Athens, and Delos.[37] More followed, along with continuing insurrection in Spain.

Reform and Civil War

The Gracchi

Like all Romans, the brothers Tiberius and Gaius Gracchus, grandsons of Scipio Africanus, wanted slave revolts and provincial rebellions efficiently suppressed.[38] The militia's failures alarmed them. After service in Spain, Tiberius concluded that the desperation of the Italian peasantry was to blame. "The beasts of Italy," he said, "have a house and home: they know where they can find shelter. But the men who risked their lives in fighting for Italy are granted only air and light: house and home are denied them and they are left to wander with their wives and children in the open air. . . . They die for foreign luxuries and riches, in name the masters of the world, in fact not even masters of their own plots of land."[39]

In 133 B.C.E. the Assembly elected him tribune. He wanted to distribute Roman public lands to veterans, but the Senate resisted. Insiders had long leased that land at favorable rates and didn't want to surrender them.[40] Tiberius proposed to grant citizenship and votes to Italian veterans, but senators feared losing their privileges. Instead, they preached a return to old moral virtues and a renewed commitment to religion. Tiberius's uncle, Rome's religious leader the Pontifex Maximus, demonstrated those values by leading a lynch mob that assassinated Tiberius.

His brother Gaius later pursued a similar agenda more adroitly.[41] To distribute public lands to veterans, he agreed to purchase senatorial lease-holds for full market value, a deal made possible by the 133 B.C.E. inheritance of Pergamum's bulging treasury. He then planted veterans' colonies in restive areas of northern Italy, where they helped pacify the region.[42] That success led to more, especially outside Italy where no senators had leaseholds to lose. Starting in 118 B.C.E. with a colony in southern Gaul at Narbo, which became the capital of a new province there, veterans' colonies gradually became a cornerstone of Roman policy to secure much of Western Europe and North Africa.

Indirectly, the creation of veterans' colonies promoted entrepreneurial business in Italy and Western Europe. Italian agribusinesses ended up buying many veterans' public land allotments for cash.[43] At the same time, in Gaul, Spain, and North Africa as well as Italy, new veterans' colonies built along Hellenistic lines brought free markets and private enterprises along with the wealth and commercial knowledge of the many Hellenistic refugees who settled in these new cities.[44]

In each colony temples, forums, baths, and amphitheaters surrounded a central square and market, with privately operated theaters, libraries, gymnasiums, and hotels behind. Tailors, shoemakers, bakers, and other artisans had shops in the nearby residential neighborhoods.[45] In the suburbs were villas, sometimes spaciously built to Roman standards with central heat, wall paintings, and mosaics.[46] Beyond were homesteads.[47] Since the hinterlands of the European colonies were usually unproductive, traders supplied many of their provisions through markets.

Gaius's creation of the *annona*, a subsidized food program for Rome, proved a great boon to agribusiness. Like the *annona militaris* that provisioned the army, or indeed such modern welfare programs as food stamps, the *annona* used private firms for supplies and distribution.[48] Because starvation was such a danger—there were at least thirty-seven food shortages in Rome between 201 and 31 B.C.E.[49]—this became wildly popular, especially once food became free after 58 B.C.E.[50] The *annona* eventually imported a quarter of Rome's food supply from abroad: two hundred to four hundred thousand tons of grain per year plus other items.[51] It became a mainstay of governmental policy.[52] In 22 C.E. Emperor Tiberius warned that "if it is neglected the utter ruin of the state will follow."[53] Never neglected, it continued in Rome as late as 537 C.E., long after German kings had replaced Roman emperors.[54]

To win publican support for his programs, Gaius replaced the city magistrates who had traditionally collected taxes in Asia and other Hellenistic kingdoms[55] with Roman tax farmers, a change that has been described as "the biggest killing in the financial world."[56] The publicans won another important concession as well. As senators, governors accused of wrongdoing were traditionally tried by a jury of other senators. Gaius expanded this jury pool to include equestrians, the class of publican business managers.[57] With that, "a governor who had defied big business in his province was to be tried by big business on his return."[58] Between 123 and 90 B.C.E. eighteen senators were prosecuted, four convicted. The chilling effect on governors can be imagined.[59]

Contemporaries described the publican tax collectors falling upon the Hellenistic city-states like wolves. Despite contracts specifying a customary level of taxation, they had many ways to collect more—ways that modern credit card customers might recognize. Gone were the formerly customary exceptions, deferments, low assessments, or other favors; now came collection fees, exorbitant interest on late payments, and business-friendly officials who raised assessments or allowed excess collections.[60] Insiders like M. Brutus, the father of Caesar's assassin, might advance tax money at exorbitant rates of interest: 48 percent per year, in Brutus's case.[61] Upon default, they would seize the lucrative properties and commercial activities that secured the loans, regardless of the amount in default, and sell the debtors into slavery.

To be sure, loud and piteous complaint was a regional art form and probably exaggerated publican depredations. The speedy payments that followed a tax amnesty that Cicero arranged indicate that coffers were not as depleted as claimed.[62] Nor were the publicans alone in abusing the provincials. Many officials were arrogant, greedy, and indifferent to local needs.[63] Nonetheless, as in Africa and Spain, the publicans were ruthless. The king of Bithynia, declining in 104 B.C.E. to contribute soldiers to a Roman army, explained that publicans had enslaved most of his men.[64]

The cause that finally killed Gaius was Italian citizenship. In Greece and other Mediterranean societies grants of citizenship were rare, due to the scarcity of arable land; citizenship above a certain age was hereditary.[65] But Rome had never lacked for arable land and often granted citizenship to others, starting with its Latin foes. Brave allied soldiers or individuals who otherwise served Roman interests often received a reward of citizenship,[66] and slaves became citizens upon manumission. Indeed, Macedonia's conqueror Aemilius Paulus boasted that most of Rome's citizens had once been his prisoners of war.[67]

The more powerful Rome became, the more valuable were the rights and privileges of Roman citizenship. A Roman citizen could live in Rome, own Roman land, travel freely throughout Roman territory, receive *annona* handouts, serve in the army, and remove lawsuits to Roman courts, among other benefits. The Italians clamored for citizenship, but senators could not abide it. Lest Gaius achieve this reform as well, they assassinated him in 121 B.C.E.

Marius

Gaius's reforms never remedied the problems of Rome's militia; indeed, thanks to him the publicans created serious new grievances and slave revolts, provincial uprisings, and border raids continued. The navy failed to suppress piracy, and in Africa, the Numidian leader Jugurtha was killing thousands of soldiers and colonists in his raids on Roman farms. By 107 B.C.E. German invaders were threatening Italy itself.

Terrified into drastic measures, the Senate elected as consul the plebeian Gaius Marius, Rome's leading military hero, with a mandate to handle these problems at all costs. Marius delivered. He captured Jugurtha and paraded him through the streets of Rome, a scene fancifully depicted by Tiepolo in a gigantic mural at New York's Metropolitan Museum of Art. Marius then repulsed the Germans from northern Italy and drove pirates from their base in Cilicia.[68]

To accomplish these feats, Marius instituted far more radical reforms than the Gracchi had conceived and changed the course of Roman history. He replaced the seasonal, landowning militia with a full-time army open to any able-bodied Roman.[69] Committed to serving for sixteen years, these strenuously trained and highly disciplined soldiers could carry sixty pounds and march thirty-seven miles per day. They proudly called themselves "Marius's mules,"[70] and their army would remain virtually invincible for the next 350 years.

Marius's military reforms had profound political consequences as well. Unlike militia members, who as landowners were loyal to their senatorial village patrons, Marius's mules owed loyalty only to commanders who brought them loot and pay. This realignment of military loyalties would lead first to power struggles between military commanders, then between the prevailing military commander and the Senate, and ultimately to the imperial system of constitutional monarchy.

The first spark to ignite these civil wars came from the Italian demand for citizenship. In 91 B.C.E. yet another Roman champion of their cause was assassinated, and the Italians launched a savage war, known as the Social War. After three years of fighting, the Senate would finally trade citizenship for peace.

A more urgent threat had materialized, due largely to publican depredations in the East. Their Hellenistic victims had finally found a champion in King Mithridates of Pontus on the Black Sea side of Anatolia. He had secured the throne in 112 B.C.E. by murdering his father, mother, brother, and sister, who was also his wife. Unsurprisingly, Mithridates feared assassination and evidently poisoned himself gradually to build up immunity. As the poet describes,

> They put arsenic in his meat
> And stared aghast to watch him eat;
> They poured strychnine in his cup
> And shook to see him drink it up. . . .
> I tell the tale that I heard told.
> Mithridates, he died old.
> —A. E. HOUSEMAN, *A SHROPSHIRE LAD*

Mithridates was also reputedly fluent in twenty-two languages and dialects, self-disciplined, hard-riding, brave, and ruthless. By seizing part of Galatia and marrying his daughter to King Tigranes of Armenia, this steely prince became Rome's most formidable enemy since Hannibal.

The Social War gave Mithridates an apparent opportunity to drive Rome from the East. In 88 B.C.E. he instigated the Anatolian Vespers, a midnight slaughter of up to 150,000 Italian businessmen, their families, and local companions in Asia, formerly Pergamum. He then invaded and confiscated the victims' estates.[71] At his behest Cilician pirates ravaged Delos and the Aegean, and his promise to cancel debts, restore democracy, and send gold to Athens led to the murder there of many Romans while local aristocrats fled.[72]

The nearly empty Roman treasury lost its richest source of revenues, and many influential Romans faced bankruptcy.[73] A young Cicero, with a fortune lodged in Ephesus, passionately advocated war:

The whole system of credit and finance which is carried on here at Rome is inextricably bound up with the revenues of the Asiatic provinces. If these revenues are destroyed, our system of credit will crash. . . . If some lose their entire fortunes they will drag many more down with them. Save the state from such a calamity. . . . Prosecute with all your energies the war against Mithridates, by which the glory of our Roman name, the safety of our allies, our most valuable resources, and the fortunes of innumerable citizens will be effectively preserved.[74]

The Civil Wars

Sulla

The Senate's champion Lucius Cornelius Sulla fought a bloody civil war against the Assembly's favorite, the now elderly Marius, for the privilege of attacking Mithridates. Sulla prevailed, plundering Greece and sacking Athens, which never recovered. Like Rhodes, Athens became little more than an academic, tourist, and resort destination.[75] Sulla then invaded Asia, where he evicted Mithridates and assessed a twenty-thousand-talent penalty on its citizens.[76] Sulla then returned to Italy, where the Senate elected him dictator. He cruelly pursued Marius's supporters[77] and, before retiring as the richest of all Romans, promulgated a law that forbad leading an army into Italy, as he had done.

His protégés Gnaeus Pompey and Marcus Crassus might have become the next political rivals but for Crassus's greater interest in business. Pompey was a wealthy young equestrian with a flair for flattery and self-promotion who addressed Sulla as *imperator* and beguiled premature honors from him with the saucy reminder that "more men worship the rising than the setting sun."[78] His fortuitous victory over Spanish rebels gained him acclaim.

Crassus, on the other hand, would become the most successful businessman in Roman history and probably the only one to attain political leadership.[79] Born around 114 B.C.E. into a moderately wealthy senatorial family, his father committed suicide during Marius's purge of the Senate, and Crassus hid out in a Spanish cave until Sulla's return. As an aide to Sulla, he used a three-hundred-talent inheritance to purchase property confiscated from Marius's supporters and became wealthy.

Crassus made his name by finally defeating Spartacus and his slave army of two hundred thousand men in 72 B.C.E. Pompey, returning from Spain, cleverly offered to take the captives off Crassus's hands. He then had thousands crucified along the Appian Way, gaining a hero's welcome in Rome. He and Crassus were elected co-consuls.[80]

Mithridates, meanwhile, used these diversions to invade Asia again. His son-in-law King Tigranes of Armenia seized Antioch, and Cilesian pirates appeared off Italian ports, menacing vital grain shipments.[81] These developments greatly disrupted trade shipments. Lucullus, Rome's governor in Asia, inexorably dispatched Tigranes and annexed Armenia, but his slow pace outraged business interests who already hated him, due to his irritating fairness to provincials.[82]

Pompey and Crassus now engineered Lucullus's recall to a gourmet retirement[83] and persuaded the Senate to send Pompey east with dictatorial powers. Pompey swept the pirates from the sea, drove Mithridates into final exile in the Crimea, and seized his enormous estates.[84] He established client kingdoms for Rome in northern Mesopotamia and annexed vast new provinces in Syria and the Levant, increasing Rome's provincial revenues by 60 percent and succeeding Sulla as the wealthiest of Romans.[85]

Although the publicans had sought Pompey's leadership, he initiated their downfall. Their moment of political power had enabled them to single-mindedly pursue their own interests without concern for the wider community. While initially successful, this strategy set up their own destruction.

At first, the publican societies obtained tax farms in all the provinces that Pompey acquired and intensified their collection efforts everywhere.[86] But Pompey's seven years in the East let him see how publican greed and poor governance nourished events like the Anatolian Vespers. As dictator, he could and did begin to improve governing practices and to police the publicans without fear of senatorial interference.[87] So could later military leaders like Julius Caesar, Marc Antony, and the emperors. They all withdrew tax farms and restored local authority.[88]

Crassus

In the first century B.C.E. Rome was an enormous, growing, crowded city of nearly one million people.[89] Like an ancient Donald Trump, Marcus Crassus's land investments prospered as his city's land increased in value. But he was also an ingenious entrepreneur.

Save for a thousand luxurious dwellings with atriums, bathrooms, floor heating, hot and cold running water, pools, fountains, gardens, and stables, everyone lived in rickety wooden tenements. Reaching eight stories high, they stood haphazardly on a maze of muddy, excrement-filled pathways and alleys that were often no wider than a man's shoulders.[90] Tenements frequently collapsed or had to be torn down to prevent it.

An apartment's furnishings consisted mainly of a bed, with tripods for tables and campstools or cushions for seats.[91] It contained little except bedding, clothes, tableware, and jewelry. Lacking water above the ground floor, chamber pots were emptied either in the neighborhood latrine, which fed into the public sewer, on the neighborhood dunghill, or at a nearby fuller's, who used urine to clean or soften wool. Slaves served as water-carriers, porters, and sweepers.

These tenements were firetraps. Fireplaces and chimneys hadn't been invented; heat came only from an open fire in a brazier. These usually smoked away on wooden balconies and frequently set buildings ablaze. Fires quickly engulfed whole areas of the city. The poet Juvenal exclaimed, "No, no, I must live where there is no fire and the night is free from alarms!"[92] To Crassus, though, fire represented opportunity. He trained slaves as firefighters and construction workers, and after the unfortunate owner sold him the flaming building on the spot his crews would extinguish the fire and rebuild it. In this way Crassus became Rome's largest landlord.

Crassus diversified his investments to farms, silver mines, and commercial loans. Like Cato the Elder, he educated his slaves, in his case as "readers, amanuenses, silversmiths, stewards, and table-waiters," and rented them out to others. But more like a modern consulting firm than the harsh Cato, he was very much the motivational manager and believed that the more he cared for his slaves, the better they would tend his interests.

Still, Crassus was known for his love of property, a reputation that saved his life. Like many other Romans, he pursued inheritances from childless patrons. He courted one, a Vestal Virgin, so ardently that he was charged with corrupting her, a capital offense.[93] In defense, Crassus claimed that his only interest was her property, and a jury believed him. Indeed, Crassus eventually received the property.

Far from crass, a word derived from an earlier Roman known as Crassus the Rich,[94] Marcus Crassus had a winning personality, lived with a simplicity that would have pleased Cato, and was popular for his generosity and public spirit. He consistently donated 10 percent of his income to public causes, provided much free food to the poor, sponsored games, and readily loaned money to his friends without interest, though he was strict in requiring repayment.

Caesar and Pompey

One such friend was Marius's dashing son-in-law, Julius Caesar. As a youth he was so charming that he talked his way free of kidnapping pirates by promising, in effect, to mail them a check. Then he returned in force and captured them. To repay their kindness he executed them quickly rather than by the slow and painful crucifixion that was a pirate's normal fate.

Careless with money, Caesar ran up huge debts. Crassus guaranteed them, enabling Caesar to become governor of Spain, where he regained his fortune. In 60 B.C.E. the Senate's refusal to provide Pompey's veterans with public land led Caesar, who like Marius was a popular champion, to join Crassus and Pompey in a political alliance, the first Triumvirate. Caesar became consul and Pompey got land for his veterans. Eventually Crassus, unfortunately, got what he wanted as well: to lead an attack on the Parthians. Traffic on the caravan routes through Persia had increased considerably, and control of these routes may have been his goal.[95] But as his force marched across the Syrian desert in the summer heat of 53 B.C.E., the Parthian cavalry destroyed it and beheaded Crassus.

After Caesar's rabble-rousing consulship, the Senate reluctantly appointed him to the customary provincial governorship, selecting a tiny province around Ravenna called Cisalpine Gaul. Caesar, however, used it to launch his conquest of Gaul's three parts, as well as Britain and the alpine regions.

Gaul

Carthaginians, Etruscans, and Greeks had long traded for Gaul's abundant resources. Around 450 B.C.E. trade declined, and Gaul's Celtic tribes invaded northern Italy and points eastward. Except for the Greek colony of Marseilles, there remained only small, isolated farming communities. After the Second Carthaginian War, commerce began to revive with Roman trade. It centered on fortified hill towns in Spain and Gaul called *oppida*, where some populations grew into the thousands. By Caesar's time,

Gaul had sixty independent states. They spoke Celtic, practiced Druidic religions, and were ruled by tribal leaders.[96] Some minted their own coins, in weights that became standardized and widely circulated.

The population remained sparse, however. Gaul's climate was cold and wet, and the still forested land[97] was "thankless to till and dismal to behold," as Tacitus famously described Germany.[98] Since approximately 75 percent of the human diet consisted of grains,[99] these conditions kept food supplies short. Virtually the size of all the arable regions of the Mediterranean combined, Gaul supported only three to five million people when Caesar conquered it, and double that two centuries later.[100]

Still, Caesar's conquests were immensely valuable. German and Celtic chiefs provided an endless supply of slaves. Iron, silver, gold, and salt came from mines in Gaul and Austria, tin and copper from Britain. Acquisition took Caesar eight years, along with two excursions to Britain, but the prize rivaled Pompey's conquests in the East.

Nevertheless, the hostile Senate under Cicero's fiery leadership summoned him to Rome. The danger was plain. For Caesar to obey Sulla's law and leave his troops behind could mean death, but to march across the little Rubicon River that marked the border meant war. On January 12, 49 B.C.E., Caesar crossed the Rubicon. The Senate's champion Pompey assembled an army in Greece, and Caesar followed, winning the Battle of Pharsallus. Pompey fled to Alexandria and was murdered as he stepped ashore.

Pursuing, Caesar confronted an Egyptian uprising that led to the accidental burning of Alexandria's great library. He also met Cleopatra, and while he continued Pompey's work in the East, they had two children.[101] One of Caesar's expeditions defeated Mithridates' son and annexed Pontus, prompting his famous *veni, vidi, vici*—"I came, I saw, I conquered." In several provinces he disciplined publican agents, reduced taxes, and replaced publican tax farmers with city magistrates.[102] Eventually, though, he returned to Rome. Fearing that he meant to rule as dictator, Senators Brutus and Cassius assassinated him in 44 B.C.E.

They fled east to raise and finance an army. They ransacked the provinces, extracting thousands of talents from Rhodes and Lycia, and thousands more from Judea. They seized the property of Antioch's Jews and forced the residents of Tarsus to sell their children, wives, and fathers into slavery.[103] Caesar's avengers, his lieutenant Mark Antony and his adopted son Octavian, pursued them. In 42 B.C.E. they defeated and killed the senators at Philippi in Greece.

Octavian and Antony

Then Antony and Octavian unleashed a savage purge of the Senate. Cicero was hunted down and killed, his right hand and head hung in the Forum. The wife of at least one senator slept with Antony to save her husband's life; Antony's wife Fulvia had the head of another senator nailed to his door after he refused to sell her his mansion. Virtually every other senator and two thousand equestrians were slaughtered, their property confiscated.[104] Antony married Octavian's sister and for a time the two ruled as dictators—Antony in the East, Octavian in Rome.[105]

But Antony's affair with Cleopatra caused a falling out. A brief civil war ended with Octavian's victory over the fleets of Cleopatra and Antony at Actium in 31 B.C.E. The lovers committed suicide in Alexandria, and Octavian bestrode the Roman world.

Business During the Civil Wars

Many people, not just senators, lost their lives and property during the civil wars. In Italy, for instance, some 1,500,000 peasants, half the landowners, lost their farms.[106] Nevertheless, Rome's wealth grew and business multiplied. Colonial conquests added vast new territories, resources, and populations. Rome's treasury, nearly empty when Sulla departed for Greece in 89 B.C.E., had swollen to 700,000,000 sesterces (HS—worth four to the denarius) by Caesar's death forty-five years later. Huge shipments of Eastern coins, bullion, and valuables flowed into Rome, adding to the money supply and funding higher levels of investment. Not coincidentally, Caesar began minting a new coin, the gold aureus.[107]

Rome's wealth was highly concentrated, but due to the patronage system this concentration did not contract business credit, unlike the Hellenistic experience. Patronage made investment easy for those with money, allowing venture funding through their many slaves, freedmen, and clients. Avid for profits, Roman elites became eager investors. Once, profit had been a minor byproduct of frugality like Cato the Elder's; Romans primarily sought prestige and status through military prowess. But as market consumption increased, so did business opportunities and the importance of generating income from commercial investments.

Another impetus to commercialization was Rome's unification of the Mediterranean's fragmented elites. These elites gained a common language, taste, and culture. Rome's passion for all things Greek, the use of Hellenic slaves to educate upper-class children, and the spread of Hellenistic cities created a largely uniform culture in which "an African land-owner, for instance, found himself quite at home in a literary salon of well-to-do Greeks at Smyrna."[108] This generated an empirewide market for luxury goods, one enjoying comparatively low internal barriers to trade, equivalent currencies, and two common languages: Greek in the East, Latin in the West.

Neither the destruction of the republic's elite during the civil wars nor the publican loss of tax farms had a significant economic effect. Confiscated property found new owners, who were often more active and entrepreneurial than the old.[109] Investors and businessmen received new public projects even as tax farming faltered. In Italy the late first century B.C.E. was a time of great prosperity. Agribusiness dominated the arable countryside south of Rome, and vast herds of sheep, goats, oxen, and cows grazed on upland pastures. Thousands of artisans, shopkeepers, slaves, and freedmen conducted business every day in Rome's lively streets. The goods for sale there included slaves, food, and manufactured products and also real estate, shares in publican societies, debts,[110] and participation in entrepreneurial ventures.[111]

This chapter shows both the bad and the good of business. Multinational publican societies inflicted great pain in the single-minded pursuit of their short-term profits. The political power they gained was used to the great detriment of provincials, Romans, and even themselves—especially after they virtually eliminated adult supervision. By contrast, the story of the ancient world's most successful business entrepreneur, Marcus Crassus, illustrates how beneficial a creative entrepreneur could be. He saw a business opportunity that others did not and created an organization that allowed him to seize it. It also shows that great business success was not incompatible with exceptional personal honor and decency by the standards of the day. As in the case of modern tycoons like Warren Buffett and Bill Gates, Crassus's career refutes those cynics who argue that business success is morally degrading.

If any chapter of this book bears upon public policy, it is this one. It demonstrates why business, regardless of the morality of individual owners and managers, should not dominate political decisions. The interests of business are so different from those of any legitimate sovereign that it governs very badly indeed. That is why catastrophic results followed when business exerted political power for the first and only time in ancient history. When Roman business gained enough power over the Senate to intimidate zealous regulators and free itself for predation, it ultimately incited deadly uprisings like the Anatolian Vespers and Spartacus's revolt. And when it demanded forceful military responses to the uprisings it caused, those solutions led to the long-term destruction of publican societies themselves.

Certainly business has a role in formulating public policy, but what makes it so effective an institution is its pragmatic, short-term focus on profits. That focus means that businesses, in deciding what public policies to support or oppose, will seek to disregard collateral damage, even to their own long-term self-interest. If policies to reduce global warming, workplace injuries, or asthma reduce business profits in the short term, business will fight them.

Moreover, larger businesses with far-flung operations, like the publican societies, will be more indifferent to collateral or long-term consequences than smaller businesses, simply because those consequences mostly fall far away. Smaller businesses are much more likely to consider the local impact of their actions and policies. When business controls public policy, then, large businesses will be much more pernicious than smaller ones. Size matters.

10

The Principate, 31 B.C.E.–192 C.E.

Here begins the story of business in the early Roman Empire, a period called the Principate because Augustus and his successors humbly called themselves *princeps*, or "first citizens," and were elected by the Senate. During these two centuries business enjoyed better conditions than ever before, and we also know far more about it. Business would not reach these heights again for another thousand years.

Two developments during the Principate altered the history of business:

- Augustus, like Alexander, created political changes that dramatically improved business conditions. Without his work, the Roman Empire could not have lasted very long. Until its end, the provinces would have continued to be exploited, impoverished, and rebellious colonies. And Roman business would not have enjoyed the prolonged period of peace and security that was its most innovative and important business condition.
- In Judea, part of the province of Syria, certain little-noted developments would later have an even more profound effect on business than Augustus's efforts. These include the formulation and dissemination of the idea of human equality, leading ultimately to modern consumer societies; the creation of Christianity and

Table 11
Roman Chronology: Late Empire, 212–476 C.E.

212	Caracalla makes all freemen Roman citizens
224	Sasanian revolt against Parthians, Ardashir takes over
235	start of fifty years of rapid imperial turnover: twenty-five emperors in forty-seven years, only one died naturally
240	Shapur I is crowned
243	Shapur I defeats Roman attack on Mesopotamia
250–266	major outbreak of smallpox and measles in Roman Empire
251	Decius lost with army to Goths
256	Shapur I attacks Roman east, destroying Dura Europa and ravaging Syria and Cappadocia
260	Shapur sacks Antioch, captures Valerian at Edessa
260	Postumus breaks away in Britain, Gaul, Spain
267	Zenobia of Palmyra builds Levantine Empire
268	Battle of Nis: Gallienus beats Goths
269	invention of Arabic numerals in India
270–275	Aurelian begins recovery: defeats Alamanni invasion of Italy, stops Postumus
270	Gallienus abandons Dacia
271	Chinese first use magnetic compass
272	Aurelian dstroys Palmyra, captures Zenobia
276–282	Probus drives Germans back across Rhine
282–283	Carus beats Persians, dies at Euphrates
284	Diocletian elevated at Nicomedia, stabbing his rival on the spot while quoting Cicero
298	Galerius wins Mesopotamia in Persian War
301	Diocletian's Price Edict
305	Diocletian and Maximian retire, naming Galerius and Constantius emperors, Severus and Maximin II as caesars
306	Emperor Constantius killed at York fighting Picts, legion proclaims Constantine emperor; Maxentius kills Severus

(*continued*)

Table 11
(*continued*)

310	Galerius attacks Maxentius in Italy; Constantine has Maximin strangled
311	Galerius dies
312	Battle of Milvian Bridge: Constantine kills Maxentius, becomes western emperor
313	Edict of Milan: Constantine and Licinius unite against Maximin II, who dies at Tarsus
323	Constantine beats Licinius and kills his family
325	Council of Nicea: Nicene Creed, condemnation of Arius
330	Constantine founds Constantinople
332	peasants bound to land; occupations made hereditary
337	death of Constantine; after civil war among sons, Constans is emperor

its powerful church, which would strongly influence the business environment for many centuries to come; and a dispersal of the Jews, which would position their communities to play a leading role in the trade and commerce of the Middle Ages.

Augustus and the Roman Peace

After Actium, Octavian stood supreme.[1] The army hailed him as "Imperator," but we know him by the Senate's title of "Augustus." While Sulla, Pompey, and Caesar all had their enemies, Augustus could claim none, having killed them all.[2]

Yet Rome might easily have reverted to political strife. Provincial exploitation remained the city-state's policy. A proud Senate and ambitious generals stood poised to fight for primacy; the army's landless city-dwellers remained loyal to their commanders; and civil wars might leave Roman lands vulnerable to invasion like the Persian Empire or disintegration like China's Han Empire.[3]

Instead, Augustus transformed the empire into a territorial state that operated for the benefit of all its leading inhabitants, wherever they lived.

Augustus's motto was *festina lente*, "make haste slowly," and the forty-five years of his rule allowed him to painstakingly construct a new order. It legitimized Roman rule, virtually eliminated rebellions, and allowed the army to protect the empire's borders. The result was two centuries of peace, the longest in European history.[4] A Roman man stood less than one in a thousand chances of dying in battle during these two centuries.[5] For ages afterward, Europeans would fondly recall it as the *pax Romana*, the "Roman Peace."

With few exceptions, civil order and low taxes prevailed throughout a realm that stretched from the Scottish highlands to the Caucasus, encompassed fifty to sixty million people, and allowed trade and prosperity to flourish as much as ancient technology permitted. This achievement was the principal reason for the great success of business during the Principate, the period of its fullest development in ancient times.[6]

Augustus (31 B.C.E.–14 C.E.)

As Augustus walked to the Forum one day, a street poet lauded him in verse and requested alms. Augustus rejected the request with a verse he composed on the spot. The poet then offered the emperor a few coins, apologizing that he could not give more. Augustus laughed, and rewarded the poet's jest, if not his verse, with one hundred thousand sesterces (HS).[7] But the emperor was also austere and lived with his beloved wife Livia in a rather modest house on the Palatine Hill, ironically the source of our word *palace*. They ate a largely vegetarian diet, wore cloth that she and her daughters wove, and usually retired early from the lavish banquets he had to host.

THE SENATE

Augustus took great pains to win over the proud, powerful, and traditional Roman patricians. Their love of power had contributed to three civil wars, and later emperors like Nero, Caligula, and Domitian would conduct bloody purges to keep them subdued. Augustus, by contrast, formalized patrician status, gave it privileges like wearing a purple stripe on the toga, and made it hereditary, at least so long as senators had one million HS and equestrians four hundred thousand HS (at a time when comfortable living in Rome required assets of at least one hundred thousand HS).[8] As emperor, he styled himself merely first citizen and insisted on standing for annual election as consul. He always cast his proposals as benefits to the patricians and made sure they would profit from them or receive compensation.

But beneath a veneer of deference, Augustus was ruthlessly making the Senate his tool, not his partner. He repeatedly revised its membership, ejecting individuals he disliked and sponsoring, even financing, supporters. By appointing officials who became senators by virtue of their office or nominating personal friends or clients, he ended up choosing most of its members.[9] Like conservative politicians today, Augustus took puritanical social positions to distract people from a radical political agenda, repeatedly proposing curbs on conspicuous consumption.[10] Posing as the champion of Roman tradition, he changed it as fast as he could.

Most fundamentally, the Senate ceded him important powers and responsibilities. The most crucial was control over the army, which Augustus gained in his typically subtle way. He proposed to deploy the army to defend the empire's frontier provinces against barbarian attack. The idea was hardly new: Pompey, Caesar, and Mark Antony had all considered it. But since a permanently stationed force had to be maintained, rather than live off the land like expeditionary forces, it had always seemed too costly. When Augustus offered to assume responsibility for the frontier provinces, including the army's pay, the Senate happily agreed.

Augustus's vast wealth made this possible.[11] He had inherited Julius Caesar's enormous properties, including many former royal estates in Anatolia,[12] and during the civil wars he seized vast properties throughout Italy and the provinces. After Cleopatra's suicide, he also took over the Ptolemaic holdings. These covered much of Egypt, the richest of all provinces, and great portions of Cyprus and eastern Anatolia. Augustus also received a steady stream of bequests, many of them quite enormous, from Romans and provincials.[13] The most famous was from Herod's sister to Livia: balsam groves at Ein Gedi that had once brought Cleopatra four hundred talents a year.[14]

Augustus also managed his possessions for profit. While the Senate leased public lands to cronies for pittances, Augustus used a large staff of slaves and freedmen to maximize the yield from his lands. Because of his wealth and managerial skill, the Senate gave Augustus financial and operational responsibility for many public obligations. He financed construction projects, helped underwrite the *annona* and military pensions, paid the Pretorian (imperial) Guard, and provided splendid games for public entertainment. The Senate increasingly asked his staff to assume responsibilities like collecting taxes, supervising officials in the Senate's provinces, and managing the state's treasury in the temple of Saturn. Ever so obliging, Augustus made himself indispensable.

State funds would eventually merge with those of the emperors, and within a century or so the distinction between imperial and senatorial provinces faded away.[15] Like the Hellenistic kings, the emperor's control of the treasury and army assured his political supremacy. Membership in the Senate became a reward for imperial service, rather than an independent source of power. The political conflict underlying the civil wars had been resolved.

THE PROVINCES

Just as the emperor's control over political, fiscal, and military matters virtually eliminated civil war, the consent of the empire's population to his governance virtually eliminated provincial rebellion.[16]

The republic's leaders had rarely concerned themselves with provincial sensibilities. Most had served abroad only briefly on military duty and as senators were then prohibited from owning land outside Italy. Governors were military commanders who lacked the time or staff to provide welfare or administer justice.[17] To the republic, as to the Assyrians and to some modern colonial powers, provinces were there for exploitation.

But Augustus owned vast properties outside Italy and had lived abroad most of his life. He understood the value of order and justice in the provinces and began to provide them with the services necessary to legitimize governmental rule. Unlike senatorial governors, the emperor had a bureaucracy to provide them.[18] The imperial staff also told the emperor of provincial grievances, allowing him to ameliorate the worst inequities.[19] In time, adjudication would become the most consuming work of many emperors' careers.[20]

By far the most consequential of Augustus's provincial reforms was to station the army on the frontiers, making border protection its mission and his personal responsibility. Although half its civil war size, the army still numbered about three hundred thousand at the time of Augustus's death.[21] It kept Germans beyond the Rhine and Danube Rivers, stopped Berber and Taureg raids into Roman Africa, and halted the Parthians at the Euphrates.[22] Troops escorted caravans from the Nile to the Red Sea and from the Mediterranean to the Euphrates, while naval patrols suppressed piracy.

These military measures, while protecting the provinces, also reversed the previous one-sided flow of wealth to Rome.[23] Except in the construction of military roads, republican Rome had returned little of provincial tribute, taxes, and indemnities.[24] But Augustus posted the army to frontiers where they couldn't live off the land, and military doctrine forbad farming.[25] As a consequence, vast sums returned to the provinces as the imperial government paid and supplied these troops and built infrastructure to support them.

Augustus and his successors sought predictable and consistent revenues to match the predictable and consistent expenses of the now permanent army. The peaceful and prosperous conditions created by military protection and improved administration made this feasible.[26] One step was to rationalize the crazy quilt of tax treaties and local taxes. He adopted the Persian practice of basing taxes on a periodic census of local populations and land values.[27] Started in Gaul in 27 B.C.E., it was famously described in Luke 2.1: "It came to pass in those days that an edict went out from Caesar Augustus, that the whole world should be registered." The rationalization of tax collection promoted fairness and reduced tax burdens. The emperor Tiberius rebuked an overly zealous tax collector, saying "I want my sheep shorn, not shaved."[28]

Urban magistrates in the provinces lobbied for the privilege of collecting these moderate taxes. Since the publicans probably kept a third or more of the taxes they farmed, Augustus realized that this measure would greatly increase Rome's revenues.[29] No doubt to great provincial relief, then, magistrates began inexorably replacing tax farmers.[30] Such measures gave Roman rule a good name.

CITIES, CITIZENS, AND GODS

Like Hellenistic rulers, Augustus and his successors valued city-states as administrative units.[31] They frequently authorized them to expand and, with veterans' colonies and other settlements, created many new ones.[32] Emperors, like kings, also preferred aristocrats to run the cities, men who had the most to lose by disobedience. They rewarded favorites with lucrative contracts and Roman citizenship.[33]

Roman citizens enjoyed important benefits, including access to the powerful Roman legal system, which is why Saint Paul could obtain a Roman trial after being imprisoned in Jerusalem.[34] In a society so concerned with status that the first question to a witness was usually, "What is your place in society?" citizens fared better with Roman judges and juries.[35] They were also exempt from the cruel physical tortures usually inflicted on both witnesses and those convicted of crimes,[36] a privilege that allowed Paul a quick beheading once Nero convicted him.[37]

Augustus actively promoted Roman citizenship in the provinces, where he settled large numbers of military veterans. If not already citizens, veterans gained that privilege after completing their service. Citizenship drew people into Roman social networks. For one thing, the only way to benefit from access to Roman law or to defend oneself from its rulings was to enlist Roman patrons. For another, the right of citizens to travel and acquire property around the empire led to far-flung commercial and family connections. In time, then, citizens became linked into durable relationships of influential people who naturally supported Roman rule.[38]

The forging of a national identity was another critical basis for legitimacy. Until Augustus's time, people had identified primarily with small social units like one's family, patron, tribe, or city. Persian and Hellenistic monarchs had gained personal loyalty, but Augustus was the first to use nationalism as a unifying element. This evidently began in the propaganda war against Antony and Cleopatra before Actium. Augustus claimed that "Antony was the miserable slave of Cleopatra, a man with no will of his own and no sense of honor, and a traitor," and warned that "if Antony were victorious, Rome would be enslaved by the East, Italy would become a province of Egypt, and the pride of the conqueror would be exchanged for the shame of defeat."[39] This appeal was wildly successful in unifying Roman identity, as indeed nationalist appeals have proven ever since.[40]

Religion also helped create identification with Rome. No clear distinction between gods and humans existed in the pagan mythology of the day. Greek gods mingled enthusiastically with Greek maidens and, just as Alexander traced his lineage to Achilles, many people claimed them as ancestors.[41] Eastern mythology took the relation of kings to gods even more seriously; Alexander had been greeted at the Egyptian oasis of Siwa as the new Pharaoh, "Son of Ammon, Good God, Lord of the Two Lands."[42] His Hellenistic successors, eager for all the legitimacy and support they could get, accepted elevation to divinity as well. Romans also deified people, essentially to perpetuate the memory of a great man's spirit, or what they called his *genius*. The dying Emperor Vespasian remarked, "Oh dear, I fear I am becoming a god,"[43] and Augustus's formal name was "Gaius Octavianus, [adopted] son of the deified Caesar."

When Augustus received a Greek petition to worship him as a god after Actium, he evidently realized that deification could focus popular loyalty on himself, and he not only granted the petition, but fostered an imperial cult.[44] Emperor-worship soon became a universal badge of Roman affiliation in an empire with a bewildering variety of gods.[45] Augustus also used the imperial cult to cement the loyalty of former slaves by making them the cult's exclusive guardians. The role was a source of pride and prestige, especially for the former imperial slaves known as Augustales, who served as the cult's leaders and chief financial sponsors.[46]

To the people and businesses of the Roman Empire, Augustus's leadership was a happy development. He had brought about an extraordinary social and political unification that distributed the empire's wealth more widely and fostered an unprecedented and long lasting-era of security and peace. Peace reduced the cost of government, leaving more purchasing power in private hands, even while it spent more on welfare, primarily supplied and distributed by businesses. All this translated into larger markets and greater efficiency for business.

The emperor died at age seventy-six in 14 C.E. at Nola, in Campania. The murder of Caesar was ancient history, the civil wars old nightmares. A ship from Alexandria chanced to pass Augustus's funeral barge near Naples. Dressed in mourning white and wearing garlands, the passengers and crew lined the deck and shouted thanks to him.[47] The Principate had become the accepted order of things, and the emperor was seen as the fount of peace, prosperity, and good government.[48]

Augustus's Successors

Augustus's successors were, by and large, a fearful and greedy lot. His wife Livia's children by her first husband Claudius were the first, the Claudian dynasty. Tiberius, coveting the gold and copper mines of the richest man in Spain, had him hurled to death from the Tarpaean Cliff on the Capitoline Hill on the false charge of committing incest with his daughter.[49] Fearing revolt and seeking the forfeiture of valuable properties, as Roman law decreed for treason, Tiberius and later Claudians had many patricians convicted of it. The most moderate, Claudius, killed thirty-five senators and three hundred equestrians during his twelve-year rule.[50] Nero, whose mother Agrippina poisoned Uncle Claudius to secure him the throne, was perhaps the most fearful and greedy of all. He exterminated most of Rome's noble families and acquired huge tracts of their land in Africa and elsewhere.[51] Later emperors continued to murder the rich and seize their properties. In the early third century, for instance, Emperor Septimius Severus confiscated many Spanish estates after they had become large and prosperous.[52] Emperors also tried to monopolize lucrative products. Hadrian, for instance, monopolized the cedars of Lebanon.[53]

These depredations scandalized the upper-class authors who tell of them. But they also constituted a very crude form of progressive taxation that translated into new demand for business goods and services. From the time Rome was fighting for its life against Hannibal, important expenditures had channeled through private contractors. The policy continued when Rome began providing welfare through the *annona* and expanded with the military *annona* that followed Augustus's creation of a standing army. In fact, a careful study of the empire's expenditure in 14 C.E. shows that fully 84 percent of it went to the Roman and military *annonas* and veterans' pensions.[54]

In essence, the state served as purchasing agent for all those people, creating a demand for goods and services that businesses supplied. Few of those so served would otherwise have participated so fully in the market economy. Moreover, much of this spending took place in frontier provinces, where military manpower, which varied from two hundred to four hundred thousand men, was primarily located. Such places could not fully support them from local production. For example, Rome stationed twenty thousand soldiers at the mouth of the Rhine, a region that could feed fewer than fourteen thousand inhabitants. It took a tremendous logistical effort, mostly provided by private businesses, to overcome such shortages.[55] In addition, many veterans settled near their last frontier outposts,[56] and the bases themselves required huge outlays for facilities and transport. Thousands of miles of road were built, while in Rome itself, the *annona* fed almost as many people as the army did.

The need for imported provisions in Rome and the Western frontier provinces created an enormous market for business services and for goods that originated in Italy, Africa, and Spain. By the first century B.C.E. the government was buying something like 12,500 talents per year of grain for the *annona* at Rome and would eventually add olive oil, wine, and even pork.[57] Most of this came from agribusinesses, while other private enterprises stored and shipped the food.[58] In 57 B.C.E., for example, Pompey as the Prefect of the *Annona* made three-year contracts with private merchants in Africa, Sicily, and Sardinia to purchase and ship grain to Rome.[59] No ancient government had ever bought food on such a massive and consistent scale.

The *annonas* supported business in another way. The vast fleets, caravans, and wagon trains delivering supplies to Rome and to the legions on the frontiers gave well-connected shippers the opportunity to piggyback on public transport for little more than the cost of a bribe.[60] By the second century C.E., for instance, olive oil from Spain's Guadalquivir River valley was accompanying silver shipments to Rome and its military outposts.[61] As we know from modern bribery scandals and lobbying expenditures, the cost of obtaining government help was trivial compared to the benefit. The effect was a large subsidy to private commerce that allowed far more of it than would otherwise have existed. Not surprisingly, then, Spanish olive merchants hailed a Prefect of the *Annona* as their patron; African merchants helped erect a monument to another one.[62]

Apart from their purges of the Senate, Claudian rule was reasonably competent. Despite corrupt aides who became Rome's wealthiest men, the emperors furthered Augustus's programs, even the sumptuary laws. Claudius brought Britain and Thrace into the empire, and Nero built a great deal of housing for the poor.[63] By trial and error they also became competent managers of what had become an incredibly far-reaching economy that was intimately tied to money and credit. The very modern sounding financial crisis of 33 C.E. is a good illustration.

Tiberius decided to save money by reducing outlays on public works. Since the government normally distributed its coinage through such outlays, this thrift reduced the money supply. As coins disappeared, interest rates rose, bankrupting many enterprises. To keep cash in Italy, the Senate then forbad senators from investing abroad, requiring most of their wealth to be held in Italian land. To raise the necessary investment funds, senators withdrew commercial deposits, called in loans, and foreclosed on mortgages—shrinking the supply of credit at the same time that Tiberius was shrinking the supply of cash.

An international panic followed, triggered by the collapse of two major customers of the Roman bankers Maximus and Vibo—the dyeing firm of Malchus at Tyre and the trading firm of Senthes and Son of Alexandria, which had lost three valuable spice ships at sea. A run on deposits then destroyed banks in Rome, Lyons, Byzantium, Corinth, and Carthage. Tiberius finally restored confidence by suspending the land-investment law and distributing 100,000,000 HS to banks for making three-year, interest-free mortgages. Credit began flowing again, and interest rates fell.[64]

In 68 C.E. the Pretorian Guard finally stopped Nero's reign of terror, and his generals fought a civil war for the throne. Vespasian (69–79) finally prevailed. He was a canny, earthy, and notoriously tight-fisted soldier, useful qualities after Nero's extravagance, but his main contribution to our story was to complete the identity of Rome with its provinces.[65]

The civil war had shown that the Roman legions were dangerously mercenary in outlook. Restricted to Italians and consisting almost entirely of the poor, landless, and unemployed, they had forced each general to bid for their support with promises of spoils. Landowning Roman citizens in the provinces, though, were eager to serve. To improve the army's quality and reduce its role as a volatile political force, Vespasian began admitting these provincial citizens to military service.[66] Within a few decades, the provinces were supplying most of Rome's troops.[67] Like Greek hoplites and Egyptians after the Battle of Rafia, provincial Romans gained more political standing. They joined the Senate in increasing numbers, becoming a majority in the second century c.e.[68] Rome had become a fully a territorial state.

After the assassination of Vespasian's youngest son Domitian (81–96), who had ruled as another Nero and demanded to be addressed as "Our Lord and God,"[69] the Senate sidestepped another civil war by electing old Nerva as emperor; he adopted the great Spanish-born general Trajan as his heir. The idea of adopting a talented imperial successor led to a series of capable emperors known as the Antonines, who ruled for nearly another century, a period that Edward Gibbon, in his late-eighteenth-century *Decline and Fall of the Roman Empire*, called "the period in the history of the world during which the condition of the human race was most happy and prosperous."[70] These emperors shared the Stoic view of the Hellenistic King Antigonus Gonatus that the ruler was chief public servant.[71] So when Antoninus Pius (138–161) learned of his elevation, he stopped his wife from celebrating, saying "now that we have passed over to empire, we have lost even what we had before."[72] His heir Marcus Aurelius (161–180), the author of *Meditations*, is often considered the most thoughtful ruler of any age.

Unfortunately, a series of misfortunes during Marcus's reign, including his leaving the throne to his crazy son Commodus (180–192), began a century of disasters that nearly destroyed the empire. Although it would revive, business could not. But that is for the future—chapter 13, to be exact.

The Western Roman Empire

By the time Marcus Aurelius became emperor, the Roman Empire had reached its fullest extent. Augustus had pacified most of Spain, but his effort to conquer Germany ended gruesomely, with his nephew Varus and twenty thousand legionnaires slaughtered and boiled in kettles in the Teutoburg

Table 12
Population of the Roman Empire (in millions)

Region	Augustus	First Century C.E.	Second Century C.E.	Justinian
Roman Empire	50 (D'Arms 1981: 14)	50–60 (Hopkins 1978: 2)	100 (R. Cameron 1991: 39)	—
Italy	4.5 (CAH 1994: 604) or 7 (Garnsey and Saller 1987: 6)	6 (Hopkins 1978: 7n13)	6.6–10.0 (Pounds 1990: 53—including 0.6–1.0 for Sicily)	5 pp (Kaegi 1992: 30)
Rome	0.8 (A. Cameron 1993b: 153)	—	1.2–1.7 (Carcopino 1968: 22)	.03 (after Justinian) (Hibbert 1985: 74)
Anatolia	13 (Peters 1970: 520)	—	—	10 (C. Mango 1994: 23) or 5 pp (Kaegi 1992: 30)
Ephesus	0.4 (Peters 1970: 520)	—	—	—
Smyrna	0.4 (Peters 1970: 520)	—	—	—
Pergamum	—	—	0.05–0.1 (Alfoldy 1988: 98)	—
Egypt	7.0–7.5 (Peters 1970: 520)	8 (Bowman 1989: 17)	—	8 (C. Mango 1994: 23) or 3 pp (Kaegi 1992: 30)
Alexandria	0.6 (Peters 1970: 520)	1 (Rostovtzeff 1972: 1139; Peters 1970: 173)	—	—
Syria (includes Levant and northern Mesopotamia)	6 (Peters 1970: 520) or 1.9–10.0 (Kaegi 1992: 27)	—	—	9 (pre-plague, includes Mesopotamia) (C. Mango 1994: 23) or 1.9 (pp) (Kaegi 1992: 30)
Palestine	0.4–2.0 (Kaegi 1992: 27)	—	—	—
Antioch	0.6 (Peters 1970: 520)	0.25–0.4 (Peters 1970: 520)	—	—
Jerusalem	0.1 (Peters 1970: 520)	—	—	—

Table 12
(*continued*)

Region	Augustus	First Century C.E.	Second Century C.E.	Justinian
Balkans (includes Thrace)	—	—	6–12 (Pounds 1990: 53)	3–4 (C. Mango 1994: 23) or 2 (Kaegi 1992: 30)
Spain	—	—	7–12 (Pounds 1990: 53)	—
Gaul	5 (CAH 1994: 604)	—	6–10 (Pounds 1990: 53)	—
Africa	11.2 (Durand 1977: 256–96)	—	—	5 (Kaegi 1992: 30)
Other (includes Britain, Alpine regions, Hungary, Bohemia)	—	—	6 (Pounds 1990: 53—including 2.5 for Britain and 3.5 for Central Europe)	—

pp = post-plague of Justinian

Forest. It is said that the anguished emperor repeatedly beat his head against a wall, crying, "Varus, give me back my legions!" After that, the Roman frontier was firmly established on the Rhine River, and once Claudius had added Britain and Thrace, on the Danube as well. Despite various probes beyond, the Euphrates stood as Rome's southeastern frontier. The empire encircled the Mediterranean Sea and included virtually all of Europe west of the Rhine and south of the Danube. Its population was fifty to one hundred million people (table 12).

The former Hellenistic regions, described earlier, still contained Rome's richest and most populous provinces, as well as some nine hundred cities.[73] Provinces in Africa and Spain had smaller populations, while the Balkan and northern European provinces were much poorer and more sparsely settled.

Italy had become very prosperous. About 40 percent of its population lived in its more than five hundred towns and cities. Rome's population had long exceeded one million; ports like Puteoli and Ostia and regional centers like Milan, Capua, and Palermo had one hundred thousand or more; and up to fifteen thousand people lived in each of twenty-five or so smaller cities.[74] The average life expectancy was only twenty-five years, due mainly to deaths in childbirth and early childhood. But those who outlived childhood, epidemics, or plague could expect to live into their sixties or older.[75]

Italians in cities and towns obtained many of their ordinary needs from markets. In large cities these operated daily. Elsewhere, market days were posted on approaching roads.[76] Commerce filled Rome's streets, alleys, and pathways. The poet Martial greeted a ban on street vendors by writing, "No pillar is now girt with chained flagons . . . nor does the grimy cook-shop monopolize the public way. Barber, tavern-keeper, cook and butcher keep within their own threshold. Now Rome exists, which so recently was one vast shop."[77] Antonine Rome enjoyed better streets, water supplies, sewage disposal, and fire protection than did the capitals of Europe in 1800.[78] But loud screeches filled the Roman nights as vast numbers of delivery carts, banned during the day, rattled along the paved streets on iron-shod wheels that lacked springs or lubricants.[79]

The provinces of Africa, with over three hundred towns, occupied a 200-mile-wide strip of coastal Tunisia, Algeria, and Morocco. Many Italians had settled there after the destruction of Carthage and with the later establishment of veterans' colonies by Augustus. Roman engineering greatly expanded the irrigated acreage, creating remarkably fertile farmland. In addition to wines, grapes, fruits, and olives, Africa rivaled Egypt as a source of Rome's grain,[80] and after 330 C.E., when Constantine directed Egypt's grain to his capital of Constantinople, became Rome's main supplier.[81] Much of it came from places like Saint Augustine's birthplace, the farm town of Thagaste. Located two hundred miles inland amid wheat fields, it had a bustling marketplace, numerous shops, and impressive public buildings, although none so large as the amphitheater, almost the size of Rome's Coliseum, which graced a nearby town.

Africa's elite, clad in the flowing robes of the day, hunted on horseback or received their subordinates at lavish country villas set amid gardens, paddocks, fishponds, and ornamental cypress trees. An inscription from Timgad, in the highlands of southern Algeria, expressed their carefree spirit: "The hunt, the baths, play and laughter: that's the life for me!"[82] Great landowners, like Augustine's patron Romanianus, also kept townhouses in Carthage, the provincial capital of two hundred thousand people. It boasted a university, the governor's headquarters, an imperial palace, and baths, amphitheater, circus, and gymnasia. Africa would remain the least troubled Roman province until the sixth century.

As in Africa, many Roman colonists followed the legions to Spain, especially after Augustus finally pacified it. Two hundred towns and cities enjoyed civic status by Vespasian's time.[83] Mining remained Spain's economic mainstay until the third century C.E.; Cadiz, with perhaps one hundred thousand people during the Antonine period,[84] was its largest city. As Roman citizens, the African and Spanish settlers could grow whatever they wanted and exported food, oil, and wine to Rome and military markets on the frontiers. When Domitian attempted to maintain Rome's grain supplies by outlawing the conversion of Italian grain fields to vineyards, their exports of wine increased, and they similarly profited after the eruption of Mount Vesuvius in 79 C.E. destroyed many Italian farms and vineyards.[85] Spain even surpassed Italy in supplying frontier military markets.[86]

Spanish farming centered on the southern province of Baetica, which exported olives, olive oil, wine, grapes, and *garum* (a fish-paste condiment that was an important source of protein).[87] Olive oil illustrates the export process. Landowners grew the olive trees, harvested the crop, and pressed the oil. Potters made shipping jars.[88] Roman officials inspected, weighed, and sealed the filled jars; and shippers barged them down the Guadalquivir River to ports like Seville, then loaded them on freighters for ports where they maintained sales offices. The voyage from Seville to Rome took about a week.[89]

The province of Narbonensis in southern Gaul, with soils and climate like Africa's and Spain's, had a similar economy. Augustus founded its capital Narbonne in 27 B.C.E. to replace Marseilles, which had dwindled after losing its hinterland for fighting Julius Caesar. Augustus later made large land grants to colonial settlements like Nimes and Vienne. Arles and Trier became cities as well.

Most Roman settlements were founded at frontier posts, mining sites, and slave-trading centers. Some became Bologna, Bordeaux, Cordoba, Geneva, Lisbon, London, Seville, and Vienna.[90] In addition to barracks, settlements typically contained warehouses for necessities like food, weapons, and armor; housing for military officers, tax collectors, and other Roman officials; civic buildings; and a market where residents obtained their supplies.

The provinces north of the Alps played a special role in the development of Roman business during the Principate. With little trade and few buildings of stone,[91] their settlements were "islands of progress" slowly expanding into the wilderness.[92] A limited ability to produce food kept them small, averaging five thousand or fewer inhabitants. The Romans would eventually improve agricultural output in northern Europe by replacing barley with rye, which suited the climate better, and inventing heavy plows with wheels, improved scythes, and a harvesting machine.[93] During the fourth and fifth centuries these improvements enabled England to provision the Rhine frontier. Still, even major centers like Paris, London, Mainz, and Cologne had fewer than 20,000 people.[94] Lyons, with 110 miles of aqueducts and 25,000 people, was the largest city north of the Alps. Augustus designated it capital of the Gauls, where Celtic leaders met in council; it was also the hub of the Roman road system, seat of a mint, and the emperor's headquarters in Gaul.[95]

Judea

He, for his birth, did not bestow himself
on Rome, but chose Judea, since he cared
among all states to elevate the humblest.
—PETRARCH, *CANZONIERO* 3

This section takes an excursion to the most studied and best-known province of the Roman Empire; more specifically, to the small and remote subprovince of Syria known as Judea.[96] Judea was quite productive, with more rainfall and forests than now, and in 63 B.C.E. supported approximately one million people, more than any time until the twentieth century. But my goal is less to describe Judea than to explain developments that would deeply affect business down to modern times.

These developments were three: the formulation of a humanistic tradition that would eventually provide the moral underpinnings of modern consumer society; the creation of Christianity, with many business ramifications in Europe from the fourth to the nineteenth century; and a series of revolts that forced virtually all of Judea's Jewish inhabitants to emigrate, creating a commercial diaspora of great importance to trade for many centuries.

Background

In 586 B.C.E. the Babylonians had conquered Jerusalem and deported many Jews to Mesopotamia. Most ancient communities abandoned their deities after such defeats or identified them with the conquering gods. But for Jews, Yahweh was the only god, so they saw defeat not as Yahweh's loss,

but as punishment for their transgressions. Their defeat and exile constituted a demand for correction.

The prophets, from Amos and Hosea in the eighth century B.C.E. to
Jeremiah just before the Babylonian conquest, had repeatedly warned
against ignoring the rights of the widow, the orphan, and the poor. To regain Yahweh's favor even exiles, in Micah's words, should "do justice, love
mercy, and walk humbly with thy God."[97]

As the Babylonian exiles were developing this reasoning, Cyrus the
Great encouraged them to write down their oral tradition, the Torah, and
return to Judea. In 444 B.C.E. Ezra the Scribe brought this writing to Jerusalem. Scribes and teachers—later called rabbis—taught its strictures for
individual conduct. From these teachings would later evolve the humanistic doctrines of Hillel and Jesus.

Nevertheless, the dominant form of right Jewish conduct in Judea long
remained, as before, the practice of ceremonies under the guidance of priests,
especially those high priests in the main cult center at Jerusalem who
wielded sovereign authority under the Persians, Seleucids, and Romans.
Judeans flocked there on major holidays, and Jews everywhere sent tithes
to the rebuilt temple in Jerusalem. Babylonian tithes arrived by caravan,
with thousands of pilgrims guarding it from theft.[98]

This prodigious flow of tribute allowed the high priests and their supporters to own the best land, so that under the Seleucids their rents supported a relaxed and luxurious Hellenistic lifestyle compatible with the
ceremonial nature of their Judaism. These ceremonial Jews came to be called
zadokim, after Zadok, the first high priest—or "Sadducees" in Greek.[99]

As rabbinic teachings took hold in the country, however, another form
of Judaism became popular. Peasants, never far from starvation, lived in
dread of Yahweh's anger at any violations of the Torah's strictures. Demanding separation from unclean ways, or perhaps from Hellenizers,[100] they became known as separatists, perushim—"Pharisees" in Greek. Although
Pharisaic teaching was humanistic, the harsh fears of its supporters also led
to extremism in defense of virtue, as a politician might say.

Strife between Sadducees and Pharisees grew, but the Pharisees also
produced startling innovations. Under the sympathetic regent Salome Alexandra, they pioneered universal education for boys, and marriage contracts
that Jews still use. Among the earliest of all protective measures for women,
these prohibited husbands from divorcing at will and leaving wives and
children destitute.[101] In addition, Hillel and others prepared commentaries
on Jewish law that emphasized the humane treatment of other people.[102]

To settle a civil war between Salome Alexandra's sons, Pompey came to Jerusalem in 62 B.C.E. After accepting large bribes from both, he appointed one the high priest.[103] That man, in turn, gave all secular power to his friend Antipater and, after Antipater's death, to his son Herod.

Antipater and Herod worked hard to curry Roman favor. They sent regular tribute to Rome and enslaved many Jews for expressing hostility to Rome.[104] Herod eventually persuaded the Roman Senate to name him King of Judea, which he seized in 37 B.C.E. after three years of fighting. One of the most interesting of all ancient characters, Herod sumptuously reconstructed Solomon's temple, created Judea's first port at Caesarea, built himself several palaces, and constructed the fortress at Masada.[105] He also made generous donations to such Roman causes as the Olympic Games and revered cities like Athens and Rhodes.

These expensive activities required such heavy taxes[106] that many people lost their land to Jerusalem financiers or Herod himself.[107] Peasants often faced dismal choices: day work at starvation wages, virtual serfdom to the wealthy, the dole in Jerusalem, or turning brigand.[108] Discontent and brutal responses mounted during Herod's last years.

Revolt

Lacking Herod's skill at placating Rome, his successors had to send ever-larger tributes to the emperors; tax revenues may have doubled by his grandson Agrippa's reign.[109] Unemployed young men gravitated to Jerusalem, where they lived on charity, even as competition between rabbinic schools undermined legal authority and encouraged lawlessness.[110] The atmosphere grew highly combustible.[111] Anti-Roman uprisings became common, especially after Agrippa died in 44 C.E., and Emperor Claudius imposed direct Roman rule.

Thereafter, even inadvertent Roman acts of idolatry, Sabbath violation, or arrogance drew furious reactions and triggered murderous cycles of retaliation. Roman officials like Pontius Pilate, ultimately convicted of corruption, could be brutal or dishonest.[112] But even decent ones like Petronius had difficulties. Ordered to erect a giant statue of Caligula on a sacred site, he asked the emperor to reconsider. Instead, Caligula ordered him to commit suicide for disobedience; luckily, news of Caligula's death arrived first.[113]

One Jewish sect stood apart. The Galilean rabbi Jesus, whose humane teachings and stress on the equal worth of all people resembled those of Pharisees like Hillel, also taught his followers to expect the imminent arrival of the day of judgment.[114] Accordingly, they ignored Roman misdeeds. By 40 C.E. the Pharisee Paul had joined the sect and reestablished it in Antioch and other cities around the eastern Mediterranean. Viewing Jesus as the Messiah (*christos* in Greek), they became known in the second century as Christians.

The Jews, however, proceeded to carry out a series of bloody revolts. In 67 C.E. they drove out the Roman legate, triggering an invasion by Vespasian that his son Titus completed after Vespasian became Rome's emperor. The temple caught fire and was ultimately razed, leaving only the base, part of which now forms the famous "wailing wall." Some rebels fled to Masada, where they committed mass suicide after a three-year siege.[115] Titus enslaved thousands, and the booty financed construction of the adjacent Coliseum by the Jewish captives.[116]

Diaspora

Many Jews had long since settled abroad. Some had fled the Babylonians to Egypt,[117] and others were deported to Persia and Mesopotamia. Hellenistic rulers, who gave Jews equal status to Greeks, attracted Jewish communities to their cities; indeed, a priest of the Anatolian cult of Cybele proclaimed that every land was full of Jews.[118] Since Pompey's day thousands of Jewish slaves had reached Europe, creating many Jewish communities there after emancipation. By 70 C.E. Jews accounted for 10–20 percent of the Roman Empire's total population.[119]

Jewish communities were coherent, and the elaborate observances required of their members made them distinctive. In every other respect, however, Jews lived like everyone else. Roman officials generally protected Jews and their communities, as the story of Saint Callistus illustrates. Callistus, the Christian slave of an imperial freedman, had invested badly for his master. He tried flight, then suicide, and finally martyrdom, which he hoped to achieve by demanding his money at the synagogue on the Sabbath. Instead, he was beaten and hauled before Rome's prefect, who condemned him to the mines for disturbing the peace. Callistus survived to become the first pope in 217 C.E.[120]

Jews also proselytized vigorously. After the 67 C.E. revolt, Greeks demanded their expulsion from Hellenistic cities. The emperor refused; in reaction, Greek mobs in Antioch, Alexandria, Damascus, and Tyre lynched many Jews. Retaliation came in 115. Fanatics known as Zealots launched horrendous attacks in Cyrenaica.[121] Their uprising spread to Egypt, terrorizing the Nile Valley. On Cyprus another Jewish uprising demolished the island's capital, Salamis. After Roman legions quelled these uprisings, however, nearly all the Jews in Cyrenaica, Egypt, and Cyprus were killed in turn. For centuries afterward, the Cypriots would kill any Jew who landed there, even the shipwrecked.

Judea itself did not participate in these uprisings, but a last, desperate outburst occurred there in 131. Emperor Hadrian (117–138) decided to rebuild Jerusalem as Aelia Capitolina, centered on a forum, theater, and temple to Jupiter. In reaction Simon, called *bar Kochba*, "son of the stars," seized Jerusalem, held it for two years and even minted his own coins. But Hadrian easily recaptured Jerusalem and spent two more years mopping up Simon's bitter guerrilla resistance. According to Dio Cassius, 50 strongholds and 985 villages were razed. So many were enslaved that for a time a slave sold at the price of a horse.

After this, Jews remained a majority only in Galilee. Hadrian's successor Antoninus Pius allowed Jews to resume their rituals and rabbinic ordinations throughout the empire, provided they renounced proselytization. Their uprisings had earned them such enmity that this probably seemed a good trade at the time. Later, though, it would impede the growth of Judaism.

In Antioch, the Jesus sect had initially continued to observe Jewish law.[122] But Paul soon dispensed with circumcision and Jewish ritual as impediments to conversion. He claimed that on the day of judgment all pagans would go to hell while only believers in Jesus as the Son of God would enjoy a glorious new age.[123] Perhaps the Jews feared the impact of Paul's threats to the pagans, a fear that would eventually materialize in horrible persecutions; Paul and his followers, for their part, were undoubtedly eager to distance themselves from the increasingly unpopular Jews.[124] They became bitter enemies.

Although Nero had famously persecuted the Jesus sect after a fire in Rome, it steadily gained converts. The humanitarian doctrines of Jesus appealed to slaves, women, and other mistreated people, while the magic and mystery of his followers' theology gave it great emotional power. Ardent proselytization and easy conversion steadily increased its numbers. By the end of the second century C.E. the Christians, as they were then called, constituted about 10 percent of the empire's population.[125]

History happens in a lot of ways. Augustus and Alexander created conditions that made money, markets, and free enterprise widespread and important features of the states they created. By contrast, the developments that emerged from the turmoil in Judea came about through a confluence of cultural, social, and political circumstances, just as in classical Greece such a confluence had led to the first free-market economy.

Augustus converted Rome from a colonial power into an enormous, peaceful, and unified territorial state. What Pliny the Younger called the "boundless majesty of the Roman Peace" lasted for about two centuries.[126] As the next chapters will elaborate, this allowed business to flourish to an extent not seen again until the High Renaissance.[127]

From Judea came the humanism of Hillel and Jesus, the church, and the Jewish diaspora. Each proved important in later ages. The egalitarian precepts of Jesus would ultimately provide religious support and moral justification for popular participation in economic prosperity, a participation that has fueled modern economies since the seventeenth century. The church became the Roman Empire's co-sovereign in the fourth century, and Europe's until modern times. Its bishops and doctrines helped shape business practices during those centuries. And the Jewish diaspora would become a mainstay of business from the late Roman period to at least the end of the Middle Ages.

But back in ancient Rome, during the period of the Roman Peace, what happened to such crucial aspects of the business environment as the development of Roman Europe, the distribution of wealth, the status of business, the influence of law, and the nature of labor? Read on.

11

Roman Society

I have written a great deal about what made business important during Roman times, specifically from the conquest of Carthage in 200 B.C.E. to the end of the Principate around 200 C.E. This chapter will focus more on what business was actually like during that time:

- the demand for goods and services, fueled by private purchasing power in the empire's cities
- the nature and operation of business enterprises, contracts, agents, and property transactions as molded by Roman law
- the sources and conditions of labor
- the status of business and its practitioners

Wealth

Roman wealth was a vital aspect of the Principate's business environment. By this time, Rome held much of the Western world's wealth. Some belonged to the state; most of the rest belonged to no more than 200,000 people— the emperor, 300 or 600 senators (depending on the period), 20,000–40,000 equestrians, and about 150,000 decurions, as Romans called their municipal notables.[1] The senators and equestrians alone owned about half the empire's assets and received a quarter of its income.[2]

Among the largest fortunes were those of the imperial freedmen Pallas and Narcissus, totaling three to four hundred million sesterces (HS). As chief aides to Claudius and Nero,[3] Pallas and Narcissus exercised powers comparable to, and often greater than, those of senatorial governors, and under the Roman system of paying office holders for performing their duties, they reaped the financial rewards. But their enrichment soon led equestrians to replace freedmen in the imperial service, and by the Antonine era they held all the top posts.[4] Senators dominated the army and retained their lucrative monopoly on provincial governorships.

In general, then, high social status led to high office and the spoils that went with it. Salaries were low, but top military officers received most of the booty from successful military operations and along with bureaucrats could expect to receive rich payments from princes, municipalities, and publican societies, among others, for performing their official duties. Public office was and remained the main source of personal wealth. John the Lydian, a somewhat later example, was an official for Constantinople's pretorian prefect. He earned nine solidi per year in salary, but cleared another thousand in "fees."[5]

East vs. West

Although the Hellenistic East was always the most productive part of the empire, virtually all the wealthiest men lived in Italy. Even after Constantine created a larger second Senate at Constantinople in 330 c.e., the Roman senators paid about twelve times more in taxes than their Eastern counterparts.[6] The largest fortunes seem to have been gathered in the early days of the Principate, starting with friends and associates of Augustus. To mention just a few: Mycaenas's name is still a byword for great wealth; Nero's father Ahenobarbus owned two hundred thousand acres in Italy; Augustus's best friend Agrippa built the port facilities of Ostia from his personal funds; and Seneca, tutor to the emperor's children, left an estate of three hundred million HS.[7]

The richest Easterner was Herodes Atticus of Athens, who lived under Hadrian in the second century c.e. His family had joined the Athenian elite by the late second century b.c.e. and gained Roman citizenship under Nero. His grandfather became enormously wealthy until Domitian had him condemned for treason and sold off his estates for one hundred million HS. But he had hidden some of his cash, and with it Herodes' father recouped the family fortune. Herodes then multiplied it with moneylending on a grand scale and property investments. He left a trust providing one hundred drachmas per year to every Athenian citizen—which, alas, they never received.[8] His properties included houses, villas, and estates in Marathon and Athens, and *latifundia* in Corinth, northern Attica, the island of Euboea, the Peloponnese, Egypt, and on the Appian Way and in Apulia in Italy.[9]

Great landowners did not hold huge tracts like the royal grants of Macedonian barons or Persian satraps. Their scattered holdings, like those of Herodes, were haphazardly gathered from inheritances, dowries, the bequests of patrons, and opportunistic purchases.[10] Pliny the Younger, for instance, inherited from his parents an estate near Como plus houses there, in Rome, and on the Bay of Naples. His uncle, Pliny the Elder, left him an Umbrian villa. He gained other properties as dowries from his three wives or as legacies from patrons. Land generated about 90 percent of his income, business investments the rest.[11] Scattered holdings suited wealthy Romans because efficient farm sizes were small and dispersion protected them against natural disasters. Many knew the sad tale of the admiral who sank one hundred million HS into Umbrian vineyards that were then destroyed in a single storm.[12]

Holdings in Africa and the Western provinces became significant exceptions to this rule, a fact that would ultimately play an important role in the destruction of Western business. In Africa, the Carthaginians had created enormous *latifundia*—agribusiness estates—employing up to twenty thousand workers,[13] and these passed to senators once they could invest abroad. Half the land had fallen into the hands of just six senatorial families by Nero's day.[14] He confiscated and sold their properties, but huge *latifundia* remained common there. Wealthy Romans could also acquire large estates for low prices in Spain and Gaul. One such was Montmaurin, built near Toulouse in the first century C.E. It had twenty-five hundred acres of farmland plus pastures and forests. The central buildings covered forty-five acres, sheltering animals, equipment, storehouses, the labor force, the manager, and the owner when present.[15] Large provincial holdings also resulted when Rome granted tribal leaders their tribal lands.[16] By the time of Marcus Aurelius, senators and tribal leaders owned twice as much land as the Roman state itself.[17] Even so, due to frequent imperial confiscations, private holdings remained too small and scattered for use as feudalistic power bases.[18]

Uses of Wealth

Private investment expenditures were primarily to acquire property. Since many public works were financed through private liturgies with an eye toward securing public office, these might be investment expenditures as well. Nevertheless, expenditures on the buildings, roads, aqueducts, sewage systems, drainage and irrigation projects, fortifications, and harbors that remain today as visible evidence of Roman activity were surprisingly small. Soldiers or slaves did most of the work, but even paid labor was very cheap.[19] For example, one of the largest public works in antiquity, Claudius's draining of the Fuscine Lake, employed thirty thousand men for eleven years. Even if every laborer received the going rate of three HS per day of work, the entire project would have cost only about thirty million HS a year.[20]

The largest investment expenditures were for slaves and ships. Most of the slaves purchased during four hundred years of the late republic and Principate were used in businesses like agriculture, mining, forestry, grazing, or manufacturing. Many also served landlords, attached to their tenements as janitors, water carriers, or garbagemen.[21] Unlike free people, slaves attached to a property were considered part of it, sold along with its machinery and animals.[22] Slaves averaged less than twenty years of life,[23] so the annual replacement rate was at least 5 percent. If Rome had two million slaves, this meant an annual investment of about two hundred million HS.[24]

Much of Rome's commercial shipping carried grain for the *annona*. Given its routine but risky nature, shipping was not very profitable, and the emperors had difficulty finding the amount they needed. But after a hungry mob cursed Emperor Claudius in the forum and pelted him with stale bread because of inadequate *annona* deliveries, shipping became an imperial priority. Claudius insured merchants against the loss of their grain ships, even in winter, and offered a bounty for the construction of new ones.[25] Just the Egyptian grain for the *annona* took nearly twenty-nine thousand tons of new shipping every year;[26] assuming total shipping needs were double that, the annual investment in ships was probably at least fifty-eight million HS.[27] Even this didn't suffice; the state ultimately had to force shipowners into guilds and make their obligations to the *annona* hereditary.[28]

No other business investments were so large. Businesses rarely needed much plant or equipment because manufactured output—primarily baked goods, textiles, metalware, and pottery—required little capital investment.[29] Working capital requirements were also minimal. Sales were customarily for cash or barter. Merchants carried few accounts receivable, and inventory costs were sharply reduced by the freight subsidies from piggybacking on state shipments. Overhead was also low, since a trading business generally consisted only of the merchant, his family, and a few dependents.

Law

Roman law, praised as "the bedrock of the Roman art of government,"[30] also had a major impact on business.[31] Like coinage, provisions of Roman law were social inventions that reduced the cost of transactions among strangers.[32]

Although many of the empire's local governments had their own legal systems until well into the third century C.E., the entrepreneurs and financiers of major businesses were usually Roman citizens or their slaves, and entitled to use Roman law.[33] As a result, Roman law governed many businesses throughout the empire's vast territory.[34] The multilayered legal system did, however, enable creative jurists to adopt the best practices of each region for the entire empire.[35] This flexible and evolving legal system determined the powers and privileges of business entities, helped them organize and control employees, improved their access to credit, and made their dealings with others more trustworthy.

Roman law operated on distinct tracks, much like the distinct civil and criminal systems in modern societies. The civil law governed property, contracts, debts, and even consumer fraud. Patronage, a customary system based on loyalty, received civil and criminal support much as administrative law does today.[36] The *aediles*, officials who had originally been elected to supervise grain supplies, administered the *ius commercii* in the marketplaces. They leased out the stalls, tested weights and measures, controlled money changers, enforced contracts, regulated prices during emergencies, and decided contractual conflicts. *Aediles* could hold court, but normally settled disputes and imposed fines on the spot as they strolled around the market with a retinue of slaves armed with metal-tipped whips.[37]

Roman law originally consisted of oral rulings by the Pontifex Maximus, Rome's primary religious authority. As in Greece, the rising political power of commoners had imposed codification. According to legend, envoys went to study Solon's laws in 450 B.C.E. Athens and brought back Hermodorus of Ephesus to help them write Rome's laws, known as the

Twelve Tables. Cicero claimed that, in his youth, lawyers had to memorize them, but by imperial times there was a large and growing accumulation of additions and revisions.

Because of these changes, magistrates would issue edicts specifying the laws they expected to apply. Their rulings then brought more changes, especially once emperors began deciding numerous individual cases.[38] Professional jurists like Gaius, Ulpian, and Papinian helped emperors and magistrates cope with the growing body of law during the first two centuries C.E. They shaped and adjusted it into a useful instrument for those who dealt with it. But after the turmoil of the third century C.E., which reduced the role of business in Roman society, legal innovations ceased. Justinian's *Digest*, a compilation of jurists' opinions published in 534 C.E. (the main source of our knowledge of Roman law), cites no jurist later than Papinian, who died in 223.

To begin suit, a citizen wrote out and filed a complaint against another person. If the form of the complaint exactly matched the kind of case that Roman law was prepared to handle and various fees were paid to the court clerk, including stipends for the magistrate's jurists,[39] the pretor would then instruct the magistrate or, in large cases, a jury.[40] Here is one:

> Titius shall be the judge. If it is evident that Numerius Negidius ought to pay Aulus Agerius 10,000 sesterces, provided that in this matter nothing has been done or is being done through dishonesty on the part of Aulus Agerius, the judge shall declare liable Numerius Negidius to Aulus Agerius for 10,000 sesterces; if it is not evident, he shall absolve Numerius Negidius.[41]

At this point, litigants needed to enlist patrons. The court took no role in producing the defendant or enforcing its judgment.[42] Without a sheriff, civil litigation could proceed only if patrons agreed to support the litigation and the judgment.[43] As a result, even a litigant as wealthy as Saint Augustine's fourth-century African patron Romanianus had to spend much of his time courting patrons in Milan to support his lawsuit.[44]

Nevertheless, litigation and legal innovations flourished,[45] especially once Claudius authorized fees for advocates in 47 C.E.[46] These developments made it safer for businessmen to contract with strangers because they could punish bad faith and get legitimate disputes resolved. Laws could reduce the risk of loss due to dishonesty or an inability to resolve disputes. For instance, one law made wine merchants liable for bad wine unless the

buyer had tried it before buying.[47] Law's relatively clear rules and definitions also made negotiations easier.

Some legal innovations allowed people to organize and accomplish
things they could not otherwise do. Four were of particular importance:
the creation of corporations, agency law, the treatment of debt, and property law.

Corporations

No previous society had conceived of an impersonal legal entity. Even
partnerships had no authority as entities and evaporated when their project ceased or any partner departed.[48] Roman law gave publican societies
perpetual life and the ability to own property, make contracts, and hire
employees; it divided rights of ownership from managerial authority, creating new entities, corporations, with powers that surpassed those of individuals and partnerships.

Contracts and Agents

Roman contract and agency law evolved with commercial society. The
Twelve Tables enforced contracts of sale between free heads of household
only if they personally made the contract. Two thousand years after the
Code of Hammurabi had allowed Babylonian agents to act for their masters, no Roman could do the same.[49] This disability became increasingly
inconvenient as Rome became richer. For instance, agribusiness bailiffs
lacked the power to make binding agreements on the owner's behalf to sell
crops, extend credit to buyers, or buy slaves, tools, and provisions.[50]

Contract law evolved accordingly. The first change was to enforce an
agent's contract if he was the principal's dependent and had written authority to make the contract. Next came the acceptance of customary as
well as written authority and, later, of apparent as well as customary authority.[51] Ultimately, the law honored agreements by agents like clients and
freedmen who were not dependents.[52]

The difficulty of trusting agents other than slaves or family members
had always limited the size and geographical scope of the ancient firm.
Partnerships were limited to single, time-limited projects like trading voyages, while ongoing businesses were sole proprietorships or family enter-

prises. Even those employing slaves or seasonal workers were limited by the span of supervisory control. No institutional or legal mechanisms, other than the state's support for slavery, facilitated the extension of trust beyond the family circle.

Here again, Rome's legal system created a revolutionary advance. Patronage, backed by law, was the first institutional arrangement that made it practical for businesses to trust employees in responsible positions without minute supervision, even if they were not slaves or family members.[53] By making clients nearly as trustworthy as family members, patronage made the large, loosely supervised, and geographically dispersed publican societies possible.

Debt

Harsh debt laws help explain why Roman banks were less important and respectable than earlier Greek and Hellenistic banks. Rome's law originally allowed creditors to confine a defaulting debtor in chains until his debts were paid. Absent payment, the creditors could sell the debtor and his family into slavery or literally divide his body among themselves.[54] The efficiency of Roman farming was a victim, since the perils of rent default kept good farmers from leasing additional land instead of having to buy it.

The harshest penalties were ultimately abolished, a measure that Livy likened to the inauguration of freedom, but the law continued to punish default severely. Men of low status could be savagely whipped or beaten, and since rent was considered a debt, this terrifying possibility constantly threatened most Romans.[55] Romans of high standing were not fully exempt. In 85 C.E. the imperial prefect for Egypt rebuked a creditor named Phibion, saying, "You deserve to be flogged for keeping in your custody a man of quality and his wife."[56] Even men of quality forfeited all their property upon the smallest default, a provision put to merciless use during the Roman civil wars. Julius Caesar, a man of many debts, introduced Rome's first bankruptcy law by exempting defaults due to acts of God, but not until the reign of Vespasian were sons freed from their fathers' debts. After 130 C.E. magistrates limited the sale of property to the amount necessary to satisfy a defaulter's debts.

Property and Labor

Most ancient societies regarded land as so important that they imposed elaborate controls on its disposition. But to the Romans, who had easily acquired all the land they wanted through conquest, it was as disposable as any other possession.[57] Roman law made land purchases and sales much easier than ever before, allowing the first real estate market in Western history to develop in Rome.[58] The only procedure necessary was a ceremony called *mancipiato*.[59] In front of five witnesses and a man holding bronze scales, the buyer would take the property in one hand—in the case of land, a clump of its dirt—and a piece of bronze in the other and recite, "I declare this [thing] to be mine by the law of the Quirites and purchased by me with this piece of bronze upon these bronze scales." He would then strike the scales with the bronze and hand it to the seller.[60] Roman lawyers extended this system abroad via the legal fiction that a Roman citizen's land was Italian, regardless of physical location.[61] Romans also used *mancipiato* to sell slaves—hence, the word *emancipation*.

Since these transactions were simple and inexpensive to make, Rome was rife with land speculation. This created public benefits by favoring more effective usage, as when Marcus Crassus bought burning tenements on the spot and then deployed his superior renovation skills.

Apart from slaves, Romans worked far less than in the modern Western world. Farmers were chronically underemployed due to their small plots,[62] and the workday in the cities was less than six hours in winter, seven in summer.[63] Although there were no weekends or Sundays off, the number of holidays was about equal to the number of working days. All told, Romans worked about 60 percent as much as modern Americans.[64]

Men dominated the workforce and ran most of the businesses (table 13). Women and children helped their fathers or husbands, who had legal control over them.[65] Women's slavelike legal status made it hard for them to function independently, and the law specifically barred them from trades like law, banking, and jewelry.[66] Women worked as seamstresses, women's hairdressers, midwives, nurses, retail clerks, and performers. A few female performers became rich and famous; more women probably achieved a degree of prosperity through prostitution.[67]

Most work was agricultural. In Egypt, agriculture employed 68 percent of the labor. Another 12.5 percent worked as household servants, and 19.5 percent worked in manufacturing, trade, or public service. Statistics

Table 13
Location/Activity of Adult Males, ca. 15 C.E.

Location/Activity	Number	Percent
Slaves	2,000,000[a]	13
Peasants	11,000,000[b]	73
Cities	1,600,000[c]	6.7
Soldiers	300,000[d]	2
Officials	100,000[e]	0.67

a. Finley 1983b: 80.
b. Hopkins 1978: 15 says 80% in agriculture.
c. To derive the male population figures, I assumed that men were 30% of the population in cities, with populations of 1,000,000 for Rome, 500,000 for Alexandria, 300,000 for Antioch, 200,000 for Carthage, and 2,000,000 for other cities.
d. Garnsey and Saller 1987: 68.
e. The number of civilian officials is my estimate. There is obviously some overlap between the number of men living in cities and those working in the army or officialdom, but the vast majority of the urban populace worked in trade or lived on the dole.

Table 14
Employment in Roman Egypt

Industry	Percent
Textiles	25
Food processing	22.5
Woodworking	17
Metals	9.5
Building materials	6.5
Leather	3
Glass and pottery	2.5
Miscellaneous	12.5

Source: Applebaum 1992: 145, with data from White 1984: 191.

about the distribution of manufacturing employment exist for only one province (table 14).

RURAL LABOR

Agricultural labor outside Italy, parts of Greece, and Pergamum consisted primarily of free peasants and serfs. Peasants either owned their land and paid taxes or rented their land as sharecroppers. Serfs were also sharecroppers, but could not leave their land without the owner's permission. There were also landless and impoverished agricultural laborers, often employed as herdsmen. These arrangements rarely changed during the Roman Era.[68] In Italy, though, two major shifts took place. Many free peasants lost their land to agribusiness-oriented villas; before Vespasian opened the army to provincial citizens, some became professional soldiers. During the second century C.E., as peaceful conditions sharply reduced the supply of slaves, their average cost quadrupled.[69] With former peasants so desperate for subsistence that they agreed to become *coloni* ("serfs") tied to the land,[70] villa owners sharply reduced the number of slaves on Italian farms and increased the number of *coloni*.[71]

HIRED LABOR

Hired labor was actually more common in rural areas, where peasants and *coloni* were underemployed and farmers needed help at peak season, than in the cities, where it was regarded as "servile obsequiousness," in the sneering words of the callow Emperor Gratian.[72] Still, freemen did take paid jobs. Apart from helping to unload and distribute the *annona*,[73] they worked in mining and construction, on ship crews, in taverns and inns, and the like. They bore the same relationship to the slaves who generally constituted the permanent workforce that temporary workers do to permanent employees today. Since the employer had no investment in them, they were assigned to the most unpleasant and unhealthy work, received no health benefits, and could be laid off at a moment's notice.[74]

There were exceptions to hired labor's lowly status. One was apprenticeship. Fathers often apprenticed their sons to artisans, even paying for the lad's upkeep. Hired labor was also more respectable in regions with heavy unemployment. Examples included Egypt, where weavers often worked for others and were paid by the piece or the day,[75] and Europe during the later Roman Empire.[76]

Freedmen were the largest group of free Romans working as employees. This was considered respectable for freedmen, who owed their former masters days of service and often remained loyal to those who had raised, educated, protected, financed, and freed them. Ten percent of farm bailiffs were freedmen,[77] and many worked for their former masters in other positions of importance and discretion. Hired labor wasn't the stigma to this group that it was to freeborn Romans, and in many cases there was probably no other way for them to make a living.

SLAVES

Slaves, predominantly men, constituted about 13 percent of the Roman Empire's fifteen million adult males in 15 C.E.[78] Most of them tended farms and animals in Italy.[79] Others worked as servants or in manufacturing and other business enterprises.[80] Most slaves lived short and miserable lives. Many were worked to death as field hands or in the mines, where for many years it was cheaper to replace them after horrid conditions had inevitably crippled them, than to feed and clothe them.[81] Domestic slaves fared better, but only to a degree. Promiscuity, as Seneca remarked, "is a crime in the freeborn, a necessity for a slave, and a duty for the freedman."[82] Many of the late republic's slaves were educated Hellenes, whose spirit of rebellion constantly smoldered. They terrified the Romans, who inflicted brutal punishments at the first sign of insubordination.[83]

As the supply of new slaves dropped and their price increased under the Roman Peace, owners became motivated to provide better treatment. Late republican writers like Varro and Columella had counseled the use of persuasion instead of the whip.[84] Later, masters encouraged slaves to reproduce and improved their living conditions. By the second century C.E. slave quarters had doubled in size,[85] and slaves received clothing and medical treatment and were removed from malarial regions.[86] By fleeing to a statue of the emperor, a slave could even force a sale by a sadistic master or one who had imposed prostitution.[87]

But coercion—with humiliation, torture, and terror the preferred techniques—remained the principal Roman solution to management problems. Collective responsibility, as when a master was murdered, remained routine. So when a slave or *colonus* fled, the authorities could torture to death his family and even the neighbors.[88] This created a docile but untrustworthy workforce that showed little initiative and required close supervision. Since even the supervisors had to be watched, few enterprises could operate with more than a boss, a few supervisors, and the workers they could watch. Given the lack of technology, increases in scale just led to higher supervisory costs, with no offsetting improvements in productivity. These constraints kept Roman manufacturing firms small, with a hundred or fewer employees. State enterprises sometimes employed many more, but, for them, the uneconomical supervision cost didn't matter.[89]

To overcome the limitations of coercion, some Roman entrepreneurs gave their best slaves incentives like business opportunities and manumission.[90] These techniques weren't new. Rich Athenians in the third century B.C.E. had set up their slaves in business and allowed them a cut of the profits, and the Carthaginian writer Mago, who died around 375 B.C.E., had advocated similar measures even earlier.[91] By the Antonine period, though, Romans routinely freed their household slaves after a decade or two of service.[92] In the imperial household, a slave who rose to high position could expect manumission at thirty years of age.[93]

Manumission was a powerful incentive for slaves to serve their masters well.[94] Nor was it a total loss for the master; freedmen still had to provide a number of days' service, as long as the work wasn't prostitution or otherwise degrading. One contract required a freed slave named Monarchia to either bear and rear a male child for her mistress's sons or pay fifty denarii.[95] As clients of their masters' families, freedmen owed loyalty, attendance, and help and had to bequeath them a good part of their property.[96] Freedmen often made better agents than either slaves or free clients. They were of known competence and trustworthiness and unlike slaves had legal powers. In addition to freedom, manumission made slaves or their children Roman citizens who could make and enforce contracts, convey and inherit property, and leave an estate.[97] It was mainly through their freedmen that wealthy Romans invested in business enterprises.

If manumitted by a wealthy master, a slave could enjoy superior access to capital and business opportunities.[98] Thanks to the intimate and binding ties of patronage, wealthy patrons were in fact the main source of business investment, which is why so many businesses belonged to slaves and freedmen. So desirable was access to these business opportunities that some people actually sold themselves into slavery for it[99]—much like the modern-day entrepreneurs who virtually indenture themselves to venture capitalists.

Manumission for the slave's beloved was perhaps even more appealing. Slaves could not marry, and their out-of-wedlock family could always be sold away.[100] Manumission and marriage let concubines become wives, with social respectability and legal protections. Although women had few legal rights with respect to property and trade, the Roman bride lived in her husband's home as his equal.[101]

GUILDS

Collegia were Roman societies devoted to social and religious functions. According to Plutarch, they could be traced back to King Numa Pompilius (715–673 B.C.E.), who organized musicians, goldsmiths, carpenters, dyers, shoemakers, and other artisans into societies with their own courts, councils, and religious observances.[102] By the late third century B.C.E. there were also *collegia* of playwrights and actors and of professional athletes.[103]

Collegia provided the same social and religious services that guilds provided in the Hellenistic kingdoms, and the members similarly elected a hierarchy of officers to administer their affairs.[104] Roman *collegia* sought patrons to provide them with political protection and financial support. Cicero was a patron of several, as were many wealthy imperial freedmen. Like the Ptolemies, the emperors found guilds useful and kept increasing their powers. Augustus allowed them, for instance, to regulate members' trade.[105] Such powers were primarily meant to assure delivery of the *annona*, an urgent requirement since the urban mob strongly influenced public opinion throughout the empire[106] and represented the greatest threat to an emperor's personal safety.[107] But *collegia* also worried the emperors, who saw them as potential sources of discontent. As Trajan wrote to Pliny the Younger, "If people assemble for a common purpose, whatever name we give them and for whatever reason, they soon turn into a political club."[108] Accordingly, when this same emperor organized the *annona's* suppliers, from shipowners to stevedores, into similar associations, he regulated them more intensively, in the fashion of Ptolemaic guilds, and called them *corpora*. Each received monopoly powers and great authority and in return was responsible for its members' work.[109]

When Marcus Aurelius granted such guilds the right to inherit property, some became very wealthy. The bakers of Rome owned land in Europe and Africa and warehouses in Portus.[110] At Ostia, the guilds had quarters in a magnificent colonnade, still to be seen, facing a temple to the "Divinity of Imperial Supplies." They occupied sixty-one rooms, each about four square meters. Black-and-white mosaics on the colonnade pavement denoted the resident guilds—caulkers, rope-makers, furriers, wood merchants, etc. A particularly elaborate mosaic depicts a corn measurer, one knee to the ground, dividing a measure of grain with his tool.[111] Many rooms belonged to shipowners grouped by their port of origin: Alexandria, Carthage, Bizerta, Narbonne, Arles, and some that are long forgotten. Another lavish building housed the imperial freedmen's guild. Three hundred at a time could sacrifice and banquet in its hall, and members met there every day to exchange news of ships, property, and prices, just like commercial exchanges in the major ports of North America during the eighteenth century.[112]

Status

The status of businessmen in Rome, as in Greece, was somewhat ambiguous.[113] On the one hand, despite the heavy involvement of wealthy Romans in publican societies, agribusiness, and commerce, upper-class writers like Cicero professed a disdain for business. He considered agriculture the sweetest, most fruitful, and fitting way to make money. Skilled professions like architecture and medicine were respectable, but he disdained artisans, including artists, because they worked with their hands. Trade was also mean, unless on a large enough scale for profits to be invested in land.[114] Such attitudes barred publicans, even those of equestrian rank, from public office,[115] and even a suspicion that someone had once worked for a living could disqualify him from the Senate. In the provinces, where many fortunes came from business, magistrates were expected to have put such activities behind them.

Romans had reason for this disdain. The low wages of slaves and freedmen kept earnings down; "few fortunes were made in trade."[116] Work was mostly menial, so punishing and dangerous that it destroyed men or was, as Xenophon put it, sedentary and feminizing.[117] Work was therefore primarily for helpless people: slaves, freedmen, women, and the landless.[118] More shameful yet was work for others, displaying a lack of self-mastery.[119]

Business also reeked of immorality. Cicero thought marketing was a form of lying. But the sulfurous odor came primarily from a cultural conflict, one that remains alive today. Markets do have ethical rules, but they differ from the ethics of society in general, particularly agrarian and military societies. To them, the rules of the market appear deceitful and portray bad character.[120] Soldiers and farmers find it difficult to see business as a game whose special rules apply no more to real life than do those of poker.[121]

Just as the city-slicker habits of modern financial types seem alien and morally suspect to ordinary people today, the alien origins, appearance, and habits of Roman businessmen reinforced distrust then. Workers and managers were usually slaves or former slaves—foreigners, almost by definition—while free businessmen were often immigrants who, like the metics of the Hellenistic world, had to work for a living because they couldn't rely on farming, patronage, or welfare. Traders were called "Syrians" because many were Greeks from southern Italy or hailed from the Eastern part of the empire. Greeks and Jews were especially prominent in trade with the Hellenistic East, where they spoke the language and had the contacts. These "Syrians" lived separately and had different looks, cultures, and practices than the locals.

Another negative was that business establishments were often dens of vice. Lightly regulated bars, restaurants, hotels, and brothels provided sexual entertainment much as modern watering holes provide sports broadcasts. Since other types of retail establishment were scarcer than today, many businessmen must have seemed partial to vice, a view that probably contributed to their reputation for extraordinary sexual appetites![122]

On the other hand, business owners did not share society's contempt for their work.[123] Many of their tombs proudly depict their trades, shops, and products.[124] The Roman baker Eurysaces, who may have employed as many as a hundred men, left an elaborate monument portraying the various stages of the baking process.[125] The one businessman portrayed in Roman fiction, the freedman Trimalchio of Petronius's *Satyricon*, takes enormous pride in the fortune he made.[126]

Like Trimalchio, many businessmen were freedmen, Roman citizens whose descendents, like the poet Horace and Emperor Vespasian, could become senators and even emperors.[127] During the late republic and early Principate, Roman citizenship was rare and offered valuable rights and privileges. Citizenship placed these businessmen among the empire's elite, legally equal to the *princeps* ("first citizen").

Nor was business left exclusively to slaves, freedmen, and others of low status. Despite Cicero's snobbery, many equestrians and senators participated in the creation and management of manufacturing, trading, and public contracting enterprises.[128] True, they normally invested in businesses through intermediaries and, since most of their wealth and status came from land, viewed business as a sideline.[129] But in practice, investment easily became entrepreneurial. Cicero's own circle included such entrepreneurs.[130] C. Vestorius of Puteoli entertained Cicero and introduced Egyptian dye-manufacturing methods to Italy. Like Crassus, he also bought and restored damaged buildings.[131] Cicero's pal Atticus financed banking and moneylending through his slaves and freedmen.[132] He may also have been the first commercial publisher. After Cicero's death, he had his slaves churn out copies of his friend's works for Rome's public library, which was founded by Julius Caesar, and for its numerous provincial imitators.[133] Other friends of Cicero's, the Lucceius family, were contractors who paved two Roman streets, operated in Delos and Cilicia, had banks in Rhegium, owned property in Puteoli, kept storehouses in the Forum Boarium (Rome's meat market), and leased slaves to other entrepreneurs.[134]

Such wealthy families maintained diverse investment portfolios and ran extensive business networks through their slaves and freedmen. Twenty-five senators were known to be moneylenders in the first century B.C.E.,[135] and at least eighteen senatorial families of the early empire, including members of the imperial families, had commercial or manufacturing interests. One, the Sestius family of Cosa in southern Italy, shipped wine in pottery jars all over Italy and to Delos, Athens, Spain, Switzerland, and France. They also made tiles and probably helped finance the ships that transported their goods as well.[136]

Business became yet more respectable as the Roman Peace allowed increasing prosperity. Writers like Seneca, Pliny the Elder, and Juvenal claimed that trade, especially long-distance sea trade, was the easiest way to make a fortune.[137] In the West, and for a much longer time in the East,[138] business success could lead to social elevation, if not for the entrepreneur, then for his children and grandchildren.[139] Even at the senatorial level, the emperors killed off so much of the old nobility—by Trajan's reign only one in twenty senators bore an ancient name[140]—that their replacements were often descendents of successful businessmen. Some became emperors. Vitellius, briefly an emperor in 69 C.E., descended from the union of a prostitute with a freedman who had been a cobbler. Vespasian's grandfather, a provincial moneylender, was said to start as a muleteer.[141] A later emperor, Pertinax, meaning "persistence," was named for the principal quality of his father, a Genoese freedman in the lumber business.[142] One, perhaps mythically, was even a merchant, an Alexandrian named Firmus, who amassed a fortune in the late third century. A huge man who could eat an entire ostrich in a day and drain two buckets of wine at one sitting, he lived in a mansion with glass windowpanes, a large library, and two legendary twelve-foot elephant tusks. Grown rich on trade with India, he became active in Egyptian political affairs and, if he actually existed, may even have been acclaimed emperor at one point.[143]

Business success so often led to social elevation, in fact, that officials repeatedly legislated against it. In 22 C.E. the Senate barred anyone born a slave from gaining equestrian status. The problem, it seems, was that freedman innkeepers were claiming equestrian status to gain exemption from taxes on hotels, gaming, and prostitution.[144] So many former crafts-men became Roman senators in Constantinople after 335 C.E. that the em-perors repeatedly barred tradesmen from the imperial service, which by then had become the route to senatorial status.

But the relatively comfortable status of businessmen did not last. As more and more inhabitants of the Roman Empire became citizens, citizen-ship lost its status value. By 120 C.E. citizens were classified as *honestiores* or *humiliores*. *Honestiores* were the elite: senators, equestrians, and decuri-ons. All others, including merchants, were *humiliores*, who eventually be-came subject to flogging, torture, forced labor, and condemnation to gladi-atorial shows, beast hunts, and crucifixion.[145] Merchants in the marketplace could be flogged with leaded whips, which humiliated and often crippled or killed them. *Honestiores* increasingly monopolized the best opportuni-ties, and business became a less attractive route to social advancement. When civil order broke down in the third century, the status of *humiliores* drifted toward serfdom and, as in the Hellenistic kingdoms, the practice of business became increasingly degraded.

Many people today see business and government as polar opposites. Capi-talist ideologues argue that business can do almost everything (even fight wars) better than the state and oppose most funding of state activity as a waste of resources. In the ancient Middle East, however, business really began and received its earliest nurture from the state. State efforts con-stantly brought otherwise isolated people into exchange economies and expanded markets. And in the Roman Empire, while enlightened mone-tary, regulatory, and taxation policies stimulated the creation of purchas-ing power, the state transferred it to hundreds of thousands of soldiers, veterans, and welfare recipients who might otherwise have remained largely outside the market system. Millions of the Roman Empire's inhab-itants looked to markets for much of what they needed in daily life, giving business a substantial economic role.[146]

Perhaps because I am an attorney, I take particular interest in the cre-ative role that law played in the business story. Roman law worked very differently than the civil or common law that now prevails in advanced Western countries; it far more closely resembled the legal traditions now evident in China and Japan. But like all good law, it proved capable of evolving with the felt necessities of the time, and, like money, this social innovation made productive new forms of organization and activity possible.

In discussing the status of Roman business, the question of business morality looms large. A crucial difference between businesses and business people is sometimes overlooked. Regardless of what U.S. Supreme Court Chief Justice John Roberts (no relation) may proclaim,[147] businesses are not persons, or even business people, and in themselves have no more morality than do automobiles. Like automobiles, they obey the driver, not the rules of the road. The morality of business, then, comes down to that of the driver. In business, however, both personal morality and business demands determine the driver's course, and when they deviate, the driver's decision becomes more difficult. The more remote the consequences of an action or the more urgent the bureaucratic considerations, the more business demands will prevail over personal morality. That was true in Rome, and it remains true today. The public policy implications are clear. Either regulate businesses well enough to ensure moral behavior, or keep them small enough to let personal morality predominate in management's decisions.

12

Roman Businesses

We know much more about Roman business operations than those of earlier societies. Except where noted they did not change much over time; this chapter will therefore treat a fairly broad period, ranging from 200 B.C.E. to 200 C.E. and sometimes beyond, as a single unit of time. The businesses described here fell into three broad categories:

- the manufacturing, primarily artisanal, of metals, processed food (primarily bread), textiles, and pottery
- trade, including retail, long-distance, and market activities
- services, most prominently entertainment and finance

Manufacturing

Of the empire's full-time nonagricultural workers, an estimated 20 percent were engaged in mining, refining, and working metals; 17 percent were in transport; 11 percent were butchers; and bakers, masons, and weavers each accounted for 10 percent. Carpenters, skippers, leatherworkers, shipwrights, and potters followed in declining percentages.[1] There were also many part-time textile workers.

Much manufacturing took place where the raw materials were found. Ore was refined at the mine mouth; marble was roughly shaped into blocks and pillars at the quarry; wood was stripped and trimmed in the forest; sheep were sheared and the fleeces washed on the farm. Fabrication took place both in rural communities, where labor was seasonally available,[2] and in the cities. Given the state of technology and the still largely subsistence economy's limited demand for manufactured goods, production remained in small units that used simple tools and traditional methods.

Most manufacturers were artisans who lived in and sold their goods from the workshop.[3] Rome had some 300 sandal makers,[4] as well as producers of clothing, kitchenwares, furniture, and agricultural equipment.[5] But the empire's manufacturing heartland was in the Hellenistic East, especially Alexandria.[6] Alexandrines made articles of papyrus, linen, silk, wool, perfumes, glass, ivory, jewelry, dyes, and much of the Roman world's silver plate.[7]

The empire's common market allowed a degree of regional specialization. Capua, originally known for its bronze-smelting business, became famous for the medicines and perfumes it made from the by-products.[8] Tarsus was famous for its wool. Another Anatolian city, Laodicea, gave its name to several types of cloak.[9] The Silk Road ended at Levantine ports like Sidon and Tyre. Long known for their textiles, they duly became specialists in silks. Glass became another Phoenician specialty after the invention of glassblowing in the first century B.C.E.[10] Using local beach sand and soda imported from Egypt, large furnaces produced slabs of glass that weighed up to eight thousand kg. As a result, the business centered on a few capital intensive factories that sold pieces of these slabs to glassblowing workshops around the Mediterranean.[11] Ennion of Sidon's glass has been found in Egypt, Italy, and even Russia. Ennion himself eventually moved to Italy and opened a factory near Rome.[12]

Metals

Mining, done by hand except for Archimedean pumps to remove water seepage, required workers in vast numbers. At any one time, approximately 150,000 prisoners and slaves labored in Roman mines, 40,000 in the Spanish silver mines alone.[13] Imperial lead- and ironworks in fourth-century Britain, primarily employing miners, were the largest industrial enterprises in Roman history.[14]

Mining was the most miserable job in antiquity. Most miners were slaves or prisoners.[15] Diodorus's description of a Roman Era gold mine in Egypt seems representative:

> The hardest of the earth which contains the gold they burn with a good deal of fire, and make soft, and work it with their hands; but the soft rock and that which can easily yield to stone chisels or iron is broken down by thousands of unfortunate souls. A man who is expert in distinguishing the stone supervises the whole process and gives instructions to the laborers. Those who have been consigned to the mines, being many in number and all bound with fetters, toil at their tasks continuously both by day and all night long, getting no rest and jealously kept from all escape. . . . What they hew out they throw down on the floor—all this without pause, and under the severe lash of the overseer. . . . There is absolutely no consideration nor relaxation for sick or maimed, for aged man or weak woman; all are forced to labor at their tasks until they die, worn out by misery, amid their toil.
>
> The boys who have not yet reached manhood go in through the shafts to the rock galleries, and laboriously pick up what is hewn down, piece by piece, and carry it to the head of the shaft into the light. Men who are more than thirty years old take a fixed weight of the quarried stone and pound it in stone mortars with iron pestles until they reduce it to pieces of the size of a [lentil seed]. The women and older men then take these: they have a number of mills in a row and throw the stone on them, standing beside them at the handle in twos and threes, and grinding their fixed weight of stone until it is as fine as wheat flour.[16]

Mines were usually state property, licensed as in Athens to private operators: publican societies under the republic or, later, imperial agents—who at different times might have been slaves, freedmen, or equestrians.[17] The ore would be refined at the mine mouth and the metal fabricated into products right there, or sold to forges and blacksmiths. Metalwares included weapons, armor, coins, and tools. Blacksmiths made the tools, others made armaments and coins. In Capua, the main Italian center for metalwork, most forges were privately owned and operated.

The first state arms factories began to appear in the first century c.e.,[18] but no imperial monopoly developed until two centuries later. Arms factories usually specialized, making shields, bows, arrows, helmets, or armor. Workers included free craftsmen, slaves, and convicts,[19] increasingly subject to regimentation and harsh discipline. Late Roman armorers were branded in the face to prevent desertion, and so closely controlled that Emperor Valentian I (364–375 C.E.) had one executed for reducing a breastplate's weight by overpolishing it.[20]

Precious metals were minted into coins in many cities. Roman coins found at Oxyrhynchus in Egypt came from mints at Antioch, Alexandria, Nicomedia, Cyzicus, Constantinople, Rome, Aquilaea, Arles, Treves, Tarraco, and even London.[21] The mints fed worn coins into furnaces, along with fresh bullion. *Scalpatores* engraved dies for stamping out copper or brass coins and cast the molds for silver and gold coins, while laborers used these forms to make the coins.

The first rung in a republican senator's career ladder was to become a moneyer, supervising a mint. But Julius Caesar and the early emperors gave the job to their slaves and later to equestrians as contractors, not officials; one third-century equestrian ran five mints producing bronze and silver coins.[22] *Numellarii* handled the mint's purchases and sales. They assayed bullion and worn coins bought from money changers or collected as taxes and dispensed newly minted coins to government officials to pay soldiers and other government obligations.

Food Processing

The most important urban manufacturing business was food processing, especially milling grain and baking bread. Bread constituted about 70 percent of the Roman diet, but home baking was impossible for most city families because ovens and fuel were large, expensive, and readily caused fires.[23] Instead, people took their grain to millers and bakers. Pompeii, a city of 15,000, had no fewer than forty bakeries.[24] Rome had 254,[25] some specializing in particular types of pastry or bread.[26] Trajan, to encourage the profession, offered freedmen bakers the full citizenship rights that would normally have accrued only to their grandchildren.[27] Many of Rome's mills and bakeries were located across the Tiber in Trastevere, where remains are still visible on the Janiculum Hill.[28] Convicts and slaves did much of the hot, dirty work. Some Roman bakers established taverns or brothels above their underground bakeries and dropped customers through trapdoors to become bakery slaves.[29]

Certain bakers became quite wealthy.[30] Eurysaces may have employed over a hundred men. Bas-reliefs on his elaborate tomb at the Porta Maggiore in Rome depict the various stages of grain processing: cleaning and sieving the grain; grinding it between wheels powered by horses, donkeys, or men, often criminals in chains; rolling and kneading the dough; baking loaves of bread in large ovens; and finally delivering them to magistrates for weighing.[31]

Bakers generally milled their own flour, but not all millers were bakers.[32] Mills were important assets. Diocletian's Price Edict at the end of the third century C.E. lists a donkey mill, a slightly larger horse mill, and a watermill valued respectively at five, six, and eight times the cost of a hand mill.[33] Roman literature suggests that watermills were common after the second century C.E.[34] Although few traces of mills survive, archeologists have found one at fourth-century Barbégal, a few miles outside of Arles, where eight pairs of waterwheels were set down a cascading stream, apparently feeding all 12,500 of the provincial capital's residents.[35]

Textiles

After metals and food processing, the largest private manufacturing business in the ancient world—in fact, in all Europe until the nineteenth century—was textiles.[36] Textiles generated considerable wealth. The second richest city in Italy was Padua, a wool center where more than five hundred rich men reputedly lived, second only to Rome.[37] While Augustus's women spun and wove his cloth at home,[38] most Romans bought cloth on the market. According to Columella, even in the countryside it was customary not to wear homespun, but rather to buy cloth and clothing in shops.[39] Homespun cloth itself was often finished and cleaned by professional fullers.

Wool was by far the most common fiber; in Latin literature, the word is practically synonymous with clothing. The finest came from Anatolia's Tarentine sheep, whose fleece was so valuable that each sheep wore a protective felt jacket. Northern Italian centers like Parma, Padua, and Mutina specialized in snow-white wool; jet-black wool came from Spain; and some Anatolian fleeces were dark red.

Linen was the other common fiber. For four thousand years men had obtained it the same way. The flax plant's stalks were dried and combed to remove the seeds, which made linseed oil. Then the stalks sat in warm, stagnant water for two to three weeks to loosen the bark, which when peeled exposed fibers to be spun and woven into linen. Dye was rare; finishing consisted of smoothing the surface with a heavy hand roller.[40]

In Roman Europe, flax grew in the Rhone and Po Valleys, southern Spain, and the French coast. Linen came into increasing demand as the Roman military presence increased in Syria. An imperial factory made linen at Arles in the fourth century C.E., but the main production centers were in Alexandria and other Eastern cities.

Cotton and silk were rare and expensive. Most of Rome's cotton, which Herodotus had described as a fruit,[41] came from India; some was from the Sudan, Egypt, and Elis in Greece. Romans used cotton canvas for sailcloth, tents, and the like, but cotton clothing was unusual. Among the most valuable possessions of a wealthy man named Stephan, who died at Ravenna in 564 C.E., was a silk-and-cotton shirt in scarlet and leek-green that was worth three and a half solidi, or about four months' worth of food for a laborer.[42]

Cleopatra wore nothing but silk.[43] Marcus Aurelius's dissolute son Commodus was famed for his long-sleeved tunic of pure silk interwoven with gold thread. Emperor Severus Alexander gave all his clothes to charity every year, except those that were silk. In the dark days of the third century, Emperor Aurelian forbade his wife to wear silk because a pound of silk was worth a pound of gold, and Aurelian's treasury was bare.[44]

Silk weaving had long been a specialty of the Aegean island of Cos where, according to Aristotle, a woman named Pamphilia invented the business.[45] But after the first century C.E. oriental imports took over the market.[46] Silk thread and even whole cocoons traveled 230 days over the Silk Road from central Asia, bound for weavers in Antioch, Sidon, Tyre, and Alexandria. Persia also exported silk textiles.[47]

In perhaps the first instance of industrial espionage, the late Roman Emperor Justinian sent priests to steal the secret of China's superior silk. In Samarqand they acquired silkworms and mulberry seeds, smuggling them past the Chinese guards in hollowed out staffs.[48] Mulberry trees and silk worms soon flourished on the southern shores of the Black and Caspian Seas. Silk became an imperial monopoly in 541 C.E., and palace workshops began churning out fine silk fabrics.[49] Later emperors confined the wearing of silk to the imperial family and its favorites, who could buy it only in the imperial store, called the House of Lamps.[50] Silk remained a Byzantine monopoly in Europe for centuries afterward.[51]

Other fibers used in cloth making included mallow, nettles, a giant mollusk (*pinna nobilis*) found in the Balearic Islands off Spain, rabbit fur, and goat hair. Ancient writers also report napkins made of asbestos that were cleaned by throwing them into the fire.[52]

Textiles, usually manufactured near the fiber source to minimize shipping costs, were important items of trade.[53] As the poet Petronius put it, "Here the Numidian, there the Ceres [Chinese], wove for the Roman new fleeces, and for him the Arab tribes plundered their steppes."[54] Military purchase orders for linen went to hundreds of villages in Egypt,[55] and the cities most famous for their woolens were all located in sheep country. One, Laodicea in Anatolia, gave its name to a popular garment, the Laodicena. Padua made carpets and tunics so tough that only a saw could cut them, according to the Roman poet Martial.[56] Pompeii, the closest textile center to Rome, used wool from Apulia that Pliny the Elder considered Italy's finest.[57]

Woolens

Roman fashions never changed, except for some shifts in the hemline.[58] Still, Romans bought and sold various qualities of cloth and finished garments. The best woolen cloak could cost twenty times the worst.[59] The rich wore togas and clothing made from the finest wool, imported from Anatolia. The wool that Augustus's wife and daughters spun probably came from his estates there as well. The coarsest wool, used for army cloaks and the poor, came originally from Italian peasants and later from Gaul.

Roman woolen factories used methods and equipment that improved on earlier techniques[60] and involved several distinct steps. These would remain largely unchanged, apart from the sequence, until the Industrial Revolution. Some artisans still use them today.[61]

The first step was shearing the sheep, originally a matter of plucking. By the end of the first century C.E. Romans used iron shears like modern ones, shaped to reduce the loss of wool. Sheep were very small; a typical fleece weighed a pound or two compared to sixteen pounds and more today.[62] Fleeces were sorted according to fiber length, the longer the better, then beaten and washed to remove debris. Sometimes this step took place in special centers with good water. Hieropolis in Syria became famous for its soft water. Lanolin came out in the wash and was sold separately as a cosmetic, as it is today.

Romans next dyed the fleece and combed it to untangle the fibers.[63] Dyeing was tricky. Dyers commonly used mordant (a biting agent) to hold the color. One was decayed urine. Roman dyers also imported "fuller's earth"—alkaline soil. Sarda, from Sardinia, was favored for white garments, while varying amounts of alum and iron could be added to color garments. The dyes themselves came from plants and chemicals: yellow from saffron, red from madder, blue from indigo, and some shades of purple from indigo and antimony.[64] The dyer heated fleece in a stone or metal vat along with the mordant, while mixing, fermenting, or dissolving chopped leaves, flowers, and other ingredients in other vats. Into them he dipped the fleece to obtain the color he wanted. This process took such expertise that dyers often specialized in particular colors.

After combing to remove tangles, the fleece would be spun into thread. Spinning wheels didn't appear until the thirteenth century; instead, the spinner, always a female,[65] put a mass of wool on a forked stick—the distaff—in her left hand. She pulled out and twisted a few fibers from the bottom of the mass, tying them to a spindle. She then twirled and dropped the spindle, which drew, twisted, and wound the thread as it fell. The spinner fastened the thread to the next wool mass and repeated the process until the spindle was full.

Weavers, of either sex, used a loom that was a simple frame up to three meters wide leaning against a wall. Vertical (warp) threads tied to weights hung straight from a rod at the top; after the first century C.E. they were tied to a bottom pole. Then horizontal (weft) threads were attached to small blocks of wood and shuttled over and under the vertical threads. The weaver pushed the weft threads down with a notched stick to press them into place.[66]

Fulling the fabric was the largest and most complex step in turning fleeces into cloth. It was a major business because all cloth required finishing to be wearable, and few could afford a private fullery.[67] Fullers took various chemical and mechanical steps to clean fabric, soften it, shrink it to its final form, bleach it if white, and perhaps finish the texture by raising the nap and trimming it.[68] Best segregated from residential life because of their stench, these complex industrial processes required a significant investment in equipment and skilled workers. Other industries supplied the dyes and chemicals.[69]

Since cleaning soiled cloth required the same equipment and processes, fulleries also served as public laundries. Some fullers specialized in cleaning, some in finishing cloth for others, and some controlled the entire process: buying fleeces, subcontracting the spinning and weaving, finishing the cloth, and selling it.

The first stage of fulling was to trample the cloth in a tub of water and cleaning chemicals. A Roman relief in the Loire town of Sens depicts a fuller gripping handrails while he tramples cloth in a square tub under-foot,[70] and Seneca mentions a dance step, the fuller's hop.[71] The cleaning chemicals included ingredients like potash and fuller's earth, but the most important was putrefied urine, which produced ammonia. Fullers set out pots to collect urine from passersby,[72] and they also collected animal urine. There was even a trade in the prized urine of camels. When Vespasian sought to raise funds by installing urinals in Rome and taxing fullers on the collections, Suetonius accused him of selling urine as a business enterprise. It wasn't the inventory that Suetonius found unseemly, but the entrepreneurial spirit.

The trampled cloth, washed many times in clean water, was finally hung out to dry. Linen bleached in the sun, and wool over a slow-burning pot of lump sulfur. Damp wool's nap could be raised by currying it with thistles stuck into a flat board, then trimmed to a uniform height. As a final step, some fullers pressed the cloth between two boards compressed by large screws, a press still used in the early nineteenth century.[73]

Fulleries required good water supplies and lots of space. The largest fullery in Pompeii had a gatehouse and two buildings with courtyards. One building had a small kitchen with a furnace and flour-mill to feed the slaves. A workshop contained six treading stalls standing above a storage area for urine. Four large rinsing vats sat on a slope, with water piped down through each. A strongly supported second floor may have been used for storing inventory. Cloth would have been spread in the courtyards and over balcony railings to dry.[74] Such a fullery employed between nineteen and twenty-seven people: a foreman, six to eight tramplers, and four to six each for rinsing, napping and bleaching, and shearing and pressing.[75]

Finished cloth came in various colors, although most were white. Cloth varied in thickness, finish, and texture. Summer fabrics could be gauzy, while a soldier's all-weather tunic and cloak, which also served as a blanket, required very durable cloth.[76] Sales were either direct or through auctions, normally to wholesalers. Retailers included *sagarii*, who sold inexpensive cloaks and blouses to peasants, soldiers, slaves, and sailors; *vestiarii*, who were tailors for the rich; *forenses*, who sold in the forums and markets; and *centonarii*, who were rag peddlers.

Roman clothing required almost no cutting and only minor tailoring. Men typically wore a loincloth, an undershirt, a tunic made of two pieces that were sewn together across the shoulders and along the sleeves, and a cloak for outerwear. Togas were a nuisance to put on and rarely worn. Women wore a *palla*, which could be draped artfully and pinned, or a longer tunic. Until the third century, sleeves were almost always short, and the most tailored garments were *feminalia*, long trousers for mounted knights in severe climates like Dacia. The only other tailoring was fancywork around the collar or hem and stripes of rank on togas.

Most of what we know about the textile industry's firms and structure comes from Pompeii, which offered unusually favorable conditions for industrialization. Set near Rome amid the largest sheep-raising farms and grazing lands of Italy, its River Sarno could take shallow-draft vessels to the Bay of Naples, carrying textiles to market and importing the chemicals its fullers and dyers required.

Pompeii had six dyeing and eleven fulling establishments, six other firms that washed fleeces and were closely associated with the fullers, and another six spinners and weavers called *textrinae*.[77] Each firm employed several people. For instance, a three-loom *textrina* needed about twenty skilled workers: a foreman, three to five wool combers, three weavers with three assistants, and nine spinners.[78] But even though Pompeii was a major manufacturing center by Roman standards, the textile industry employed only seven hundred to one thousand people there, about 5 percent of the city's population of fifteen thousand.[79] The business share of economic activity was still a small one.

Pottery and Marble

Although not the largest Roman industry, pottery making is the best known to us due to its durability, the ingenious work of archeologists, and its location primarily on farms, enabling upper-class Romans to write about it. Common products included oil lamps for lighting; bricks, which after the fire of 64 C.E. became Rome's standard building material; and jars, the packaging of the day for storage and shipping.[80] Jars contained such items as wine, oil, olives, fish sauce, salted fish, fruits, vegetables, honey, ointments, medical products, and grain.[81]

Pottery making was widespread. Clay deposits were common and farm laborers could mine it off-season. Kilns required only one operator and an assistant or two and could fire thousands of pieces at a time. While kilns rapidly exhausted local wood supplies,[82] so that centers of production like Arezzo, Lyons, La Gaufresenque, and Lezoux flourished only briefly,[83] they were portable, and wood was common.

Skilled potters were the scarcest resource. One man, even using many assistants, could make only two hundred vases a day. P. Cornelius, the most productive known potter, employed fifty-eight slaves, most working as firemen, shippers, and helpers.[84] Accordingly, a few families built considerable, long-lasting businesses by training skilled potters and keeping them busy. C. Ateius of Arezzo's firm operated for over eighty years; even more remarkably, Marcus Aurelius's family, the Afers, controlled brick production in Italy between 40 and 192 C.E.[85] The founder, an orator from Nîmes, employed three freedmen as foremen and six slaves at the time of his death. His great granddaughter, Marcus Aurelius's mother, had twenty-seven freedmen and nineteen slaves working her kilns.[86]

Although brick was Rome's basic building material, Augustus's boast, that he had found Rome a city of brick and left it a city of marble, looked plausible.[87] Imperial Rome imported vast quantities of marble, turning what had formerly been an artisanal business into something resembling mass production. The emperor took over major quarries and trained specialized craftsmen to produce columns and sarcophagi of standard size. These might be stockpiled for decades, even centuries.[88] Romans paid fantastic sums to transport huge monoliths from quarries in Greece, the Egyptian desert, and central Anatolia to their cities. Strabo described columns quarried in central Anatolia being hauled more than three hundred kilometers over land, then sailed to Rome.[89]

Trade

We commonly think of traders as entrepreneurs who buy goods at one time or place and sell them at another. Marx likened them to "the gods of Epicurus, in the spaces between the worlds."[90] But Romans usually divided trade into several functions. Financiers provided the inventory and cash for working capital; others, sometimes the financiers' slaves or clients, accompanied the goods to market; still others might sell at the destination. Skippers, soldiers, and veterans often played a major role in the trading process.[91]

Retail Markets

Most free Romans in the cities, even freedmen, worked for themselves as artisans, traders, shopkeepers, bargemen, donkey drivers, carters, and caravan leaders.[92] Artisans usually worked with one or two assistants, rarely more than five or six—usually members of their own family or apprentices.[93] Since patricians often set up their slaves in the same trades, profits were skimpy.[94] At best, an artisan might own his shop—which also served as sales counter and home—a bed, some bronze cooking vessels, and a slave.[95] But difficult times could force him to sell even his children to raise the money for taxes.[96] The shops of artisans and other retailers resembled small vendors' shops today, with goods piled on a counter, displayed on shelves, or hanging from strings. Wine was poured from barrels into the customer's jug, and shoppers were always squeezing the fruit to test its ripeness.[97]

Retail sales also took place through peddlers and at markets or fairs. Towns made money from markets, so the right to hold one was jealously guarded, and towns lobbied the authorities to prevent competition. Even Emperor Claudius had to ask the consuls' permission to hold a market on his land. Moreover, the authorities closely monitored markets and fairs as potential breeding grounds for political disorder.[98] Fairs, which usually sold only local goods (in hard times perhaps including peasant children),[99] were the principal marketplaces in Syria, Anatolia, and North Africa.[100] They often sat astride urban or tribal boundaries, allowing free access without the need to cross a border. The most famous Italian fair was at Campi Macri, established in 176 B.C.E. as an army supply depot where the Via Emilia from Rome to Ravenna crossed a river between Modena and Reggio Emilia. It operated for more than two centuries.[101]

Major markets were often held in permanent buildings constructed around a fountain known as a *tholus*, which sat under a pillared, decorative gazebo and was surrounded by sundials, cisterns of fresh water, and latrines. Goods sold at a local market in the temple of Serapis in Oxyrhynchus included such materials as rushes, wood, dung and cow-pats; fodder and fresh, prepared, and preserved human foods; wool, yarn, and textiles; tinware and pottery; and decorative items like embroidery and garlands.[102]

Vendors, usually women or slaves,[103] would typically rent stalls from the market's owner. They operated with so little capital that they had to restock themselves from wholesalers, sometimes several times a day. The *aediles* who supervised the markets kept a scale, weights, and liquid measures under lock and key, setting them out with a table containing slots for dry measures on market days. They patrolled the market with a retinue of powerful slaves, maintaining order through on-the-spot decisions and fines. There was no nonsense about fair trial or due process.

In Rome itself, weekly food markets gradually yielded to shops, bars, and bazaars.[104] There were huge shopping malls as well. Trajan's Market had at least 175 shops built on three levels around an atrium.[105] Other markets specialized in various goods. At the Forum Boarium, a bronze statue of an ox oversaw the sale of livestock and salt by the Tiber.[106] Rome's Forum provided a financial market for the publican societies' stocks and guarantees, real estate in Italy and the provinces, negotiable debts, ships, warehouses, slaves, and cattle.[107]

Since the purity of wine and oil was important, the vendors of those commodities sought to enhance their brands by owning the entire distribution system. Sometimes they grew the crop, produced the wine or oil, and owned the retail shops. Others bought in bulk before harvest, had their own crews pick and process the fruit, and shipped it to Rome in their own large jugs. They sold directly to the rich, but to common people through specialized shops in the ports.[108]

Long-Distance Trade

The value of interregional and international trade amounted to about four billion sesterces (HS) per year.[109] Although a small share of total economic activity, since most trade was local,[110] it represented vastly more commerce than ever before, and more than Europe would experience for many centuries to come. Most interregional trade consisted of food shipments from Egypt, North Africa, Spain, and Gaul to Rome, other cities, and military posts on the frontiers. As historian Lionel Casson writes: "The Roman man in the street ate bread baked with grain grown in North Africa or Egypt, and fish that had been caught and dried near Gibraltar. He cooked with oil from North Africa in pots and pans of copper mined in Spain, ate off dishware fired in French kilns, and drank wine from Spain or France."[111]

There was more luxury trade than ever before, sometimes over extraordinary distances. By the Antonine period, wealthy Romans dressed in wool from Miletus, linen from Egypt, cotton from Greece or India, and silk from China. Arabia and India supplied gems and pearls, Yemen and Ethiopia sent perfumes. Colored marble quarried in Egypt or Anatolia faced Roman houses, and Romans ate food seasoned with Indonesian pepper off Spanish silver dishes while quaffing African or Aegean wine in Syrian glasses, all while Greek statues gazed down on set tables of Moroccan lime wood.[112]

Pliny the Elder, writing in the first century C.E., reported that trade with India, China, and Arabia each had reached fifty million HS a year.[113] Although Romans originally bought their imports with gold and silver, after Nero's time they sent horses, donkeys, saffron, grain, wine, or manufactured goods like glass, metalware, linen, and cloth of purple and other colors.[114] Of fifty-four imports that paid duty at Alexandria, twenty-three were spices, ten were precious stones, and ten were fabrics.[115] Rome also traded extensively with German barbarians, who offered amber and slaves for Roman and more exotic objects, such as the Coptic bronze handle from Egypt and the north Indian bronze Buddha found at a fifth-century C.E. site at Helgö in Scandinavia.[116]

Goods in long-distance trade normally passed from hand to hand;[117] few Romans saw India, and Rome received only formal embassies from India or Ceylon.[118] A Chinese emissary reached Mesopotamia in 97 C.E., while Chinese accounts mention a Roman embassy to Vietnam in 166 C.E.[119] (where Roman finds have been unearthed)[120] and the presence of Romans in China in 226 and 284 C.E.[121] But Chinese silk came mainly through the ports of India or was forwarded along the silk route through central Asia and Persia to the Levantine silk factories on the Mediterranean.[122]

Alexandria was the major port for Eastern trade.[123] Strabo, who sailed up the Nile in 25/24 B.C.E., reported 120 ships leaving for India,[124] about six times more than the Ptolomies had ever sent.[125] They sailed some two hundred miles up the Nile to Coptos under the guard of river police. Then caravans guarded by Arab mercenaries, probably from Palmyra, would cross to the Red Sea port of Berenice, stopping at wells dug along the route.[126] From Berenice, ships could reach Muza in southern Arabia, where goods like cinnamon, ivory, ginger, and rhinoceros horn (considered an aphrodisiac then as now) arrived from African ports as distant as Dar es Salaam and Zanzibar.[127] Or they could continue to Aden, which grew spices like frankincense and myrrh. Other ships simply followed the monsoon winds directly to the west coast of India and returned the same way.[128]

The most frequently visited Indian ports lay along the Malabar coast and in Ceylon, but Roman sailors knew the east coast as far north as the Ganges River delta.[129] Indian ports transshipped many products from farther east, including huge quantities of Sumatran pepper. Rome had a warehouse for pepper during the early empire[130] and in 410 C.E. gave three thousand pounds of it to keep the Visigoth chief Alaric from sacking Rome.[131]

Palmyra was a crucial intermediary in Rome's trade with the Far East. Beginning around 200 B.C.E. an improved saddle had allowed camels to carry up to five hundred pounds of cargo. Traveling with six camels to a man, camel caravans could haul freight less expensively than donkeys, carts, and wagons, at least in arid regions where wagons had to carry water for their draft animals. By 300 C.E. camels had replaced carts and wagons in those parts of the empire.[132] The oasis of Palmyra was the chief beneficiary, since it was the only stop camels needed to travel directly from the Mediterranean to the Euphrates.[133]

Palmyra furnished livestock, provisions, guards, and staff for the caravans, some becoming traders themselves. Palmyrene merchants operated along the Euphrates River and in Babylon, Alexandria, and Persia; they also traveled to Africa and India.[134] Palmyra's cavalry guarded caravans not only along the route to the Euphrates and between Berenice and Coptos on the Alexandria route, but also along the two-thousand-kilometer spice road that ran up the Red Sea from Yemen through Mecca, Medina, and Petra to Gaza or Damascus.[135] All this made the oasis city fabulously wealthy—its glorious ruins are a tourist attraction today—and during the third century its rulers Odeanthus and his wife Zenobia briefly controlled territory that stretched from Egypt to Anatolia.

Many traders were Greek or Syrian slaves or freedmen working for their patrons.[136] But during the late republic and Principate, Roman financiers, trading partnerships, and publican societies probably claimed most of the profits. A local representative would obtain trade goods, perhaps in payment of taxes, and later send them on to Rome or wherever prices were favorable. Publicans could often use their own ships.

Against such competition, independent traders made little money. Even in Alexandria, wealth from trade was only a small fraction of the wealth from land.[137] Trading profits in the late Roman Empire were so low that one seventh-century trader, known as Jacob the Jew, took cloth worth 144 solidi from Constantinople to Spain and Africa on a voyage through pirate-infested waters that must have lasted most of a year, yet made only the 15 solidi he would have earned as a common laborer.[138]

The slave trade was probably the most important type of commerce, funneling a river of lost humanity to Rome.[139] Rome needed some 100,000 new slaves every year. While many were purposely bred, slave traders brought about 15,000 from Gaul every year.[140] They also procured slaves from German tribes, which frequently raided one another to support this commerce, and trafficked in sold or abandoned babies.[141] Many slaves appeared as the spoils of war, for even during the *pax Romana* Roman armies frequently fought skirmishes and small wars on the borders, with slave traders close behind. Yet others had been captured by brigands, pirates, and creditors. Some people even sold themselves or their children into slavery, either to pay their debts or in the hope that slavery would lead to a better life. At least during the late Principate, most slaves probably came from Spain and Gaul,[142] while Roman literature suggests that a disproportionate number of children were sold into slavery from Greece and Anatolia.

At the slave markets in Delos and Rome, skilled and expensive slaves were sold from shops whose luxurious appointments conveyed the high quality of their offerings. A Roman market, the *Saepta*, specialized in homosexual slaves,[143] while slaves destined for the farms or the mines were auctioned off in the streets. The slave on the block in Rome wore a placard stating his nationality, health, and tendency to run away. Any dealer who failed to provide this information was liable for the consequences.[144]

Unlike the Greeks, Romans hated and despised slaves, terming them *faex*, or "scum." Most slave traders were evidently Roman citizens, but the business was considered distasteful, and slavers were widely seen as dishonest. They were not proud of their calling, and few traces of them remain.

The Annona

The most celebrated trading venture was the *annona's* yearly delivery of grain from Egypt and North Africa to Rome and its distribution there. Although the public treasury paid, private enterprises did the work.

The Egyptian harvest came between April and June. The grain was threshed and dried on the farm before an endless procession of donkeys carried it to the Nile villages,[145] which sent most of it downriver to Alexandria's granaries. By late June or early July, privately owned ships were loaded. Some ships carried up to 1,300 tons,[146] but the average capacity was 340–400 tons by the end of the second century C.E.[147] By comparison, the ships that sailed between New England and Europe on the eve of the American Revolution carried 100–300 tons.[148] The *annona* ships then formed an enormous fleet that sailed directly to Puteoli, on the Bay of Naples, crossing the thousand miles in about forty days.[149] Romans eagerly awaited the first glimpse of the fleet and exuberantly celebrated its arrival. The return to Alexandria, running before prevailing winds, took only half the time,[150] but the sailing season was usually too short for a second trip.

North Africa's grain was harvested over a longer period. The *annona* supplied four-wheeled wagons to haul the harvest to ports, while landowners provided two pair of oxen for each wagon.[151] Grain ships, usually smaller than those from Egypt, then sailed for Puteoli and perhaps other ports.

From Puteoli, small ships took grain to the Tiber, a three-day voyage, and were then towed upriver to unload at warehouses in Rome. Goods could also reach Rome over a seventy-mile road, but the freight charge was 23 percent of the cargo's cost,[152] nearly 50 percent more than the cost of the entire trip from Alexandria to Puteoli. To bypass Puteoli, Augustus's pal Agrippa dug a new harbor at Ostia and built a magnificent port there. But silt from the rushing Tiber kept Ostia's harbor shallow, and Puteoli remained in business. Nearly a century later, Trajan constructed a silt-free harbor called Porta, with warehouses spread over about seventy-five acres of land and linked to the Tiber by a canal. Porta served as Rome's main seaport until it was abandoned in the ninth century.[153]

In port, *saccarii* carried the sacks of grain from the hold to *mensores* for weighing before taking them to one of the warehouses or onto a barge. Divers known as *urinatores* retrieved sacks that fell into the harbor. *Sabuarii* then loaded the empty ships with sand as ballast for the return voyage.

The Tiber was extremely busy, with three hundred trips a day from Porta to Rome.[154] Privately owned until the mid-second century C.E. and publicly owned after that,[155] Rome's warehouses were often enormous complexes. The Galba warehouse covered more than seven acres, holding merchants' oil, wine, fish, marble, and tunics in rooms built around three courtyards.[156]

The Trading Process

A number of state-fostered conditions helped make trading less expensive during the Principate. Augustus and his successors kept regulations and commercial taxes minimal,[157] while few wars, embargoes, or prohibitions interfered with shipping. Piracy and brigandage virtually disappeared, and the empire's internal customs duties were much lower than those prevailing at other times and places.[158] In addition, the operation of the state's taxation and payment system promoted the use of money and markets virtually everywhere, expanding demand for goods and services.[159]

Trade also enjoyed enormous hidden subsidies. To ship the food and other supplies it provided, Rome built and maintained an immense system of lighthouses, harbors, docks, roads, canals, and warehouses. Olive jars from one Spanish supplier, for instance, have been found in York, Basel, Budapest, Carthage, Alexandria, and Rome's port of Ostia.[160] Perhaps even more valuable was the subsidy that merchants received by adding their shipments to those of the state at virtually no cost. Considering how expensive shipping was, this alone probably supported much of the empire's interregional and international trade.

Other trading costs also fell.[161] One was the cost of information about values: the quality of wheat offered to the *annona*; the cost and feasibility of transporting wheat or other distant goods; the condition of grapes that wine merchants were buying; the weight and purity of coins, to cite a few examples. If available at all, such information could be expensive to acquire.

Commonalities of speech, money, and culture throughout the Roman Empire also helped reduce information costs. The Romans made their denarius the same weight as the Athenian drachma. They minted both, and state payments distributed them everywhere. This made valuations, purchases, and sales simpler and cheaper. The continuation of Greek as the common language of the East and the spread of Latin in the West likewise reduced communication barriers.

More frequent travel and better policing also helped. During the Roman Peace, pirates and brigands were scarce, while the unprecedented volume of trade and the state's own activity provided many opportunities for travel. Frequent communication gave Roman traders much better information about conditions in other parts of the empire than anyone had previously had, and linguistic, monetary, and cultural uniformity made the information easier to evaluate.

Higher levels of trust, due to patronage and law, also reduced trading costs. Traditionally, businesses had confined all but cash transactions to slaves or family members. Rome was probably the first Western society whose traders could routinely contract with unrelated parties and employ significant numbers of unrelated agents without close personal supervision. Peace allowed the formation of stable business networks, whose relationships allowed for increasingly efficient transactions.[162]

It must be noted, however, that despite Rome's enormous purchasing power, it had to pay fair prices for most of what it acquired. Since Roman patricians, including imperial families, were the producers of the goods involved in interregional trade, even the *annona* paid market prices. With provincial prosperity, many cities competed with Rome for trade goods. Romans also had to bid against the elites of rich and powerful states like Persia, India, and China for distant luxury goods. The Parthians, for instance, traded very widely after about 50 C.E.; their coins have been found on the Volga, in the Caucasus, and in Chinese Turkistan.[163] Their successors, the Sasanians, were even more competitive, trading as far afield as Japan.[164]

Services

Romans enjoyed many of the same services we use today:

- Art, medicine, hospitality, and entertainment made life more enjoyable.
- Education, mail, and legal counseling facilitated social life.
- Roman businesses, no less than today's, depended on transport and finance.

Slaves provided many services, including garbage collection, building maintenance, and food preparation. But other services were furnished for profit,[165] often paying their top practitioners very well. Rome had private hospitals and medical specialists in urology, gynecology, obstetrics, ophthalmology, eye and ear problems, dentistry, and veterinary medicine.[166] Augustus was sickly; his attending doctor, a freedman named Antonius Musa, gained a following among Roman senators and became extremely wealthy. He received the senatorial right to wear gold rings, and in his honor all physicians were exempted from taxes.[167] A female dancer named Dionysia earned two hundred thousand HS in one year, the actor L. Roscius Gallus made three hundred thousand HS a year, and another named Aesop—no relation to the Greek fabulist—left a fortune of two hundred million HS.[168]

But no matter how successful professionals might be, Roman patricians saw them as menials. No youth of proper character would want to be a renowned and well-paid sculptor like Phidias or Polyclitus, the creators of such wonders as the statues of Zeus at Olympia and Hera at Argos, because, in Plutarch's words, "it does not of necessity follow that, if the work delights you with its grace, the one who has wrought it is worthy of your esteem."[169]

Finance

Practically the only business service at the time was finance. Although Rome's banking institutions operated like earlier ones and were less economically important than in Greece or even Mesopotamia, Romans enjoyed better financial support than did earlier societies, in terms of both the money supply and the availability of credit.

While peasants living at subsistence levels used few coins[170] and often paid taxes in kind rather than money,[171] cash transactions were commonplace in all the empire's cities, large towns, and military centers, as well as throughout the former Hellenistic provinces and Italy.[172] From the time Rome subjugated the Greek city-states of southern Italy to the beginning of the third century C.E., its money supply was large and fairly stable. For instance, the total Roman coinage per capita in the early years of the Principate came to approximately 80 percent of the current U.S. money supply.[173]

Rome's sources of silver allowed it to mint enough virtually pure silver denarii to reliably maintain this money supply (table 15). After Augustus conquered northern Spain, twenty thousand pounds a year of gold from

Table 15
Sources of Roman Silver

Date	Amount	Source
241–231 B.C.E.	tribute from First Carthaginian War	28,500,000 denarii
201–161 B.C.E.	tribute from Second Carthaginian War	60,000,000 denarii
188–168 B.C.E.	Seleucid indemnity	90,000,000 denarii
167 B.C.E.	booty from Macedonia	70,000,000+ denarii
201 B.C.E.–200 C.E.	output of silver mines in Spain	100,000,000+ denarii per year[a]

Source: Randsborg 1991: 126 (fig. 71) and Jones 1974: 114.
a. Badian 1972: 34.

its mines, joined later by those of Romania, furnished the eight-gram gold aureus as well.[174] This was used for international trade, the payment of taxes, and other large payments.

More importantly, the steady gold supply allowed Rome to anchor its entire coinage with the aureus, whose gold content fell only slightly over time. Caesar's aureus had 8.2 grams of gold, Augustus's 7.8, and Nero's 7.25. Although the silver content of the denarius was halved by Trajan's reign (98–117),[175] it held its value because 25 denarii could always buy one aureus.[176] Hence there was little inflation: military pay, for instance, increased only slightly throughout this period.[177]

This ample money supply lubricated trade and markets. According to Cicero, plenty of money was available at 6 percent interest,[178] and the rates for reliable borrowers never got much higher.[179] Interest rates remained at 4–6 percent in Rome and 8–12 percent in the provinces until the third century C.E.[180]

Credit

Credit was part of many business transactions: 308 of over 900 business contracts listed in Egypt in 45–47 C.E. involved credit,[181] as when shop-keepers provided goods in return for a mere deposit, with the balance due later.[182] Others who provided credit included money changers, pawnbrokers, silver specialists in the markets, patrician financiers, publicans, the state, civic treasuries, temples, foundations, moneylending partnerships, loan clubs, and individuals.

Roman bankers, silver dealers, and money changers operated like their Athenian predecessors, except that they largely served plebeian families and market vendors.[183] As in Athens, bankers were slaves, freedmen, and foreigners; in Rome, often Greeks from Syria. In Gaul, "Syrian" was the common term for banker.[184]

The most respectable bankers were the silver dealers, *argentarii*, who served as agents for the government mints in exchanging new for old coins and served as notaries to verify payments. People would pay debts in front of *argentarii*, who recorded payments in an account book and testified to them if necessary.[185] In the provinces, *argentarii* served as financial agents for both the government and private clients. Cicero's friend Atticus had one pay his son's allowance while he was at university in Athens.[186]

Money changers, who changed and loaned money in the marketplace and made tiny consumer loans secured by pawned goods,[187] were licensed and regulated, with most of their fees established by law.[188] Since people regularly clipped coins to adjust their value, the weighing, assaying, and valuing of coins was an ongoing task. In the markets, coins had to be exchanged: gold for silver, silver for bronze, bronze for copper, Roman for Greek, etc. Some money changers issued their own currency, bags of small coins with a specified value.[189] Like silver dealers, money changers had to safeguard their own coin inventory and became depositories and paymasters for others. One at Pompeii held deposits of thirty-eight thousand HS.[190]

Like the Greeks, Roman bankers would make book transfers from payer to recipient when both were clients.[191] This was very convenient for people frequenting the same marketplace. But nothing like the Ptolemaic branch banking system existed, nor did any system for handling book transfers between banks, like today's clearinghouses. Since amounts due from one banker to another were considered debts, and bankers were *humiliores* whose default would trigger savage punishment, the risks of operating clearinghouses weren't worth the potential fees.

But grander entities—such as publican societies, patrician families, and the state itself—did use book transfers to move cash over long distances.[192] Since so much of the empire's credit came from Rome and had to be repaid there, many international debts could be settled simply by transferring coins within its seven hills.[193] Multinational publican societies, whose agents often held huge sums of cash, provided a service similar to that of ATMs.[194] Someone needing funds could present an authorization letter and a passwordlike seal or token of identification and receive cash, with the amount to be deducted from his account in Rome or, if he was on government business, from what the society owed to the government.[195] The same could happen in reverse: money deposited in Alexandria could be retrieved in Rome.[196]

On the whole, bankers played less of a financial role than their Hellenistic counterparts.[197] Instead, the empire's elite provided most of the late republican and Principate credit. One reason was that loans were more secure: Roman law strongly supported creditors, debtors routinely paid interest even on late rent and dowries,[198] and creditors could readily sell their loans.[199] Roman creditors posted information about debtors on the *columna Moenia*.[200] Patronage gave the rich a trustworthy way to extend credit through their clients and dependents.[201] Slaves, freedmen, relatives, and other clients often received investment funds from their patrons. For slaves, it might be a small sum, known as a *peculium*, to start a business. Those who prospered could pay back the patron, invest the profits, and ultimately buy their freedom and retain the business for themselves.

For instance, in 37 C.E. an imperial freedman gave his slave ten thousand HS to lend to a food broker. The slave added three thousand more HS of his own. A year later, the broker paid off the imperial freedman and one thousand HS of the slave's loan. The slave extended the unpaid balance for another year at 12 percent interest. The following year, he extended the loan a final thirty days, with a late penalty of 1 percent of the balance per day after that.[202]

Most investments were secured, as when a Roman centurion living at Ein Gedi, on the Dead Sea, made a large, short-term loan to one Judah, who later died in the Bar Kochba uprising. It appears that the same lawyers were writing security agreements then as now:

> In the consulship of Manius Acilius Glabrio and Torquatus Tebanianus one day before the *nones* of May, in En-gedi village of lord Caesar, Judah son of Elazar Kthousion, En-gedian, to Magonius Valens, centurion of Cohors I Miliaria Thracum, greetings. I acknowledge that I have received and owe to you in loan 60 *denarii* of Tyrian silver, which are 15 staters, upon hypothec of the courtyard in En-gedi belonging to my father Elzaar Kthousion . . . which money I will repay to you on the kalends of January in the same year during the said consulship, and the interest of the said money I will deliver to you monthly at the rate of one denarius per hundred *denarii* per month. If I do not repay you on the specified terminal date as aforewritten, you will have the right to acquire, use, sell and administer the said hypothec without any opposition.[203]

Entertainment

Entertainment was the largest service business, and prostitution its most frequent form. Prostitution was evidently as common to the many inns and taverns that fronted Roman roads and crowded city centers as cable TV is to hotels and motels today.[204] The word *fornicate* derives from the Latin for "arch" because of the trade under the arches of the Forum.[205] Prior to Christianity, Romans had no prudery about paid sex, and the authorities derived important tax revenues from it. Innkeepers, often women, were assumed to be prostitutes, madams, or witches. Only in very late Roman times did church disapproval begin to impinge on prostitution, as when the prostitutes of Palermo rioted against the local bishop's appointment as Imperial Inspector of the Brothels in 630 c.e., apparently fearful that he would hurt business.[206]

In addition to taverns and the arches of the Forum, there were many other places that offered public entertainment.[207] The empire had more than three hundred amphitheaters, not to mention private theaters in senatorial homes. Fourth-century Rome had four theaters, a concert hall, five amphitheaters with attached gladiatorial schools, four circuses for racing chariots, four staging places for mock naval battles, and one athletic stadium. The largest amphitheater, Rome's Coliseum, could seat 45,000–55,000 people, while the Circus Maximus held up to 350,000 for chariot races.[208] In 27 c.e. as many as 50,000 people perished when a wooden amphitheater in the Roman suburb of Fidnae collapsed. Its owner, a freedman, had apparently cut corners on its construction, leading the Senate to confine the construction and operation of public venues to men of equestrian or higher rank.

Holidays provided the usual occasion for a show. In addition to gladiatorial combats and chariot racing, performing companies staged mimes, dramas, comedies, dances, and athletic events. Mime shows combined lewd comedy with spectacular violence, not unlike Hollywood's action films. Also popular were X-rated erotica, known as Milesian tales in honor of Miletus's celebrated prostitutes. *The Golden Ass* by Apuleus is a surviving example.

The performing companies were business firms that investors or performers owned in partnership, forerunners of Disney or Time Warner. Performers included partners, employees, and slaves. Their shows, free to the public, were usually financed by men holding or seeking office. This expense consumed a great deal of upper-class wealth.[209] In the late Roman period, Senator Symmachus spent two thousand pounds of gold to subsidize games during his son's year as consul.[210]

Chariot races had been popular since Homer's day. Organized into red, blue, yellow, and green factions in the fourth century b.c.e., chariot stables still existed in twelfth-century Constantinople, some fifteen hundred years later. The faction masters, some of high rank, others former charioteers, would negotiate fees with the praetors who sponsored chariot racing in Rome, much as sports agents negotiate contracts with professional teams today. Indeed, professional sports owners might do well to recall the unfortunate Praetor Fabricius Veiento, who tried to substitute dog races when he found the chariot-racing fees too exorbitant.

Stables employed as many as 250 people, including a treasurer, several foremen, stable masters and their assistants, charioteers, men to operate the starting gates, and grooms to hold the horses in them, throw water to cool the horses as they ran, and ride alongside the chariots to guide and encourage them. Top charioteers became celebrities. At the funeral of one, a fan threw himself on the burning pyre. Gaius Appuleius Diocles, who won 34 percent of his several thousand races over a twenty-year career in the second century C.E., accumulated over thirty-five million HS, more than any but the wealthiest senators.[211]

Emperors were wary of the charioteers and their stables because their passionate fans could easily become threatening mobs. During crises in the third century C.E., not daring to ban chariot racing, they bought control of the stables instead. Imperial ownership terminated chariot racing as a business, but fans still menaced the emperor's life on occasion. In 529 C.E. Constantinople, as the deeply unpopular Emperor Justinian attended the races with his wife Theodora, the crowd in the hippodrome began chanting "Nika!" meaning "conquer," and acclaimed a new emperor. Units of the imperial guard joined in, and Justinian prepared to flee. But Theodora, once Constantinople's leading courtesan, declared: "If you, my Lord, wish to save your skin, you will have no difficulty in doing so. We are rich, there is the sea, there too are our ships . . . as for me, I stand by the ancient saying: the purple is the noblest winding-sheet."[212] With that, troops attacked the mob. Half of Constantinople and thirty thousand people perished before order was restored.[213]

The most spectacular entertainments of all were gladiatorial combats. Originally funeral sacrifices, gladiatorial battles became public entertainment in the second century B.C.E. While some gladiators were freemen, most were slaves, too valuable to fight to the death. That fate was for condemned criminals who had been sentenced to fight each other or wild animals to death. The capture and delivery of wild animals for these popular features became a business in its own right.

Private gladiatorial schools housed, fed, and trained huge numbers of gladiators. The school of Gaius trained twenty thousand gladiators at a time. Prominent men often owned these schools. Cicero and his pal Atticus owned a troupe. Augustus inherited Julius Caesar's and owned others in Gaul and Spain. Caligula established one, and Domitian had three.[214]

Gladiators performed in troupes, which they sometimes owned, that included wild animals and their "hunters," along with coaches, masseurs, dieticians, and physicians.[215] Gladiators were the pop stars of the day, with enormous sex appeal and flocks of groupies. Marcus Aurelius's wife Faustina once confessed her lust for a certain gladiator whom she had passed on the street. In response, the great stoic had the gladiator killed and made Faustina bathe in the blood before he would return to her bed.[216] Not coincidentally, perhaps, their son Commodus fancied himself a gladiator. A terrible emperor in the mold of Nero and Domitian, he was assassinated by his wrestling coach.

The slaves and freedmen who managed gladiatorial troupes would negotiate prices with the spectacle's financiers. Performers, even slaves, normally kept a portion of the fee if they won, and freedom might follow especially good performances. The night before a performance, all the gladiators, even the condemned prisoners, paraded through town to advertise the spectacle and then ate a banquet in front of their fans. The next morning, they marched into the arena. The early fights pitted animals against men or each other in various combinations and scenarios. The condemned criminals met their fates around lunchtime, and the afternoons were devoted to gladiatorial combat. The shows became increasingly bizarre, with an almost unimaginable variety of violent and sadistic displays: "Scenes from history, mythology, and literature were also enacted: one man's arm was held over a fire to represent Mucius Scaevola; the castration of Atys [consort of Mithra] was reproduced, as was the living pyre of Hercules on Mount Oeta; and the mythological union between Pasiphae and the bull became a reality."[217]

The church tried to stop gladiatorial shows, but the effort took nearly a century to succeed. The emperor finally banned them in the fifth century after a monk named Telemachus was stoned to death for trying to stop one.[218]

I began this book wondering how a Roman blacksmith shop differed from the small manufacturing business that I was running. Not much, it turns out. My company's workers were not slaves, but many jobs were routine and unskilled; Roman middle managers supervised with whips, and mine sometimes wished to. My company had machinery, computers, sophisticated accounting, and certain financial services that sped work or reduced labor, but the basic processes were what Romans would have used.

More generally, Roman consumers bought the same kind of goods and services that modern ones do, albeit with many fewer choices of color, quality, and function in each category. For instance, clothing was as important then as now, but of course ours is much more varied and effective. More revolutionary have been transformations in transportation and communication, which have become modern necessities. There are, of course, new categories of consumption like education, documentation, and electronic entertainment, as well as those resulting from the commercialization of formerly private (or slave-provided) services like hairdressing.

Much greater differences appear in the areas of wealth creation and business-to-business sales. Ancient businesses created some wealth by stimulating demand and reducing the cost of supplying it. But most ancient wealth consisted of the natural resources and agricultural production needed for food, clothing, and shelter. The human need for those requirements was the overwhelming source of demand; and even in the Greek, Hellenistic, and Roman economies, the exchange of labor for food constituted the principal economic transaction. Moreover, given the Malthusian nature of society, the amount of wealth changed very slowly, and its pursuit was a zero-sum game: more for some meant less for others.

In the modern world, by contrast, desires constantly change and expand with the rapidly mutating array of goods and services. Modern finance has expanded the purchasing power necessary to translate those desires into a demand for sales. And the resources necessary to satisfy this demand have drastically changed as well. Chief among those resources today is human imagination, made valuable by intangibles like skills, education, intellectual property, and the quality of institutions. In modern economies such intangibles represent fully 80 percent of the productive resources,[219] while labor and land—minor inputs today—constituted the inputs in ancient economies. Moreover, unlike the ancient world with its Malthusian constraints, modern wealth per capita constantly grows; hence, the acquisition of wealth has ceased to be a zero-sum game.

Another important difference between ancient and modern business is the extent of business-to-business exchange. Transport aside, the sale of goods and services to other businesses played a subsidiary role in the ancient economy. While credit played a significant role in the ancient economy and operated along the same principles as modern credit, it had nothing like its modern importance, largely because modern institutions, including laws, government regulation, credit markets, probability theory, and massive computational capabilities have greatly increased the trustworthiness of repayment.[220] In addition to finance, modern businesses buy many other services, helping the service sector to account for more than 60 percent of U.S. gross domestic product.[221]

13

The Downfall of Ancient Business

Here I will discuss the disintegration of business in Western Europe during the third century and why it could not recover even as the Roman Empire returned to great prosperity later on.[1] Business survived, however, in Africa and the eastern half of the Roman Empire. Byzantium and the Arab forces that triumphed in the seventh century therefore inherited an urban system of money, markets, and entrepreneurial business that it would return to Europe during the early Renaissance.

End of the Antonines

In 165 c.e., four years after Marcus Aurelius took office, Roman legions returned from war against the Parthians in Mesopotamia bearing the plague, probably smallpox. Recurring for decades, it killed between one quarter and one third of the population.[2] As Romans reeled, German raiders crossed the Danube, attacked Greece, and even reached Italy. Berbers from North Africa plundered Spain. Marcus, who had never before seen an army much less commanded one, would spend his entire imperial career at war.[3]

The economic toll of plague, invasion, and war was enormous. Silver mines in southern Spain and gold mines in Dacia were abandoned, while other Spanish mines that once yielded half of Rome's gold began to decline.[4] Marcus had inherited a treasury of 2,700,000,000 sesterces (HS), but the expense of the wars, the loss of tax revenue due to the plague, and faltering mints forced him to auction off crown jewels and imperial furnishings.[5] The addled son who succeeded him squandered yet more money on games and extravagances until the Praetorian Guard arranged his assassination in 193.[6]

The Severan Dynasty (193–235): Devaluation and Desertion

The Praetorian Guard then auctioned off the emperorship. Pertinax, the son of a wealthy Genoese timber merchant, won by promising the Praetorian Guard the same bonus that Marcus had given upon his elevation, but of course the treasury was now practically bare. He could not pay up and was killed as well. Civil war followed, ultimately won by Septimius Severus (193–211).

Homeland security had suddenly become Rome's priority. The troops realized that people would pay any price for it, and the Praetorian Guard's auction foreshadowed decades of increasing military demands. Septimius instructed his family, "Be of one mind: enrich the soldiers; trouble about nothing else."[7] He raised soldiers' wages from three to five hundred denarii per year, the first increase in a century, and his son Caracalla (211–217) granted 50 percent more.[8] They also enlarged the army by 50 percent, primarily to fight discretionary wars against the Parthians, who were ancient enemies of the Severan family's Syrian fiefdom, the city-state of Emesa.[9]

These wars gained little, but so weakened the Hellenized Parthians, who had been fairly peaceable neighbors, that by 227 they fell to a very aggressive Persian dynasty, the Sasanians. Conjuring up the glory of their alleged ancestors Cyrus and Darius, Sasanian rulers persistently tried to expand their empire, often at Rome's expense. Tellingly, three small, empty chairs sat below their throne: one for the emperor of China, one for the khan of the steppe nomads, and one for the emperor of Rome.[10]

More immediately, Severan military expenses greatly increased imperial outlays just as the disheartening consequences of the plague and dwindling supplies of silver and gold were reducing revenues. In response, Septimius confiscated many private mines and other properties. Caracalla granted Roman citizenship, and the obligation to pay an inheritance tax, to everyone except slaves. But since about 90 percent of imperial revenues came from property taxes, which were already maximized,[11] these measures could not balance the budget. So the Severans did what the Ptolemies had done when they ran out of silver: they began to debase the coinage—that is, to pay soldiers and other suppliers in coins of reduced precious metal content.

Silver in the denarius had declined only from 99 percent to 75 percent in the 150 years between Augustus and Marcus Aurelius, but Septimius reduced it to 50 percent, and Caracalla reduced it further. Rapid debasement initiated an accelerating and self-reinforcing process. Mints obtained much of their silver from worn coins exchanged for new ones. But now people hoarded the older ones and starved the mints,[12] forcing new issues to contain even less silver. As gold mines disappeared, the story of gold coins was similar.

Debasement ruined government contractors. They could not survive on the true value of the payments they received and in the absence of developed credit markets had no way to hedge the value of future payments through option purchases. Publican societies had to cease tax farming during the Severan era and soon disappeared completely.[13] More generally, debasement favored barter over cash in virtually all exchanges, reducing market activity and business transactions throughout the economy.

As government contractors and markets disappeared, the supply system that had maintained Roman military units on the frontiers broke down. Again the Severans tried palliatives. Septimius lifted the traditional prohibition against troops raising their own food. Some generals minted their own coins to purchase supplies. Most often, however, frontier units relocated to more productive areas and began living off the land, while in-kind payments, rather than money, became common even for taxes.[14]

The relocation of troops provoked repeated strikes and riots, even in rich provinces like Egypt and Asia.[15] But relocation proved especially damaging to the cities of Western Europe, whose dank hinterlands could hardly sustain their own populations. As military requisitions and pillaging reduced local food supplies further,[16] peasant farmers began deserting the land for the wilds or to join gangs of brigands.[17] By midcentury, according to archeological surveys, only 57 percent of Italy's farms were occupied, 69 percent of southern Gaul's, 45 percent of northern Gaul's, 61 percent of northern Spain's, and 43 percent of Belgica's.[18] The cities of those provinces, their transport imperiled by outlaws and their economies hobbled by the collapse of the military supply chain, gradually imploded.[19]

The Later Third Century

In 235 troops assassinated the last Severan emperor and, hoping for bonuses, acclaimed a sergeant named Thrax as emperor. Sasanians, German raiding parties, and pirates everywhere launched attacks.[20] Twenty-five emperors would come and go during the next fifty years.[21] The low point was probably Valerian's (253–260) horrible death. The Sasanians had sacked Antioch, killing or enslaving many of its residents. Then, as the Sasanian king's inscription at Bishapur in Iran still boasts, "Valerian the Caesar came against us with 70,000 men . . . and we fought a great battle against him, and we took Valerian the Caesar with our own hands. . . . And the provinces of Syria, Cilicia and Cappadocia we burnt with fire, we ravaged and conquered them, taking their peoples captive."

The Sasanian king flayed Valerian alive and covered a footstool with his skin.[22] Such disasters also precipitated revolts and secessions within the empire, one of which took away several Western provinces for nearly two decades. Perhaps most memorable was the secession of virtually the entire Fertile Crescent under the gifted and erudite Zenobia, widow of Palmyra's ruler. Ultimately captured, she was led to Rome in golden chains and retired to a villa in Tivoli.[23]

Meanwhile, monetary problems continued. A bushel of wheat cost three denarii in 100 C.E., ten denarii in 200, two hundred denarii in 270, and ten thousand denarii in 314.[24] By the late third century, the denarius was only 5 percent silver, and gold had largely disappeared.[25] In the fourth century even the value of brass sesterces plummeted forty-five-fold as their brass content diminished; silver coins were rarely issued.[26] These devaluations prevented any revival of government contracting.[27]

In its place, the emperors were slowly building an in-kind taxation and supply system based on authoritarian commands rather than market incentives, an undertaking symbolized by Septimius Severus replacing the old imperial title of *princeps* ("first citizen") with *dominus* ("master").[28] A growing imperial bureaucracy became capable of gathering and distributing in-kind tax payments, operating state factories to produce armaments and many other goods, and, like the Ptolemies, assigning monopoly powers and privileges to guilds in return for their services at its prices. By the century's end virtually every Roman in manufacturing, shipping, and trade belonged to one of more than 150 guilds.[29] Even the smallish provincial Egyptian town of Oxyrhynchus had 90 different guilds, with 33 fixing their members' prices.[30]

One reason that the warrior emperors of the late third century began to recover Roman territories was their adaptation of an expensive new Parthian military technology, the armored knight. As heavy cavalry units, such knights became so militarily crucial that the emperors moved to Milan, where the horses had good grazing. Militarily successful as they were, however, these knights required horses specially bred for sturdiness, the fabrication of extensive armor, and attendants, fodder, stables, and long training for each knight. By century's end military expenses were double those of Septimius Severus[31] and five times those of Augustus.[32]

Even though plague had reduced output everywhere[33] and desertions crippled the Western provinces,[34] the government's increased expenses (and the lack of public debt) prevented any abatement of tax demands. In fact, the remaining taxpayers had to pay property taxes for the deserted properties. Enormous tax increases, sometimes even tripling, became ruinous.[35]

Those most seriously afflicted were the principal customers of business, the decurions, especially those in the Western provinces.[36] Taxes also afflicted decurions because of their role as tax collectors. For centuries, they had vied for municipal magistracies, which allowed them to collect imperial taxes. They had to guarantee the emperor's payment, but since collections were always greater, the position had been most lucrative.[37] Now, however, the guarantee often exceeded what they could collect. This liability was so onerous that some third-century Christians were persecuted by being forced to serve as magistrates.[38] In time, anyone with wealth was dragooned, including women, merchants, and illiterates.[39]

In contrast to the decurions, the richest and luckiest people could escape tax burdens by purchasing exemptions or entering exempt occupations like the imperial bureaucracy or the priesthood.[40] The rest suffered from increased coercion. By Caracalla's time, all Romans below decurion rank could be tortured and beaten like slaves; by the fifth century even decurions became subject to whipping. Crimes meriting the death penalty tripled to thirty-six by the end of the third century, and executions became more hideous: no longer the swift stroke of a sword, but rather burning at the stake, crucifixion, or being torn apart by wild animals.[41] Mere survival forced virtually everyone to lie, cheat, and help neighbors do the same, spreading an ethos of cynicism, selfishness, and corruption.[42]

Late Rome

By the late third century, Roman armies had regained virtually all the empire's former territory. Plague had disappeared, and deserted lands were repopulated and farmed again. Production reached new heights in many regions, including some of the Western provinces.[43] The ruling classes thought of their world as Rome restored.[44]

But the late Roman world was not the one that for four centuries had allowed business to flourish. New institutions absorbed the bulk of purchasing power and had little use for business except as taxpayer. The saving grace for business seems to have been corruption, a prevalent feature of late Roman society that liberated for use in the markets of Mediterranean cities some of the purchasing power that late Roman institutions would otherwise have absorbed. Here, in brief, is the late Roman story.

Western Europe

In Western Europe, business largely disappeared after the third century. Its main customers, the decurions, were gone, and many of the cities where business operated had lost out to a new, self-sufficient institution as the dominant local power. This was the manor, a fortified holding that rich Romans assembled in response to the third century's disasters. These manors successfully privatized sovereign powers, leading first to the fatal weakening of imperial rule in the Western provinces and ultimately to feudalism.

Some Romans retained great wealth during the disasters that beset Rome in the third century, having either diversified or protected their landholdings. As in Greece during the early Hellenistic Era and in central Italy after Hannibal, such wealthy individuals could profit by acquiring land that destitute farmers sold for a pittance or just in return for protection.[45] Great manors came to cover large parts of the Western European provinces,[46] and many of their owners became Roman senators.[47] Indeed, by the end of the fourth century such senators controlled most of the resources in Italy, Gaul, Spain, and Africa,[48] and the Senate was five times wealthier than under Augustus.[49]

In Rome, which still contained 500,000–750,000 people, including 3,000 dancing girls and 3,000 dancing masters,[50] senators' palaces enclosed small towns that included hippodromes, forums, temples, fountains, and many baths, as well as prisons and slave quarters.[51] Country villas became spectacular showplaces, adorned with gigantic private bath-houses, sprawling gardens, stone and bronze sculptures, mosaics, frescoes, huge storage facilities, and housing for hordes of laborers.

Senators like Ausonius (ca. 310–395), who owned vineyards in the Moselle Valley as well as the site of Chateau Ausone, now a famous winery near Bordeaux,[52] even survived barbarian invasions, since the invaders worked out accommodations with the owners of well-protected villas.[53] With the decline of Western cities, they also became the local intermediaries with the emperor, collecting taxes and supplying the army's recruits.[54] They avoided or even profited by imperial exactions, bribing officials to value their property far below its worth, paying taxes late if at all, and collecting other peoples' taxes long before they were due.[55] Far wealthier and more powerful than city magistrates had ever been, they could also extract concessions from the emperor in return for their cooperation.[56] These included laws tying peasants to the land and delegating to their landlords judicial and punitive powers over them.[57]

Business was largely irrelevant to these new powers. Their manors, and the church properties that many became, produced virtually all their own needs or bartered with neighboring manors for the rest.[58] They bought little from business and had no reason to facilitate markets or commerce.[59] If the roads were dangerous and life outside was difficult, it was hardly their concern. By the fifth century, only a few sea captains and Syrian or Jewish traders could eke out a living by providing silk, spices, or exotic supplies to senatorial families, barbarian upstarts, and churches.[60] Long-distance trade, which had declined sharply in the third century, never recovered (table 16).[61]

Nor could the emperors regain their power. A succession of imperial commanders in Great Britain revolted, sometimes shearing away provinces for years on end. The last Roman legions left Britain to pursue German tribes that crossed the frozen Rhine in 405 and "scattered through Gaul like a shrapnel burst."[62] Their commander, who styled himself Constantine III, controlled much of Gaul and Spain until his defeat and death at Arles in 411. By this time, thanks to imperial concessions and tax avoidance, the great landowners of Italy, Gaul, and Spain had in practice achieved independence.[63] They paid lip service to the emperor and served as Roman senators, but readily shifted their allegiance to powerful interlopers like German warlords or Constantine III. The Western emperor's difficulties were exacerbated by corruption. Although the nominal army was nearly double that of Marcus Aurelius,[64] it was actually much smaller and weaker.

Table 16
Merchant Shipwrecks in Northwestern Europe

Years (c.e.)	Wrecks Found
1–99	120
100–199	122
200–299	53
300–399	39
400–499	11
500–599	20
600–699	5

Drained of resources and troops by concessions to these magnates and by the pervasive corruption of the day, the Western emperors took refuge behind the Po River marshes at Ravenna. Isolated there amid endless palace intrigues, they desperately tried to buy off or divert their enemies. Nevertheless, between civil wars and invasions the deterioration of the Western empire continued. In 410 the Visigoths briefly seized Rome, but the loss of Africa triggered the final fall.

An ambitious imperial general named Aetius persuaded the regent, the child emperor's mother Galla Placida, to fire the governor of Africa, Boniface. Boniface dug in, summoning Vandals from Spain for reinforcement. They began seizing African property for themselves, besieging the port of Hippo as Saint Augustine lay dying there in 432. Aetius, meanwhile, poisoned his superior to become the imperial chief of staff. The alarmed Galla Placidia now appealed to Boniface for help. Boniface sailed with his army to Italy, where after a pitched battle he died of his wounds. According to a charming medieval legend, the two generals had "decided to struggle by single combat, and Boniface, with his dying breath, commended his wife to his victorious enemy as the only man worthy of her love."[65]

Worthy of her love Aetius may have been, but he could not stop the Vandals from completing their conquest of Africa in 439, a potential disaster for Rome. Many senators owned valuable estates there, and Rome, still a city of 500,000 people, depended heavily on its food.[66] The Vandals, however, offered to protect Roman property and maintain the flow of food to Rome if the emperor would ratify their rule in Africa. Now of age, Valentinian III agreed. To seal the bargain he betrothed his infant daughter to the Vandal leader's son.

A few years later, Aetius fought another great battle, driving Attila and the Huns out of Gaul in 451.[67] But Aetius, raised among the Huns, refused to slaughter them as they fled, and Attila was able to descend on Italy the following spring, where he sacked Milan and obliterated Aquilaea, driving its refugees onto Adriatic sandbars where they founded Venice. Italy quailed, but after meeting Pope Leo I at Pavia, Attila mysteriously departed. He died that winter, and the Hun confederation dissolved.

In 455 Valentinian cut down Aetius, stabbing him to death in the Ravenna throne room as the general was reporting to him. Petronius, the ambitious prefect of Rome, saw his chance and persuaded officers loyal to Aetius to assassinate Valentinian during a visit to Rome, which they did. Petronius immediately proclaimed himself emperor and married Valentinian's widow. He also married his son to Valentinian's daughter, breaking her betrothal to the Vandal prince.

The enraged Vandals then sacked Rome so savagely that their name remains a term for wanton destruction. Petronius was killed, and Valentinian's wife and daughter were abducted to Carthage and married off once again. Over the next twenty years succeeding emperors failed to revenge the sack of Rome and recover the senators' estates in Africa. In 476, therefore, when the imperial military commander Odovacer, son of a bodyguard to Attila, retired the child emperor Romulus to Lucullus's old estate near Naples and proclaimed himself king of Italy, the Roman Senate cheered.[68]

The Roman East

Eastern provinces had also suffered invasions, civil wars, and secessions during the third century,[69] but the absence of heavy forests, the tillability of the soil, and the moister climate of the day made them much more productive. They could feed themselves as well as soldiers relocated from frontier posts. Land was not abandoned, cities kept their wealthy citizens and their governmental functions, and the elites of the East derived their status and income from imperial office, not semi-independent fiefdoms. The emperors therefore remained powerful. But while business in the cities continued, new institutions relegated it to a more marginal role than it had enjoyed under Hellenistic and earlier Roman rule.

Bureaucracy

Diocletian (283–305) began his long reign dramatically.[70] At Nicea the grizzled general stood with his predecessor Numerian's father-in-law Lucius Afer before "thousands on thousands of warriors in numberless myriads as far as the eye could see, the mightiest force on earth, . . . roaring in perfect unison that they would obey him, die for him, follow him to the end of the world." Diocletian swore that he had not sought the throne and was innocent of Numerian's death. He then turned, accused Afer of poisoning Numerian, drew his sword, and slew him on the spot.

The imperial bureaucracy had grown from several hundred under Marcus Aurelius to thirty to thirty-five thousand,[71] and many more people worked in state factories and other operations. If small by modern standards,[72] the bureaucracy's size was unprecedented for the ancient world, and of course its functions were more limited. Diocletian's contribution was to provide an effective management structure. He doubled the number of provinces and organized them under two emperors, one for the Greek-speaking provinces east of the Adriatic Sea, and the other for the Latin-speaking provinces to the west. Under each emperor was a caesar, who like all governors and diocesan vicars had large staffs—Antioch's governor had fifteen hundred. The civil and military services each had a hierarchy reporting to the emperors, headed respectively by counts and dukes. This system lasted another four centuries.[73]

Diocletian also created a tax system that extracted 50 percent more from the empire's economy than Augustus had taken.[74] More importantly, it operated on in-kind payments and command distribution. In other words, it replicated on a vastly larger scale the economic systems of the ancient Middle East, capturing and diverting from business channels a large share of the available purchasing power.

The bureaucracy further undercut business by imposing price, labor, and other regulatory controls that sharply reduced profits and opportunities.[75] These controls were, however, a necessary accompaniment to Diocletian's new order, whose budgeting and taxation system tried to track every asset in the empire, "every field, orchard, vineyard, every laborer, slave and child, every horse, ox and pig," and value them in terms of land or labor.[76] For this to work, everyone had to remain in place. Peasants could not desert their farms, urban laborers could not change jobs, and assets could not change values or be devoted to new purposes. Diocletian tried to freeze thousands of prices in his Price Edict of 301 C.E., and over the fourth century "men were increasingly 'frozen' in their class"[77] through such measures as tying peasants to their land and organizing urban labor into tightly regulated hereditary orders that excluded rural migrants.[78] Such restrictions on individual freedom reduced business activity and profits.

The Church

Emperor Constantine (306–337) built the church into a late Roman institution parallel to the imperial bureaucracy. It, too, enfeebled business by absorbing vast amounts of purchasing power into self-supporting establishments and regulating private conduct to business's detriment.

Paradoxically, promoting the church served the same practical purpose for Constantine and his successors as persecuting it had for earlier emperors: to marshal religious sentiment in support of imperial rule.[79] Imperial rule had desperately needed religious support as third-century disasters undermined the old reasons for its legitimacy. Roman armies that once protected the populace and enriched the cities with their salaries and purchases now allowed barbarians to invade as the army itself plundered the countryside. Taxes, once moderate, had become oppressive. Citizenship, formerly an exclusive benefit, now imposed tax burdens on everyone. The inducements that had won the loyalty of provincial civic leaders had turned into costs from which they had fled or revolted.[80] This loss of legitimacy was grave because, as Nobel Prize–winning economic historian Douglass C. North puts it, "The costs of maintenance of an existing order are inversely related to the perceived legitimacy of the existing system."[81]

Plague, war, and taxes had no easy remedy, so imperial advisers, like modern political consultants, sought to manipulate public perceptions. Hence the imperial court, harking back to Darius the Great, began to emphasize the symbolism of moral authority, hoping that the appearance of majesty would help preserve the reality. Septimius Severus began calling himself *dominus*. Diocletian adopted elaborate court ceremonies in the Persian style and required those who entered his presence to prostrate themselves.[82] Emperors adopted remote and dehumanized images, as in a contemporary description of Emperor Constantine II parading into Rome in 357:

In spite of the din he exhibited no emotion, but kept the same impassive air as he commonly wore before his subjects in the provinces. Though he was very short he stooped as he passed under a high gate; otherwise he was like a dummy, gazing straight before him as if his head were in a vice and turning neither to right nor left. When a wheel jolted he did not nod, and at no point was he seen to spit or to wipe or rub his face or nose or to move his hand.[83]

More importantly, as during all troubled times, the third century summoned forth religious passion, and the embattled emperors saw in their divinity an opportunity to inspire loyalty.[84] In easier times this attribute had seemed more an honor for good deeds than literal godliness,[85] but the Severans began requiring the army and civil service to swear their *devotio* to the emperor, and later emperors demanded public worship through the offering of sacrifices.[86]

To Christians, who by the late third century were approaching 10 percent of the empire's population,[87] such idolatry was evil. They refused to offer sacrifices and objected to the auguries from animal entrails that preceded battles and other important undertakings. Participants, they provocatively proclaimed, would go to hell.[88] Since it is always tempting to find scapegoats for hard times, and these subversive views threatened order and imperial legitimacy, persecutions followed.

Diocletian initiated the worst, after priests complained that Christians making the sign of the cross were preventing them from reading the omens of an augury before battle. He ordered all Christians to offer sacrifices to the emperor and had his Caesar Galerius (305–311) pursue those who refused. Galerius sadistically tortured Christians long after Diocletian retired. But the tactic backfired. The courage of Christian martyrs greatly impressed everyone. Then, in what seemed a sign of God's wrath, Galerius died slowly from an agonizing and gruesome disease. On his deathbed he published an edict of toleration "in virtue of our extreme clemency and our immemorial practice of dealing gently with all men."[89]

A few years later Constantine's father was killed near York, and Constantine launched a civil war to succeed him as emperor of the West. Legitimacy was closely tied to religious sentiment, and Christianity had become respectable, even admirable. Constantine's Jewish mother had become a devout Christian, and his own conversion followed his triumph in 312. As the story goes, before the decisive Battle of Milvian Bridge outside Rome, he saw a shining cross in the sky emblazoned with the words *in hoc signo vinces*, "with this sign you will conquer." He vowed to convert if he won, and he did.

With his sister's husband, the Eastern Emperor Licinius, Constantine proclaimed the Edict of Milan, ending all persecution of Christians. Except his own; a few years later Constantine defeated Licinius in battle and despite his sister's pleas executed Licinius and her children. Licinius's son by a previous wife was castrated and sent to the imperial harem in Carthage. Later, Constantine had his own wife and their children murdered.

After consolidating his rule, Constantine set about granting the church such privileges, powers, and preferences that within the century most Romans had joined,[90] and the bishop of Rome, the pope, owned more property than all the Roman senators combined.[91] Charismatic bishops like Jerome and Augustine also secured huge private gifts.[92] Augustine courted Proba, widow of the richest Roman,[93] and Jerome got Melania and her husband Pinianus to donate estates in various parts of Italy, Sicily, Spain, North Africa, and Britain that were yielding 1,150 pounds of gold per year. One of these, near Rome, included sixty-two hamlets and allegedly some 24,000 field slaves.[94] Constantine also stripped the previously sacrosanct pagan temples of their valuables, a boon to the imperial treasury that he regarded as practically a sacred duty.[95] In consequence, as Isidore of Pelusium wrote in 420, "The religion of the Greeks, made dominant for so many years, by such pains, by the expenditure of so much wealth, and by such feats of arms, has vanished from the earth."[96]

Constantine's theological contribution was more important.[97] At the Council of Nicea, a summit meeting of Christian bishops that he called in 325, the emperor formulated the Nicene Creed in response to a dispute between an Alexandrian priest named Arius and his bishop. The bishop claimed that through Jesus and the disciples, only the bishops and the priests they ordained had the authority to save a soul from eternity in hell. As part of the trinity that constituted God, Jesus's word was God's. Arius asserted a simpler and more familiar concept: Jesus was not God, but rather a divine intermediary like the familiar demigods of paganism.[98] This view was indeed congenial to pagans because it allowed them to petition Jesus directly, like a demigod, and most barbarian conversions were to Arian Christianity. But the Arian view undercut church authority. For if Jesus was not God, neither bishops nor their church had any power over the afterlife. Which view would prevail? The decision was Constantine's, and his choice was to condemn Arianism as heresy.[99] To avoid hell, every Christian would need a pass from the church.

In return, the bishops recognized the emperor's authority over life on earth; imperial Rome was a manifestation of the Christian world order that derived from God's will.[100] The church also provided practical support for the emperor's sovereignty. With its vast organization, disciplined hierarchy, and effective fundraising, it readily replaced the declining *decurion* class, whose liturgies had earlier supported most welfare efforts.[101] It assumed other sovereign functions. One of the earliest was to adjudicate civil disputes under Roman law.[102] In time, however, church officials also came to adjudicate local disputes, provide public amenities, and even repair bridges, dikes, and canals.[103] One stylish bishop symbolized his dual civil and ecclesiastical roles by wearing the black or red shoes that represented the different powers on alternate days.[104]

These developments made ecclesiastical authorities the judges in most commercial disputes and gave them great power over day-to-day business activities. While not inevitably hostile to business interests, churchmen strongly disapproved of charging interest, thereby making credit extremely scarce. Church officials also fought such business mainstays as luxury and vice.[105]

The church rivaled the imperial bureaucracy as a sink for purchasing power. Its tithe was roughly equivalent to the imperial property tax,[106] and no more than 25 percent of its enormous income returned to general circulation through alms to the poor.[107] The rest of its mostly in-kind revenue supported hundreds of thousands of bishops, priests, and monks in austere self-sufficiency or was hoarded in ceremonial displays.[108]

Corruption

If the bureaucracy and the church had truly absorbed the purchasing power they claimed, as standard accounts suggest,[109] business in the late Roman Empire might have disappeared altogether. But there are serious doubts about the thoroughness of late Roman regulation,[110] and a considerable amount of purchasing power evidently continued to support private commerce—at least in the larger port cities, some of which issued their own coins to support commercial activity.[111] The *chrysargyron*, Constantine's business tax payable only in coins, lasted for centuries despite the extreme difficulty in collecting it, a fact that suggests the revenues were worth the trouble. As a later bishop named Zosimus describes, he did not even allow poor prostitutes to escape. The result was that as each fourth year came round when this tax had to be paid, weeping and wailing were heard throughout the city, because beatings and tortures were in store for those who could not pay owing to extreme poverty. Indeed mothers sold their children and fathers prostituted their daughters under compulsion to pay the exactors of the chrysargyron.[112]

The great church historian Peter Brown notes that tombs in the Roman catacombs show that Christian artisans were thriving in fourth-century Rome and, despite obviously reduced prosperity, still active in the fifth century.[113] In fact, Italy and Africa under Arian rulers in the sixth century enjoyed a revival of money, markets, and business. Rome again became a magnet for students and a center of entertainment, while all Italy was busy with repairs to public structures.[114]

The main reason for believing that markets and business continued to function during the late Roman Empire, even if on a more local and petty level than during the Principate, was the prevalence of corruption. It was practiced on such an enormous scale that at the end of the fourth century the church prohibited all imperial officials from church office on a presumption of low moral character.

Corruption transformed the coercive power of late Roman institutions into private wealth. Military commanders routinely inflated the number of their troops, then pocketed the excess salaries and supplies. Judging from the size of battles, phantom troop levels far exceeded actual numbers. For instance, an army supposedly double the size of Marcus Aurelius's could barely field twenty thousand men at the Battle of Adrianople in 378, and most later battles involved many fewer men.[115] Civilian corruption was also endemic. The more coercive the government became, the more common and acceptable was the use of bribery to escape its exactions.[116] Virtually every official had discretion to sell—to tax or not, license or not, appoint or not—and they constantly invented new charges and fees.[117] While Rome had always expected its officials to charge fees for performing their official duties, even minor officials now became immensely wealthy.[118] Recall that John the Lydian earned nine solidi in salary, but over a thousand, more than 99.9 percent of his income, in "gifts" for the performance of his duties.

The remote emperors, screened from information by famously corrupt functionaries, were helpless to stop it.[119] For instance, when certain

Libyans denounced Romanus, their notoriously corrupt late-fourth-century governor, an imperial investigator arrived in Tripoli. Because he brought the payroll and accepted the usual fees for this service, Romanus could accuse the investigator himself of corruption. Intimidated, the investigator cleared Romanus, and the whistleblowers had their tongues torn out.

Saint Augustine fondly imagined that both bribers and bribees would "lavish their goods on the poor."[120] Whether indirectly in that manner or directly through market purchases in the Mediterranean cities where wealthy Romans usually lived, it seems likely that the fruits of corruption served to support a considerable level of late Roman business.

But by the mid-sixth century God's work was afoot in Constantinople, where orthodox Christian emperors became increasingly militant. When the fanatical Justinian (527–565) became emperor, he closed the ancient Academy of Plato in Athens, sending its pagan scholars fleeing to Sasanian Persia. Justinian then launched attacks on the Arians. All went well until the Roman senators, who had supported Justinian against their Arian Ostrogothic kings, realized that his victory would cost them dearly in taxes. They renewed their support for the Ostrogoths, who persuaded the Sasanians to attack Syria. Justinian's great General Belisarius then left Italy for Mesopotamia, from which his army returned with the bubonic plague in 541. The so-called Plague of Justinian devastated the empire and adjacent kingdoms, killing three hundred thousand people in Constantinople alone.[121] Between the plague and the fighting, by Justinian's ultimate victory in 553 Italy was devastated.[122] Milan had been sacked and razed with a loss of three hundred thousand men,[123] while Rome was reduced to a mere thirty thousand people surrounded by malarial swamps.[124]

Meanwhile, a series of earthquakes were destroying Ephesus and other Eastern cities. The weakened empire began to disintegrate. Hungarian and Slavic tribes invaded, corrupt lowlifes seized the imperial throne, and the Sasanians repeatedly assaulted the Levant, ultimately seizing the relic of the true cross from Jerusalem.[125] As the dwindling Roman Empire and Sasanian Persia battered each other, Mohammed died in 632 and veteran Arab mercenaries of these wars rallied to his successor. As they descended upon the Levant, one last Roman army gathered to confront them. But for months its disoriented leader, the ill Emperor Heraclius, idled in the Syrian desert heat before leading it to annihilation on the Yarmuk River. Jerusalem and the rest of the Fertile Crescent quickly capitulated to the Arabs, and within decades so did Roman provinces from

Anatolia to Gibraltar. Just as the Roman population had converted to Christianity under the inducements of Constantine during the fourth century, so it now began converting to Islam. A Byzantine Empire based at Constantinople survived as a Christian outpost, but the Roman Empire was gone.

The decline of business during and after the third century was not due to the plagues and invasions that afflicted the empire. The loss of life, territories, and markets would certainly damage business at any time. But crises can also mobilize resources that, channeled through business suppliers, lead to great prosperity.

The downfall of business was due, rather, to policies chosen in response to the crises. In the first instance these amounted to vast increases in military spending, far beyond those necessary to safeguard the borders. Then, like the Ptolemies after their silver supplies had disappeared, the emperors resorted to short-term sleights-of-hand—devaluations—to support their spending. These rendered money unusable, evaporated credit, and terminated government contracting, in the process also destroying the trade that depended on government transport.

As the private enterprise-based supply system fell apart, the Western cities depending on that system declined, a trend exacerbated by military relocations. Deteriorating cities and abandoned lands put the provincial elite at a great disadvantage. Burdened with taxes that abandoned lands could not pay and liable as tax collectors for all shortfalls, the class disappeared, as did the businesses that had served them.

A new political and social structure emerged in the Western provinces as wealthy Romans acquired great manors, replaced the magistrates of declining cities as the local authorities, and enserfed the peasant population. By the fifth century these magnates had largely freed themselves from imperial authority, leading ultimately to the Western empire's dissolution and demise. As sovereign states emerged in the Western provinces, their feudalized institutional structure no longer supported business apart from the occasional trader in luxuries.

The far richer Eastern and Mediterranean cities did not experience similar economic misfortunes during the third century. They retained their populations and markets, land prices did not collapse, and there was no reorganization of property into large, self-sufficient manors. Nevertheless, other structural changes in Roman society prevented business from resuming its former role even after the economy recovered.

The authoritarian, bureaucratic state and the wealthy church became, in effect, co-sovereigns. They each curtailed the economic and personal freedoms that had previously allowed business to flourish. Economic freedom suffered from the loss of purchasing power to heavy taxation and church tithes and gifts, prohibitions against virtually all forms of credit, and the ruin of the urban elite. Autocratic government and religious repression restricted the freedom of individuals to pursue pleasure or profit as they saw fit.

Taken as a whole, late Rome's major institutions—the great landowners of the Western provinces, the imperial bureaucracy, and the church—internalized society's purchasing power, reducing demand that business had formerly served. What remained for business, at least in the Mediterranean cities and the Roman East, was largely the purchasing power that leaked into private hands through corruption. Quite possibly more extensive than usually credited, this business life was inherited by Rome's successors—the Byzantine state and the Arab caliphates.

Concluding Note

I would like to conclude this book with a personal view of what the story of early business has taught me. One of the questions I hoped to understand was this: what, exactly, is new in modern business? The answer, discussed below, surprised me; and with it came answers, or at least partial answers, to other questions I have long entertained, such as the role of business in creating wealth, the function of finance, the place of morality in business, and the role of business in society.

Wealth

The crucial difference between modern business and that of ancient times is not one of size, the complexity or technology of operations, the products or services sold, or the nature of work and employment. If not found in the businesses of antiquity, these features are nevertheless just extensions and variations of what did exist. The main difference lies in the role that modern business plays in the creation of material wealth,[1] thanks to systems of innovation and marketing that never existed in antiquity.[2]

The importance of business in creating wealth, although often asserted, is rarely explained. It has been hard to understand because the nature of wealth itself is somewhat elusive. My own understanding gained a lot from the story of classical Athens.

In the Middle East before money, markets, and business became prominent at Athens, and in most places for a long time afterward, wealth consisted almost entirely of productive land and surplus production paid in rents and taxes. All the pyramids and other surviving monuments of ancient civilizations, or whose ruins hint at former magnificence, came from that surplus. In Athens and other Greek city-states, however, there was never so much surplus—yet the city-states grew far richer, per capita, than any of the Middle Eastern empires. A mysterious miracle was taking place, much like the miracle that makes resource-poor nations like Japan, Holland, and Denmark wealthy today.

Mercenary service abroad generated some of Greece's wealth. This was due to the enduring competitive advantage of Greek phalanxes, an advantage derived both from the success of the phalanx and from the unique culture that made it inimitable.[3] Modern businesses like Apple Inc. constantly strive to achieve similarly enduring competitive advantages for themselves.

Of more general relevance now, though, was the wealth that Athens and other Greek city-states derived from the creation and quickening of markets. Lively markets exposed people to goods they had never known about and sparked a desire for those goods. To satisfy those desires, people who had produced only the necessities for subsistence, rent, and taxes now sought to earn purchasing power. To do so, they deployed their skills, assets, and time to create goods and services that others wanted.[4] In effect, then, money, markets, and businesses created wealth by stimulating a combination of desire and purchasing power. Economists call it "demand."

Market-created demand accounts for much more of our wealth than of antiquity's. As the "market" is practically universal, innovation and marketing reach almost everywhere. Virtually everyone quickly learns about the desirable new offerings that businesses constantly create and market. And like the Athenians, people respond by generating purchasing power to acquire them, increasing the general level of wealth.

More than desire, which normally remains strong,[5] the key variable in demand is purchasing power, almost always in the form of money or credit. But money and credit are not the only forms of wealth; they are just the forms easiest to use in exchange for other things. Finance is the discipline concerned with purchasing power. It began when people first sought purchasing power and helped them use assets like land, crops, and houses as security for loans of more easily exchanged valuables, such as silver or barley. In modern economies, finance still converts other forms of wealth into purchasing power (mortgages, securitization), increases the value of purchasing power by protecting the underlying assets (insurance, portfolio management), and improves the use of purchasing power (creating markets, allocating risks). Given the importance of purchasing power to demand and sales, finance governs the health of all businesses.

The centrality of Wall Street comes not just from the importance of purchasing power, but primarily from the dominant form of purchasing power, which is credit. Even in ancient times, credit was probably the major form of purchasing power. The principal varieties of credit have always been trade credit, equity investment, and loans—mostly loans. The availability of this credit has always depended primarily on trust: the creditor's trust in the debtor's promise of repayment. When trust falls, credit contracts and business falters; when trust expands, credit flows and business flourishes.

Let me summarize the foregoing: (1) desire combined with purchasing power equals demand; (2) by stimulating demand, business creates wealth; (3) purchasing power is the key limitation on the amount of demand and wealth that business can stimulate; (4) the main type of purchasing power is credit; and (5) the main variable that determines the amount of credit available is trust in the borrower's promise of repayment. This explains the importance to business of finance and the importance to finance of trust.

Although trust is a psychological phenomenon, rationality plays a significant role as well. Antiquity developed various ways to make the promise of repayment rationally more trustworthy, such as confining transactions to family or clan members and using oaths, moral systems, and laws to motivate the promisor's faithful performance. Legal codes, the Hellenistic invention of international arbitration, and the Roman use of patronage extended the possibilities of trust even to strangers.

Technology, financial theory, improved data, and innovations like new markets and financial instruments have recently created a rational basis for greatly increased levels of trust in promises of repayment, justifying extensions of credit that would previously have been irrational. Nevertheless, especially after the 2007–2008 Great Recession, many voices decry the increased levels of debt as overly risky by historical standards. In doing so, they are ignoring these very real advances in our ability to evaluate promises of repayment. The recession does not devalue recent financial accomplishments; rather, it indicates how treacherous and difficult the achievement of trust can be.

For instance, consider some of the financial instruments blamed for the Great Recession. Those most severely criticized—subprime mortgage-backed securities, securities created by bundling them in various combinations, and derivatives of those securities—all had economic rationales. They created benefits and could have been rational investments. Unfortunately, the underlying mortgages were frequently fraudulent, and creditors were insufficiently wary. The problem was fraud, which lapses in financial regulation permitted to flourish.[6]

The problem of lax regulation, which triggered the Great Recession, is actually endemic to modern commercial society. The rapid pace of intellectual innovation outruns social adjustments in the form of legal, regulatory, and normative constraints—adjustments that usually develop by trial and error over a long period of time. For example, it took a century after the invention of motor vehicles to create rules of the road, such as driving norms and safety features, that subdue carnage on our highways. Similarly, carnage like the Great Recession results because our financial rules of the road did not keep up with the innovations of recent decades. This lag allowed finance to become something of a Wild West, with rampaging outlaws and weak sheriffs. But should we reject financial innovation because the sheriffs have trailed behind? Should Wild West desperados have kept the first settlers from crossing the Mississippi? This brings me to the issue of business morality.

Morality and Business

The social status of business and the standing of those who work in businesses have been major concerns of this report. Since ancient business was largely conducted by slaves and women, their low status necessarily tainted public attitudes toward the activity. In addition, however, there was a taint due to perceptions of business morality. The perception of business morality remains very much a public concern today.

The pursuit of profit has long been morally suspect. Its self-serving nature borders on the sin of greed, while the special rules that govern markets, which differ in certain ways from the moral rules of society, have generated distrust. In historically anti-Semitic Europe, the old association of business with Jews also prejudiced its reputation.

This dubious view of business morality is mistaken, not because businesses are inherently moral, but because they have no inherent morality at all, good or bad. The vast majority of businesses reflect the morality of their owners and managers. Since business leaders, more than most people, exercise great power over others—customers, employees, suppliers, communities, etc.—I would expect that on any measure of comparative morality they would come out rather well.

But apart from the personal morality of their leaders, businesses can be expected to pursue sales and profits as expediently as possible under prevailing legal and social circumstances.[7] If they can increase profits by polluting, cheating customers, or bribing officials, they will; if a strict adherence to legality seems more prudent, they will do that. In short, they will adapt to whatever course serves their sales and profits best.

If the ancient business experience serves as a guide, businesses likely to act in this brutally amoral way are often found where they can function with little accountability, like those selling expensive items to one-time customers. Also tending to the amoral are far-flung, bureaucratic firms whose leaders are well insulated from the consequences of their choices. That is why, in the ancient world, the most notorious businesses were far-flung and bureaucratic organizations like the publican societies or pirate/traders like the Phoenicians in their black boats, calling on distant tribes.

Although not themselves moral entities, businesses depend heavily on the morality of society. This is not just a matter of trustworthiness and the availability of credit. Nobel Prize–winning economic historian Douglass C. North notes that "strong moral and ethical codes of a society is the cement of social stability which makes an economic system viable."[8] The enforcement of these codes becomes especially important as the size and complexity of operations increase, since then the benefits and opportunities for cheating do as well.[9] More specifically, says economist Richard Nelson, "for markets to work, participants must have a moral code that emphasizes and supports truthfulness and playing by the rules. . . . Economies with such moral conditions have prospered, those without them have not."[10]

This brings to mind the role that current business leaders seem to be playing in undermining those favorable moral conditions. Because business was held in such low repute until recently, the behavior of business leaders had little effect on social attitudes. But now successful entrepreneurs and the leaders of large firms enjoy the highest levels of prestige and social influence. Unfortunately, in too many instances they have lied, committed fraud, and flouted the laws. Worse, when called to account they routinely deny wrongdoing on the ground that their behavior was not criminal. In other words, they seek to substitute the difficult and rarely invoked standard of criminality for the prevailing moral code "that emphasizes and supports truthfulness and playing by the rules," in Nelson's words. This is dangerous, for as the businesses of Western Europe discovered during Rome's third century, if the only wrong behavior is that which the sovereign prohibits and if the sovereign cannot or will not enforce those rules, business cannot really function. This leads me, finally, to reflections on public policy.

Business and Public Policy

Viewed from one perspective, much of this book is about how public policy shapes business, and in particular about how public policies created money, markets, and business and developed them into the recognizable forerunners of today's major institutions. It did so in four main ways, which continue to condition business today: providing knowledge, creating markets, enforcing rules, and reducing transaction costs.

Providing Knowledge

Because public policy encompasses far more human activities and broader concerns than business does, governments have often had more reason than business to develop new forms of knowledge. The mathematics, accounting, forward time orientation, and writing that Middle Eastern bureaucratic empires originated and made available for business use come immediately to mind. In modern times, the broader concerns of government generate military and other types of research, including basic research of distant or uncertain payoff. Indeed, business increasingly confines its scientific work to development, leaving basic research to governments, universities, and foundations.

Creating Markets

The original public role in creating markets was simply the expansion of sovereignty over larger territories. Since businesses could usually operate throughout a given sovereign's territory with relatively few barriers to activity, larger territories equated to larger markets. The creation of markets by enlarging tariff-free territories continues in the modern world, primarily by treaties like the North American Free Trade Agreement (NAFTA). The Greek city-states and their Hellenistic and Roman imitators literally created markets, which they owned and managed. More frequently emulated today are the city-states like Ugarit that turned themselves into marketplaces. The British did this with Hong Kong in the nineteenth century,[11] and Dubai is currently doing the same.

Enforcing Rules

Perhaps the most obvious and enduring of public policy's roles in fostering business has been the creation and enforcement of rules. Practically from the time that cities began, control over weights and measures was one way of imposing order on commercial activity. Business also benefited from public policies like policing markets and creating legal systems that enforced contracts and agency relationships. In modern societies, which by their size and complexity depend more heavily on legal systems than did smaller, more customary societies, the nature and amount of business depends very heavily on how well public policies support the rule of law. For example, the privatization of the Russian economy after 1989, which occurred before any significant rule of law had been established, led to a destruction of Russian wealth on the same scale as World War II's.[12]

Reducing Transaction Costs

By creating coins and managing their availability, ancient governments greatly facilitated market transactions. Many other public actions also reduced transaction costs. To mention just a few: sovereigns maintained the peace, reduced piracy, and enforced international law; improvements in sovereign legitimacy reduced internal strife; and the construction of roads and navigation aids reduced transport and informational costs. The most dramatic ancient reduction of transaction costs was Augustus's establishment of the Roman Peace, an accomplishment that reduced taxes, permitted transport and interregional commerce to flourish, and by allowing business relations to ripen over long periods of time facilitated negotiations, credit, and the volume of transactions.

Issuing money sufficient to the economy's size and growth rate remains a central task of public policy, even if prudently left to independent central banks like the Federal Reserve. But compared to antiquity the scope of both public and private activity has ballooned, and we understand much more about the public consequences of behavior that once seemed entirely private in nature. As a result, public policy affects much more activity than was conceivable in antiquity, and in many more ways. It includes government decisions about subsidies, taxes, trade barriers, and direct regulation, of course, but also matters like zoning, public transit, health insurance, and employment rights.

The concerns of business about public policy have grown accordingly, and modern democracies are far more susceptible to business persuasion than were the sovereigns of old. Money, the currency of business, plays a vastly greater role in political success than ever before. In addition, it is widely accepted that business generates wealth, even if the mechanisms described here are not widely known. Consequently, our political leaders are attentive to business concerns both out of self-interest and out of concern for the public welfare.

As I write, however, the old problem of the publicans looms ever more ominously. The publicans had a valid role in seeking to influence Roman public policy, but when Gaius Gracchus ceded them commanding influence, their narrow and self-interested concerns brought Rome to the brink of destruction and led to their own demise afterward. In the United States and other developed countries, for reasons described above, political power has been consolidating in the hands of powerful business interests. In the United States, corporate political control may already have culminated, with the Supreme Court's decision in *Citizens United v. Federal Election Commission*.[13] In giving corporations free rein to control the political process through campaign spending, that case may have committed the same fateful error that Gaius Gracchus did in Rome. History does not repeat itself, but familiar patterns do recur.

NOTES

Preface

1. Businesses also arose in Southeast Asia, India, China, and other places, but there is little evidence that those developments led to the business environment and structural characteristics that produced what I am calling here modern business.

2. Braudel 1979–86, 1995b; A. Chandler 1977, 1990; Hicks 1969; McNeill 1991, 1977; North 1981, 1990, 2005; North and Thomas 1973; Williamson 1985, 1996; and Williamson and Winter 1991.

Introduction

1. Scheidel, Morris, and Saller 2007:12. I, too, have relied heavily on the institutional economic ideas of Nobel Prize–winner Douglass C. North.

2. N. Ferguson 2009:12.

1. The Beginning

1. The concepts and information in this chapter come mainly from Clark 1952; Dalton 1967; Diamond 1999; Earle and Ericson 1977; Highwater 1981; Jaynes 1976; McNeill 1991; and Polanyi, Arensberg, and Pearson 1971.

2. McNeill 1991:6.

3. Boyer 2002 and Schoek 1987. On the evolutionary origins of religious belief, see Wolpert 2006.

4. Dalton 1967. See generally Boyer 2002 and North 2005. Spinoza argued that the source of priestly power was belief in afterlife; Nadler 2001:142.

5. Quotation from Highwater 1981:55–56.

6. Etzioni 1988:51.

7. Jaynes 1976. See also Nash 1967:524. Recent psychological research and neuroscientific findings support this possibility, in that 80 percent or more of all behavior can be explained by animal instinct rather than rational thought; see Westen 2008.

8. North 2005:76. Schlesinger 1964:11 argues that the central idea of classical Greek tragedy is to portray the hero as promising to alter fate. This hubris, or attempted usurpation of the gods' role in controlling fate, led Middle Eastern societies to limit the swearing of oaths; see also Schlesinger 1968.

9. Polanyi 1971:75, 77.

10. Diamond 1999:272; Polanyi 1971:75, 77; Dalton 1977:196.

11. Diamond 1999:350–51.

12. For the phrase "cradle of business," see Sutherland 1969:16.

13. Clark 1952:175.

14. Clark 1952:244.

15. Einzig 1966:416.

16. Polanyi 1971:250.

17. Polanyi 1971:73–77.

18. Black and Mendenhall 1993:50–51.

19. Highwater 1981:89.

20. Highwater 1981:95, quoting Robert Ornstein Jr. For the impact of time orientation on individual promises, see Schlesinger 1978:24.

21. The basic historical approach in this section comes from McNeill 1991 and North 1981. Main sources are Algaze 1993; Diakonoff 1982, 1969; Diamond 1999; Kramer 1963; Larsen 1979, 1982; Leemans 1950, 1960; Oppenheim 1977; Saggs 1989; Silver 1985, 1995; and Snell 1997. Many aspects of early Egyptian and Mesopotamian society are difficult to ascertain for sure, but it would be tedious to litter the text with constant reminders that our understanding is highly speculative. I have tried instead to provide a narrative based on my best interpretation of the sources cited.

22. East 1967:138–39.

23. For a full discussion, see Diamond 1999:131–75.

24. Oppenheim 1977:41–42 and McNeill 1991:30–32.

25. Saggs 1989:36.

26. Moore and Lewis 2009:27.

27. McNeill 1977:40.

28. Saggs 1989:39; Silver 1985:57; Diakonoff 1969:6.

29. Van de Mieroop 2005:18.

30. Yoffee 1981:23–24.

31. Saggs 1989:23–24.

32. Saggs 1989:133–36; see also Wilford 1997.

33. McNeill 1977:54–55. For acreage, see Silver 1985:163.

34. Thomas 1984.

35. Saggs 1989:130. For date plantations, see Silver 1995:109.

36. Snell 1997:57.

37. Silver 1995:66–67.

38. Sherratt 1997:10–11.

39. Sherratt 1997:5.

40. Snell 1997:56.

41. See generally Meyer 2003. For widows and orphans, see Snell 1997:35.

42. McNeill 1991:68n4.

43. L. Casson 1991:8 and Leemans 1960:122–24.

44. Saggs 1989:131, 139.

45. McNeill 1991:84–85.

46. Saggs 1989:133–36; see also Wilford 1997.

47. L. Casson 1991:8.

48. Saggs 1989:144.

49. McNeill 1991:41; Clark 1952:269; and Sherratt 1997:17.

50. Letters from al-Amarna, quoted in Saggs 1989:145.

51. Yoffee 1981:12.

52. W. Bernstein 2008 2008:24–25.

53. Snell 1997:40–41.

54. Leemans 1950:44.

55. For instance, a contract at Mari was concluded when the parties "have eaten from the platter, drunk from the goblet, and anointed each other with oil"; Silver 1995:32.

56. Silver 1995:73.

57. Leemans 1950:11; see generally Silver 1985.

58. Yoffee 1981:8.

59. Moore and Lewis 2009:49. See also Leemans 1950:113–17.

60. Wilford 1993:1.

61. Snell 1997:38, 41.

62. Moore and Lewis 2009:34–36.

63. McNeill 1991:92.

64. Leemans 1960:132. They could travel on their own behalf, for investors, or for principals.

65. Leemans 1950:9. The earliest written record dates to 2430 B.C.E. at Girsu; Snell 1997:21.

66. Finley 1983a:17.

67. Silver 1995:122 suggests this.

68. Silver 1995:122.

69. Silver 1995:94.

70. Webber and Wildavsky 1985:57.

71. Silver 1985:50.

72. Leemans 1950:63–66.

73. Oppenheim 1977:303.

74. Silver 1985:118ff.

75. Jacob Janssen, quoted in Silver 1985:83.

76. McNeill 1991:48.

77. It's convenient to ascribe steps like secularization to particular people like Sargon, but we don't usually know the detailed chronologies. In Sargon's case, his grandson Naram-Sin (2236–2200 B.C.E.) discarded the old religious titles and completed the secularization of government; Diakonoff 1991:89–90.

78. North 1981:53.

79. Snell 1997:32.

80. McNeill 1991:46.

81. Comin, Easterly, and Gong 2007:5–6.

82. Silver 1985:12–16.

83. McNeill 1991:52.

84. Larsen 1979:80–81.

85. McNeill 1991:55–60; see generally Nissen, Damarov, and Englund 1993.

86. Webber and Wildavsky 1985:77.

87. For the ecological advantage, see Gall and Saxe 1977.

88. Genesis 41.33–36.

89. McNeill 1991:62.

90. My thanks to Frederick Terna for suggesting this line of speculation.

91. Webber and Wildavsky 1985:77.

92. Seife 2000:11.

93. Maine 1861:165.

94. Association of Chartered Accountants 1999.

95. Snell 1997:60.

96. Code of Hammurabi §32, at Leemans 1960:6–7.

97. Baskin and Miranti 1997:314.

98. Snell 1997:60.

99. Code of Hammurabi §148, quoted in Brunstad 2000:524n104.

100. W. Ferguson 1969:31.

101. The classic definition is Polanyi 1971:264:a unit of exchange, which is both a measure and a store of value. For more recent variations, see Schaps 2001:94.

102. Vilar 1976:26 and Leemans 1950:14.

103. Leemans 1950:2–3.

104. Stos-Gale 2001:73–4.

105. Schaps 2001:94.

106. Baskin and Miranti 1997:314.

107. Sutherland 1969:17.

108. Sutherland 1969:25–31.

109. Sutherland 1969:31 and Polanyi 1971:266.

110. Silver 1985:124.

111. Silver 1985:125–26.

112. W. Bernstein 2008 2008:27.

113. U.S. Federal Reserve 2005.

114. The following discussion is based on Leemans 1950. While credit transactions are known for Egypt, far more have been found in Mesopotamia; see Silver 1985:83.

115. This observation is the central insight behind Keynesian economics; see Skidelsky 1999.

116. Leemans 1950:16. In Babylon there was for many centuries a class of money-lenders; Silver 1985:84–85.

117. Goetzmann and Rouwenhorst 2005:chap. 1.

118. Leemans 1950:16.

119. Silver 1985:83.

120. Code of Hammurabi §119, at Leemans 1950:16.

121. These particular examples are from Silver 1985:85–86.

122. Goetzmann and Rouwenhorst 2005:chap. 1.

123. Baskin and Miranti 1997:314–15.

124. Goetzmann and Rouwenhorst 2005:chap. 1. It is known that Dimuzi made loans to fishermen and farmers, so absent any indication of his use of the 250g of silver I presume that he did so with this wealth as well.

125. Harrison 2002.

126. Quoted in Saggs 1989:141.

127. Saggs 1989:134.

128. Aubet 1993:89ff.

129. Silver 1985:61.

130. The classic discussion of such communities is Curtin 1984.

131. Curtin 1984:69.

132. Saggs 1989:143.

133. Yoffee 1981:12.

134. This account is based on Larsen 1982.

135. See Silver 1995:53 for economic discussion.

136. Silver 1985:41–43.

137. Silver 1995:42.

138. Larsen 1982:229–32.

139. Silver 1985:105.

140. Snell 1997:36.

141. Leemans 1950:9.

142. Association of Chartered Accountants 1999.

143. Oppenheim 1977:80–84.

144. Snell 1997:35–6.

145. Snell 1997:56.

146. See generally Finley 1983b:86.

2. Middle Eastern Empires, 1600–323 B.C.E.

1. Frye 1963:120.

2. For general history and geography I relied primarily on East 1967; Frye 1963; McNeill and McNeill 2003; and Peters 1970. The perspectives of Polanyi, Arensberg, and Pearson 1971 remain important, even though some of the discussions are now outdated.

3. I have taken these dates from chronologies compiled in Ross 2003.

4. Trading partners included the Mitanni, Babylonians, Hittites, Assyrians, and the people of Cyprus, Crete, and the Aegean Islands; Kinder and Hilgemann 1964:25.

5. Saggs 1989:138.

6. L. Casson 1991:15. Astarte was sometimes known as "Our Lady of Byblos."

7. L. Casson 1991:13.

8. L. Casson 1991:6.

9. We know rather little about Minoan society. Its written language, Linear B, remains primarily from the palace of Knossos, preserved at the moment of its destruction; Finley 1981:40–42. For the story of Linear B, see Chadwick 1958. More recently, with additional discoveries of Linear B at various sites, doubt has been thrown on the dating of Linear B, and therefore of the Mycenaean takeover, moving it forward to 1385 B.C.E. or so; see Rutter 2000:lesson 25.

10. The discussion of the Cyclades relies on Renfrew 1972.

11. L. Casson 1991:19 and McNeill and McNeill 2003:97n54.

12. Hammond 1986:46.

13. Fine 1983:6.

14. Renfrew 1972:11.

15. Renfrew 1972:332. Linear B consists almost entirely of accounts recording the receipt and delivery of goods; Finley 1981:40–42.

16. Finley 1981:45–48.

17. L. Casson 1991:26–27.

18. Frankenstein 1979:264.

19. Ugarit was, in fact, the first of many ports of trade down to present-day Hong Kong and Singapore; see Revere 1971:50ff.

20. Louvre Dept. of Oriental Antiquities, window 19, 1/19/09.

21. Arnold 1971:182–83 and Kohlmeyer 1985:250–51.

22. Saggs 1989:79–84.

23. Aubet 1993:61. The capacity of a ship excavated at Ugarit, 200 tons, was the average size of Atlantic trade ships in the late eighteenth century; see Albion, Baker, and Labaree 1994:93.

24. Kohlmeyer 1985:250.

25. Saggs 1989:148.

26. Louvre Dept. of Oriental Antiquities, window 19, 1/19/09.

27. Both from Saggs 1989:147.

28. Moore and Lewis 1999:22.

29. Moore and Lewis 1999:95–96.

30. Moore and Lewis 1999:97.

31. Silver 1985:51, quoting a study of Ugarit merchants.

32. Hammond 1986:73.

33. Hammond 1986:52.

34. For drought, see Aubet 1993:55. For Romanian origins of invasion, see Finley 1981:58.

35. Troy's fall is dated to 1184 B.C.E.; McNeill and McNeill 2003:93–94, 192. For Mycenaean participation in the Hittite Empire's destruction, see Diakonoff 1991:327.

36. Aubet 1993:57.

37. Aubet 1993:115, citing the *Iliad*.

38. McNeill and McNeill 2003:117–18.

39. Clark 1952:200.

40. Clark 1952:201.

41. McNeill and McNeill 2003:120.

42. Snell 1997:83.

43. Oded 1979:69.

44. McNeill and McNeill 2003:136n27.

45. Frye 1963:98.

46. Miles 1995:212.

47. Frye 1963:105.

48. McNeill and McNeill 2003:127 and Frye 1963:55.

49. Kinder and Hilgemann 1964:31.

50. Oded 1979:101–2.

51. The factual basis of the following account is found in Oppenheim 1971:319–20; Moscati 1968; and Aubet 1993.

52. Wilford 1997. For Tyre, see Aubet 1993:19.

53. Aubet 1993:9.

54. Aubet 1993:92, 298.

55. 1 Kings 5.

56. Moore and Lewis 1999:24.

57. See generally Moscati 1968:83ff.

58. Genesis 37.3.

59. Moore and Lewis 1999:28.

60. Aubet 1993:59.

61. Aubet 1993:40–41.

62. Moore and Lewis 1999:22–28.

63. Moore and Lewis 1999:29.

64. Aubet 1993:96.

65. Moscati 1968:98.

66. Moore and Lewis 1999:26.

67. Frye 1963:64.

68. Ezekiel 27.3–8.

69. Frankenstein 1979:265.

70. Aubet 1993:91–94.

71. Moore and Lewis 1999:22.

72. Herodotus, *Histories*, quoted in Moscati 1968:101.

73. Aubet 1993:111.

74. Aubet 1993:244.

75. Sahlins 1974.

76. *Odyssey* 15, quoted in Moscati 1968:87. See Dougherty 2001:44.

77. Cunliffe 2008:28 makes a similar point when he contemplates a Roman merchant trading wine in Gaul for slaves: "To a Gaul . . . to find a trader who would willingly give an amphora of wine for a worthless captive must have seemed like manna from heaven. Who was duping whom?"

78. Arnold 1971.

79. Aubet 1993:117.

80. Aubet 1993:appendix 2.

81. Moore and Lewis 1999:110.

82. Fine and Leopold 1993:264.

83. Muhly 1985:263.

84. Aubet 1993:64.

85. The primary sources for this account are Aubet 1993; Moore and Lewis 1999; and Moscati 1968.

86. Moscati 1968:115.

87. From Diodorus, quoted in Moscati 1968:126–27.

88. Diodorus 5.35, 4–5, quoted in Aubet 1993:237.

89. Moore and Lewis 1999:31.

90. Aubet 1993:96.

91. Aubet 1993:166.

92. Moore and Lewis 1999:33.

93. Aubet 1993:64, 273.

94. W. Bernstein 2008 2008:35.

95. Frye 1963:54.

96. Diakonoff 1991:252.

97. The estimate is from Oded 1979:20–21n5. The percent of the population is based on the assumption that the total population of the Assyrian Empire at any time, excluding Egypt, was something like four million people. Over 300 years that's about ten generations, or forty million people.

98. Frye 1963:50–55.

99. The account of Assyria's fall and Persian history comes from McNeill and McNeill 2003; Frye 1963; Fine 1983; and CAH 1964.

100. Herodotus, *Histories* 69–70.

101. Herodotus, *Histories* 60.

102. My description of the Persian Empire is taken largely from Bairoch 1988; Fine 1983; Frye 1963; and Peters 1970.

103. As of 323 B.C.E.; Bairoch 1988:27.

104. Green 1991:301.

105. Bairoch 1988:28–29.

106. This discussion of legitimacy relies heavily on the Nobel Prize–winning work of economic historian Douglass North and successors like Daron Acemoglu, cited in the bibliography.

107. Quoted in Frye 1963:78.

108. North 1981:100.

109. Green 1991:334.

110. CAH 1964:63, 91–92.

111. Green 1991: 372–73.

112. Frye 1963:90–92.

113. McNeill and McNeill 2003:128.

114. Under the Assyrians, local commissions had reassessed property annually, based on the expected harvest. But local assessors were easily corrupted and annual reassessment discouraged improvements because it quickly led to higher taxes. Instead, Darius created a central ministry to assess land based on average historical yields. The central ministry was less corruptible than local assessors, and the method didn't penalize landowners for improving productivity. A number of modern theorists, including the early-twentieth-century economist Henry George, believe that the resulting land tax was the fairest and most economically favorable tax possible. The virtues of such a land tax are eloquently argued in George's *Poverty and Wealth*.

115. Frye 1963:101.

116. Frye 1963:117.

117. CAH 1964:98.

118. Frye 1963:98.

119. L. Casson 1994:53.

120. L. Casson 1994:56.

121. W. Bernstein 2008: 56 dates the adoption of dromedaries to the Assyrian Empire, but more scholarly sources put it a bit later; see Bulliet 1975.

122. All the surviving records seem to be from Babylonia, largely because records there were kept on permanent clay tablets, while elsewhere the writing material of preference was papyrus, little of which survives. But the generalization seems plausible.

123. Silver 1985:131.

124. Aubet 1993:49.

125. McNeill and McNeill 2003:133.

126. Shiff 1987.

127. Silver 1985:50–51.

128. CAH 1964:97.

129. The description of the Murasu archives is taken from Stolper 1985.

130. Stolper 1985:27–28.

131. Ville 1996.

132. Herodotus, *Histories* 103.

133. Silver 1985:121.

134. Silver 1985:119; see also Nehemiah 13.16.

135. Frankenstein 1979:287.

136. Merchants who knew each other could simplify payments by keeping books of account and using weighed and sealed purses of gold or silver of specified value. But due to problems of trust, these techniques weren't available for consumer transactions; Silver 1985:126.

137. Frye 1963:110.

138. Frye 1963:106.

139. Frye 1963:109.

140. North 1981:102 referring to Weber 1976. As to the Depression-era central bankers and the hoarding of gold as the principal cause of the 1930s Depression, see Ahamed 2009:378–79.

141. Frye 1963:118–19.

142. Frye 1963:119.

143. Frye 1963:119.

144. Fine 1983:541.

145. Frye 1963:119.

3. Markets and Greece

1. My conception of Greek history is based mainly on Burn 1988; Fine 1983; Finley 1981; Grant 1987; Hammond 1986; and Starr 1989. After writing this chapter I read Hanson 1999, who argues for a similar view of the hoplites.

2. Plato, *Phaedo* 109b.

3. Quoted in Finley 1981:126.

4. Finley 1981:6.

5. Burn 1988:13.

6. Fine 1983:51.

7. Sparta at its most populous may have had about 8,000 men over the age of twenty-one and perhaps 45,000 male helots, providing a total population of around 200,000. See n10 and Figueira 1986:116.

8. Starr 1989:38.

9. Fine 1983:51 and Starr 1989:24; Since only adult men could be citizens, I assume that the total population was four times the number of citizens, plus 30 percent for slaves.

10. Although an Athenian population of about 300,000 seems to be generally agreed, historians are uncertain about the population of the Greek diaspora. Pounds 1990:34 estimates 1,500,000 for the entire Greek world.

11. Silver 1985:66.

12. Silver 1985:66.

13. The unattributed facts in the following paragraph are based on Finley 1981 and Hanson 1999.

14. Hammond 1986:84.

15. Grant 1987:xiii.

16. Hammond 1986:98.

17. Finley 1981:75.

18. Fine 1983:36.

19. Quoted in Hanson 1999:133.

20. Hanson 1999:310–11.

21. Finley 1981:132.

22. Grant 1987:13.

23. Finley 1992:151.

24. Keegan 1993:244.

25. Finley 1981:81. The etymological derivation represents a real conceptual derivation as well.

26. Fine 1983:41.

27. Fine 1983:63.

28. Anonymous 2008.

29. Fine 1983:9 and Finley 1981:83. As Hanson 1999:xx says: "All cultural complaints against trading, censure against commerce, and envy and disdain for the factory owner, shipowner, or speculator originate in the distance of such figures from the conservative, rural traditions of the great majority of the [ancient Greek] population."

30. Oliver Wendell Holmes Jr., "The Profession of the Law," quoted in Lerner 1943:33.

31. Some pottery fragments dated to 825 B.C.E. are probably older; Hammond 1986:94.

32. For this insight, Clifford Brown referred me to Gunnell 1968:72, who says: "It was through the work of Homer, Hesiod, the Greek poets and dramatists, and the philosophers that the idea of the self and its temporal limitations as well as the idea of history or the existence of social order in time emerged."

33. Van de Mieroop 2005:30.

34. Hanson 1999:41ff.

35. Hanson 1999:83.

36. Grant 1987:7.

37. The following discussion is based on Fine 1983:69–96.

38. Morris 1994:32.

39. Austin and Vidal-Naquit 1977:54.

40. Hornblower and Spawforth 1996:1536.

41. Grant 1987:83.

42. Finley 1992:106. For land subdivision, see Finley 1952.

43. Hanson 1999:116.

44. Shakespeare, *Merchant of Venice* 1.3.

45. Fine 1983:98–99.

46. Finley 1992:116. For dollar equivalents, see table 5.

47. This formulation avoids the scholarly controversies about whether the armaments or the yeomanry came first. See Hanson 1999:226–29.

48. Hanson 1999:68.

49. Fine 1983:99.

50. Fine 1983:99.

51. Finley 1981:98.

52. Hanson 1999:221.

53. Ste. Croix 1981:24–25.

54. Austin 1988:729.

55. Fine 1983:246.

56. Hammond 1986:126. For graffiti, see Fine 1983:84.

57. Austin 1988:729.

58. *International Herald Tribune* 2007.

59. Cook 1983:219.

60. Parke 1931:233.

61. Parke 1931:235.

62. McNeill 1991:198.

63. The following story is taken from Grant 1987; Fine 1983; and Finley 1981.

64. Grant 1987:39.

65. Fine 1983:193.

66. Fine 1983:1. For Periander's revenge, see Hammond 1986:147.

67. Hammond 1986:156.

68. Grant 1987:42.

69. Jaynes 1976:285.

70. My description of Solon's reforms is based on Fine 1983 and Finley 1981:120–21. As so often the case, it is convenient to attribute everything that happened to this one attractive figure, whether he himself actually did it or not.

71. From *The Suppliants*, quoted in Finley 1981:101.

72. Finley 1981:120–21.

73. Hammond 1986:160.

74. Finley 1992:162.

75. Finley 1992:162.

76. Whitby 1998:120–21.

77. Isager and Skydsgaard 1992:146.

78. Quoted in Fine 1983:250.

79. Fine 1983:212–13.

80. W. Bernstein 2008 2008:48.

81. Isager and Skydsgaard 1992:145.

82. McNeill and McNeill 2003:201.

83. Finley 1981:124.

84. Fine 1983:392–94.

85. McNeill and McNeill 2003:202.

86. Sallares 1991:58, 61.

87. Figueira 1986 and Finley 1992:30–31.

88. For Spartan customs, see Burn 1988:20–21; Hammond 1986:101; and Fine 1983:162–63.

89. McNeill and McNeill 2003:255.

90. Ste. Croix 1981:346.

91. Fine 1983:263.

92. Rostovtzeff 1957:751.

93. Fine 1983:218.

94. Polanyi, Arensberg, and Pearson 1971:83.

95. Aubet 1993:117.

96. Finley 1981:120n1.

97. Sutherland 1969:67.

98. Fine 1983:136; see also Grant 1987:21.

99. Austin and Vidal-Naquit 1977:56–58.

100. Austin and Vidal-Naquit 1977:57 and von Reden 1995:181.

101. Bogaert 1966:313 and Schaps 2004:104.

102. Hammond 1986:661.

103. Grant 1987:291–92.

104. Von Reden 1995:195.

105. For a rigorous and mathematical statement of the issues in these paragraphs, see Brunner and Meltzer 1971. I disagree here with von Reden 1995, who argues that coins reflected rather than created the new set of social relations exemplified by markets and democratic political structures.

106. North 1990:108 emphasizes low transaction costs.

107. E. Harris 2002:70.

108. Quoted in Finley 1981:135.

109. Austin 1988:741.

110. Polanyi, Arensberg, and Pearson 1971:67.

111. E. Cohen 1992:24.

112. Aristotle, *Politics* 2.4.12 §§1267–69, quoted in Finley 1952:53.

113. Finley 1952:58.

114. E. Cohen 1992:66–67.

115. 1998 Statistical Abstract of the United States, table 826: "Money Stock and Liquid Assets: 1980–1997," 525.

116. Finley 1952:63n64. For average acreage, see Applebaum 1992:41.

117. Applebaum 1992:41.

118. Finley 1952:58.

119. Ste. Croix 1981:118.

120. On temple slaves, see W. Ferguson 1969:93n9.

121. As contemporary plays portray them; W. Ferguson 1969:94.

122. Rostovtzeff 1957:1145.

4. Business in Athens

1. This discussion is primarily based on Bogaert 1966; E. Cohen 1992; and Millet 1983.

2. Finley 1952:103.

3. Davies 2001.

4. Kim 2002:10 (map 1.1).

5. Bogaert 1966:313.

6. Bogaert 1966:307.

7. E. Cohen 1992:19n82.

8. http://www.federalreserve.gov/releases/h6/Current/ (accessed July 9, 2008).

9. Quoted in E. Cohen 1992:111. Except as otherwise cited, all facts and quotations in this and the next five paragraphs are from E. Cohen 1992:65–148.

10. Hyperides, *Against Athenogenes* (330–324), quoted in E. Cohen 1992:120.

11. Bogaert 1966:367.

12. Minchinton 1990:172 and Crook 1967:214.

13. Millet 1990:182.

14. Finley 1952:103.

15. Finley 1992:117.

16. Millet 1983:48, citing a speech of Demosthenes.

17. Millet 1983.

18. Finley 1952:85, quoting an Athenian author.

19. Deuteronomy 23.19–20.

20. L. Casson 1994:30.

21. See generally Persky 2007.

22. Finley 1992:198.

23. E. Cohen 1992:32n20, explicitly refuting Finley's argument that thirty known bankers indicates a small level of business.

24. E. Cohen 1992:13n48.

25. Bogaert 1966:370.

26. Mossé 1983:62.

27. Bogaert 1966:371.

28. E. Cohen 1992:151n170. Compare Goldsmith 1987:30.

29. Finley 1952:87.

30. E. Cohen 1992:201.

31. E. Cohen 1992:8.

32. E. Cohen 1992:231.

33. Green 1990:375.

34. E. Cohen 1992:56–57.

35. Millet 1983:36.

36. E. Cohen 1992:146–47.

37. Meijer and van Nijf 1992:49.

38. Hopper 1979:69.

39. Hopper 1979:49.

40. Hopper 1979:49, 67–8.

41. Rostovtzeff 1957:1270–74, for Alexandria in the Hellenistic period, but certainly true earlier and elsewhere.

42. Frayn 1993:6. Pompeii and Herculaneum were no different in this respect from the Greek cities of the East; Rostovtzeff 1957:1274.

43. Veyne 1987:133.

44. Contemporary fragment quoted in Austin 1988:738.

45. Duncan-Jones 1990:37.

46. Hopper 1979:60.

47. Hopper 1979:60.

48. Hopper 1979:70.

49. Goldsmith 1987:30. The value of the slaves seems too low by this estimate, however.

50. Reger 1994:87.

51. Finley 1992:107.

52. W. Harris 1993:86.

53. Applebaum 1992:47–48.

54. Hopkins 1983:xii.

55. Hopper 1979:130–31.

56. Applebaum 1992:45.

57. Austin 1988:743 and Applebaum 1992:46.

58. Hopper 1979:129.

59. Mokyr 1990:21.

60. Mokyr 1990:196–97.

61. Applebaum 1992:28.

62. Finley 1983b:89–90.

63. Applebaum 1992:55. There were twenty-one more studied, but their status is unknown.

64. Hanson 1999:245.

65. Austin 1988:746 and Hanson 1999:105.

66. For Periclean Athens, estimates vary from twenty to four hundred thousand, with sixty to seventy thousand "the best guess"; Grant 1987:2n60.

67. Finley 1992:83.

68. Finley 1992:73–74. Finley 1983b:80 estimates that the percent of slaves in Greece and Rome was about the same as it was in the U.S. South, 30–35 percent, giving him a figure of sixty thousand for Athens in the fifth century B.C.E. (and two million for Rome in the second century C.E.).

69. Applebaum 1992:46.

70. Fine 1983:439.

71. This description of Chios is based on Grant 1987:148–50.

72. Reed 2003:55, citing comments of other scholars.

73. E. Cohen 1992:77.

74. Applebaum 1992:51.

75. Radice 1973:111.

76. E. Cohen 1992:78.

77. E. Cohen 1992:100.

78. Applebaum 1992:51.

79. Lacey 1968, quoted in E. Cohen 1992:78n81.

80. Applebaum 1992:59.

81. Sallares 1991:58, 61.

82. Adams 1993:66.

83. Applebaum 1992:37.

84. Green 1990:365.

85. Aristotle, *Politics* 8.2.4, quoted in Grant 1987:22.

86. See Demosthenes' denunciation in *Against Aristogeiton* 1.50–52, quoted in Meijer and van Nijf 1992:45.

87. E. Cohen 1992:82.

88. Fine and Leopold 1993:96.

89. North 2005:100–101.

90. Finley 1992:48.

91. Prior and Kirby 1993.

5. Hellenistic History

1. For Hellenistic history in general, I relied mainly on Finley 1992; Frye 1963; Grant 1990c; Green 1990; Gruen 1984; Jones 1940; Rostovtzeff 1957; Ste. Croix 1981; Tarn and Griffith 1974; and Walbank 1993.

2. Quoted in Hopper 1979:193.

3. Green 1990:5–7.

4. Green 1990:11.

5. Green 1991:155–56.

6. Revere 1971:60.

7. Green 1991:316.

8. Oldach et al. 1988.

9. Borza 2007:431n54.

10. Grant 1990c:92.

11. Green 1991:20.

12. Tarn and Griffith 1974:64.

13. Green 1990:524.

14. Jones 1940:166.

15. Quoted in Ste. Croix 1981:310.

16. Ste. Croix 1981:300.

17. Quoted in Green 1991:10–11.

18. Rostovtzeff 1993:276; Grant 1990c:127; and Sallares 1991:73.

19. The population of Athens has been much discussed. I follow Sallares 1991:60, who puts Athens as low as 100,000 people, with a total population for Attica including Athens at 150,000–200,000.

20. Metropolitan Museum of Art 1994a.

21. L. Casson 1994:54.

22. Green 1990:13.

23. Green 1990:369.

24. Grant 1990c:43.

25. Peters 1970:166.

26. Peters 1970:166.

27. Rostovtzeff 1957:1150–51.

28. Egypt around 300 B.C.E. was estimated to have six million people; Aperghis 2001:76. Josephus estimated Egypt's population at the time of Jesus at seven to eight million people, and since the Romans were taking a census for tax purposes, historians assume this number to be valid; see Bowman 1994:17; Grant 1990c:78–79; Kaegi 1992:27; Peters 1970:173, 517, 520; and Rostovtzeff 1957:1137–38.

29. Bowman 1994:204–6; Walbank 1993:121, 176; and Grant 1990c:37–38, 76.

30. Green 1990:396. Poem quoted in Tarn and Griffith 1974:53.

31. Tarn and Griffith 1974:325–38; and Green 1990:609–13.

32. Gabrielsen 2001.

33. Mokyr 2008:76. Mokyr notes that economic models demonstrate that such transfers sustain cooperative outcomes even in the absence of good legal enforcement of contractual obligations (2008:77–78).

34. Grant 1990c:146; and Rostovtzeff 1957:691.

35. Gabrielsen 2005:236.

36. McNeill 1991:289n53.

37. Bowman 1994:111–13.

38. Quoted in Bowman 1994:111–12.

39. Berthold 1984:55–56n64 says there were about forty thousand citizens, plus a large population of foreigners and slaves.

40. Starr 1989:54.

41. Green 1990:108. An alternative theory is that the Winged Victory celebrates the Battle of Cos, where Macedonia's Antigonus Gonatus defeated the Ptolemaic fleet in 260 B.C.E.; Cary 1965:138.

42. Green 1990:380. See also Rostovtzeff 1957:686–87.

43. Peters 1970:177.

44. Berthold 1984:53.

45. The king was Seleucus III, the mistress was Mysta; Berthold 1984:102.

46. Higgins 1988:126.

47. Quoted in Berthold 1984:67.

48. Higgins 1988:137.

49. Rostovtzeff 1957:686–87.

50. Diamond 1999:159.

51. Hornblower and Spawforth 1996:766 ("Ipsus").

52. Frye 1963:145.

53. Peters 1970:239.

54. Bowman 1994:96; and Adams 1993:17–25.

55. Peters 1970:242.

56. Green 1990:425.

57. Green 1990:531.

58. Bowman 1994:225.

59. Alfoldy 1988:56.

60. Starr 1989:60.

61. Berthold 1984:227.

62. Berthold 1984:219.

63. Bowman 1994:26.

64. Green 1990:431.

65. Green 1990:513.

66. Peters 1970:143; and Frye 1963:176–77.

6. The Hellenistic Business Environment

1. McNeill 1991:276.

2. Tarn and Griffith 1974:147.

3. Tcherikover 1975:149.

4. Jones 1940:7.

5. Quoted in Finley 1983a:25.

6. Quoted in Walbank 1993:29.

7. For the economic and political theory, see Acemoglu and Robinson 2008.

8. Jones 1940:108.

9. Garnsey and Saller 1987:32.

10. Jones 1940:4 and Finley 1992:153.

11. McNeill 1991:282.

12. Finley 1992:170.

13. Walbank 1993:142.

14. Walbank 1993:151; and Jones 1940:4.

15. Quoted in Walbank 1993:128.

16. Frye 1963:137.

17. Frye 1963:137.

18. Whittaker 1993:4.

19. Ste. Croix 1981:114–15.

20. Rostovtzeff 1957:1116–17.

21. Hopkins 1983:53.

22. McNeill 1991:287; and Ste. Croix 1981:124.

23. Tarn and Griffith 1974:295.

24. Quoted in Grant 1990c:98.

25. White 1993:214.

26. McNeill 1991:292.

27. Grant 1990a:152 and Gies and Gies 1995:22.

28. Walbank 1993:185–86.

29. Applebaum 1992:74.

30. For Euclid, see Green 1990:456. For Fermat, see Singh and Ribet 1997:69.

31. Cunliffe 2008:11–12.

32. Walbank 1993:191–92.

33. Durant 1944:313.

34. Peters 1970:401.

35. Walbank 1993:188–89.

36. Walbank 1993:160.

37. Applebaum 1992:81.

38. Quoted in Mokyr 1990:27n10.

39. Rostovtzeff 1957:1166.

40. See discussion of White 1993 in Green 1993:233–34.

41. CAH 1994:21.

42. Walbank 1993:160.

43. Peters 1970:169.

44. Grant 1990a:43.

45. Rostovtzeff 1957:650.

46. Grant 1990a:70.

47. Rostovtzeff 1957:697, 1166; and Frye 1963:145.

48. Cipolla 1974:49.

49. Rostovtzeff 1957:650.

50. Rostovtzeff 1957:632–33.

51. Applebaum 1992:81.

52. Scarborough 1993:220.

53. Running before a good wind, a ship could cover 90–135 km in a twelve-hour sailing day; Grant and Kitzinger 1988:359.

54. Finley 1992:126.

55. Garnsey, Hopkins, and Whittaker 1983:168. For grain prices, see M. Mango 2001:96.

56. Green 1990:367.

57. Applebaum 1992:87.

58. Ste. Croix 1981:12.

59. Described in Landels 1981:161.

60. W. Bernstein 2008 2008:56.

61. Green 1990:367; and McNeill 1991:295–96.

62. L. Casson 1994:68–69, citing the legend of Theseus.

63. L. Casson 1994:68–69.

64. Grant and Kitzinger 1988:354.

65. Durant 1944:323–24.

66. Durant 1944:324.

67. Gies and Gies 1995:30.

68. Rostovtzeff 1957:1037–38.

69. Walbank 1993:44.

70. Walbank 1993:202.

71. Landels 1981:164; and L. Casson 1994:66.

72. Grant and Kitzinger 1988:359; and D'Arms and Kopff 1980:8.

73. http://members.aol.com/Sokamoto31/ny.htm.

74. Durant 1944:325.

75. Landels 1981:153.

76. From the description by the third-century B.C.E. Greek writer Athenaeus, translated in Meijer and van Nijf 1992:154–56.

77. Grant and Kitzinger 1988:359.

78. Duncan-Jones 1990:9–29.

79. Green 1991:401.

80. Rostovtzeff 1957:1218.

81. Finley 1992:147.

82. Quoted in Finley 1992:147.

83. Grant 1974:86.

84. Anderson 1978:63.

85. Garnsey and Saller 1987:58.

86. Alfoldy 1988:97.

87. Kauffman 2006:44 provides a general explanation of this phenomenon: "Every economic good occupies a niche defined by its relations to complementary and substitute goods. As the number of economic goods increases, the number of ways in which to adaptively combine those goods takes off exponentially, forging possibilities for all-new niches. The autocatalytic creation of niches is thus a main driver of economic growth." See also Atkeson and Kehoe 2007:66.

88. Walbank 1993:192.

89. See generally Rosenberg 2008 and Nelson 1996:chap. 3.

90. McNeill 1991:288.

91. Applebaum 1992:90.

92. Frye 1963:151.

93. Described in Walbank 1993:196.

94. *Aeneid* 6.848–53 (Vergil 2008), Anchises to his son Aeneas.

95. Gies and Gies 1995:36.

96. Gies and Gies 1995:32; and McNeill 1991:374.

97. Ste. Croix 1981:118.

98. Pompey's father-in-law Pythodorus, from the small Anatolian city of Tralles, had four thousand talents (Tarn and Griffith 1974:113); Hiero of Laodicea on the Lycus gave more than that to his home city in gifts alone (Ste. Croix 1981:120); Antiochus IV's satrap in Jerusalem, Joseph ben Tobiah, had three thousand talents (Tcherikover 1975:135); and in 65 B.C.E. a Syrian outlaw paid Pompey a fine of one thousand talents (Bowersock 1983:30).

99. CAH 1994:639.

100. Garnsey and Saller 1987:56; and Hopkins 1978:17–18.

101. A long decline in the price of grain at Delos during a period of steady population growth suggests this; Green 1990:372.

102. D'Arms and Kopff 1980:149–50.

103. Todd and Millet 1990:8–9; and Halpern and Hobson 1993:10.

104. D. Cohen 1995:188.

105. Blackstone 1962:379–80.

106. Jones 1977:5.

107. Quoted in Ste. Croix 1981:141.

108. Ste. Croix 1981:300–301.

109. Ste. Croix 1981:304.

110. For equivalent efforts by U.S. conservatives, see Bandow 2000; Taylor and Meier 2003; McDermott and Eliot 1996; and Howard 1994.

111. Green 1990:46.

112. Tarn and Griffith 1974:88. The kings also sat in judgment of individual cases; 1974:90.

113. Tarn and Griffith 1974:80.

114. Tarn and Griffith 1974:88–89.

115. Walbank 1993:251; Rostovtzeff 1957: 3 and Tarn and Griffith 1974:89.

116. Rostovtzeff 1957:680.

117. Quoted in CAH 1994:630.

7. Hellenistic Business

1. The principal sources for this chapter are Austin 1988; Berthold 1984; L. Casson 1991, 1994; Frayn 1993; Grant 1990c; Green 1990; Hopper 1979; Peters 1970; Rostovtzeff 1972; Tarn and Griffith 1974; and Walbank 1993.

2. Garnsey, Hopkins, and Whittaker 1983:i.

3. Rostovtzeff 1972:9.

4. Finley 1992:7.

5. L. Casson 1994:17–18.

6. McNeill 1991:96.

7. Metropolitan Museum of Art 1994b.

8. Grant 1990c:6.

9. L. Casson 1994:24; and Hopper 1979:91.

10. Frye 1963:59.

11. L. Casson 1994:124.

12. McNeill 1991:96.

13. Rostovtzeff 1972:247.

14. L. Casson 1991:2.

15. Meijer and van Nijf 1992:6–67.

16. Hopper 1979:91.

17. Barraclough 1984:77 (map 1).

18. Morley 1996:111.

19. Rostovtzeff 1972:10.

20. Gaylin 1989.

21. The Bosporan kings in the Crimea and the Greek colonists in southern Italy and Sicily may have done so, since Athens and other Greek city-states were providing them with good markets. In Athens, where Solon and Cleisthenes had encouraged farmers to grow exportable crops, some of the wealthier landowners, like Pericles, may have done so as well.

22. Green 1990:68.

23. Rostovtzeff 1972:1203–4.

24. Sharecropping was the landholder's equivalent of owning debt, as compared to owning equity, which requires more active management but yields higher returns.

25. Reger 1994:7.

26. Quoted in Ste. Croix 1981:4.

27. On peasant conservatism, see Gallant 1991:7: peasants "actively seek to minimize subsistence risk and so avoid activities which would increase the level of risk."

28. Morley 1996:5.

29. Morley 1996:11.

30. Rostovtzeff 1972:4.

31. Rostovtzeff 1972:10.

32. Grant 1990c:1; see also Walbank 1993:8–110.

33. Grant 1990c:1.

34. Bowman 1989:9.

35. Grant 1990c:2.

36. Grant 1990c:43.

37. Thompson 1983:8.

38. Finley 1992:106.

39. Rostovtzeff 1972:52ß.

40. Rostovtzeff 1972:182.

41. See Varro's comments at Rostovtzeff 1972:188.

42. Frye 1963:46.

43. Rostovtzeff 1972:50.

44. Rostovtzeff 1972:158; and Ste. Croix 1981:56ff.

45. Hopper 1979:90.

46. Ste. Croix 1981:71.

47. Burford 1972:3–4.

48. Wood 1988:4.

49. Tarn and Griffith 1974:69; see Walbank 1993:79.

50. Quoted in Durant 1944:504.

51. White 1993:14.

52. Burford 1972:42.

53. Ste. Croix 1981:71.

54. Tarn and Griffith 1974:17–18.

55. Tarn and Griffith 1974:13.

56. Tarn and Griffith 1974:78.

57. Tarn and Griffith 1974:273.

58. Finley 1992:51.

59. Finley 1992:53.

60. Jones 1940:4.

61. Tarn and Griffith 1974:14–15.

62. As describe by Dio Chrysostomus; Meijer and van Nijf 1992:6–7.

63. Plutarch, *Lives* 74.

64. Grant 1990c:24; and Green 1990:62.

65. Green 1990:73.

66. For ten years, see Bogaert 1966:306. For brief inflation, see Reger 1994:157, 252.

67. Green 1990:73.

68. The description of banking is taken from Bogaert 1966 unless otherwise noted.

69. L. Casson 1991:100.

70. Quoted in Hendy 1985:249–50.

71. Hendy 1985:49–50, citing John Cassian. At the time Cassian was writing there was only the one Roman currency.

72. Quoted in Rostovtzeff 1972:88.

73. Bogaert 1966:79.

74. Bogaert 1966:292.

75. Reger 1994:3.

76. Green 1990:74.

77. Bogaert 1966:34.

78. Bogaert 1966:72.

79. Bogaert 1966:35–40.

80. Grant 1990c:4–5; Bowman 1989:13; and Rostovtzeff 1972:285.

81. Bogaert 1966:344.

82. Bowman 1989:8, 115, 117. Bowman is describing Roman Egypt, but the description probably applies to later Ptolemaic Egypt as well.

83. Bowman 1989:13.

84. Bogaert 1966:55–56.

85. Rostovtzeff 1972:22.

86. Bowman 1989:16; Finley 1952:7; and Bogaert 1966:57, 361, 370.

87. Grant 1990c:4–5.

88. Bogaert 1966:5–6.

89. Wild 1970:10.

90. Finley 1992:44–45.

8. The Early Roman Republic

1. This section relies on Ferrill 1988; Keller 1974; Pallotino 1975; and Wells 1999.

2. Keller 1974:60–68.

3. Ferrill 1988:47.

4. Smith 1988:35. Alfoldy 1988:6 translates Smith's fifteen thousand "citizens."

5. Brunt 1988:145.

6. Keegan 1993:265.

7. Dudley 1993:42.

8. The discussion of Rome's political structure relies mainly on Alfoldy 1988 and Finley 1983a.

9. For patronage I have relied on Alfoldy 1988; Brunt 1988; D'Arms and Kopff 1980; Garnsey and Saller 1987; Saller 1989; and A. Wallace-Hadrill 1989.

10. Plutarch, *Pericles*.

11. Nippel 1995:2.

12. Veyne 1987:151. The discussion of this paragraph follows Nippel 1995.

13. Quoted in MacMullen 1988:105.

14. Crook 1967:52–54.

15. Saller 1989:57. This designation seems to have been very confusing to historians.

16. A. Wallace-Hadrill 1989:63.

17. "A mighty tide of morning callers"; Vergil, *Georgics* 2.461.

18. Quoted in Saller 1989:58.

19. Saller 1989:58.

20. Dudley 1993:25.

21. Quoted in Garnsey and Saller 1987:148.

22. G. Hamilton 1996 and Casson and Rose 1997:2–3.

23. Aubert 1994:285.

24. D'Arms and Kopff 1980:155–56.

25. Finley 1992:64. Andreau 1999:68–70 doubts that the *peculium* was enough to capitalize slave businesses, but remains silent about funds advanced from patrons to clients—who may well have included such slaves.

26. The account of the Carthaginian wars is based on Dudley 1993; Goodman 1997; and Rostovtzeff 1960.

27. Alfoldy 1988:29–30.

28. Ferrill 1988:52.

29. Rostovtzeff 1960:41.

30. Rostovtzeff 1960:50.

31. Rostovtzeff 1957:51.

32. Duncan-Jones 1990:36.

33. Rostovtzeff 1957:1150–51.

34. Duncan-Jones 1990:36.

35. Durant 1944:40–41.

36. Alfoldy 1988:37, citing Polybius.

37. L. Casson 1991:145–46.

38. Rostovtzeff 1960:79 and CAH 1994:579.

39. Rostovtzeff 1960:86.

40. Jones 1974:114–15.

41. Durant 1944:40.

42. Dudley 1993:184.

43. CAH 1994:579.

44. Dudley 1993:137.

45. Badian 1972:16.

46. CAH 1994:636; see generally, Badian 1972:66ff.

47. Rostovtzeff 1957:17.

48. Malminder 2005:32–33.

49. Hopkins 1978:52.

50. Adams 1993:66–68.

51. Adams 1993:97–102.

52. Aubert 1994:332–33.

53. Aubert 1994:338.

54. Lintott 1993:87.

55. Alfoldy 1988:50; and Rostovtzeff 1960:88.

56. Badian 1972:45.

57. Goodman 1997:172. See also Veyne 1987:158; and generally D'Arms and Kopff 1980.

58. Brunt 1988:145.

59. Much remains to be known about them, such as the number of publican societies and how long they lasted.

60. Badian 1972:38; and Aubert 1994:327.

61. Aubert 1994:325–26. For staffs, see Badian 1972:46–47.

62. Aubert 1994:337.

63. This is evident from the praises Cato received for being an honest censor.

64. Hopkins 1978:45. See also Durant 1944:336.

65. Aubert 1994:329.

66. Alfoldy 1988:52.

67. About 50 percent of all citizens served around seven years on average; Hopkins 1978:30.

68. Quoted in Alfoldy 1988:46.

69. Whittaker 1993:60.

70. The following account is from Talbert 1984:54–66.

71. Quoted in Alfoldy 1988:61. Sallust (86–34 B.C.E.), born a plebeian, became a tribune, senator, governor of Africa, and one of Julius Caesar's supporters.

72. Nelson and Zeckhauser 2008:3–4.

73. Talbert 1984:63. Veiento went no further.

74. Quoted in Talbert 1984:54.

75. D'Arms and Kopff 1980:83.

76. CAH 1994:612.

77. Morley 1996:117. See also Moritz 1958:67.

78. Hopkins 1978:2.

79. Finley 1983b:82.

80. Hopkins 1978:16 (fig. 1.2).

81. Garnsey and Saller 1987:90.

82. Hopkins 1978:107–11.

83. Hopkins 1978:118.

84. Alfoldy 1988:67.

85. Frayn 1984:128.

86. Crook 1967:156.

87. An Italian population of 5,000,000–8,000,000 in the early empire is "the broad consensus of modern scholarly opinion"; Parkin 1992:5. An additional 600,000–1,000,000 lived in Sicily; Pounds 1990:53. For 2,000,000 slaves, see CAH 1994:608 and Finley 1992:92–93. I find this number improbably high, however. It derives largely from contemporary estimates, which are notoriously unreliable. Even if slaves worked

every one of the 123,000 acres planted to vineyard around Rome with the same man-power that one well-documented farm used (Settefinestre; see below), the total number of slaves involved would be less than 17,000. Of course, there were many farms growing other products, but vineyards were among the most important cash crops for which slave labor would have been used.

88. CAH 1994:616.

89. Frayn 1984:115.

90. CAH 1994:616; and Frayn 1984: 123.

91. Alfoldy 1988:68–69, 145.

92. This area was the Roman measure of land, the *jugerum*; Pounds 1990:63–64.

93. Duncan-Jones 1990:126.

94. Rostovtzeff 1957:61.

95. CAH 1994:612.

96. Morley 1996:11.

97. Hopkins 1978:3.

98. Goodman 1997:148.

99. CAH 1994:614.

100. Vallee 1998.

101. Garnsey and Saller 1987:60.

102. W. Harris 1993:12n7.

103. Hopkins 1978:9n16.

104. Aubert 1994:117.

105. Duncan-Jones 1990:127 (table 42).

106. Finley 1976:106.

107. Aubert 1994:176–77.

108. In the second century C.E. at Veientanus, near Rome, there were 86 large villas and farms and 230 smaller holdings; Randsborg 1991:42. At Veleia in northern Italy at the beginning of the second century there were 17 estates holding 125 farms, of which many were leased to peasants; Duncan-Jones 1990:127. In the Hermapolite nome of Egypt around 350 C.E., there were 441 landowners, with 16 owning 51 percent of the land; Bowman 1994:87, 99.

109. Aubert 1994:176–77.

110. Aubert 1994:176–77.

111. Quoted in Ste. Croix 1981:187.

112. White 1975:213.

113. Kolhatkar 2006:99. Columella's comment is at Aubert 1994:185.

114. Paterson 1998:159.

115. Frayn 1984:145.

116. Frayn 1984:77 (fig. 7).

117. Carandini 1980:7.

118. CAH 1994:614. One hectoliter = 26.4 gallons.

119. Aubert 1994:173.

9. The Late Roman Republic

1. My understanding of Roman history before the third century C.E. relies most heavily on Alfoldy 1988; CAH 1994; Dudley 1993; Ferrill 1988; Finley 1976, 1992; Garnsey and Saller 1987; Goodman 1997; Rostovtzeff 1957, 1960; and Ste. Croix 1981.

2. Cato's biography appears in Plutarch's *Lives* 411ff., and all quotations below are from this work.

3. Thanks to Plutarch, more is known about Cato's investments than any other Roman's.

4. Rostovtzeff 1957:22.

5. Rostovtzeff 1957:21.

6. Rostovtzeff 1957:818.

7. Dudley 1993:62.

8. CAH 1994:593. Presumably the publicans provided the military with bribes and gifts, but these could hardly amount to a significant share of their profits.

9. Adams 1993:79, citing Livy.

10. Badian 1972:76–77.

11. Quoted in Adams 1993:82.

12. Alfoldy 1988:55.

13. Quoted in Alfoldy 1988:61.

14. Green 1990:428.

15. Quoted in Badian 1972:45.

16. Rostovtzeff 1960:71; and Green 1990:427–28.

17. Alfoldy 1988:46.

18. Badian 1972:41.

19. Jones 1974:114; and Green 1990:414.

20. Rostovtzeff 1960:73.

21. Walbank 1993:238.

22. See, e.g., a memorial to the diplomats of Abdera, quoted in Walbank 1993:238.

23. Rostovtzeff 1957:17; and Alfoldy 1988:49.

24. CAH 1994:593.

25. L. Casson 1991:169.

26. Rostovtzeff 1957:744–45, based on shipwrecks containing statues in bronze and marble, furniture, decorative bowls and candelabra, bas-reliefs, columns, bases and capitals in marble, and slabs of marble.

27. Grant 1990c:122.

28. Rostovtzeff 1957:752–56; and Alfoldy 1988:61.

29. W. Ferguson 1969:428.

30. Rostovtzeff 1957:741.

31. Dudley 1993:60–61.

32. Ste. Croix 1981:347.

33. Hopkins 1978:28.

34. Rostovtzeff 1957:739.

35. Alfoldy 1988:54.

36. Edmondson 1993:170–74.

37. Alfoldy 1988:68; and Green 1990:529–30.

38. Alfoldy 1988:59.

39. Alfoldy 1988:53, quoting Plutarch.

40. Garnsey and Saller 1987:5.

41. Dudley 1993:73.

42. Dudley 1993:65.

43. Rostovtzeff 1957:33–34.

44. Rostovtzeff 1960:156; Rostovtzeff 1957:35; and Pounds 1990:53–54.

45. Description from Whittaker 1993:116.

46. Dudley 1993:180; and Pounds 1990:49.

47. Pounds 1990:62.

48. For the *annona* I relied mainly on Sirks 1991. Other important sources include L. Casson 1980 and Loane 1938.

49. On incidents, see Aldrete and Mattingly 1999:174; Tacitus quoted in 1999:176–77.

50. Hopkins 1978:38.

51. Loane 1938:13n9. The number of Romans who received the *annona* is unclear: 10 percent lived on church charity in late antiquity (Sirks 1991:21n52), but other sources suggest a much larger percent of Romans received free food at earlier times. Barnish 1987:160–63 seems to conclude that about 29 percent of the city's population received the dole. L. Casson 1980:22 estimates that the state supplied twelve million of the sixty million modii (four hundred thousand tons) of grain Rome consumed, or 20 percent.

52. Aldrete and Mattingly 1999:203.

53. Quoted in Rickman 1980:263.

54. A. Cameron 1993b:99.

55. After designating Pergamum the province of Asia, Gaius imposed a new harvest tax and allowed the publicans, instead of city magistrates, to collect it; Rostovtzeff 1960:101.

56. Dudley 1993:72.

57. Brunt 1988:145.

58. Dudley 1993:74.

59. Brunt 1988:152.

60. Badian 1972:81.

61. CAH 1994:594.

62. Badian 1972:14.

63. Ste. Croix 1981:356. For Cicero's story about Verres in Asia, see Hopkins 1978:42–43.

64. Green 1990:556.

65. Sallares 1991:190–200.

66. Rostovtzeff 1960:96; and CAH 1994:592.

67. Quoted in Alfoldy 1988:51.

68. W. Ferguson 1969:428.

69. Plutarch, *Caius Marius*. Marius was elected one of the two consuls.

70. Dudley 1993:77. They actually averaged twenty years of service; Hopkins 1978:30.

71. Dudley 1993:80.

72. W. Ferguson 1969:441; and Green 1990: 560–63. Information about Athens is far better than about anywhere else in Greece.

73. Dudley 1993:80.

74. "For the Manilian Law," is quoted in Durant 1944:140.

75. Green 1990:64.

76. Green 1990:564.

77. Rostovtzeff 1960:113.

78. CAH 1994:197.

79. My account is based on Ward 1977 and on Plutarch. The quotations are from Plutarch's *Life of Crassus*, unless otherwise indicated.

80. Durant 1944:138.

81. Dudley 1993:90.

82. W. Ferguson 1969:428.

83. Lucullus retired to his Roman town house, where he sponsored epicurean feasts and introduced cherry trees from Pontus. He bought Sulla's estate on the Bay of Naples, paying more than thirty times what Sulla had paid Marius for the same property (a measure of Rome's increasing wealth). The last Roman emperor retired here after his abdication in 476 C.E.; Dudley 1993:70–71 and Durant 1944:132. On real estate see Finley 1992:103.

84. Starr 1989:74.

85. Bowman 1994:35.

86. Badian 1972:105.

87. Jones 1974:93.

88. Badian 1972:109, 116–17; and Peters 1970:380.

89. The description of Rome is taken largely from Carcopino 1968, who describes the city under Augustus, a few decades after Crassus.

90. Carcopino 1968:22.

91. Chairs were for professors or priests (the origin of the term for a university appointment).

92. Quoted in Carcopino 1968:33.

93. A capital offense for both; if convicted, he would be executed and she, buried alive.

94. Bailey 1978:40n18.

95. Dudley 1993:97–98.

96. Wells 1984:52.

97. Wells 1984:40.

98. Quoted in Klingaman 2008:35.

99. Garnsey, Hopkins, and Whittaker 1983:118.

100. For population at time of Caesar, see CAH 1994:605. For population in the second century C.E., see Pounds 1990:53.

101. Both Caesar and Pompey reduced taxes in the East, reformed the tax system, and got rid of publicans; Peters 1970:380.

102. Peters 1970:380.

103. Peters 1970:384; and Durant 1944:203.

104. Durant 1944:201–2.

105. Their rule was called the Second Triumvirate because one Lepidus, who commanded Roman forces in Africa, served for a time before Octavian had him removed.

106. Hopkins 1978:7.

107. Durant 1944:192.

108. Brown 1973:14.

109. Goodman 1997:23.

110. Andreau 1999:18.

111. Rostovtzeff 1957:30–31.

10. The Principate.

1. On Augustus I have relied mainly on Alfoldy 1988; Brunt 1988; Dudley 1993; Durant 1944; Goodman 1997; Hopkins 1978; and Rostovtzeff 1960.

2. Dudley 1993:107.

3. Hopkins 1978:92.

4. Dudley 1993:124.

5. Williams 1997:9.

6. Rostovtzeff 1960:165–66.

7. Durant 1944:234. Sigmund Freud tells a joke from Macrobius's *Saturnalia*, said to have originated in Augustus's Rome, if not with the emperor himself: a monarch touring his provinces met someone who looked just like him. He asked if the fellow's mother had worked in the palace. "No, your highness, but my father did"; Beard 2008.

8. Hopkins 1978:39.

9. Durant 1944:215.

10. Brunt 1988:439.

11. Rostovtzeff 1960:174.

12. Goodman 1997:240.

13. Rostovtzeff 1960:173.

14. Horsley 1995:210.

15. Rostovtzeff 1960:229; and Goodman 1997:108.

16. Dudley 1993:137.

17. Richardson 1976:55; and Rostovtzeff 1960:227.

18. Rostovtzeff 1960:228–29.

19. Richardson 1976:62–63.

20. Millar 1977.

21. Goodman 1997:118.

22. Garnsey and Saller 1987:88.

23. Goodman 1997:100.

24. Hopkins 1978:38.

25. MacMullen 1988:175–76.

26. Goodman 1997:100.

27. Adams 1993:78; Webber and Wildavsky 1985:77; and Crook 1967:147.

28. Quoted in Ste. Croix 1981:363.

29. Brunt 1988:153–54.

30. Adams 1993:94–95.

31. Jones 1974:95.

32. Rostovtzeff 1957:49.

33. Adams 1993:95.

34. MacMullen 1988:88.

35. MacMullen 1988:88.

36. MacMullen 1988:138.

37. Morley 1996:78–79.

38. MacMullen 1988:120.

39. Rostovtzeff 1960:144.

40. Rostovtzeff 1957:29; and Goodman 1997:190.

41. Green 1991:5.

42. Quoted in Green 1991:274.

43. Green 1991:200.

44. Jones 1940:101.

45. Hopkins 1978:221, 230–31.

46. Goodman 1997:175.

47. Dudley 1993:142.

48. Dudley 1993:140–41.

49. Tacitus, quoted in Goodman 1997:201.

50. Durant 1944:274. The Durants evidently got this from Seneca's *Apocolocyntosis*, which contains a section called "The Pumpkinification of Emperor Claudius," a daydream. Claudius arrives in heaven where "Augustus denounces him: 'Since the divine Claudius has killed his father-in-law Appius Silanus, his two sons-in-law Magnus Pompeius and L. Silanus, his daughter's father-in-law Crassus Frugi, a man as like himself as one egg is to another, Scribonia his daughter's mother-in-law, his wife Messalina, and others too numerous to mention, I propose that strict punishment be meted out to him, that he be granted no rest from adjudicating cases, and that he be got out of the way as soon as possible, departing from heaven within thirty days and from Olympus within three.' The motion carried and Claudius was sent to Pluto's Hell for further trial. There he was found guilty of 'Senators killed, thirty-five; Roman knights, two hundred and twenty-one; other persons, as many as the sands on the seashore.' His punishment: 'It was decided that a new punishment ought to be arranged, that for him must be devised some vain task and the hope of gratifying some desire, without end or consummation.' So he was given a bottomless dice box to gamble with, and the dice constantly slipped out, frustrating him no end. But finally Caesar appeared, claimed him as a slave, and he ended up working as a law clerk."

(trans. A. P. Ball [orig., Columbia University Press, 1902], available at http://www
.forumromanum.org/literature/apocolocyntosis.html [accessed 6/28/08]).

51. On extermination, see Rostovtzeff 1960:196. On Africa, see Goodman
1997:56.

52. Keay 1988:100–101.

53. Alfoldy 1988:95. For cedars, see Goodman 1997:248.

54. Goldsmith 1987:55 (table 4.2).

55. Brown 1997:12–13.

56. From Augustus to Titus, veterans were paid 900 HS (225 denarii)/year and
retired with 12,000 HS; Goodman 1997:118.

57. The *annona* added oil in 200 C.E., and pork and wine later, in the 270s; Morley
1996:55.

58. Silver 1985:80. But see L. Casson 1980:22.

59. Sirks 1991:25.

60. Garnsey and Saller 1987:60 and Whittaker 1993:54. For piggybacking on military shipments, see Keay 1988:95. For piggybacking on private landowner shipments,
see Greene 2000:44.

61. Keay 1988:98.

62. Aldrete and Mattingly 1999:191.

63. Kleberg 1957:102–5.

64. The story of the crisis is from Durant 1944:332.

65. Dudley 1993:167.

66. Rostovtzeff 1957:103–5.

67. Goodman 1987:120.

68. Alfoldy 1988:120.

69. Dudley 1993:169.

70. Gibbon 1946:61.

71. Rostovtzeff 1960:208.

72. Quoted in Rostovtzeff 1957:122.

73. Counted as of the fourth century C.E. (Brown 1992:25), but never much
changed (A. Cameron 1993b:129).

74. For five hundred villages, see Frayn 1993:162 (speaking of the early empire).
For 30–40 percent in cities, see Hopkins 1978:6; and Morley 1996:182. For the population of Rome, see Hopkins 1978:7n13; and Garnsey and Saller 1987:6. For Puteoli largest outside Rome, see Randsborg 1991:92. For one hundred thousand in Ostia, see
Dudley 1993:202, but see Morley 1996:182, estimating thirty thousand. For Capua and
Salerno, see D'Arms and Kopff 1980:106. For twenty-five cities of fifteen thousand
each, see Morley 1996: 182.

75. Duncan-Jones 1990:104.

76. Frayn 1993:38–39.

77. Quoted in Carcopino 1968:47.

78. Mokyr 1999:20.

79. L. Casson 1988:356.

80. Dudley 1993:182–83.

81. MacMullen 1988:30.

82. Brown 1969:20.

83. Dudley 1993:181.

84. Dudley 1993:184.

85. Garnsey and Saller 1987:59.

86. Goodman 1987:200.

87. Sirks 1991:39; and Keay 1988:75.

88. Paterson 1998:163.

89. Keay 1988:103.

90. I am summarizing here a complex process, described in Rostovtzeff 1960:216–25.

91. Goodman 1987:213.

92. Pounds 1990:51.

93. Garnsey and Saller 1987:57; and Randsborg 1991:31–32.

94. Brown 1997:13.

95. Pounds 1990:57–58; and Dudley 1993:131.

96. The history of Judea related here relies primarily on Bowersock 1983; Buehler 1974; Cahill 1998; S. Cohen 1988; Cohn 1994; *Encyclopaedia Judaica*; Goodman 1987; Miles 1995; Millar 1993; Peters 1970; Safrai 1994; Smallwood 1976; Tarn and Griffith 1974; and Wylen 1996.

97. Micah 6.8.

98. *Encyclopaedia Judaica* 6.18 ("Diaspora").

99. Buehler 1974:58–59.

100. Buehler 1974:88–89.

101. Wylen 1996:66.

102. Schiffman 1992; and Huie 1998.

103. Smallwood 1976:28. The bribes included a solid gold vine from the temple worth seven hundred talents; S. Cohen 1988:23. While in Jerusalem, Pompey visited the famous temple. Leaving his guards and their eagle standards in the courtyard he wandered around, then departed. The Pharisees, claiming that the eagle standards had desecrated the temple with idolatry, so vilified Pompey that nearly two centuries later a Jewish mob tore down his tomb in Alexandria; Smallwood 1976:27.

104. Goodman 1987:10.

105. Wylen 1996:72–73.

106. Wylen 1996:210–11; Brown 1973:36; and Horsley 1995:219n50. Tenancy was a Hellenistic innovation in Judea during the third century B.C.E.; Goodman 1987:67.

107. Goodman 1987:56–58.

108. Horsley 1995:219–20.

109. Millar 1993:51.

110. Goodman 1987:65, 75.

111. Smallwood 1976:257.

112. Millar 1993:55.

113. Wylen 1996:75.

114. Cohn 1994:208.

115. Smallwood 1976:343–49.

116. Johnston 2001.

117. Miles 1995:200.

118. Miles 1995:219. The Sibylline Books were from the cult of Cybele, very important in these parts.

119. Smallwood 1976:384 and *Encyclopaedia Judaica* 6.10 (Philo estimated one million Jews in Egypt in the first century C.E.).

120. The following paragraphs are based on Smallwood 1976:358–69.

121. The insurrectionists allegedly slaughtered 220,000 people and greatly depopulated the land. They were said to have worn the intestines of their victims as belts, among other atrocities.

122. A. Cameron 1993b:183.

123. Cohn 1994:208.

124. Goodman 1997:325.

125. MacMullen 1986:83.

126. Quoted in Dudley 1993:179.

127. Hornblower and Spawforth 1996:1537 ("Trade, Roman").

11. Roman Society

1. Alfoldy 1988:88–89, 127, 147.

2. Estimate by Whittaker 1993:12.

3. Alfoldy 1988:108.

4. Hopkins 1978:182.

5. Hopkins 1978:41. For John the Lydian, see Ste. Croix 1981:488.

6. Hendy 1985:203.

7. Alfoldy 1988:108. For Ahenobarbus, see Anderson 1978:61.

8. Ste. Croix 1981:359n10.

9. Finley 1992:100–101.

10. Garnsey and Saller 1987:70.

11. Garnsey and Saller 1987:64–69.

12. Garnsey and Saller 1987:67.

13. Durant 1944:40.

14. Alfoldy 1988:107.

15. Finley 1992:112.

16. Goodman 1997:208.

17. Under the Antonines; see Jones 1974:126.

18. Hopkins 1978:49.

19. Aubert 1994:368.

20. The drainage was not completed until 1875, and further work was done repeatedly throughout the Middle Ages; Dudley 1993:164. Working days are net of Roman holidays.

21. Peters 1970:339n26 and Hopkins 1978:109. On slavery generally see Alfoldy 1988; Finley 1992, 1983b; Hopkins 1978; Ste. Croix 1981; and Whittaker 1993, 1987.

22. Wells 1999:13–14.

23. Duncan-Jones 1990:104.

24. For one hundred thousand slaves costing a typical average of two thousand HS, see Anderson 1978:135; and Alfoldy 1988:203.

25. Suetonius, *Claudius*, in Meijer and van Nijf 1992:101.

26. Claudius required ships to remain six years in service (Garnsey and Saller 1987:88), so I assume this is the useful life of such ships. That means one sixth of the shipping tonnage had to be replaced annually, or just under 29,000 tons.

27. This is a speculative calculation. It assumes that Rome consumed 172,000 tons of Egypt's grain annually; Bowman 1989:38. Landels 1981:166 notes that since a ship usually made only one voyage per season between Alexandria and Italy, this required a fleet of 172,000 tons. Bowman says that Egypt may have supplied 30 percent of the *annona*'s grain, a number that comes from one ancient text called "isolated" and "unreliable" by Garnsey and Saller 1987:85, but it's the only estimate we have. If correct, then even though other routes allowed more trips, Rome might have needed double the Egyptian tonnage to supply all its needs. How much did 58,000 tons of shipping cost? Fairly careful estimates suggest that it cost up to 1,000 HS per ton for a 400-ton ship sailing the route from Alexandria to Ostia; Garnsey and Saller 1987:49. But smaller ships undoubtedly cost more per ton, so the 1,000-HS-per-ton figure is conservative.

28. Sirks 1991:31–34.

29. Garnsey and Saller 1987:43–44.

30. J. Wallace-Hadrill 1988:11.

31. In this section I have relied primarily on Alfoldy 1988; Crook 1967; Finley 1976; Frayn 1993; Jones 1974; Kolbert 1979; Nippel 1995; Ste. Croix 1981; and Wolff 1951.

32. North 1981:109.

33. By contrast, in many underdeveloped societies today—and even in the developed societies a century ago—the multiplicity of legal systems has greatly complicated the ownership of property, and the resulting confusion has been a major obstacle to the creation of wealth and its use for productive purposes. See DeSoto 2003.

34. See DeSoto 2003 for an excellent discussion of the role of law in the creation of wealth.

35. Crook 1967:214.

36. Wolff 1951:71.

37. Rome also had a *ius gentium* for non-Romans, and the censor punished crimes against the state like treason and sedition, serious crimes against persons like rape and murder, and the economic crimes of counterfeiting, smuggling, and brigandage; Nippel 1995:113. Citizens accused of capital crimes could appeal to the emperor; Crook 1967:70.

38. Crook 1967; and see generally Millar 1977.

39. According to a price list from the African town of Timgad in 362 C.E., 7½ bushels of wheat went to the governor's chief of staff and his aides to begin a lawsuit

before the governor, plus 2 bushels per mile to the clerk for travel to notify the defendant—100 bushels if service was overseas; MacMullen 1988:151.

40. In large cases the jury might include up to a hundred people; Crook 1967:79.

41. Quoted in Wolff 1951:77.

42. As the first sentence in the Twelve Tables says, "If a man is summoned to appear in court and does not come, let witnesses be heard and then let the plaintiff seize him. If he resists or absconds, the plaintiff can use force"; Kolbert 1979:13.

43. See generally Crook 1967 for legal procedures.

44. Brown 1969:90.

45. MacMullen 1988:118–19; and CAH 1994:547.

46. Goodman 1997:185.

47. Paterson 1998:155; see Justinian, *Digest* 18.

48. CAH 1994:635.

49. Aubert 1994:44–45. Recall that the Code of Hammurabi provided that an agent's sale of his master's merchandise could not be invalidated if the agent had provided his master a price quotation under seal; Association of Chartered Accountants in the United States 1999.

50. Aubert 1994:171.

51. Aubert 1994:5–6, 9–12, 59.

52. Aubert 1994:413.

53. In recent years, economists and social scientists have developed the concept of "social capital," a set of informal norms that facilitates cooperation; Fukuyama 1999:14–16. Where high levels of social capital exist, as in a patronage relationship, agency costs are typically much reduced; Fukuyama 1999:201ff. and Fukuyama 1995.

54. Ste. Croix 1981:165.

55. Ste. Croix 1981:259.

56. Quoted in Ste. Croix 1981:167.

57. Hopkins 1978:14n20. Rawson 1976 contrasts the Roman lack of attachment to land with the passionate attitude of the English nobility at the time of Jane Austen.

58. D'Arms 1981:86.

59. Morley 1996:79.

60. Kolbert 1979:58.

61. Crook 1967:140.

62. Finley 1992:106 explains that peasant holdings were usually too small to fully occupy an entire peasant family.

63. Carcopino 1968:184.

64. Carcopino 1968:206. A typical American worker might have ten holidays, two weeks vacation, weekends off, and an eight-hour day, which comes to 1,920 hours per year. The Roman work year of seven hours a day for ninety days plus six hours a day for ninety days equals 1,170 hours.

65. Crook 1967:107–9; and Aubert 1994:44–45.

66. Carcopino 1968:181.

67. Applebaum 1992:158–62.

68. Alfoldy 1988:144.

69. The cost was 270 denarii under Augustus; Finley 1952:70. For a year's upkeep, see Hopkins 1978:39–40. For early-second-century cost, see Hopkins 1978:109; and Peters 1970:339n26.

70. Finley 1983b:133. The precise status of these *coloni* varied with time and place; in general, the restrictions became increasingly severe as the empire aged, until at last it could be stated that the only distinction between a slave and a *colonus* was the latter's obligation to serve in the army; Whittaker 1987:110.

71. Finley 1983b:140.

72. Quoted in Ste. Croix 1981:182.

73. Aldrete and Mattingly 1999:201.

74. Applebaum 1992:112–13.

75. Goodman 1997:273; and Jones 1974:358.

76. Alfoldy 1988:208; and Ste. Croix 1981:243.

77. Aubert 1994:157.

78. This assumes that 25–30 percent of population were adult men, or approximately fifteen million.

79. Hopkins 1978:7n13; and Garnsey and Saller 1987:73. The size of the slave population after Augustus is a matter of uncertainty. With the end of the great military conquests and of Mediterranean piracy, slave prices rose, and therefore it would be logical to conclude that the number of slaves declined; Jones 1974:128. On the other hand, Finley 1983b:131 and other scholars (e.g., Whittaker 1993:171) believe there was little or no decline until the third century. As Finley observes, we know only that it existed in the second century C.E. and was largely gone by the time of Charlemagne.

80. Finley 1983b:81.

81. Badian 1972:33–34.

82. Quoted in Finley 1983b:96.

83. Recall that if a master was killed, the law required that all his slaves be tortured to death; Hopkins 1978:120.

84. Applebaum 1992:104. The choice between persuasion and the whip is known, in modern human resource theory, as "theory x versus theory y management"; see McGregor 1985.

85. Whittaker 1987:98.

86. Applebaum 1992:136; and Whittaker 1987:98.

87. Hopkins 1978:222.

88. Alfoldy 1988:146.

89. Finley 1992:74.

90. Alfoldy 1988:143.

91. For Athens, see Grant 1990c:132. For Mago, see Rostovtzeff 1957:10.

92. Alfoldy 1988:141.

93. Crook 1967:63.

94. Alfoldy 1988:141.

95. Inscription from the Aegean island of Calymna around 100 C.E., quoted in Hopkins 1978:157.

96. Crook 1967:51. The freed person could not be obligated to perform degrading work, however, such as prostitution; 1967:52.

97. Although freedmen had to gain their former masters' permission to sue; Crook 1967:2, 51.

98. Garnsey and Saller 1987:124.

99. Alfoldy 1988:141; and Veyne 1987:145.

100. Ste. Croix 1981:148.

101. Carcopino 1968:85.

102. Applebaum 1992:116–17.

103. Potter and Mattingly 1999:267.

104. Applebaum 1992:121.

105. Carcopino 1968:183.

106. What Rostovtzeff 1957:1306 says of the Hellenistic kings was true of the Roman emperors as well.

107. For the dependence of emperors on the urban mob, see Brown 1992:149.

108. Trajan was instructing Pliny to forbid the formation of a fire brigade in Bithynia's capital of Nicomedia; Pliny, *Letters* 10.34, quoted in Goodman 1997:232.

109. Sirks 1991:406.

110. Applebaum 1992:143.

111. Description from Carcopino 1968:175–76.

112. D'Arms 1981:147–48.

113. A. Wallace-Hadrill 1991. The discussion of status relies especially on Alfoldy 1988; Aubert 1994; D'Arms 1981; Garnsey, Hopkins, and Whittaker 1983; Hopkins 1978; Talbert 1984; and Veyne 1987.

114. Cicero, *De officiis* 1.150–51, cited in Finley 1992:41–42.

115. This was true even in the Principate; Badian 1972:51.

116. Applebaum 1992:105, cited in Hopkins 1978:54.

117. "Because these men are forced to remain seated in the shade and sometimes even to spend entire days at fireside"; quoted in Veyne 1987:122.

118. Veyne 1987:119; and Applebaum 1992:96.

119. Whittaker 1993:2.

120. The dominant ideal for the economy was stability, a virtue particularly prized in rural economies; Green 1990:363.

121. Thaler 2010; and Carr 1968.

122. Aubert 1994:21–22.

123. Crook 1967:193.

124. Crook 1967:193; and Veyne 1987:132.

125. Applebaum 1992:152.

126. See his speech in Meijer and van Nijf 1992:74.

127. Andreau 1999:48.

128. Veyne 1987:143.

129. Brunt 1988:172–73.

130. Brunt 1988:169.

131. D'Arms 1981:49.

132. Brunt 1988:171.

133. Carcopino 1968:193.

134. D'Arms 1981:64.

135. Andreau 1999:12.

136. Andreau 1999:78.

137. Andreau 1999:8.

138. Peters 1970:528.

139. Alfoldy 1988:128.

140. Rostovtzeff 1957:150n14.

141. Alfoldy 1988:52.

142. Grant 1985:103–4.

143. Bowman 1994:39–40.

144. Aubert 1994:25.

145. Alfoldy 1988:109ff.

146. Ten percent of the population lived in cities of 10,000 or more; Goldsmith 1987:34.

147. *Citizens United v. Federal Election Board*, 558 U.S. 50 (210), J. Roberts concurring opinion.

12. Roman Businesses

1. Randsborg 1991:127–28.

2. Whittaker 1993:113.

3. Rostovtzeff 1957:550.

4. Burford 1972:64.

5. Frayn 1993:73.

6. Durant 1944:323.

7. Rostovtzeff 1957:74.

8. Frayn 1993:43.

9. Jones 1974:353. Diocletian's Price Edict, a 305 C.E. decree that listed many consumer products and their prices, specifically mentions several types of cloak made in the Anatolian city of Laodicea.

10. Garnsey and Saller 1987:136; see also Hopper 1979:136.

11. Window 1, Room 41, Early Medieval Europe A.D. 300–1100, British Museum.

12. Dudley 1993:197.

13. Goldsmith 1987:263; and Badian 1972:33–34.

14. Whittaker 1993:116.

15. Ste. Croix 1981:142, 197.

16. Quoted in Sutherland 1969:30, as a reasonably true picture in general.

17. On private contractors, see Bowman 1994:95. On publicans, see Badian 1972:32.

18. W. Harris 1993:17n44.

19. Alfoldy 1988:206.

20. Burford 1972:92–93.

21. Alston 1998:188.

22. Senators evidently remained responsible for the mints producing tiny copper coins known as *ases*.

23. Pounds 1990:64.

24. Durant 1944:321.

25. Alfoldy 1988:206.

26. Frayn 1993:60.

27. Carcopino 1968:60.

28. Hodge 1990:119.

29. Ste. Croix 1981:156–57. Theodosius put a stop to this in 390 C.E.

30. Garnsey and Saller 1987:87.

31. Applebaum 1992:152.

32. Moritz 1958:73.

33. Moritz 1958:102.

34. Hodge 1990:119–20.

35. Hodge 1990:115. See also Greene 2000:39.

36. Rostovtzeff 1957:551. The description of cloth relies mainly on Moeller 1976; Wild 1970; and Wilson 1938.

37. Dudley 1993:200.

38. Jones 1974:351.

39. Moeller 1976:7.

40. Wild 1970:27.

41. Wilson 1938:3.

42. Randsborg 1991:159–60.

43. Rice 1967:125.

44. The stories about Commodus, Severus Alexander, and Aurelian are from Wilson 1938:5.

45. Wilson 1938:4.

46. Rice 1967:125.

47. Wild 1970:13.

48. A story told by Procopius; see Collins 1991:130; and Hopkirk 1980:21.

49. Brown 1973:155–56.

50. Rice 1967:126.

51. Rice 1967:124, 126.

52. Wild 1970:21.

53. Jones 1974:39.

54. Quoted in Carcopino 1968:174.

55. Jones 1974:356.

56. Wilson 1938:66.

57. Meijer and van Nijf 1992:103.

58. The description of wool manufacturing relies primarily on Frayn 1984; Wild 1970; and Wilson 1938.

59. Jones 1974:353.

60. Wild 1970:79.

61. This description is based on Guttmann 1988:23–26, with Roman details from Moeller 1976; Wild 1970; and Wilson 1938.

62. http://www.peacefulpastures.com/fleece.html.

63. Dyeing became part of the finishing process in the Middle Ages.

64. Moeller 1976:13–14.

65. Wild 1970:35–36.

66. See Ovid's description in *Metamorphoses* 6.53–58, quoted in Wilson 1938:22.

67. Wild 1970:82.

68. Guttmann 1988:25.

69. Moeller 1976:14.

70. Wild 1970:82.

71. Moeller 1976:19.

72. Wild 1970:83.

73. Moeller 1976:26. There is a question about how common these were. Moeller thinks many fullers used them; Wild 1970 thinks they were rare.

74. Moeller 1976:45–46.

75. Moeller 1976:79.

76. Wilson 1938:65.

77. Moeller 1976:54.

78. Moeller 1976:78.

79. Moeller 1976:81.

80. Applebaum 1992:153.

81. Aubert 1994:284.

82. Aubert 1994:211.

83. These might have been partnerships of potters, but more likely it was of landowners; Aubert 1994:211.

84. Applebaum 1992:154.

85. D'Arms 1981:155–56.

86. Applebaum 1992:154.

87. Dudley 1993:154.

88. Wood-Perkins 1980:325–38.

89. Meiggs 1982:341.

90. Quoted in Ste. Croix 1981:25.

91. Elton 1996:82.

92. Ste. Croix 1981:199. The discussion of markets relies heavily on Frayn 1993 and Morley 1996.

93. Applebaum 1992:163–64.

94. Applebaum 1992:105.

95. C. Mango 1994:41.

96. Alfoldy 1988:207.

97. Applebaum 1992:146.

98. Frayn 1993:122–23.

99. Barnish 1987:171.

100. Alston 1998:196.

101. Frayn 1993:141.

102. Bowman 1994:107.

103. Frayn 1993:19.

104. Frayn 1993:33–34.

105. Moeller 1976:65.

106. Silver 1995:7, quoting Rose 2004.

107. Rostovtzeff 1957:31; and Andreau 1999:18.

108. Frayn 1993:162–63.

109. Goldsmith 1987:46.

110. Pounds 1990:66. The only measure of trade as a share of the economy comes from Constantine's tax on commerce that collected about 5 percent of the imperial tax revenues in the East during his reign, almost entirely from Eastern trade; Jones 1974:35–37.

111. L. Casson 1991:198.

112. L. Casson 1991:198–99.

113. Ste. Croix 1981:232.

114. L. Casson 1991:205; see also the Periplus quoted in Goodman 1997:271.

115. Elton 1996:82.

116. Randsborg 1991:139.

117. Rostovtzeff 1957:1247.

118. L. Casson 1991:198.

119. L. Casson 1991:202. Peters 1970:523 claims it went to China. It is not clear if "Antun" in the Chinese account refers to Antoninus Pius or Marcus Aurelius.

120. Randsborg 1991:146.

121. L. Casson 1991:205–6.

122. Peters 1970:521.

123. Rostovtzeff 1957:156–57.

124. Duncan-Jones 1982:33.

125. L. Casson 1991:203.

126. Rostovtzeff 1957:156–57.

127. Dudley 1993:203.

128. The winds blew toward India in the spring and toward Egypt in the fall.

129. L. Casson 1991:204–5.

130. Starr 1989:73.

131. L. Casson 1991:203.

132. McNeill 1987:1115; see generally Bulliet 1975.

133. Palmyra was two hundred kilometers from the Euphrates, but on the upstream journey travelers had to disembark considerably downriver and proceed overland about five hundred kilometers to Palmyra; Millar 1993:331.

134. Millar 1993:332.

135. Rostovtzeff 1957:155n19; and Millar 1993:515. There were also Palmyrene agents at Alexandria.

136. Garnsey, Hopkins, and Whittaker 1983:174.

137. Hopkins 1983:54.

138. C. Mango 1994:43. In the seventh century an Alexandrian laborer earned 1/24 of a solidus per day; 1994:40.

139. My discussion of slave trading relies on Alfoldy 1988; Finley 1983b; W. Harris 1980 and Hopkins 1983.

140. Tchernia 1983 and Hopkins 1983:98.

141. Finley 1983b:80. Outside Italy, most slavery was urban and domestic; Whittaker 1993:95.

142. CAH 1994:630.

143. W. Harris 1980:126.

144. Morley 1996:104.

145. Bowman 1994:105.

146. L. Casson 1988:359.

147. D'Arms 1981:8.

148. Albion, Baker, and Labaree 1994:23.

149. Duncan-Jones 1982:17, 24.

150. Loane 1938:11n3.

151. Rickman 1980:264.

152. Jones 1974:37.

153. Sirks 1991:253–56.

154. Applebaum 1992:163.

155. Rickman 1980:271.

156. Carcopino 1968:177.

157. Rostovtzeff 1957:54.

158. Both Rostovtzeff 1957:162 and Jones 1974:128 list the suppression of piracy first among the causes for Rome's blossoming trade.

159. Goodman 1997:146.

160. Keay 1988:104.

161. This discussion is based on the extended definition of transaction costs at North 1981:19.

162. A detailed description of such a process is provided in Boyce 2003.

163. Frye 1963:188.

164. Goods from the mid-eighth century are preserved at Nara; Randsborg 1991:146.

165. As late as Cicero's day an advocate could not take fees for his legal services. But his grateful "friends" no doubt endowed him well with lucrative gifts and bequests; Crook 1967:90; and Finley 1992:57.

166. Durant 1944:313.

167. Wilford 1998.

168. Potter and Mattingly 1999:269.

169. Plutarch, *Life of Pericles* 2.1–2, quoted in Finley 1992:54.

170. Garnsey and Saller 1987:50; contrast D'Arms 1981:149–50.

171. Duncan-Jones 1982:198. But coin hoards suggest a greater usage than some historians allow; Howgego 1992:20–21.

172. Morley 1996:78; Duncan-Jones 1982:6; W. Harris 1993:20; and Bowman 1994:91.

173. Goldsmith 1987:40–41 estimates silver in 14 C.E. of 100 HS per capita and total coinage a third larger in value. Adding them yields 0.93 times the subsistence level of about 250 HS per person reported by Hopkins 1983:39–40 and Duncan-Jones 1982:54. For the United States, taking the population at 300,000,000 and the minimum wage as the subsistence level, the ratio in 1997 was 1.2 for the M2 money supply; 1998 Statistical Abstract of the United States, Table 826, "Money Stock and Liquid Assets: 1980–1997," 525.

174. Howgego 1992:6.

175. Goldsmith 1987:37.

176. Goldsmith 1987:37.

177. It began at 900 HS and under Trajan was 1,200 HS. But retirement was reduced from thirteen to ten years' pay, leaving total compensation little changed; Hopkins 1983:75 and Goodman 1997:118.

178. Crook 1967:211.

179. W. Harris 1993:21.

180. Goldsmith 1987:44; Brunt 1988:169, 175; and Crook 1967:211. For higher rates under the Middle Eastern empires and in Europe after Rome, see Baskin and Miranti 1997:318.

181. Howgego 1992:15.

182. That is, one could purchase goods on a layaway plan, by making a deposit and paying later; Crook 1967:218–20.

183. Howgego 1992:14.

184. Durant 1944:331.

185. Crook 1967:233.

186. Crook 1967:232.

187. Duncan-Jones 1982:2.

188. Goldsmith 1987:43.

189. Goldsmith 1987:43. These first came into existence at Rome before 100 B.C.E., but had been known in the East for a long time.

190. Goldsmith 1987:44.

191. CAH 1994:634.

192. Howgego 1992:28.

193. Morley 1996:78.

194. Brunt 1988:169.

195. Bogaert 1966:345.

196. Aubert 1994:1.

197. "One reason for the lack of sophistication of Roman financial institutions could be that they were not regularly used by the elite"; Morley 1996:78.

198. For rent, see Finley 1976:109. For dowries, see Veyne 1987:146–47.

199. Veyne 1987:149.

200. Andreau 1999:12.

201. Finley 1992:64.

202. L. Casson 1980:26–29.

203. Quoted in Goodman 1997:260–61.

204. On the number of bars, inns, and hotels, see Kleberg 1957.

205. Applebaum 1992:161.

206. Veyne 1987:305.

207. Information about entertainment that is otherwise not footnoted is from Goodman 1997.

208. Dodge 1999:230, 237.

209. Potter 1999:258. My description of entertainment relies mainly on Aubert 1994; Potter 1999; and Toner 1995.

210. A. Cameron 1993a:117–18.

211. Potter 1999:296–301.

212. Norwich 1997:199.

213. Collins 1991:116.

214. Potter 1999:321.

215. Toner 1995:45.

216. Toner 1995:36.

217. Toner 1995:37.

218. Hibbert 1985:70.

219. Kling and Schultz 2009:38 (exhibit P). Eighty percent of the wealth per capita in high-income countries now derives from intangible capital, as opposed to natural resources and capital goods.

220. That perspective may appear to clash with the distrust of finance engendered by the current Great Recession. But the two phenomena are unrelated. While various new tools and institutions have made it much easier to predict repayment, and thereby permitted a tremendous expansion of purchasing power based on credit, predictions of repayment can be thwarted by misbehavior if the regulatory mechanisms for catching and punishing misbehavior work badly. The financial problems that generated the Great Recession came about not because financial tools and concepts are defective, but through the failure of regulatory mechanisms, both internal as in corporate governance and incentive pay, and external as in the operation of unsupervised markets and lax regulatory enforcement.

221. Statistical Abstract of the United States 2010, Table 653, http://www.census .gov/compendia/statab/2010/tables/10s0653.pdf (accessed April 12, 2010).

13. The Downfall of Ancient Business

1. For the description in the following paragraphs I have used mainly Brown 1973; A. Cameron 1993a, 1993b; Grant 1974; MacMullen 1988; Millar 1993; Peters 1970; Rostovtzeff 1957; and Williams 1997.

2. McNeill 1977:103.

3. Williams 1997:9; and Millar 1993:117.

4. Howgego 1992:8. For gold, see Goldsmith 1987:41.

5. Ste. Croix 1981:468.

6. Rostovtzeff 1960:266. See also "Commodus" and "Pertinax" in Grant 1985.

7. Quoted in Rostovtzeff 1960:267.

8. Ste. Croix 1981:491; and Garnsey and Saller 1987:88, using three hundred thousand for Augustus's army and four hundred thousand for Septimius Severus's. These numbers are highly controversial, but the direction of change seems clear.

9. Grant 1990a:203. Septimius's imperious wife came from the ruling high priests of Emesa's sun god Gabal.

10. Brown 1973:19–20, 160.

11. Grant 1990a:57.

12. A. Cameron 1993a:6.

13. Aubert 1994:325–26.

14. Ferrill 1986:495.

15. Bagaudae in MacMullen 1988:22–23. Egypt and Anatolia in Peters 1970:526.

16. A. Cameron 1993a:5 and Webber and Wildavsky 1985:139.

17. Ste. Croix 1981:478.

18. Lewit 1991:27.

19. On bandits and pirates, see Ferrill 1986:526. On city economies, see Brown 1973:43. See generally Duncan-Jones 1990:46. Still, by 400 C.E. there were still more than eighty towns with populations over 5,000; MacMullen 1988:21.

20. Brown 1973:22.

21. Williams 1997:18.

22. Peters 1970:594–95; quotation in Brown 1973:20.

23. Grant 1974:37 and Peters 1970:600.

24. Adams 1993:104.

25. Adams 1993:104; and Grant 1974:67–68.

26. Grant 1990a:54.

27. Williams 1997:135.

28. For a study of this practice in the Middle Ages, see Ellenius 1998.

29. Applebaum 1992:118.

30. Alston 1998:184.

31. Grant 1974:54, 62; and Williams 1997:24–25.

32. Grant 1974:66.

33. By one estimate, the empire lost 15 percent of its productive acreage during the third century; Grant 1974:56.

34. Garnsey and Saller 1987:39–40.

35. Anderson 1978:96, 99.

36. Webber and Wildavsky 1985:111.

37. Williams 1997:132.

38. Grant 1974:84.

39. Brown 1992:25–26.

40. MacMullen 1988:195.

41. MacMullen 1988:139–40.

42. See generally MacMullen 1988.

43. Lewit 1991:49, 63.

44. Brown 1973:34.

45. Brown 1997:44–45; and Hicks 1969:104.

46. Finley 1983b:147.

47. MacMullen 1988:28.

48. Ste. Croix 1981:381.

49. Brown 1973:34; see also A. Cameron 1993a:118.

50. Morley 1996:6.

51. Olympiodorus, quoted in Grant 1990a:73.

52. Brown 1973:34.

53. Anderson 1978:115; and A. Cameron 1993b:48–49.

54. Brown 1992:26; see also Alfoldy 1988:169.

55. Brown 1973:36; Grant 1974:88; and Finley 1983a:147.

56. Whittaker 1993:14.

57. Ste. Croix 1981:250.

58. Alfoldy 1988:187.

59. A. Cameron 1993b:89, 121; see also Morley 1996:6.

60. Lebecq 1990:73.

61. Based on the reasonable assumption that there was a direct relationship between the quantity of shipping and the number of shipwrecks discovered.

62. Brown 1973:112.

63. Whittaker 1993:14.

64. Grant 1974:62.

65. Grant 1990a:16.

66. On senators estates, see Grant 1990a:79. On food, see Barnish 1987:164.

67. The following account is drawn largely from Collins 1991.

68. Collins 1991:97.

69. Northwestern Europe experienced at least sixteen civil wars and major invasions between 200 and 400; Europe south of the Danube suffered more than thirty; Lewit 1991:34, 87.

70. Much of the discussion of Diocletian is based on Williams 1997.

71. A. Cameron 1993a:107.

72. The U.S. federal government had about fifteen times the number of federal civil servants per capita, according to the Census Bureau's estimate for the year 2000; www.census.gov/statab/freq/98s0676.txt. See also A. Cameron 1993a:106.

73. MacMullen 1988:79–80. For staff sizes, see Keay 1988:179–80.

74. Grant 1990a:54.

75. Williams 1997:31.

76. Williams 1997:120. Except where otherwise stated, the facts in this section come from Williams 1997.

77. Peters 1970:508–9. Land taxes were based on *juga*, the area that a yoked ox team could plow, which varied in size depending on the land, and a head tax on the capita, the residents, under which one man = two women = several livestock.

78. Alfoldy 1988:203.

79. For early Christianity generally I have relied mainly on Brown 1992; A. Cameron 1993a; Grant 1974; MacMullen 1986; Peters 1970; and Ste. Croix 1981.

80. Alfoldy 1988:180.

81. North 1981:53.

82. A. Cameron 1993a:12.

83. Ammianus Marcellinus, quoted in Grant 1985:243.

84. Neal 2000:330 observes: "The role of religion in establishing and especially maintaining the legitimacy of the governance structure in any society tends to be overlooked in this secular age. The very word religion, derived from the Latin *religare*, to tie together, and the exercise of religion has been an extraordinary force for the cohesion of people and the eventual metamorphosis of their societies and economies."

85. Ste. Croix 1981:395.

86. Alfoldy 1988:183.

87. There were 70,000–80,000 Christians in Rome in 312, when its population was probably about 800,000; Grant 1974:303. MacMullen 1986:83 estimates there were 5,000,000 Christians in total.

88. Goodman 1997:326.

89. Quoted in Peters 1970:612.

90. MacMullen 1986:101.

91. Duncan-Jones 1990:122; and Ste. Croix 1981:495.

92. Collins 1991:73.

93. Finley 1992:101–2.

94. Brown 1969:340.

95. The temples, always previously considered sacrosanct, yielded so much gold that Constantine could issue a sound gold coinage, the 99% pure solidus, worth about 25 of Augustus's denarii. It remained much in demand for hundreds of years afterward; C. Mango 1994:40; Brown 1973:27; and MacMullen 1986:49–50.

96. Quoted in Brown 1973:34.

97. Its clergy were exempted from taxes, military service, and penal servitude, and church members received preference in the imperial service. Constantine also provided the bishops a substantial and enduring source of revenue by authorizing them to judge civil litigation, much of it involving business; MacMullen 1986:56.

98. Collins 1991:61.

99. I take my understanding of Arianism and the controversy from Brown 1997:71 and 1973:90. See also Colish 1997:7.

100. Brown 1997:83–85; and Alfoldy 1988:188.

101. Rostovtzeff 1957:149.

102. MacMullen 1988:56.

103. C. Mango 1994:36.

104. This was the Patriarch Cyrus of Alexandria; Bowman 1989:81.

105. Veyne 1987:305.

106. Property taxes averaged about 10 percent, as did the tithe; Webber and Wildavsky 1985:110 and Hopkins 1978:16.

107. Ste. Croix 1981:496.

108. On hundreds of thousands, see Brown 1997:32. On austerity, see Brown 1997:66 and Ste. Croix 1981:434. On hoarding, see A. Cameron 1993a:121.

109. Sirks 1991:21, for one, argues that regulation applied only to activities connected with the *annona*. Consequently, he says, the view that Rome was highly regulated should be dropped.

110. See generally Barnish 1987:168, who argues that the capture of North Africa by the Vandals in the early fifth century led to a monetization of the economy around Rome.

111. Brown 1992:27.

112. A. Cameron 1993a:53–54, quoting Zosimus 2.38, writing after the tax's abolition in 499.

113. Brown 2008b.

114. See generally Barnish 1987:168.

115. Grant 1974:62.

116. Ste. Croix 1981:488.

117. MacMullen 1988:151.

118. Unless otherwise noted, this discussion of corruption is drawn from MacMullen 1988.

119. C. Mango 1994:33; and MacMullen 1988:148.

120. Quoted in MacMullen 1988:156.

121. McNeill 1977:109–14.

122. J. Wallace-Hadrill 1988:45.

123. Norwich 1997:223; and J. Wallace-Hadrill 1988:40.

124. Hibbert 1985:74.

125. Norwich 1997:263. I have relied for the balance of this paragraph mainly on Brown 1973; Collins 1991; C. Mango 1994; and Norwich 1997.

Concluding Note

1. Throughout this discussion of "wealth," I mean material wealth, not the social assets or spiritual wealth that the term sometimes encompasses.

2. The focus of this remark is on the practice and role of business, not on the political, social, and economic conditions that have been so much the focus of this study. Economic historians have, of course, described various dramatic and important changes in those conditions, changes without which the modern economic environment could not exist. See, e.g., Polanyi 1944 and many others.

3. Nelson 1996:118: "It is organizational differences, especially differences in abilities to generate and gain from innovation, rather than differences in command over particular technologies, that are the source of durable, not easily imitable, differences among firms."

4. Friedman 2009:52–53.

5. Sometimes, however, desire fails. If those who accumulate purchasing power find no use for it, and like the Persian rulers just hoard it in their treasuries, the result is depression. That happened to the Persian Empire, and Japan's stagnation during the last twenty years has a similar cause. Through trade surpluses Japanese firms

accumulated huge amounts of purchasing power in the late twentieth century. They found no desirable uses for their money and, in the functional equivalent of hoarding, invested it in unproductive assets like U.S. real estate and low-yielding bonds in depreciating currencies. Recent U.S. war expenditures have a similar look. This seems to be an endemic problem of empires. See Kennedy 1989.

6. It is fairly easy to see why securitizing mortgages is valuable, since that process provides purchasing power to the mortgage market by letting investors buy not risky single mortgages, but bundles of mortgages that, as a portfolio, enjoy a somewhat lower risk. Spreading the risk even further through the "fund of funds" device of bundling mortgage-backed securities into even larger bundles may be justifiable as a way of further reducing risk by spreading the investment across diverse security classes. Credit default swaps, as the insurance contracts on these securities are called, make sense in the way that all insurance makes sense. I base my description on M. Lewis 2010.

7. Technically, to maximize their return on investment, a calculation that "discounts" future benefits by some percentage to reflect its lesser value. Nor does the concept of maximizing profit, when taken in the fairly broad way I am speaking, conflict with the economic concept of "satisficing," which holds that managers seek a satisfactory level of return instead of maximization. That is true, but when managers do so they are in effect capturing some of the company's profit for themselves, in the form of leisure and simplicity of work.

8. North 1981:47.

9. North 1990:35: "The returns on opportunism, cheating and shirking rise in complex societies."

10. Nelson 2009:1159.

11. Noted economist Paul Romer, husband of the Council of Economic Advisers chairwoman Christina Romer, has formed a company to create "charter cities," markets like Ugarit or Hong Kong, ports of trade, in underdeveloped countries; Mallaby 2010.

12. Friedman 2009:73.

13. Citizens United v. Federal Election Commission, 558 U.S. 50 (2010).

BIBLIOGRAPHY

Abbott, F. F., and A. C. Johnson. 1968. *Municipal Administration in the Roman Empire*. New York: Russell & Russell (orig. 1926).

Abu-Lughod, J. L. 1989. *Before European Hegemony: The World System,* AD *1250–1350*. New York: Oxford University Press.

Acemoglu, D., and J. A. Robinson. 2008. "Persistence of Power, Elites, and Institutions." *American Economic Review* 98/1:267–93.

Acemoglu, D., S. Johnson, and J. A. Robinson. 2005. "The Rise of Europe: Atlantic Trade, Institutional Change, and Economic Growth." *American Economic Review* 95/3:546–79.

Adams, C. 1993. *For Good and Evil: The Impact of Taxes on the Course of Civilization*. Lanham, Md.: Madison.

Adkins, L., and R. Adkins. 1997. *Handbook to Life in Ancient Greece*. New York: Facts on File.

Ahamed, L. 2009. *Lords of Finance: The Bankers Who Broke the World*. New York: Penguin.

Albion, R. G., W. A. Baker, and B. W. Labaree. 1994. *New England and the Sea*. 2nd ed. American Maritime Library 5. Mystic, Conn.: Mystic Seaport Museum.

Aldrete, G. S., and D. J. Mattingly. 1999. "Feeding the City: The Organization, Operation, and Scale of the Supply System for Rome." In Potter and Mattingly 1999.

Alfoldy, G. 1988. *The Social History of Rome*. Baltimore: Johns Hopkins University Press.

Algaze, G. 1993. *The Uruk World System: The Dynamics of Expansion of Early Mesopotamian Civilization*. Chicago: University of Chicago Press.

Allen, R. E. 1983. *The Attalid Kingdom: A Constitutional History*. Oxford: Clarendon.

Alston, R. 1998. "Trade and the City in Roman Egypt." In Parkins and Smith 1998.

Anderson, P. 1978. *Passages from Antiquity to Feudalism*. London: New Left Books.

Andreau, J. 1987. *La vie financière dans le monde Romaine: les métiers de maniers d'argent (IV siècle av. J-C–III siècle ap. J.-C)*. Rome: École française de Rome.

———. 1999. *Banking and Business in the Roman World*. Translated by J. Lloyd. Cambridge/New York: Cambridge University Press.

Anonymous. 2008. "Homer and the Eclipse." *Science* (June 27): 1701.

Aperghis, M. 2001. "Population-Production-Taxation-Coinage: A Model for the Seleukid Economy." In Archibald et al. 2001.

Applebaum, H. 1992. *The Concept of Work: Ancient, Medieval, and Modern*. Albany: State University of New York Press.

Archibald, Z. H., J. K. Davies, and V. Gabrielsen, eds. 2005. *Making, Moving, and Managing: The New World of Ancient Economics*. London: Oxbow.

Archibald, Z. H., J. K. Davies, V. Gabrielsen, and G. L. Oliver, eds. 2001. *Hellenistic Economics*. New York/London: Routledge.

Arnold, Rosemary. 1971. "Separation of Trade and Market: Great Market of Whydah." In Polanyi, Arensberg, and Pearson 1971.

Association of Chartered Accountants in the United States. 1999. *Accounting: A Virtual History*. Available at http://www.acaus.org/history/hsanc.html.

Atchity, K., ed. 1997. *The Classical Roman Reader*. New York/Oxford: Oxford University Press.

Atkeson, A., and P. J. Kehoe. 2007. "Modeling the Transition to a New Economy: Lessons from Two Technological Revolutions." *American Economic Review* 97/1:64–88.

Aubert, J.-J. 1994. *Business Managers in Ancient Rome: A Social and Economic Study of Institores, 200 BC–AD 250*. Leiden: Brill.

Aubet, M. E. 1993. *The Phoenicians and the West: Politics, Colonies, and Trade*. Cambridge: Cambridge University Press.

Austin, M. M. 1988. "Greek Trade, Land, and Labor." In Grant and Kitzinger 1988.

Austin, M. M., and P. Vidal-Naquet. 1977. *Economic and Social History of Ancient Greece: An Introduction*. Berkeley: University of California Press.

Badian, E. 1958. *Foreign Clientelae (264–70 BC)*. Oxford: Oxford University Press.

———. 1972. *Publicans and Sinners: Private Enterprise in the Service of the Roman Republic*. Dunedin: Dunedin Press.

Bailey, D. R. Shackleton, ed. 1978. *Cicero's Letters to Atticus*. New York: Penguin.

Bairoch, P. 1988. *Cities and Economic Development from the Dawn of History to the Present*. Chicago: University of Chicago Press.

Balmuth, M. S., ed. 2001. *Hacksilber to Coinage: New Insights into the Monetary History of the Near East and Greece*. New York: American Numismatic Society.

Bandow, D. 2000. "Exploding Jury Awards Bode Ill for U.S. Economy in 21st Century." http://www.cato.org/dailys/03-06-00.html.

Barnish, S. J. B. 1987. "Pigs, Plebeians, and Potentates: Rome's Economic Hinterland." *Papers of the British School at Rome*: 157.

Barraclough, G., ed. 1984. *The Times Atlas of World History*. Rev. ed. Maplewood, N.J.: Hammond.

Baskin, J. B., and P. Miranti Jr. 1997. *A History of Corporate Finance*. New York: Cambridge University Press.

Beard, M. 2008. "Isn't It Funny?" *New York Review of Books* (July 17): 32.

Bernstein, P. L. 1996. *Against the Gods: The Remarkable Story of Risk*. New York: Wiley.

Bernstein, W. J. 2008. *A Splendid Exchange: How Trade Shaped the World*. New York: Atlantic Monthly.

Berthold, R. M. 1984. *Rhodes in the Hellenistic Age*. Ithaca: Cornell University Press.

Berthoud, A. 1981. *Aristote et l'argent*. Paris: François Maspero.

Black, J. S., and M. Mendenhall. 1993. "Resolving Conflicts with the Japanese: Mission Impossible?" *Sloan Management Review* 34/3 (Spring): 49–59.

Blackstone, W. 1962. *Commentaries on the Laws of England*, vol. 3: *Of Private Wrongs*. Boston: Beacon.

Bogaert, R. 1966. *Banques et banquiers dans les cités grecques*. Leiden: Brill.

Borza, E. 1990. *In the Shadow of Olympus: The Emergence of Macedonia*. Princeton: Princeton University Press.

——. 2007. "Alexander the Great: History and Cultural Politics." *Journal of the Historical Society* 7/4:411–42.

Bowersock, G. 1983. *Roman Arabia*. Cambridge: Harvard University Press.

Bowman, A. K. 1989. *Egypt after the Pharaohs, 332 BC–AD 642*. Berkeley: University of California Press.

——. 1994. *Life and Letters on the Roman Frontier: Vindolanda and Its People*. London: British Museum.

Boyce, G. 2003. "Network Knowledge and Network Routines: Negotiating Activities between Shipowners and Shipbuilders." *Business History* 45/2:52–76.

Boyer, P. 2002. *Religion Explained: The Evolutionary Origins of Religious Thought*. New York: Basic Books.

Braudel, F. 1979–86. *Civilization and Capitalism, 15th–18th Century*. 2 vols. Translated by S. Reynolds. New York: Harper & Row.

——. 1995a. *A History of Civilizations*. Translated by R. Mayne. New York: Penguin.

——. 1995b. *The Mediterranean and the Mediterranean World in the Age of Philip II*. Translated by S. Reynolds. Berkeley: University of California Press.

Brewer, J., and R. Porter, eds. 1993. *Consumption and the World of Goods: Consumption and Culture in the 17th and 18th Centuries*. New York/London: Routledge.

Brown, P. 1969. *Augustine of Hippo: A Biography*. Berkeley: University of California Press.

——. 1973. *The World of Late Antiquity*. New York: Harcourt, Brace, Jovanovich.

——. 1992. *Power and Persuasion in Late Antiquity: Towards a Christian Empire*. Madison: Wisconsin University Press.

——. 1997. *The Rise of Western Christendom: Triumph and Diversity, AD 200–1000*. Malden, Mass.: Blackwell.

——. 2008a. "Review of G. W. Bowersock's *Mosaics as History*." *New York Review of Books* (April 17): 40–42.

———. 2008b. "Review of *Picturing the Bible: The Earliest Christian Art.*" *New York Review of Books* (March 20): 49–53.

Brunner, K., and A. Meltzer. 1971. "The Use of Money: Money in the Theory of an Exchange Economy." *American Economic Review* 61:784–805.

Brunstad, G. E., Jr. 2000. "Bankruptcy and the Problems of Economic Futility: A Theory on the Unique Role of Bankruptcy Law." *Business Lawyer* 55/2:499–591.

Brunt, P. A. 1988. *The Fall of the Roman Republic and Related Essays.* Oxford: Oxford University Press.

Buehler, W. W. 1974. *The Pre-Herodian Civil War and Social Debate: Jewish Society in the Period 76–40 BC and the Social Factors Contributing to the Rise of the Pharisees and the Sadducees.* Basel: Reinhardt.

Bulliet, R. W. 1975. *The Camel and the Wheel.* Cambridge: Cambridge University Press.

Burford, A. 1972. *Craftsmen in Greek and Roman Society.* London: Thames & Hudson.

Burn, A. R. 1988. "Historical Summary of Greece." In Grant and Kitzinger 1988.

Bury, J. B. 1958. *History of the Later Roman Empire.* New York: Dover.

CAH. 1964. *The Persian Empire and the West.* 2nd ed. Cambridge Ancient History 4. Cambridge: Cambridge University Press.

———. 1994. *The Last Age of the Roman Republic, 146–43 BC.* 2nd ed. Cambridge Ancient History 9. Cambridge: Cambridge University Press.

Cahill, T. 1998. *The Gifts of the Jews: How a Tribe of Desert Nomads Changed the Way Everyone Thinks and Feels.* New York: Doubleday.

Cameron, A. 1993a. *The Later Roman Empire.* London: Fontana.

———. 1993b. *The Mediterranean World in Late Antiquity, AD 395–600.* London: Routledge.

Cameron, R. E. 1991. *A Concise Economic History of the World: From Paleolithic Times to the Present.* Oxford: Oxford University Press.

Carandini, A. 1980. "Il vigneto e la villa del fondo di Settefinestre nel coanso: un caso di produzione agricola per il mercato transmarino." In D'Arms and Kopff 1980.

———. 1983. "Columella's Vineyard and the Rationality of Rome's Economy." *Opus* 2:177–204.

Carcopino, J. 1968. *Daily Life in Ancient Rome: The People and the City at the Height of the Empire.* New Haven: Yale University Press.

Carr, A. Z. 1968. *Business as a Game.* New York: New American Library.

Cartledge, P., E. E. Cohen, and L. Foxhall, eds. 2002. *Money, Labor, and Land: Approaches to the Economies of Ancient Greece.* London/New York: Routledge.

Cartledge, P., P. Millet, and S. Todd, eds. 1990. *Nomos: Essays in Athenian Law, Politics, and Society.* Cambridge: Cambridge University Press.

Cary, M. 1965. *A History of the Greek World from 323 to 146 BC.* Rev. ed. London: Methuen.

Casson, L. 1980. "The Role of the State in Rome's Grain Trade." In D'Arms and Kopff 1980.

———. 1988. "Transportation." In Grant and Kitzinger 1988.

———. 1991. *The Ancient Mariners.* Princeton: Princeton University Press.

———. 1994. *Travel in the Ancient World.* Baltimore: Johns Hopkins University Press.

Casson, M. 1991. *The Economics of Business Culture: Game Theory, Transaction Costs, and Economic Performance*. Oxford: Clarendon.

Casson, M., and M. B. Rose. 1997. "Introduction to Special Issue: Institutions and the Evolution of Modern Business." *Business History* 39/4:1–9.

Chadwick, J. 1958. *The Decipherment of Linear B*. Cambridge: Cambridge University Press.

Chaganov, A. 1966. *The Theory of the Peasant Economy*. Homewood, Ill.: Irwin.

Chandler, A. D. 1959. "The Beginnings of 'Big Business' in American Industry." In *The History of American Management*. Edited by J. Baughman. New York: Prentice-Hall.

———. 1977. *The Visible Hand*. Cambridge: Harvard University Press.

———. 1990. *Scale and Scope: The Dynamics of Industrial Capitalism*. Cambridge: Harvard University Press.

Chandler, A. D., P. Hagstrom, and O. Solvell, eds. 1998. *The Dynamic Firm: The Role of Technology: Strategy, Organization, and Regions*. Oxford: Oxford University Press.

Chandler, T. 1987. *Four Thousand Years of Urban Growth: An Historical Census*. Lewiston/Queenston: St. David's University Press.

Charlesworth, M. 1926. *The Trade Routes and Commerce of the Roman Empire*. New York: Macmillan.

Chastagnol, A. 1998. *L'evolution politique, sociale et economique du monde romaine de Diocletian à Julien: la mise en place du regime du Bas-Empire*. 3rd ed. Paris: Société d'Edition d'Enseignement Superieur.

Cipolla, C. 1974. *The Economic History of World Population*. 6th ed. Harmondsworth, U.K.: Pelican.

Cizakca, M. 1996. *A Comparative Evolution of Business Partnerships: The Islamic World and Europe, with Specific Reference to the Ottoman Archives*. Leiden: Brill.

Clark, J. G. D. 1952. *Prehistoric Europe: The Economic Basis*. Palo Alto: Stanford University Press.

Clayton, P., and M. Price. 1988. *The Seven Wonders of the Ancient World*. London/New York: Routledge.

Cochran, T. 1981. *Frontiers of Change*. New York: Oxford University Press.

Cohen, D. 1995. *Law, Violence, and Community in Classical Athens*. London/New York: Routledge.

Cohen, E. E. 1992. *Athenian Economy and Society: A Banking Perspective*. Princeton: Princeton University Press.

Cohen, S. J. D. 1988. "Roman Domination: The Jewish Revolt and the Destruction of the 2nd Temple." In Shanks 1988.

Cohn, N. 1994. *Cosmos, Chaos, and the World to Come: The Ancient Roots of Apocalyptic Faith*. New Haven: Yale University Press.

Colish, M. L. 1997. *Medieval Foundations of the Western Intellectual Tradition, 400–1400*. New Haven: Yale University Press.

Collins, R. 1991. *Early Medieval Europe, 300–1000*. Hampshire, U.K.: Macmillan.

Comin, D., W. Easterly, and E. Gong. 2007. "Was the Wealth of Nations Determined in 1000 BC?" National Bureau of Economic Research Working Papers #12657.

Cook, J. M. 1983. *The Persian Empire*. New York: Schocken.

Crawford, M. 1977. "Rome and the Greek World: Economic Relations." *Economic History Review* 30:42–52.

Crook, J. A. 1967. *Law and Life of Rome, 90 BC–AD 212*. Ithaca: Cornell University Press.

Culican, W. 1966. *The First Merchant Venturers: The Ancient Levant in History and Commerce*. London: Thames & Hudson.

Cunliffe, B. 2008. *Europe between the Oceans: Themes and Variations, 9000 BC–AD 1000*. New Haven: Yale University Press.

Curtin, P. 1984. *Cross-Cultural Trade and World History*. Cambridge: Cambridge University Press.

Curtis, B. C., S. Rajaram, and H. Gómez Macpherson, eds. 2002. *Bread Wheat: Improvement and Production*. Rome: Food and Agricultural Organization of the United Nations.

Dalton, G. 1977. "Aboriginal Economies in Stateless Societies." In Earle and Ericson 1977.

———, ed. 1967. *Tribal and Peasant Economies: Readings in Economic Anthropology*. Austin: University of Texas Press.

D'Arms, J. H. 1981. *Commerce and Social Standing in Ancient Rome*. Cambridge: Harvard University Press.

D'Arms, J. H., and E. C. Kopff, eds. 1980. *The Seaborne Commerce of Ancient Rome: Studies in Archaeology and History*. Rome: American Academy in Rome.

Davies, J. K. 1971. *Athenian Propertied Families, 600–300 BC*. Oxford: Oxford University Press.

———. 1981. *Wealth and the Power of Wealth in Classical Athens*. New York: Arno.

———. 2001. "Hellenistic Economies in the Post-Finley Era." In Archibald et al. 2001.

De Roover, R. 1975. *Business, Banking, and Economic Thought in Late Medieval and Early Modern Europe: Selected Studies of Raymond de Roover*. Edited by J. Kirshner. Chicago: University of Chicago Press.

DeSoto, H. 2003. *The Mystery of Capital: Why Capitalism Triumphs in the West and Fails Everywhere Else*. New York: Basic Books.

Diakonoff, I. M., ed. 1969. *Ancient Mesopotamia*. Moscow: USSR Academy of Sciences.

———, ed. 1982. *Societies and Languages of the Ancient Near East*. Warminster, U.K.: Aris & Phillips.

———, ed. 1991. *Early Antiquity*. Chicago: University of Chicago Press.

Diamond, J. 1999. *Guns, Germs, and Steel: The Fate of Human Societies*. New York: Norton.

Dodge, H. 1999. "Amusing the Masses: Buildings for Entertainment and Leisure in the Roman World." In Potter and Mattingly 1999.

Dougherty, C. 2001. *The Raft of Odysseus*. Oxford: Oxford University Press.

Duby, G. 1992. *The Early Growth of the Western Economy: Warriors and Peasants from the 7th to the 12th Century*. Ithaca: Cornell University Press.

Dudley, D. R. 1993. *The Civilization of Rome*. New York: Meridian.

Duncan-Jones, R. P. 1982. *The Economy of the Roman Empire*. 2nd ed. Cambridge: Cambridge University Press.

———. 1990. *Structure and Scale in the Roman Economy*. Cambridge: Cambridge University Press.

Durand, J. D. 1977. "Historical Estimates of World Population: An Evaluation." *Population and Development Review* 3/3:253–96.

Durant, W. 1944. *Caesar and Christ: A History of Roman Civilization and of Christianity from Their Beginnings to* A.D. *325*. The Story of Civilization 3. New York: Simon & Schuster.

Earle, T. K., and J. Ericson, eds. 1977. *Exchange Systems in Prehistory*. New York: Academic Press.

East, W. 1967. *The Geography behind History*. New York: Norton.

Economist. 1992. "The Overseas Chinese." *The Economist* (July 28): 22.

Edmondson, J. 1993. "Instrumenta Imperii: Law and Imperialism in Republican Rome." In Halpern and Hobson 1993.

Eichengreen, B. 1992. *Golden Fetters: The Gold Standard and the Great Depression, 1919–1939*. New York/Oxford: Oxford University Press.

Einzig, P. 1966. *Primitive Money*. 2nd ed. Oxford: Oxford University Press.

Ellenius, A., ed. 1998. *Iconography, Propaganda, and Legitimation*. Oxford/New York: Oxford University Press.

Elton, H. 1996. *Frontiers of the Roman Empire*. London: Batsford.

Encyclopaedia Judaica. 16 vols. New York: Macmillan, 1972.

Etzioni, A. 1988. *The Moral Dimension: Toward a New Economics*. New York: Macmillan.

Ferguson, N. 2009. *The Ascent of Money: A Financial History of the World*. New York: Penguin.

Ferguson, W. S. 1969. *Hellenistic Athens*. New York: Fertig.

Ferrill, A. 1986. *Fall of the Roman Empire: The Military Explanation*. New York: Thames & Hudson.

———. 1988. "Historical Survey of Rome." In Grant and Kitzinger 1988.

Figueira, T. J. 1986. "Population Patterns in Late Archaic and Classical Sparta." *Transactions of the American Philological Association* 116:165–213.

Fine, B., and E. Leopold. 1993. *The World of Consumption*. London/New York: Routledge.

Fine, J. V. A. 1983. *The Ancient Greeks: A Critical History*. Cambridge: Harvard University Press.

Finer, S. E. 1997. *The History of Government*. 3 vols. Oxford: Oxford University Press.

Finley, M. I. 1952. *Studies in Land and Credit in Ancient Athens, 500–200* BC: *The Horos Inscriptions*. New Brunswick: Rutgers University Press.

———, ed. 1976. *Studies in Roman Property*. Cambridge: Cambridge University Press.

———. 1981. *Early Greece: The Bronze and Archaic Ages*. New York: Norton.

———. 1983a. *Politics in the Ancient World*. Cambridge: Cambridge University Press.

———. 1983b. *Ancient Slavery and Modern Ideology*. New York: Penguin.

———. 1992. *The Ancient Economy*. 2nd ed. London Penguin.

Fowden, G. 1999. "Varieties of Polytheistic Experience: Review of R. MacMullen's *Christianity and Paganism in the 4th to 8th Centuries*." *New York Review of Books* 46/20 (December 16). nybooks.com/articles/archives/1999/dec/16/varieties-of-polytheistic-experience/.

Frank, T. 1933. *Economic Survey of Ancient Rome*. 5 vols. Baltimore: Johns Hopkins University Press.

Frankenstein, S. 1979. "The Phoenicians in the Far West: A Function of Neo-Assyrian Imperialism." In Larsen 1979.

Frayn, J. M. 1984. *Sheep-Rearing and the Wool Trade in Italy during the Roman Period*. Liverpool: Cairns.

———. 1993. *Markets and Fairs in Roman Italy: Their Social and Economic Importance from the 2nd Century BC to the 3rd Century AD*. Oxford: Oxford University Press.

Friedman, D. 2009. *Morals and Markets: An Evolutionary Account of the Modern World*. New York: Macmillan.

Frye, R. 1963. *The Heritage of Persia*. Cleveland/New York: World.

Fukuyama, F. 1995. *Trust: The Social Virtues and the Creation of Prosperity*. New York: Free Press.

———. 1999. *The Great Disruption: Human Nature and the Reconstitution of Social Order*. New York: Free Press.

Gabrielsen, V. 2001. "The Rhodian Associations and Economic Activity." In Archibald et al. 2001.

———. 2005. "Banking and Credit Operations in the Hellenistic World." In Archibald, Davies, and Gabrielsen 2005.

Gagarin, M. 1986. *Early Greek Law*. Berkeley: University of California Press.

Gall, P., and A. A. Saxe. 1977. "The Ecological Evolution of Culture: The State as Predator in Succession Theory." In Earle and Ericson 1977.

Gallant, T. W. 1991. *Risk and Survival in Ancient Greece: Reconstructing the Rural Domestic Economy*. Palo Alto: Stanford University Press.

Garland, R. 1987. *The Piraeus from the 5th to the 1st Century BC*. Ithaca: Cornell University Press.

Garnsey, P., and R. Saller. 1987. *The Roman Empire: Economy, Society, and Culture*. Berkeley: University of California Press.

Garnsey, P., K. Hopkins, and C. R. Whittaker, eds. 1983. *Trade in the Ancient Economy*. Berkeley: University of California Press.

Gaylin, W. 1989. *The Rage Within: Anger in Modern American Life*. New York: Simon & Schuster.

Gibbon, E. 1946. *The Decline and Fall of the Roman Empire*. New York: Heritage.

Gies, F., and J. Gies. 1995. *Cathedral, Forge, and Waterwheel: Technology and Invention in the Middle Ages*. New York: HarperCollins.

Goetzmann, W. N., and K. G. Rouwenhorst, eds. 2005. *The Origins of Value: The Financial Innovations That Created Modern Capital Markets*. New York: Oxford University Press.

Goitein, S. 1967–83 *A Medieval Society: The Jewish Communities of the Arab World as Portrayed in the Documents of the Cairo Geniza.* 4 vols. Berkeley: University of California Press.

Goldsmith, R. W. 1987. *Pre-Modern Financial Systems: A Historical Comparative Study.* Cambridge: Cambridge University Press.

Goldthwaite, R. 1968. *Private Wealth in Renaissance Florence.* Princeton: Princeton University Press.

Goodman, M. 1987. *The Ruling Class of Judaea: The Origins of the Jewish Revolt,* AD *66–70.* New York: Cambridge University Press.

——. 1997. *The Roman World, 44* BC–AD *180.* London: Routledge.

Granovetter, M. Winter, 2005. "The Impact of Social Structure on Economic Outcomes." *Journal of Economic Perspectives* 19/1:33–50.

Grant, M. 1974. *The Climax of Rome.* London: Sphere.

——. 1985. *The Roman Emperors: A Biographical Guide to the Rulers of Imperial Rome, 31* BC–AD *474.* New York: Barnes & Noble.

——. 1987. *The Rise of the Greeks.* New York: Collier.

——. 1990a. *The Fall of the Roman Empire.* New York: Touchstone.

——, ed. 1990b. *Greek Literature: An Anthology.* Harmondsworth, U.K.: Penguin.

——. 1990c. *From Alexander to Cleopatra: The Hellenistic World.* New York: Collier.

Grant, M., and R. Kitzinger, eds. 1988. *Civilization of the Ancient Mediterranean.* 3 vols. New York: Scribner.

Gras, N. S. B. 1939. *Business and Capitalism: An Introduction to Business History.* New York: Crofts.

Green, P. 1990. *Alexander to Actium: The Historical Evolution of the Hellenistic Age.* Berkeley: University of California Press.

——. 1991. *Alexander of Macedon, 356–323* BC*: A Historical Biography.* Berkeley: University of California Press.

——, ed. 1993. *Hellenistic History and Culture.* Berkeley: University of California Press.

Greene, K. 2000. "Technology, Innovation, and Economic Progress in the Ancient World: M. I. Finley Reconsidered." *Economic History Review* 53/1:29–59.

Gruen, E. S. 1984. *The Hellenistic World and the Coming of Rome.* Berkeley: University of California Press.

Gunnell, J. G. 1968. *Political Philosophy and Time.* Middletown, Conn.: Wesleyan University Press.

Guttmann, M. 1988. *Toward the Modern Economy.* Philadelphia: Temple University Press.

Hallo, W. W., and W. K. Simpson. 1971. *The Ancient Near East: A History.* Fort Worth: Harcourt Brace Jovanovich.

Halpern, B., and D. W. Hobson, eds. 1993. *Law, Politics, and Society in the Ancient Mediterranean World.* Sheffield, U.K.: Sheffield Academic Press.

Hamilton, E. 1932. *The Roman Way.* New York: Norton.

Hamilton, G. ed. 1996. *Asian Business Networks.* Berlin: de Gruyter.

Hammond, N. G. L. 1986. *A History of Greece to 322* BC. 3rd ed. Oxford: Clarendon.

Hanson, V. D. 1999. *The Other Greeks: The Family Farm and the Agrarian Roots of Western Civilization*. Berkeley: University of California Press.

Harris, E. 2002. "Workshop, Marketplace, and Household: The Nature of Technical Specialization in Classical Athens and Its Influence on Economy and Society." In Cartledge, Cohen, and Foxhall 2002.

Harris, W. V. 1980. "Towards a Study of the Roman Slave Trade." In D'Arms and Kopff 1980.

———. 1993. *The Inscribed Economy: Production and Distribution in the Roman Empire in the light of instrumentum domesticum*. Journal of Roman Archaeology Supplemental Series 6. Ann Arbor: University of Michigan Press.

Harrison, W. B., Jr. 2002. "Banks Were Victims in Fraud Cases, Not Accomplices." *Wall Street Journal* (September 18): A18.

Hendy, M. 1985. *Studies in the Byzantine Monetary Economy, c. 300–1450*. Cambridge: Cambridge University Press.

Herodotus. 1972. *The Histories*. Translated by A. de Selincourt. New York: Penguin.

Hesiod. 1990. *Works and Days*. Translated by F. L. Lucas. In Grant 1990b.

Hibbert, C. 1985. *Rome: The Biography of a City*. New York: Penguin.

Hicks, J. 1969. *A Theory of Economic History*. Oxford: Oxford University Press.

Higgins, R. 1988. "The Colossus of Rhodes." In Clayton and Price 1988.

Highwater, J. 1981. *The Primal Mind: Vision and Reality in Indian America*. New York: Penguin.

Hodge, A. T. 1990. "A Roman Factory." In *The Origins of Technology*. New York: Scientific American.

Holle, B. F. 1978. *Historical Considerations on the Origins and the Spread of Greek Coinage in the Archaic Age*. PhD thesis, University of Michigan.

Hopkins, K. 1978. *Conquerors and Slaves*. Cambridge: Cambridge University Press.

———. 1983. "Introduction." In Garnsey, Hopkins, and Whittaker 1983.

Hopkirk, P. 1980. *Foreign Devils on the Silk Road: The Search for the Lost Treasures of Central Asia*. Boston: University of Massachusetts Press.

Hopper, R. J. 1979. *Trade and Industry in Classical Greece*. London: Thames & Hudson.

Hornblower, S., and A. Spawforth, eds. 1996. *Oxford Classical Dictionary*. 3rd ed. Oxford: Oxford University Press.

Horsley, R. A. 1995. *Galilee: History, Politics, People*. Valley Forge, Penn.: Trinity.

Howard, P. K. 1994. *The Death of Common Sense: How Law Is Suffocating America*. New York: Warner.

Howgego, C. 1992. "The Supply and Use of Money in the Roman World, 200 BC–AD 300." *Journal of Roman Studies* 82:1–31.

Huie, B. T. 1998. "Who Were the Pharisees and the Sadducees?" www.aristotle.net/~bhuie/pharsadd.htm.

International Herald Tribune. 2007. Business: www.iht.com/articles/ap/2007/02/15/business/AS-FIN-Philippines-Remittances.php (February 15).

Isager, S., and J. E. Skydsgaard. 1992. *Ancient Greek Agriculture: An Introduction*. London: Routledge.

Jay, A. 1967. *Management and Machiavelli*. London: Hodder & Stoughton.

Jaynes, J. 1976. *The Origin of Consciousness in the Breakdown of the Bicameral Mind.* Boston: Houghton Mifflin.

Johnston, B. 2001. "Colosseum 'Built with Loot from Sack of Jerusalem Temple.'" *Electronic Telegraph* (June 15). telegraph.co.uk/news/worldnews/1311985/Colosseum-built-with-loot-from-sack-of-Jerusalem-temple.html.

Jones, A. H. M. 1940. *The Greek City from Alexander to Justinian.* Oxford: Clarendon.

———. 1974. *The Roman Economy: Studies in Ancient Economic and Administrative History.* Edited by P. A. Brunt. Oxford: Blackwell.

———. 1977. *Athenian Democracy.* Baltimore: Johns Hopkins University Press.

Kaegi, W. E. 1992. *Byzantium and the Early Islamic Conquests.* Cambridge: Cambridge University Press.

Katzenstein, H. J. 1973. *The History of Tyre, from the Beginning of the Second Millennium B.C.E. Until the Fall of the Neo-Babylonian Empire in 538 B.C.E.* Jerusalem: Schocken Institute for Jewish Research of the Jewish Theological Seminary of America.

Kauffman, S. A. 2006. "The Evolution of Future Wealth." *Scientific American* 295/5:44.

Keay, S. J. 1988. *Roman Spain.* London: British Museum.

Keegan, J. 1993. *A History of Warfare.* New York: Knopf.

Keller, W. 1974. *The Etruscans.* New York: Knopf.

Kennedy, P. 1989. *The Rise and Fall of the Great Powers: Economic Change and Military Conflict from 1500 to 2000.* New York: Vintage.

Kenoyer, J. M. 2003. "Uncovering the Keys to the Lost Indus Cities." *Scientific American* (July): 67–75.

Kim, H. S. 2002. "Small Change and the Moneyed Economy." In Cartledge, Cohen, and Foxhall 2002.

Kinder, H., and W. Hilgemann. 1964. *The Anchor Atlas of World History,* vol. 1: *From the Stone Age to the Eve of the French Revolution.* New York: Anchor.

Kindleberger, C. P. 1989. *Manias, Panics, and Crashes: A History of Financial Crises.* Rev. ed. New York: Basic Books.

Kingsley, S., and M. Decker, eds. 2001. *Economy and Exchange in the Eastern Mediterranean during Late Antiquity.* Oxford: Oxbow.

Kleberg, T. 1957. *Hôtels, restaurants et cabarets dans l'antiquité romaine.* Uppsala: Almqvist & Wiksells.

Kling, A., and N. Schulz. 2009. *From Poverty to Prosperity: Intangible Assets, Hidden Liabilities, and the Lasting Triumph over Scarcity.* New York/London: Encounter.

Klingaman, W. K. 2008. *The First Century: Emperors, Gods, and Everyman.* Edison, N.J.: Castle.

Kohlmeyer, K. 1985. "Ugarit." In Weiss 1985.

Kolbert, C. F., trans./ed. 1979. *Justinian/The Digest of Roman Law: Theft, Rapine, Damage, and Insult.* London: Penguin.

Kolhatkar, S. 2006. "Inside the Billionaire Service Industry." *The Atlantic* 298/2 (Sept.). sheelahkolhatkar.com/drupal/sites/default/files/Inside%20the%20billionaire%20service%20industry.pdf.

Kramer, S. N. 1963. *The Sumerians.* Chicago: University of Chicago Press.

Krugman, P. 1997. *Development, Geography, and Economic Theory*. Cambridge: MIT Press.

Kuhn, T. S. 1990. *The Structure of Scientific Revolutions*. 2nd ed. Chicago University of Chicago Press.

Kuhrt, A., and S. Sherwin-White, eds. 1987. *Hellenism in the East*. Berkeley: University of California Press.

Kuran, T. 2004. "Why the Middle East Is Economically Underdeveloped: Historical Mechanisms of Institutional Stagnation." *Journal of Economic Perspectives* 18/3:71–90.

Lacey, W. K. 1968. *The Family in Classical Greece*. Ithaca: Cornell University Press.

Landels, J. G. 1981. *Engineering in the Ancient World*. Berkeley: University of California Press.

Landes, D. 1969. *The Unbound Prometheus: Technological Change and Industrial Development from 1872 to the Present*. Cambridge: Cambridge University Press.

Larsen, M. T. 1982. "Your Money or Your Life! A Portrait of an Assyrian Businessman." In Diakonoff 1982.

———, ed. 1979. *Power and Propaganda: A Symposium on Ancient Empires*. Mesopotamia: Copenhagen Studies in Assyriology 7. Copenhagen: Akademisk Forlag.

Lazonick, W. 1991. *Business Organization and the Myth of the Market Economy*. Cambridge: Harvard University Press.

Lebecq, S. 1990. *Nouvelle histoire de la France médiévale: les origines franques Ve–IXe siècle*. Paris: Seuil.

Leemans, W. F. 1950. *The Old-Babylonian Merchant: His Business and His Social Position*. Leiden: Brill.

———. 1960. *Foreign Trade in the Old Babylonian Period*. Leiden: Brill.

———. 1968. "Old Babylonian Letters and Economic History: A Review Article with Digression for Trade." *Journal of the Economic and Social History of the Orient* 11:171–226.

LeGoff, J. 1990. *Medieval Civilization*. Cambridge: Blackwell.

Lerner, M. 1943. *The Mind and Faith of Justice Holmes*. New York: Modern Library.

Lewis, A. R. 1951. *Naval Power and Trade in the Mediterranean, 500–1100*. Princeton: Princeton University Press.

Lewis, M. 2010. *The Big Short: Inside the Doomsday Machine*. New York: Norton.

Lewit, T. 1991. *Agricultural Production in the Roman Economy, AD 200–400*. British Archaeological Reports 568. Oxford: British Archaeological Reports.

Lintott, A. 1993. *Imperium Romanum, Politics, and Administration*. London: Routledge.

Loane, H. J. 1938. *Industry and Commerce of the City of Rome (50 BC–200 AD)*. Johns Hopkins Studies in Historical and Political Science 56/2. Baltimore: Johns Hopkins University Press.

MacDowell, D. M. 1978. *The Laws in Classical Athens*. London: Thames & Hudson.

MacMullen, R. 1986. *Christianizing the Roman Empire, AD 100–400*. New Haven: Yale University Press.

———. 1988. *Corruption and the Decline of Rome*. New Haven: Yale University Press.

Maine, H. S. 1861. *Ancient Law*. Boston: Beacon.

Mallaby, S. 2010. "The Politically Incorrect Guide to Ending Poverty." *The Atlantic* (July/August): 78–84.

Malminder, U. 2005. "Roman Shares." In Goetzmann and Rouwenhorst 2005.

Manchester, W. 1992. *A World Lit Only by Fire: The Medieval Mind and the Renaissance, Portrait of an Age*. Boston: Little, Brown.

Mango, C. 1994. *Byzantium: The Empire of the New Rome*. London: Phoenix.

Mango, M. M. 2001. "Beyond the Amphora: Non-Ceramic Evidence for Late Antiquity Industry and Trade." In Kingsley and Decker 2001.

Mark, S. 1998. *From Egypt to Mesopotamia: A Study of Predynastic Trade Routes*. College Station: Texas A&M Press.

Mathiae, P. "Ebla Recovered." In Weiss 1985.

McCraw, T. K., ed. 1997. *Creating Modern Capitalism*. Cambridge: Harvard University Press.

McDermott, E. P., and A. Eliot. 1996. *Alternative Dispute Resolution in the Workplace: Concepts and Techniques for Human Resource Executives and Their Counsel*. Westport, Conn.: Quorum.

McGregor, D. 1985. *The Human Side of Enterprise*. New York: McGraw-Hill.

McNeill, J. R., and W. H. McNeill. 2003. *The Human Web: A Bird's Eye-view of World History*. New York: Norton.

McNeill, W. H. 1977. *Plagues and Peoples*. New York: Anchor.

———. 1987. "The Eccentricity of Wheels, or Eurasian Transportation in Historical Perspective." *American Historical Review* 92:1111–26.

———. 1991. *The Rise of the West*. Chicago: University of Chicago Press.

Meiggs, R. 1982. *Trees and Timber in the Ancient World*. Oxford: Clarendon.

Meijer, F., and O. van Nijf. 1992. *Trade, Transport, and Society in the Ancient World: A Sourcebook*. New York/London: Routledge.

Metropolitan Museum of Art. 1994a. *Alexandria*. New York: Metropolitan Museum of Art.

———. 1994b. *Meroë: Kingdom on the Nile, 270 BC–350 AD*. New York: Metropolitan Museum of Art.

———. 1994c. *Dynasty 25: The Kushite Period (c. 760–656 BC)*. New York: Metropolitan Museum of Art.

Meyer, D. R. 2003. *The Roots of American Industrialization*. Baltimore: Johns Hopkins University Press.

Miles, J. 1995. *God: A Biography*. New York: Vintage.

Millar, F. 1977. *The Emperor in the Roman World (31 BC–AD 337)*. London: Ithaca: Cornell University Press.

———. 1993. *The Roman Near East, 31 BC–AD 337*. Cambridge: Harvard University Press.

Miller, J. I. 1969. *The Spice Trade of the Roman Empire, 29 BC to AD 641*. Oxford: Oxford University Press.

Millett, P. 1983. "Maritime Loans and the Structure of Credit in Fourth-Century Athens." In Garnsey, Hopkins, and Whittaker 1983.

———. 1990. "Sale, Credit, and Exchange in Athenian Law and Society." In Cartledge, Millet, and Todd 1990.

———. 1991. *Lending and Borrowing in Ancient Athens*. Cambridge: Cambridge University Press.

Minchinton, W. 1990. "Review of J. I. Israel's *Dutch Primacy in World Trade, 1585–1740*." *Business History Review* 40.

Moeller, W. O. 1976. *The Wool Trade of Ancient Pompeii*. Leiden: Brill.

Mokyr, J. 1990. *The Lever of Riches: Technological Creativity and Economic Progress*. New York: Oxford University Press.

———, ed. 1999. *The British Industrial Revolution: An Economic Perspective*. 2nd ed. Boulder, Colo.: Westview.

———. 2008. "The Institutional Origins of the Industrial Revolution." In *Institutions and Economic Performance*. Edited by E. Helpman. Cambridge: Harvard University Press.

Moore, K. J., and D. C. Lewis. 1999. *Birth of the Multinational: 2,000 Years of Ancient Business History*. Copenhagen: Copenhagen Business School.

———. 2009. *The Origins of Globalization*. London: Routledge.

Morikawa, H. 1992. *Zaibatsu: The Rise and Fall of Family Enterprise Groups in Japan*. Tokyo: Tokyo University Press.

Moritz, L. A. 1958. *Grain Mills and Flour in Classical Antiquity*. Oxford: Clarendon.

Morley, N. 1996. *Metropolis and Hinterland: The City of Rome and the Italian Economy, 200 BC–AD 200*. New York: Cambridge University Press.

Morris, I, ed. 1994. *Classical Greece: Ancient Histories and Modern Archaeologies*. New Directions in Archaeology. Cambridge: Cambridge University Press.

Moscati, S. 1968. *The World of the Phoenicians*. London: Weidenfeld & Nicolson.

Mossé, C. 1969. *Le travail en Grèce et à Rome*. Paris: Presses universitaires de France.

———. 1983. "The 'World of the Emporium' in the Private Speeches of Demosthenes." In Garnsey, Hopkins, and Whittaker 1983.

Muhly, J. D. 1985. "End of the Bronze Age." In Weiss 1985.

Muldrew, C. 1998. *The Economy of Obligation: The Culture of Credit and Social Relations in Early Modern England*. London: Macmillan.

Nadler, S. 2001. *Spinoza's Heresy: Immortality and the Jewish Mind*. Oxford: Clarendon.

Nash, M. 1967. "The Social Context of Economic Choice in a Small Society." In Dalton 1967.

Neal, L. 2000. "Presidential Address: A Shocking View of Economic History." *Journal of Political Economy* 60/2:317–35.

Nelson, J. K., R. J. Zeckhauser, and M. Spence. 2008. *The Patron's Payoff: Conspicuous Commissions in Italian Renaissance Art*. New Haven: Yale University Press.

Nelson, R. R. 1996. *The Sources of Economic Growth*. Cambridge: Harvard University Press.

Nippel, W. 1995. *Public Order in Ancient Rome*. Cambridge: Cambridge University Press.

Nissen, H. J., P. Damarov, and R. K. Englund. 1993. *Archaic Bookkeeping: Early Writing and Techniques of Economic Administration in the Ancient Near East*. Translated by P. Larsen. Chicago: University of Chicago Press.

North, D. C. 1981. *Structure and Change in Economic History*. New York: Norton.

———. 1990. *Institutions, Institutional Change, and Economic Performance*. Cambridge: Cambridge University Press.

———. 2005. "Understanding the Process of Economic Change." In *Princeton Economic History of the Western World*. Edited by J. Mokyr. Princeton: Princeton University Press.

North, D. C., and R. P. Thomas. 1973. *The Rise of the Western World: A New Economic History*. Cambridge: Cambridge University Press.

Norwich, J. J. 1997. *Byzantium: The Early Centuries*. New York: Knopf.

Oded, B. 1979. *Mass Deportations and Deportees in the Neo-Assyrian Empire*. Wiesbaden: Reichert.

Oldach, D. W., R. E. Richard, E. N. Borza, and R. M. Benitez. 1988. "A Mysterious Death." *New England Journal of Medicine* 338:1764–69.

Olegrio, R. 1999. "'That Mysterious People': Jewish Merchants, Transparency, and Community in Mid-19th Century America." *Business History Review* 73 (Summer): 161–89.

Oppenheim, A. L. 1971. "A Bird's-Eye View of Mesopotamian Economic History." In Polanyi, Arensberg, and Pearson 1971.

———. 1977. *Ancient Mesopotamia*. Rev. ed. Chicago: University of Chicago Press.

Pallotino, M. 1975. *The Etruscans*. Bloomington: Indiana University Press.

Parke, H. W. 1931. *Greek Mercenary Soldiers from the Earliest Times to the Battle of Ipsus*. Chicago: Ares.

Parkin, T. 1992. *Demography and Roman Society*. Baltimore: Johns Hopkins University Press.

Parkins, H., and C. Smith, eds. 1998. *Trade, Traders, and the Ancient City*. New York/London: Routledge.

Paterson, J. 1998. "Trade and Traders in the Roman World: Scale, Structure, and Organization." In Parkins and Smith 1998.

Persky, J. 2007. "From Usury to Interest." *Journal of Economic Perspectives* 21/1:227–36.

Peters, F. E. 1970. *The Harvest of Hellenism: A History of the Near East from Alexander the Great to the Triumph of Christianity*. New York: Simon & Schuster.

Polanyi, K. 1944. *The Great Transformation*. Boston: Beacon.

———. 1975. "Traders and Trade." In Sabloff and Lamberg-Karlovsky 1975.

Polanyi, K., C. Arensberg, and H. Pearson, eds. 1971. *Trade and Market in the Early Empires*. Chicago: Regnery.

Pollard, S. 1965. *The Genesis of Modern Management*. Cambridge: Harvard University Press.

———. 1981. *Peaceful Conquest: The Industrialization of Europe, 1760–1970*. Cambridge: Harvard University Press.

Postan, M. M. 1973. *Essays on Medieval Agriculture and General Problems of the Medieval Economy*. Cambridge: Cambridge University Press.

Potter, D. S. 1999. "Entertainers in the Roman Empire." In Potter and Mattingly 1999.

Potter, D. S., and D. Mattingly, eds. 1999. *Life, Death, and Entertainment in the Roman Empire*. Ann Arbor: University of Michigan Press.

Pounds, N. J. G. 1990. *An Historical Geography of Europe.* New York/Cambridge: Cambridge University Press.

Previts, G. J., and B. D. Merino. 1998. *A History of Accounting in the United States: The Cultural Significance of Accounting.* Columbus: Ohio State University Press.

Prior, A., and M. Kirby. 1993. "The Society of Friends and the Family Firm, 1700–1830." *Business History* 35/4:66.

Pusateri, C. J. 1984. *A History of American Business.* Arlington Heights, Ill.: Davidson.

Rabb, T. K. 1967. *Enterprise and Empire: Merchant and Gentry Investment in the Expansion of England, 1575–1630.* Cambridge: Harvard University Press.

Radice, B. 1973. *Who's Who in the Ancient World.* London: Penguin.

Randsborg, K. 1991. *The First Millennium AD in Europe and the Mediterranean: An Archaeological Essay.* Cambridge: Cambridge University Press.

Rawson, E. 1976. "The Ciceronian Aristocracy and Its Properties." In Finley 1976.

Raymond, R. 1986. *Out of the Fiery Furnace: The Impact of Metals on the History of Mankind.* University Park: Pennsylvania State University Press.

Reden, S. von. 1995. *Exchange in Ancient Greece.* London: Duckworth.

Redfield, R. 1953. *The Primitive World and Its Transformations.* Ithaca: Cornell University Press.

Reed, C. M. 2003. *Maritime Traders in the Ancient Greek World.* Cambridge University Press.

Reeves, N., and R. H. Wilkinson. 1998. *The Complete Valley of the Kings.* London: Thames & Hudson.

Reger, G. 1994. *Regionalism and Change in the Economy of Independent Delos.* Berkeley: University of California Press.

Renfrew, C. 1972. *The Emergence of Civilization: The Cyclades and the Aegean in the 3rd Millennium BC.* London: Methuen.

Revere, R. B. 1971. "'No Man's Coast': Ports of Trade in the Eastern Mediterranean." In Polanyi, Arensberg, and Pearson 1971.

Ricardo, D. 1817. *On the Principles of Political Economy and Taxation.* London.

Rice, T. T. 1967. *Everyday Life in Byzantium.* New York: Putnam.

Rich, J., and A. Wallace-Hadrill, eds. 1991. *City and Country in the Ancient Roman World.* London: Routledge.

Richardson, J. 1976. *Roman Provincial Administration, 227 BC to AD 117.* London: Bristol Classic Press.

Rickman, G. E. 1980. "The Grain Trade under the Roman Empire." In D'Arms and Kopff 1980.

Robertson, J. F. 1981. *Redistributive Economies in Ancient Mesopotamian Society: A Case Study from Isin-Larsa Period Nippur.* Philadelphia: University of Pennsylvania Press.

Rogers, J. S. 1995. *The Early History of the Law of Bills and Notes: A Study of the Origins of Anglo-American Commercial Law.* Cambridge: Cambridge University Press.

Rose, H. J. 2004. *The Routledge Handbook of Greek Mythology.* New York: Routledge.

Rosenberg, N. 2008. *Inside the Black Box: Technology and Economics.* Cambridge: Cambridge University Press.

Ross, K. L. 2003. "The New Kingdom of Egypt." www.friesian.com/notes/newking.htm.

Rostovtzeff, M. 1957. *The Social and Economic History of the Roman Empire*. Oxford: Clarendon.

———. 1960. *Rome*. Oxford: Oxford University Press.

———. 1972. *The Social and Economic History of the Hellenistic World*. Oxford: Clarendon.

———. 1993. *Greece*. Edited by E. Bickerman. Oxford: Oxford University Press.

Rutter, J. B. 2000. "The Prehistoric Archaeology of the Aegean." Dartmouth College and the Foundation of the Hellenic World. http://projectsx.dartmouth.edu/history/bronze_age/.

Sabloff, J. A., and C. C. Lamberg-Karlovsky, eds. 1975. *Ancient Civilizations and Trade*. Albuquerque: University of New Mexico Press.

Safrai, Z. 1994. *The Economy of Roman Palestine*. London/New York: Routledge.

Saggs, H. W. F. 1989. *Civilization before Greece and Rome*. New Haven: Yale University Press.

Sahlins, M. 1974. *Stone Age Economics*. Piscataway, N.J.: Aldine Transaction.

Sallares, R. 1991. *The Ecology of the Ancient Greek World*. London: Duckworth.

Saller, R. P. 1989. "Patronage and Friendship in Early Imperial Rome: Drawing the Distinction." In A. Wallace-Hadrill 1989.

Sarton, G. 1959. *Hellenistic Science and Culture in the Last Three Centuries* BC. Cambridge: Harvard University Press.

Scarborough, J. 1993. "Response to K. D. White, 'The Base Mechanical Arts?'" In Green 1993.

Schaps, D. M. 2001. "The Conceptual Prehistory of Money and Its Impact on the Greek Economy." In Balmuth 2001.

———. 2004. *The Invention of Coinage and the Monetization of Ancient Greece*. Ann Arbor: University of Michigan Press.

Scheidel, W., I. Morris, and R. Saller, eds. 2007. *The Cambridge Economic History of the Greco-Roman World*. Cambridge: Cambridge University Press.

Schiffman, L. H. 1992. "New Light on the Pharisees: Insight from the Dead Sea Scrolls." *Bible Review* 8 (June): 30–33, 54.

Schlesinger, H. 1964. "Contribution to a Theory of Promising, 3: The Use of Promising as an Element of Form and Content in Drama." Paper read at Topeka (Kans.) Psychoanalytical Society, June 9.

———. 1968. "A Contribution to the Theory of Promising, 4: The Use of Forms of Promising in the Development of Religious Practices." Paper read at Topeka (Kans.) Psychoanalytical Society.

———. 1978. "Developmental and Regressive Aspects of the Making and Breaking of Promises." In *The Human Mind Revisited: Essays in Honor of Karl A. Menninger*. Edited by S. Smith. New York: International Universities Press.

Schoek, H. 1987. *Envy: A Theory of Social Behavior*. Indianapolis: Liberty.

Scott, J. 1976. *The Moral Economy of the Peasant*. New Haven: Yale University Press.

Scullard, H. H. 1979. *Roman Britain: Outpost of the Empire*. London: Thames & Hudson.

Seife, C. 2000. *Zero: The Biography of a Dangerous Idea*. New York: Penguin.

Shanks, H., ed. 1988. *Ancient Israel: A Short History from Abraham to the Roman Destruction of the Temple.* Englewood Cliffs, N.J.: Prentice-Hall.

Shaw, B. D., and R. P. Saller, eds. 1981. *Economy and Society in Ancient Greece.* New York: Viking.

Sherratt, A. 1997. *Economy and Society in Prehistoric Europe: Changing Perspectives.* Edinburgh: Edinburgh University Press.

Shiff, L. B. 1987. *The Nur-Sin Archive: Private Entrepreneurship in Babylon (603–507 BC).* Philadelphia: University of Pennsylvania Press.

Silver, M. 1985. *Economic Structures of the Ancient Near East.* London: Croom Helm.

———. 1995. *Economic Structures of Antiquity.* Westport, Conn.: Greenwood.

Singh, S., and K. Ribet. 1997. "Fermat's Last Stand." *Scientific American* (November): 68–73.

Sinnigen, W. G., and A. E. R. Boak. 1977. *A History of Rome to AD 565.* 6th ed. New York: Macmillan Books.

Sirks, B. 1991. *Food for Rome: The Legal Structures of the Transportation and Processing of Supplies for the Imperial Distributions in Rome and Constantinople.* Amsterdam: Gieben.

Skidelsky, R. 1999. "Family Values: Review of N. Ferguson's *House of Rothschild.*" *New York Review of Books* (December 16): 25.

Smail, J. 1999. "The Sources of Innovation in the Woolen and Worsted Industry of 18th Century Yorkshire." *Business History Review* 41/1:1–15.

Smallwood, E. M. 1976. *The Jews under Roman Rule* Leiden: Brill.

Smith, C. 1988. "Traders and Artisans in Archaic Central Italy." In Parkins and Smith 1998.

Snell, D. 1997. *Life in the Ancient Near East, 3100–322 BCE.* New Haven: Yale University Press.

Solomons, D. 1978. "The Historical Development of Cost Accounting." In *Handbook of Cost Accounting.* Edited by S. Davidson and R. Weil. New York: McGraw-Hill.

Sombert, W. 1969. *The Jews and Modern Capitalism.* New York: Franklin.

Springborg, P. 1992. *Western Republicanism and the Oriental Prince.* Austin: University of Texas Press.

Spurr, M. S. 1986. *Arable Cultivation in Roman Italy, c. 200 BC–AD 100.* Journal of Roman Studies Monographs 3. London: Society for the Promotion of Roman Studies.

Starr, C. 1989. *The Influence of Sea Power on Ancient History.* New York: Oxford University Press.

Ste. Croix, G. E. M. de. 1981. *The Class Struggle in the Ancient Greek World from the Archaic Age to the Arab Conquests.* Ithaca: Cornell University Press.

Stolper, M. W. 1985. *Entrepreneurs and Empire: The Murasu Firm and Persian Rule in Babylonia.* Istanbul: Nederlands Historisch-Archaeologisch Instituut.

Stos-Gale, Z. A. 2001. "The Impact of the Natural Sciences on Studies of Hacksilber and Early Silver Coinage." In Balmuth 2001.

Sutherland, C. H. V. 1969. *Gold: Its Beauty, Power, and Allure.* 2nd ed. New York: McGraw-Hill.

Suzuki, Y. 1991. *Japanese Management Structures, 1920–80*. Basingstoke: Macmillan.

Talbert, R. J. M. 1984. *The Senate of Imperial Rome*. Princeton: Princeton University Press.

Tarn, W. W., and G. T. Griffith. 1974. *Hellenistic Civilization*. 3rd ed. New York: New American Library.

Taylor, J. M., and C. F. Meier. 2003. "Jury Awards Forcing Doctors Off the Job." http://www.heartland.org/Article.cfm?artId=11621.

Tcherikover, V. 1975. *Hellenistic Civilization and the Jews*. New York: Atheneum.

Tchernia, A. 1983. "Italian Wine in Gaul at the End of the Republic." In Garnsey, Hopkins, and Whittaker 1983.

Temin, P. 2002. "Financial Intermediation in the Roman Empire." In MIT Dept. of Economics, Working Paper 02-39. Cambridge: MIT Press.

Thaler, R. H. 2010. "Underwater, but Will They Leave the Pool?" *New York Times* (January 24): N/3.

Thomas, B. 1984. "Escaping from Constraints: The Industrial Revolution in a Malthusian Context." *Journal of Interdisciplinary History* 15/4:729–53.

Thompson, D. 1983. "Nile Grain Transport under the Ptolemies." In Garnsey, Hopkins, and Whittaker 1983.

Todd, S., and P. Millet. 1990. "Law, Society, and Athens." In Cartledge, Millet, and Todd 1990.

Toner, J. P. 1995. *Leisure and Ancient Rome*. Cambridge: Blackwell.

Udovitch, A. 1981. *The Dawn of Modern Banking*. New Haven: Yale University Press.

U.S. Federal Reserve. 2005. "Money Stock Measures." http://www.federalreserve.gov/releases/h6/Current.

Vallee, B. 1998. "Alcohol in the Western World." *Scientific American* (June): 80–85.

van de Mieroop, Marc. 2005. "The Invention of Interest." In Goetzmann and Rouwenhorst 2005.

van Gastel, A. J. G., Z. Bishaw, and B. R. Gregg. 2002. "Wheat Seed Production." In Curtis, Rajaram, and Gómez Macpherson 2002.

Vergil. 2008. *The Aeneid*. Translated by R. Fagles. New York: Penguin.

Veyne, P., ed. 1987. *A History of Private Life*, vol. 1: *From Pagan Rome to Byzantium*. Cambridge: Harvard University Press.

Vilar, P. 1976. *A History of Gold and Money, 1450–1920*. Translated by J. White. Atlantic Highlands, N.J.: Humanities Press.

Ville, S. 1996. "Networks and Venture Capital in the Australian Pastoral Sector before World War II." *Business History* 38/3:48–59.

Walbank, F. W. 1993. *The Hellenistic World*. Rev. ed. Cambridge: Harvard University Press.

Wallace-Hadrill, A., ed. 1989. *Patronage in Ancient Society*. London: Routledge.

———. 1991. "Elites and Trade in the Roman Town." In Rich and Wallace-Hadrill 1991.

Wallace-Hadrill, J. M. 1988. *The Barbarian West, 400–1000*. 2nd ed. Cambridge: Blackwell.

Ward, A. M. 1977. *Marcus Crassus and the Late Roman Republic*. Columbia: University of Missouri Press.

Ward-Perkins, B. 2005. *The Fall of Rome and the End of Civilization*. Oxford: Oxford University Press.

Webber, C., and A. Wildavsky. 1985. *A History of Taxation and Expenditure in the Western World*. New York: Simon & Schuster.

Weber, M. 1958. *The Protestant Ethic and the Spirit of Capitalism*. New York: Scribner.

———. 1976. *The Agrarian Sociology of Ancient Civilizations*. London: NLB.

Webster, L., and M. Brown, eds. 1997. *The Transformation of the Roman World*, AD 400–900. Berkeley: University of California Press.

Weisberg, D. B. 1967. *Guild Structure and Political Allegiance in Early Achaemenid Mesopotamia*. New Haven: Yale University Press.

Weiss, H., ed. 1985. *Ebla to Damascus: Art and Archaeology of Ancient Syria*. Washington, D.C.: Smithsonian Institute Traveling Exhibition Service.

Wells, P. S. 1984. *Farms, Villages, and Cities: Commerce and Urban Origins in Late Prehistoric Europe*. Ithaca: Cornell University Press.

———. 1999. *The Barbarians Speak: How the Conquered Peoples Shaped Roman Europe*. Princeton: Princeton University Press.

Westen, D. 2008. *The Political Brain: The Role of Emotion in Deciding the Fate of the Nation*. New York: Public Affairs.

Wheeler, M. 1954. *Rome beyond the Imperial Frontiers*. London: Bell.

Whitby, M. 1998. "The Grain Trade of Athens in the 4th Century BC." In Parkins and Smith 1998.

White, K. D. 1975. *Farm Equipment of the Roman World*. Cambridge: Cambridge University Press.

———. 1984. *Greek and Roman Technology*. Ithaca: Cornell University Press.

———. 1993. "The Base Mechanical Arts?" In Green 1993.

Whittaker, C. R. 1987. "Circe's Pigs: From Slavery to Serfdom in the Later Roman World." *Slavery and Abolition* 8:87–122.

———. 1993. *Land, City, and Trade in the Roman Empire*. Aldershot, U.K.: Variorum.

Wild, J. P. 1970. *Textile Manufacturing in the Northern Roman Provinces*. Cambridge: Cambridge University Press.

Wilford, J. N. 1993. "Collapse of Earliest Known Empire Is Linked to Long, Harsh Drought." *New York Times* (August 24): C1.

———. 1997. "Under Beirut's Rubble: Remnants of 5000 Years of Civilization." *New York Times* (February 23): 15.

———. 1998. "Did Augustus Take the Waters Here? Ruins Hint 'Yes.'" *New York Times* (June 16): 1.

Wilkes, J. 1992. *The Illyrians*. Oxford: Blackwell.

Wilkins, M. S. 1992. "The Neglected Intangible Asset: The Influence of the Trade Mark on the Rise of the Modern Corporation." *Business History* 34:66.

Williams, S. 1997. *Diocletian and the Roman Recovery*. New York: Routledge.

Williamson, O. E. 1985. *The Economic Institutions of Capitalism*. New York: Free Press.

———. 1996. *The Mechanisms of Governance*. New York: Oxford University Press.

Williamson, O. E., and S. Winter, eds. 1991. *The Nature of the Firm: Origins, Evolution, and Development*. New York: Oxford University Press.

Wilson, L. M. 1938. *The Clothing of the Ancient Romans.* Johns Hopkins Studies in Archaeology 24. Baltimore: Johns Hopkins University Press.

Wolff, H. J. 1951. *Roman Law: An Historical Introduction.* Norman: University of Oklahoma Press.

Wolpert, L. 2006. *Six Impossible Things before Breakfast: The Evolutionary Origins of Belief.* London: Faber & Faber.

Wood, E. M. 1988. *Peasant, Citizen, and Slave.* London: Verso.

Wood-Perkins, J. 1980. "The Marble Trade and Its Organization: Evidence from Nicomedia." In D'Arms and Kopff 1980.

Wylen, S. M. 1996. *The Jews in the Time of Jesus: An Introduction.* New York: Paulist Press.

Yamamura, K., ed. 1997. *The Economic Emergence of Modern Japan.* Cambridge: Cambridge University Press.

Yoffee, N. 1981. *Explaining Trade in Ancient Western Asia.* Malibu, Calif.: Udena.

Young, D., trans. 2004. *The Poetry of Petrarch.* New York: Farrar, Strauss & Giroux.

Yui, T., and K. Nakagawa, eds. 1989. *Japanese Management in Historical Perspective.* Tokyo: Tokyo University Press.

Zakim, M. 1999. "A Ready-Made Business: The Birth of the Clothing Industry in America." *Business History Review* 73/1:61–90.

INDEX